Comm

A

A N

F O

Lennis Polnac Austin Community College

Lyman Grant Austin Community College

Tom Cameron Bremerton Community College

Prentice Hall, Upper Saddle River, NJ 07458

Library of Congress Cataloging-in-Publication Data

Polnac, Lennis.
    CommonSense : a handbook and guide for writers / Lennis Polnac,
Lyman Grant, Tom Cameron.
      p. cm.
    Includes index.
    ISBN 0-13-082178-0
    1. English language—Rhetoric—Handbooks, manuals, etc.
    2. English language—Grammar—Handbooks, manuals, etc. I. Grant,
Lyman. II. Cameron, Tom. III. Title. IV. Title: CommonSense.
PE1408.P643   1999
808'.042—dc21   98-33272
                                                  CIP

Editorial Director: *Charlyce Jones-Owen*
Editor-in-Chief, English: *Leah Jewell*
Editorial Assistant: *Patricia Castiglione*
Director of Production/Manufacturing: *Barbara Kittle*
Senior Managing Editor: *Bonnie Biller*
Production Editor: *Alison Gnerre*
Manufacturing Manager: *Nick Sklitsis*
Prepress and Manufacturing Buyer: *Mary Ann Gloriande*
Creative Design Director: *Leslie Osher*
Art Director: *Maria Lange*
Cover Design: *Maria Lange*
Interior Design: *Circa 86, Inc. and Anne DeMarinis*
Line Art Coordinator: *Guy Ruggerio*
Electronic Page Composition: *Lori Clinton*

This book was set in 10/12 Palatino by Lori Clinton and printed and bound by
R.R. Donnelley and Sons Company. The cover was also printed by R.R. Donnelly and Sons.

Printed in the United States of America

10 9 8 7 6 5 4 3 2

ISBN 0-13-082178-0

PRENTICE-HALL INTERNATIONAL (UK) LIMITED, *London*
PRENTICE-HALL OF AUSTRALIA PTY. LIMITED, *Sydney*
PRENTICE-HALL CANADA INC., *Toronto*
PRENTICE-HALL HISPANOAMERICANA, S.A., *Mexico*
PRENTICE-HALL OF INDIA PRIVATE LIMITED, *New Delhi*
PRENTICE-HALL OF JAPAN, INC., *Tokyo*
SIMON & SCHUSTER ASIA PTE. LTD., *Singapore*
EDITORA PRENTICE-HALL DO BRASIL, LTDA., *Rio de Janeiro*

Contents

Part III Critical Thinking and Critical Reading

Preface

The title of this text, *CommonSense: A Handbook and Guide for Writers*, hints at the approach we have taken throughout the book. We have tried to make the book accessible to a broad range of potential users. To accomplish this goal, we have presented information in ways that allow writers to use what they already know about language as they explore practical strategies for solving the problems most often encountered in creating written compositions.

Nontechnical Language

The presentation of concepts in the book is relatively free of the technical jargon found in most handbooks. We see the book primarily as a resource for students and writers, so we give as many explanations as possible in terms that readers who are not English teachers will understand. Generally, people who use English know the grammar of the language even though they aren't necessarily able to define grammatical terms and many of those people not only construct logical, coherent oral sentences, but also revise and edit them in print as well. It is with that knowledge, the kind innate in any speaker of English, that we want to work. As much as possible, we have couched introductory explanations in everyday language and included both operational definitions of grammatical concepts and frequent examples that clarify those definitions. We also identify key words and patterns of usage that will allow students to proofread without having to memorize grammatical terms. Where necessary, we have highlighted technical terms and defined them at the point they are used. For the most part, however, users of the handbook are referred to the glossary for definitions of grammatical terminology.

Inductive/Intuitive Presentation

Rather than presenting material as a generalized concept, we first give examples that illustrate the principle and then derive the concept from the examples. In this way we allow students to participate in discovering the principle being explained. In addition, many of the introductory explanations contain analogies or hypothetical scenarios that invite students to relate the general concepts to their own experiences. Because students will be involved in the process, they will find the presentations sensible and, we hope, understandable.

Oral and Written Language

Understanding the connections between oral and written language helps students who are not experienced writers to recognize the need for the conventions of written communication. As a result, students will find ways of converting what they already do more or less well—talking—into writing. This connection is especially important to the explanation of sentence punctuation in Part VI. While there are certainly differences between speaking and writing, instructors have never served student writers well by telling them that writing is different from the language they use daily.

The Writing Process

The emphasis on the writing process throughout the book helps students see how each part of the activity of writing, from deciding on a topic to deciding on a specific word or mark of punctuation, is inextricably connected to every other part.

As part of the focus on the writing process, suggestions and techniques for collaboration encourage students to work with others in developing, writing, and revising their work.

Critical Thinking

Although Part III focuses attention on critical thinking and critical reading, those concepts are integrated throughout the text. In a very real sense, the entire work is an exercise in developing critical thinking and critical reading skills, for choice is an important factor throughout. That is, we try not to tell the reader what to do; we make suggestions based on the evidence presented in the explanations.

Research

Part IX, "Research and Documentation," deals with collecting information, using the information in a paper, and indicating the sources of the information. While the process of writing a research paper bears many similarities to other forms of writing, the skills of summarizing, paraphrasing, and quoting receive separate treatment. Wanting to serve students in many disciplines, we have included complete information for documenting texts in the four major documentation styles: MLA, APA, CBE, and CMS. Also included are the latest MLA and APA conventions for documenting sources on the Internet and the World Wide Web.

Through cross-references, Part IX includes a focus on the rhetorical needs of the research paper's audience (Chapters 5 and 6), information about libraries and computer access to reference materials as part of the discovery process (Chapter 4), and an explanation of document design (Part X).

The Internet

Part XI includes information about the Internet and the World Wide Web. The explanations include various strategies for doing research on the Web as well as some suggestions about specific Web sites.

ESL Guidance

Questions of usage relevant to ESL students are distributed throughout Part VII since some of those explanations are also needed by native speakers.

29c   Verb Forms Indicating Something Conjectural or Desirable
29d   Verb Forms Used with Helping Verbs
29e   Two-Word and Three-Word Verbs
29f   Uses of the Basic Form of Verbs
33e   Choosing *A, An,* and *The*
33f   Choosing between Modifiers Ending in *-ed, -d, -en,* or *-t* and *-ing*
34e   Problems with Agreement of Sentence Elements
35a   Omissions
35d   Unnecessary Repetition

Acknowledgments

We wish to thank the following colleagues who reviewed the manuscript of our text and provided helpful advice: John Schaffer, Blinn College; Judith E. Funston, State University of New York, Potsdam; Andrew Tomko, Bergen Community College; Margaret P. Morgan, University of North Carolina, Charlotte; William Demaree, Elgin Community College; Gary A. Olson, University of South Florida; and Victoria Lague, Miami-Dade Community College.

Lennis Polnac
Lyman Grant
Tom Cameron

How to Use This Book

We have tried to create a book with you, the writer, in mind; consequently, it is designed to be helpful throughout the writing process. Part I begins with an introduction and overview of that process.

The next eight parts are organized in the order in which their concepts are usually faced by the writer.

- Generating content, including critical reading and thinking (Parts II and III)
- Arranging content (Part IV)
- Revising style and punctuation (Parts V and VI)
- Editing usage and conventions (Parts VII and VIII)

The next three parts focus on topics of special interest, topics that are not necessarily part of every writing project:

- Doing research and documenting sources (Part IX)
- Designing documents (Part X)
- Using the Internet (Part XI)

Other features include a fully detailed table of contents preceding this section and abbreviated tables of contents printed on the inside front and back cover. On page ii is a checklist that will help you in revising your work. In addition, at the beginning of each part is a list that will help you find information in each chapter. Last, we include a thorough index.

If you don't know what you're looking for, think about where in the writing process your problem occurs. Does the question come up while you are creating content, arranging content, or editing content? If you can answer this question, turn to the appropriate parts and consult the lists to locate the information you need.

1

The Writing Process

The Writer's Speech

Can you remember the first words you ever learned? Probably not. The process of acquiring language is very gradual. You began to acquire language by listening to your parents and other people and trying to imitate the sounds you heard. Your first approach to language, then, was through speech; as a result, the core of your experience with language is an oral, speech-based understanding. Even now, you probably speak more than you write. This understanding of language as speech is one of your most important resources as a writer.

One aspect of language that you probably began to recognize as you grew up was that individual people and distinct groups develop unique ways of saying things. Linguists call the individual pattern of language use an **idiolect**. The idiolect you speak has been formed by the cumulative experiences you have had with language; in fact, it is being formed even now. The language you use as an individual also reflects the language you share with a group of people. That pattern of language use, which linguists call a **dialect**, controls much of the vocabulary and many of the rules for sentence formation that you use. But your language is also affected by the language of commerce, government, education, and broadcasting, the common dialect we call **standard English**. This generally accepted dialect is maintained not only orally but also in writing.

1a
SPEAKING, READING, AND WRITING

Writing developed long after spoken language began. Human beings had been using language for tens of thousands of years before putting it into written form. It is not surprising, then, that speech is the basis for our understanding of language.

Since written language is based on spoken language, in many ways the two are similar. We recognize the similarities between them when we find slang expressions in print and when the style of the writing is conversational and informal. Still, written language is less flexible than spoken language. Conventions of punctuation and style sometimes become rigid and seem to be arbitrary, not necessarily dependent on meaning. For example, the practice of avoiding the use of a preposition at the end of a sentence is rarely followed in speech.

Despite these differences, however, when we read writing aloud, it becomes speech again, and we become aware of the connection between the two. Reading your work aloud can help you tap into your innate oral-based knowledge of language. Reading aloud forces you to focus on the language, its rhythms, the natural groupings of words in sentences, and the attitudes you are expressing. Paying attention to the sound of your writing will allow you to make changes so that it sounds more authentic. To dismiss speech as irrelevant to writing is to disregard the most direct path that speakers can take to effective written communication.

1a.1 Pitch

> In all languages, pitch naturally rises and falls, sometimes almost musically; English itself has a built-in rise and fall at the beginning and end of related groups of words.

Go back to the beginning of the sentence above and read it aloud as if you were saying it: notice how certain words naturally group together, and notice how your voice varies in **pitch** from the beginnings to the ends of these word groups. In general, writers who remain aware of the sound of their writing are able to communicate effectively.

Pitch also carries meaning. Say "Hurry up!" in two ways, first as if you were trying to show the excitement of a child who is about to go somewhere, and then as if you were impatiently giving an order to someone. Notice that the first version is spoken in a higher pitch than the second. Even though we may say that individual people have a "high" or "low" voice, the voices of all people change to indicate excitement (the pitch usually rises) or determination (the pitch usually drops). In effective writing, readers can discern these pitch differences as they read.

So, when you read your work aloud, you will want to pay attention to the natural phrasing of the text and to the extra meanings you are communicating through changes in pitch. If these meanings are lost in the written text, then you will have to compensate in some way—perhaps rephrasing or reorganizing so the reader has no problem hearing the spoken word in the text.

1a.2 Cadence

Read the following sentence out loud.

> Spoken language also moves rhythmically.

This sentence contains five stresses: the first part of each word is emphasized. You are forced to read the sentence above at a slow pace, but look at the next statement.

Some sentences have cadences that speed up the reading.

Notice how smoothly these words flow. These two sentences illustrate **cadence** in the spoken language. There is more to cadence, however, than movement; there is also delay. In fact, stops and pauses help to divide up spoken language; punctuation serves the same purpose in writing.

When you compose written language that allows the reader to "hear" expected changes in cadence, it will sound natural and familiar. Readers will hear a natural voice in the writing. Listening for these elements of speech in your own writing will allow you to vary the style of your writing (see Part V) as well as alert you to employ punctuation marks that guide readers to pause at appropriate points within sentences and to stop when sentences are finished (see Chapter 22).

1a.3 Attitude

When speaking, we may express our **attitude** toward the subject we are talking about by varying the relative loudness of a word, a phrase, or a sentence. We also express attitude in the way we pronounce our words, as well as through the very words we use to reveal our thoughts. In writing, we usually call these features **tone**. When we pay attention only to the meanings of words, we may fail to recognize the writer's attitude. We can best perceive attitude by being attentive to the way the writer would have said the words aloud.

Words such as *shrill* and *sarcastic* describe attitudes we perceive readily in speech, but without clues, we cannot recognize them in writing. For example, there is no way for a reader to know that the following sentence is said sarcastically.

"I really appreciated that!"

Instead, it must be written like this.

"I really appreciated that!" he said sarcastically.

Try reading the next sentence several ways, emphasizing different words each time. Notice how the meaning changes.

How do you think we are going to get there?

If these words were spoken, we would know exactly what the speaker intended because one or more of the words would be stressed or accented.

Writing requires us to use one of the conventions that shows emphasis (Section 41c), such as underlining or italicizing. When writers treat writing only as "speech written down" and pay no attention to the readers' needs, then problems arise. But when writers remain aware of how speaking and writing are both alike and different, they can guard against misinterpretation.

1b
CONVERSATION AND WRITING

When we are engaged in conversation, we are naturally involved in a give-and-take with another person, but when we write, we are necessarily removed from the reader in both time and space. We are no longer conversing; rather, we are doing a kind of monologue. We have to supply words that answer all the reader's potential questions. We also have to structure the content so it will be coherent and clear to the reader.

1b.1 Immediacy and Rapport

In conversation, the immediate situation is a given. We relate to the other person and respond to questions, to variations in tone, and to body movements. We have little question about whether all parties in the conversation are involved in the events of the moment.

In writing, however, we have no guarantees of immediacy. And since we cannot know whether we have the reader's attention, we can't be assured that we have rapport with the reader. Yet we can preserve some of the immediacy of conversation in writing by keeping the audience and the audience's interests in mind. As we are writing, it always helps to imagine that we are actually engaging in a conversation. As we write, we can think of what would be important or compelling to the reader. We can imagine what questions may be coming up in the reader's mind—and answer those questions before the reader thinks to ask them. We can use vocabulary and style that we think will have the most positive effect on the communication. If we attend to these issues, readers will feel that they are being addressed directly; they will sense that they have rapport with the writer. More importantly, they will feel that the writer is somehow present in the reading.

1b.2 Formality

Writing is almost always more formal than conversation, in part because writers don't always know who is going to read their work. When we converse, we share a back-and-forth exchange of ideas, and the topic shifts as each person focuses on his or her own interests. As we talk, we often speak in sentence fragments because all parties know what we're talking about. In fact, to speak complete sentences sometimes stops the flow of conversation.

But in writing (as in giving a speech), only one person presents the ideas. That person controls the topic and thus must organize its development to complete the communication. When we speak in public, we naturally become more careful than we are in private conversations. And when we write, our caution can be good because it makes us think about how we want the reader to react to what we have written. Instead of saying the first thing that comes to mind, as we might in a conversation with a friend, we make formal choices. The danger is that we can grow so cautious that we end up becoming too formal. Writing can become so formal that we lose rapport with the audience.

1c VARIETIES OF ENGLISH

You may have heard people greet each other in the following ways.

Good morning!	Hello.
Howdy.	G'day!
Greetings and salutations.	How ya doin'?
Top o' the mornin' to ye.	Dude!
Yo!	Hi.

Although these phrases have essentially the same purpose, they use different words and language structures, and they express meanings that are specific to the culture they grow out of. You probably recognize them as examples of different dialects but would consider all of them to be examples of the same language, English. You also probably use more than one of them, though in different situations.

What we call a **language** is actually a set of dialects—very closely related varieties of that language that have many words in common, form words in a similar fashion, and order them according to the same grammatical principles. Dialects differ within the language by making use of many dialect-specific words and terms; different dialects may order words similarly, but they make use of different word and phrase combinations. And most apparent, they sound distinctive: they employ unique pitch and stress patterns. Quite literally, the English language contains hundreds of these varieties. Linguists insist that no dialect is inherently superior to any of the others.

1c.1 Dialects

The dialect a person speaks used to depend mostly on place of birth.

Are ya'll fixin' t' go?

Are youse guys leaving?

If you recognize the first question as distinctively Southern and the second as distinctively Northern, you're right; they are regionally specific, though these actual phrases might be spoken by relatively few people in the region. Dialects are also based in ethnicity and in interaction with other languages. Some African American, Hispanic American, and Anglo-American speakers use language patterns that differ from standard usage, though it is clear that there is no uniform dialect among all members of such diverse groups. These days, the general mobility of the population and the contact that all people have with electronic media make it impossible to use ethnic or regional background as a predictor of the dialect that anyone will actually speak.

Consider your own use of English. Unless you are just learning the language, the dialect you use most naturally is probably typical of the people you grew up around, because you were born into a dialect group. But in addition to the dialect you speak because of the region you grew up in or the ethnic or cultural group that your family belongs to, you probably speak other dialects that derive from your participation on sports teams, the friends you spend time with, your membership in church- or work-related groups, the TV shows you watch, and the music you listen to. Each dialect operates according to certain **usage patterns** that you consciously or unconsciously adhere to when you talk with members of a particular group. Your use of these patterns identifies you as a group member, allowing others in the group to feel comfortable with you. Using your knowledge of each dialect, you are continually making choices about what language to employ as your own.

1c.2 Standard English

In every language there is a dialect that all groups generally subscribe to, even though no one ever quite speaks it fully. That dialect is called the **standard dialect**. In some languages (French, for example), an actual standard is established by politically or academically sanctioned committees, who base what can be called "correct" and "incorrect" on academic study and social elitism. For those languages, there is an approved or sanctioned dialect, and all other dialects are considered not just *non*standard but *sub*standard.

However, since there is no Academy of American English, you need not think of any of the dialects you have used all your life as incorrect. In fact, in most English-speaking countries, the standard dialect derives from the various other dialects. Since native speakers of these dialects try to use this common dialect to speak with each other, in one sense the standard is an amalgam of all the social, regional, and cultural influences that form the other dialects. The standard constantly changes to accommodate the needs of the people who speak it and to reflect the changes that are going on constantly in the other dialects.

The closest that America comes to a universal standard is often referred to as **Standard American English**, the language that the news media, the publishing industry, and the academic establishment collectively promote. Electronic news networks and the publishers of print media establish **style books** that identify acceptable grammatical usage and declare how certain words and phrases should be said and written. In schools and colleges, students usually find that they are expected to use Standard American English, sometimes defined by a handbook or style book but often merely negotiated with each instructor. In either of these environments, you will be expected to use the prescribed form of English. But in general, language in English-speaking countries is grounded in democratic ideals, and there is no absolute standard that all speakers are expected to abide by in every situation.

Other social forces, however, help maintain a generally agreed-upon standard. In all languages, the dialect that enjoys prestige above all others typically has come to be the standard because it is the one spoken by those in power—those with money, those with political and social status. College-educated citizens, professionals, people in business, and others often view the ability to use the standard dialect as a gauge of intelligence and worth. So, workplace and academic requirements establish expectations that we would find it difficult not to fulfill. If you typically use a nonstandard dialect as your native language, you would probably find it difficult, even foolish, to employ the standard dialect for communication in your personal life. However, you are likely to find it in your best interest to use the standard dialect for much of your public speaking and writing, for it allows you to communicate fully with the largest audience of speakers and readers of English. There is considerable pressure on speakers of all nonstandard dialects to use a standard one.

The Writer's Resources

Imagine trying to build a house without tools such as a hammer and a saw, without workers other than yourself, without any outside sources of information. Tools make jobs easier, and so do colleagues and other resources. When you write, you can use rather simple tools such as pencils, pens, and paper or more complex ones such as typewriters and computers. You can consult with other writers and with experienced professionals. And you can make use of resources of your own making—journals, drafts, and even other papers you have already written—as well as reference books and online computerized resources.

2a THE JOURNAL

No doubt you have often thought about things that happened to you and tried to figure out why they happened. Those kinds of reflections and speculations are the stuff that journals are made of. Putting personal musings and private deliberations into written form is a way of exploring who you are and arriving at a better understanding of what you have to write about. Keeping a personal journal will give you a powerful tool for getting your thoughts into writing so that you can work with them further.

A **journal** is similar to a diary, but whereas a diary is simply a record of the day's events, a journal contains an exploration of the possible implications of those events as well as any other related ideas that come to mind.

A journal is like a mirror. It reflects the mind of the person writing it. If you are able to use the journal to its fullest, it will allow you to see more clearly your own thinking processes, your emotions, and your feelings about what has happened or what is happening to you.

A journal is like a laboratory where you can experiment freely with language. That freedom gives you an opportunity to look at your writing in a number of different ways and to develop a writing style that suits you.

A journal gives you an opportunity to practice with language. If you keep a daily journal, you will probably discover that the repetition of writing every day enables you to record your thoughts more easily.

A journal gives you a framework for exploring events in your life. Writers often translate journal writing into other kinds of writing, for even though writing about experience in a journal is a private act, it will give you a means of discovering what you *could* say publicly if you chose to do so. These discoveries about the significance of both recent experiences and experiences that took place a number of years ago may find their way into more formal writing later on.

CommonSense Suggestions

Keeping a Journal

Record random thoughts, ideas, and insights (Section 7a.1, "Freewriting").

Record your observations of what is going on around you (Section 14b).

Record things that you find interesting, such as descriptions of people and places (Section 14a).

Write down interesting quotations you run across in your reading or in conversation with other people.

Reproduce bits of dialogue you recall from conversations you have had or overheard.

Jot down your reactions to what you read.

Imitate examples of other people's writing that you find effective (Part V).

Explore events in your life (Section 4a).

2b
THE PORTFOLIO

Portfolios have long been used by artists, architects, photographers, and models to show the kind of work they are capable of. A portfolio of your written work will have a similar function. Over time, the body of work you have written will increase. By looking back at your finished products, you will learn something about your progress in writing. According to your purpose, you can design several different kinds of portfolios.

A **process portfolio** can help you document the progress of your work on writing projects. Keeping drafts intact for further reference will allow you to track the history and growth of a paper, and if you choose to exclude material from a subsequent draft, you will still have a copy of it in an earlier draft. (See Section 7d for a discussion of kinds of drafts.) In addition to drafts, a process portfolio will contain any journal work you have done prior to or during the drafting of the paper, the plans you work from, and any critiques of your work, whether from peers or instructors and supervisors. Of all the kinds of portfolios you could keep, the process portfolio is the most immediately useful.

A **personal portfolio** will probably include samples of your writing from different times in your life. It is similar to a journal in that the content reflects who you are, but the variety of works included will be broader. You may want to include copies of letters or memos; old school papers, reports, and essays; and creative writing projects, such as poetry and fiction. From a personal portfolio you may assemble other portfolios for specific purposes.

A **course portfolio** is often used to judge performance or establish final grades in a writing course. Such a portfolio usually includes prescribed work. For example, an instructor might require that you include a sample of your journal writing and a couple of specific assignments (e.g., an argumentative paper and a descriptive paper). You may eventually use the course portfolio as a resource when you are applying for jobs, especially if those jobs require writing skills.

2c
THE WRITING GROUP

Sometimes your writing will be a collaborative effort. Often, in the workplace as well as in the classroom, you may participate in drafting a document with a number of other people. Although **collaboration** requires you to open yourself to criticism from others, it is also an opportunity to expand your style and learn from colleagues through peer editing.

The initial stages of collaboration may involve brainstorming activities—oral discussions similar to the freewriting activities discussed in Chapter 7. This kind of initial discussion is particularly valuable when the topic under discussion involves issues that are multifaceted. Because each member of the group brings a different perspective to the question, such discussions often make possible avenues of discovery that might never occur to a writer working alone.

Of course, collaboration also brings with it certain difficulties. Negative criticism can undermine the working relationship of the group. Instead of looking for and focusing on errors, members of the group will be better served if they make suggestions for change and improvement.

Working collaboratively in a writing group requires some skills in reading and responding to the writing others have produced. Depending on the kind of writing you are responding to, you will find Part III, "Critical Thinking and Critical Reading," helpful.

2d
THE WORD PROCESSOR

A **word processor** allows you great freedom in composing. With it you can move words, paragraphs, and whole pages around with ease. The process of rewriting and editing is greatly simplified. **Editing** becomes a simple matter of moving blocks of text around on the screen, rearranging them however you please. You can also easily insert words, even entire paragraphs, into an existing text and so expand your ideas from draft to draft. When you revise part of your work, you are no longer faced with the prospect of having to type the whole thing all over again.

Many word processing programs have tools that simplify editing documents. The **spell checker** is probably the most helpful and the most frequently used. If you use the spell checker regularly, you can eliminate almost all spelling errors from your writing. The **thesaurus** allows you to find synonyms for a word typed on your screen. Most on-screen thesauruses are not quite as extensive as printed versions, but as a first option, they can be useful since you can pull down a list very quickly without turning away from your computer. Some word processing programs have **bibliography** and **footnote** makers. Depending on how familiar you are with documentation techniques, these programs can be helpful, especially if you are using a traditional format that requires footnotes at the bottom of a page. **Grammar checkers** are occasionally helpful, but experienced writers typically find them ineffective. If you are apprehensive about questions of usage, you may find that a grammar checker will give you helpful hints about some elements of usage, such as the use of passive voice.

If you can learn to compose on the word processor, you may find that you will be able to record your thoughts faster and so more closely approximate the thinking process. Some writers adapt very easily to composing on the word processor. Others may go back and forth between computer screen and printed draft, marking and editing a draft and reentering the changes on the computer. With a little practice, you will be able to find your own best process for using a word processor effectively.

2e
THE INTERNET

Sometimes described as a network of networks, the **Internet** has rapidly become an indispensable tool for writers. It places at your fingertips an almost unimaginable amount of information. All you need is a computer, a modem, a telephone connection, and a commercial or educational service. Some colleges offer email or Internet access to students free or for a minimum fee. Government and military institutions, individual companies, and private institutions also provide Internet access for their employees or customers.

Once you have access to the Internet through your computer, you can connect to millions of other computers throughout the world. You are able to "talk" to organizations and individuals that provide a vast array of documents, such as the complete texts of books, periodical articles, technical reports, scientific studies, and legislation. To locate this material, you have to use various search commands (see Part XI, "The Internet").

2f
REFERENCE WORKS

From time to time, all of us have to locate sources for information we need. But it's not always convenient to run to the library when we need to look up a word, find some bit of information, or check the accuracy of a fact we may remember imperfectly. Consequently, writers need to invest in at least a few reference works.

Essential Desk Reference Resources

Dictionary

A **dictionary** is the single most important tool you can have for writing. You will use a dictionary not only to check spelling but also to look up definitions of words. Nobody knows all the definitions of all the words in English. Frequently, you will need to know whether you can use a word in a particular context. A dictionary will tell you whether you can or not.

Some good general-purpose dictionaries are *Funk and Wagnalls New Standard Dictionary*, *Webster's Collegiate Dictionary*, and *The American Heritage College Dictionary*. Such dictionaries usually contain about 200,000 definitions.

Thesaurus

A **thesaurus** is a collection of synonyms. It is useful when you are trying to find a word that is different from the one you have in mind. You may be looking for a word that has the same **denotation** (a literal meaning) as one you have used previously but do not want to repeat. Or you may want a word with the same denotation but a **connotation** (an emotional impact on the reader) that is different from the only word you can think of.

Thesauruses come in two different formats: an alphabetical listing of words with accompanying synonyms or a division of synonyms into general classes. When using the first type, you simply look up the word to find synonyms listed with it. When using the second type, you must first look the word up in an index and then find the class to which the word belongs before you can find the appropriate synonyms.

Usage Guide

A **usage guide** gives extensive explanations of conventional standards of usage for almost any question about grammar. Two guides have been perennial favorites: *Fowler's Modern English Usage* by H. W. Fowler and *Modern American Usage* by Wilson Follett.

Almanac

Almanacs contain a variety of facts, figures, and statistics about everything from census information to economics to sports; they are published annually. Two of the most informative are *The World Almanac and Book of Facts* and *The Universal Almanac*.

Encyclopedia

Encyclopedias give you information about people and places and things, facts that are not included in dictionaries. Multivolume encyclopedias are rather expensive and take up a lot of room in a home library. One- or two-volume desk encyclopedias such as those listed here are affordable and handy to have at your fingertips.

> *The Columbia-Viking Desk Encyclopedia (two volumes)*
>
> *The Barnes and Noble Encyclopedia (one volume)*
>
> *Compton's Encyclopedia (CD-ROM)*
>
> *Microsoft Encarta (CD-ROM)*

Other Helpful Works

You will also find it useful to have most of the following resources, depending on your interests and writing activities.

> A book of quotations
>
> A handbook to literature
>
> An atlas
>
> A handbook (obviously this one)

CommonSense Suggestion

Make sure you own at least one dictionary and one thesaurus. These are the two most important tools for any writer.

The Writer's Tasks

When people write, they go through a series of activities, called a **process**. Although the writing process is similar for most writers, no two people follow exactly the same pattern. For that matter, writers seldom use exactly the same sequence of activities from one time to the next. You will not find an explanation of *the* writing process in this book—because there is no *single* process that all writers follow all the time. Instead, you will be encouraged to discover *your* process (or processes). The better you understand the unique process you use, the more control you will have over your writing.

You can think of the writing process as a series of three tasks that you will perform continuously as you bring any writing activity toward completion: you will generate content based on personal experience, research, or a combination of both; you will focus (and refocus) the ideas for clarity, unity, and coherence; and you will refine the language for correctness of usage, adherence to conventions, and stylistic effect. Although generating content usually starts the process, the tasks may occur in any order, and you are likely to perform all three many times, sometimes simultaneously. As you generate content, you may be focusing ideas and even correcting certain errors in usage. You may generate additional material after you have gained some focus and organized what you had previously produced. Stylistic changes may prompt you to refocus your ideas and to generate additional content. The writing process may take a number of different forms depending on the nature of the topic and on the unique thinking processes of each individual writer, but any process will necessarily include all three tasks.

> *Task 1—Generating content* (personal experience, research)
>
> *Task 2—Focusing ideas* (clarity, unity, coherence)
>
> *Task 3—Refining language* (usage, conventions, style)

In addition, how you accomplish each of these three tasks will be affected by three **shaping influences**: your self-knowledge, your purpose, and your audience. The three tasks will be controlled in part by your values, your experiences, and the unique way you use your language (your self-knowledge); in part by whether you are trying to express yourself, entertain an audience, persuade a reader, or explain a topic (your purpose); and in part by whether your intended reader is a friend, a colleague, or the general public (your audience). Paying attention to these three shaping influences as you perform each of the three tasks will enable you to make your writing more effective. Self-knowledge is discussed in Chapter 4; purpose, in Chapter 5; and audience, in Chapter 6.

Shaping Influences

Self-knowledge	Values, experiences, language use
Purpose	To express, to entertain, to persuade, to explain
Audience	Friends, colleagues, the general public

As you gain an understanding of your own individual writing process, you will be able to avoid some of the troublesome roadblocks that plague many writers. Being aware of the three tasks and the three shaping influences will help you make the most effective use of the drafts you create and the revisions you make.

3a GENERATING CONTENT—TASK 1

Take a look at the following piece of writing by Adam Rowe, a student at Austin Community College. This passage reflects an attempt simply to put thoughts into words. Being preoccupied with generating the content of the paper, the writer has not paid much attention to focusing ideas (Task 2) or refining language (Task 3). The passage highlights the need for writers to put into words whatever comes to mind, to make forays into unknown territory in order to get something, anything, written down.

John Coltrane was a genius. The first time I herd a Coltrane album I was a friend of my father's house. I remember hearing the paino intro to my favorite things and being instantly hooked. The hypnotic and spiritual emotion Coltrane played with was devastating. At that very moment I decided I was going to learn the saxophone. I was about seven years old when this occurred and I have studied music ever since.

> In generating content, the writer does not worry about spelling and mechanics.

> Writer expresses his personal values.

Coltrane was not just an acomplished improviser he was also one of the most influential composers in the history of jazz. He developed the technieques of cyclic and modal composition. Both of these compositional styles have been extreemly influential since their conception. Just go out and buy an album by almost any contemporary saxophonist and you will hear Coltrane's influence. I remember reading somewhere about the how the really fast way he played made the writer imagine that the sound just sort of poured out in long bursts. He also did something called multiphonics. For a long time I couldn't figure what he was doing but then in high school a teacher and a couple of older guys I had met showed me this trick Coltrane did with his breath and lips which I still have trouble with it but I'm starting to

> Writer begins to discover his purpose.

> Writer shares his knowledge of the subject.

> Writer shows an awareness of the audience.

> Writer recalls previous reading.

> Writer explores his personal knowledge of the subject.

continued on next page

get it. Also you have to use special

multiphonic fingerings. Man I don't know, that

guy I've read practiced all the time it sure

seems like it.

   Nowadays everybody pays hommage to Coltrane.

Branford Marsalis, Sonny Stitt, Cannonball

Adderly, and David Sanborn all acknowledge a

greate debt to the master. My favorite albums

of his now are Giant Steps and A Love Supreme.

He was a giant that's for sure.

Writer expresses his values and personal experience.

   Often writers have difficulty getting started, generating content at all. If that happens to you, there are a number of techniques, explained in Chapters 4 and 7—narrowing a topic, freewriting, mapping, and questioning—that you can use to express thoughts and feelings in writing. Since the task of generating content is not something you do only in the beginning of a writing project, the same techniques will help you whenever you need to create new material in your paper.

   Depending on the purpose of your writing and the audience you are addressing, you may find that your experience and your knowledge of the topic are not sufficient, and so you may need to generate content by doing background reading and research. The techniques of research and documentation (identifying sources) are discussed in Chapters 4, 43, and 44.

CommonSense Checklist

Generating Content—Task 1

Self-knowledge

Have you identified all your personal experiences that relate to the topic?

Have you explored everything you know about the subject?

→

continued from previous page

Purpose

Do you know what purpose you want to achieve in your piece of writing?

Does a consideration of your purpose suggest the need for any additional information (e.g., research material that would support an argument or explain the topic more thoroughly)?

Audience

Have you included information your audience will need in order to understand the topic?

3b
FOCUSING IDEAS—TASK 2

Consider the following version of the essay about saxophonist John Coltrane, which you first encountered in Section 3a. You will notice that this version is more focused, a focusing that is affected by self-knowledge, purpose, and audience (the three shaping influences). Look in particular at how the writer has attempted to bring shape and substance to his topic.

Adam Rowe

Professor Davis

English 1613

15 August 1996

    John Coltrane: Master of Modern Saxophone

    John Coltrane was an enornous genius. No jazz musician before of science has had as profound an influence as he. This essay will focus on three criteria by which I have come to this conclusion.

Writer begins to follow MLA style.

Writer adds title to focus reader on subject.

Writer clarifies purpose.

continued on next page

1. Technical mastery of the instrument in the vehicle of improvisation

2. Compositional innovativeness

3. Amount of influence exerted on jazz musicians who came after him

The legend of Coltrane's mastery of the saxophone goes back to his early days in Philadelphia. He and his cousin Mary would practice by playing and singing for hours on end to old Lester Young and Billie Holliday albums. Years later, after he was an accomplished bandleader, Coltrane's basic daily routine was: wake up and practice for at least two hours, eat a quick breakfast, practice until time to go to the club, play the first set at the club, go in the back and practice between sets, play the second set at the club, go home and finger his horn quietly so as not to wake the family, and fall asleep with the horn strapped around his neck. He spent an average of ten hours a day playing the saxophone. John Coltrane also changed the vocabulary of modern saxophone technique. His techinical innovations include overblowing, multiphonics, and the method of improvisation that the jazz critic Ira Gitler

Writer tells reader how essay is organized.

Writer omits statement about himself.

Research helps create new material.

continued on next page

called "sheets of sound." Overblowing is a
method of producing a multitude of different
timbres for the same pitch. the most famous
example of Coltranes use of overblowing is in
the first movement of his Impulse Records
masterpiece, <u>A Love Supreme</u>. To practice
multiphonics is to pracitice playing more than
one note at a time on the saxophone. As a
saxophone player myself I can tell you that
this is no easy task. To achieve a multiphonic
the musician must drop the air and lip pressure
in the armbrochure and use special multiphonic
fingerings. A well-known example of Coltranes
use of multiphonics is in his 1957 Atlantic
recording of the Sonny Rollins tune
"Harmonique." In 1959 the jazz critique Ira
Gitler coined the phrase "sheets of sound" to
describe the technical side of Coltranes
improvisations. This is basically a description
of the way the Coltrane broke away from the
standard jazz 16th and 8th note rhythms.
Coltrane would go well above the 16th note even
in charts that called for a high tempo (above
130 beats per minute.)

John Coltrane is personally responsible for
two major compositional revolutions in the
world of jazz music. The first is called cyclic

Writer adds
quotation
from
authority.

Writer
includes
personal
expertise.

Writer
combines
ideas from
two sentences
into one
sentence.

Added
statement
brings
coherence to
paragraph.

continued on next page

composition. This form of composition is more commonly called the Giant Steps cycle, named for the Coltrane album on which it first appeared. The method of cyclic composition starts with the chord progression of any old standard or bebop chart. After this progression has been established, the composer then picks a diatonic interval to cycle the progression with. Coltrane usually used the interval of the dominant (5th) and the subdominant (4th). By moving the basic chord progression around the circle of keys and ending back at the beginning, cyclic composition give the listener and intense tension followed by a delicious resolution. Coltrane worked with this compositional style for the first half of his career as a composer. By the early 1960s Coltrane had begun to feel trapped by his own compositional innovation. He felt that the quality of his improvisations was being dininished by the complexity of the chord progressions in his compositions. To remedy this Coltrane invented what would come to be known as modal improvisation, his second contribution to jazz composition. Modal composition brakes down the compositional process to it's bare miminum. The piece starts

Added information further defines topic.

Writer corrects some grammatical and mechanical inconsistencies, but others remain or are created.

Added statement brings coherence to paragraph.

continued on next page

with a melody and then the composer picks a group of scales or modes for the improvisers to use in the piece. The improviser is then left free to explore the tonal and harmonic possibilities of the composer's choice of sounds. Coltrane would use the method of modal composition until his death in 1967.

John Coltrane has had outstanding influence on nearly every major improviser and composer who followed him. The school of free jazz, which was founded in 1969, was started by two Coltrane disciples: Eric Dolphy and Ornette Coleman. It is difficult to find a contemporary bebop chart that doesn't cycle. Modern improvisers such as David Sanborn, Branford Marsalis, Sonny Stitt, and Cannonball Adderly all rely on the improvisational techniques invented and mastered by John Coltrane.

Added information brings depth to topic.

Coltrane did more for modern jazz than any other musician. His technical innovations were many years ahead of their time. His compositional genius is matched only by Thelonius Monk. His is influence on contemporary improvisation is unsurpassable. What I mean to say is that in my opinion, he is a giant among giants. I think the greatest saxophone player ever.

Writer expands and focuses ending of essay.

As you can see from the draft above, focusing your ideas may involve moving words, phrases, sentences, and passages from one place in the work to another. It may mean creating new material that clarifies what you have already written (Task 1). Writing of this kind helps unify the work and makes the writing more coherent. A work will be unified if all parts are related to a main idea (see Section 13a). The same is true of each individual paragraph as well. A work will have coherence if information presented is understandable and makes sense to a reader (see Chapter 16). In addition, the essay should have valid logical relationships between all the ideas that are presented to the reader. Many strategies for achieving these results are explained in Parts III and IV.

CommonSense Checklist

Focusing Ideas—Task 2

Self-knowledge

Is the logic of the arrangement of the ideas consistent with your values?

Are there ideas in the work that are not consistent with your values?

Purpose

Is the structure of the work appropriate to the purpose?

Are there any logical fallacies?

Does the organization make the relationships between ideas clear?

Have you made appropriate use of transitions and repetitions to clarify relationships?

Audience

Is the topic focused so that the audience can understand it?

Are there ideas in the work that are not related to the main idea and thus could confuse the audience?

Does sentence punctuation clarify the meaning of your work?

3c
REFINING LANGUAGE—TASK 3

Consider the following version of the student essay from Sections 3a and 3b. Can you see how the writer has refined his work?

Adam Rowe

Professor Davis

English 1613

20 August 1996

John Coltrane: Master of Modern Saxophone

John Coltrane was an enormous genius. No jazz musician before or since has had such a profound influence. The legend of Coltrane's mastery of the saxophone goes back to his early days in Philadelphia. He and his cousin Mary would practice playing and singing for hours on end to old Lester Young and Billie Holliday albums. Years later, even after he was an accomplished bandleader, Coltrane's basic daily routine was to wake up and practice for at least two hours, eat a quick breakfast, practice until time to go to the club, play the first set at the club, go in the back and practice between sets, play the second set at the club, go home and finger his horn quietly so as not to wake the family, and fall asleep with the horn strapped around his neck (Lyons 235). He spent an average of ten hours a day playing the saxophone. Fellow band musician Elvin Jones said of Coltrane, "The most impressive thing about working with Trane was a feeling of steady, collective learning" (qtd.

Writer moves material to beginning of essay to provide background for readers.

Following MLA style, writer documents source of research.

Writer adds quotation.

continued on next page

in Thomas 139). As a result of this single-
minded dedication to the saxophone, Coltrane
achieved a technical mastery of the instrument
that allowed him to use it as a vehicle of
improvisation, changed jazz by his compositional
innovativeness, and exerted an important
influence on jazz musicians who came after him.

    John Coltrane changed the vocabulary of
modern saxophone technique. His technical
innovations include overblowing, multiphonics,
and the method that the jazz critic Ira Gitler
called "sheets of sound" to describe the
technical side of Coltrane's improvisations
(Nisenson 49). Overblowing is a method of
producing a multitude of different timbres for
the same pitch. The most famous example of
Coltrane's use of overblowing is in the first
movement of his Impulse Records masterpiece, <u>A
Love Supreme</u>. To practice multiphonics is to
practice playing more than one note at a time
on the saxophone. To achieve a multiphonic
sound the musician must drop the air and lip
pressure in the embouchuré and use special
multiphonic fingerings. A well-known example of
Coltrane's use of multiphonics is in his 1959
Atlantic recording of the Sonny Rollins tune
"Harmonique," in which he achieved his "sheets

Writer revises statement of main idea.

Writer corrects spelling.

Writer revises fused sentence and error in possession.

Writer decides to omit personal statement.

Writer adds clarifying word and corrects spelling.

continued on next page

of sound." This is basically a description of the way Coltrane broke away from the standard jazz sixteenth and eighth note rhythms. Coltrane would go well above the sixteenth note even in charts that called for a high tempo (above 130 beats per minute.)

Coltrane is responsible for two major compositional revolutions in the world of jazz music. The first is called cyclic composition. This form of composition is more commonly called the Giant Steps cycle, named for the Coltrane album on which it first appeared. The method of cyclic composition starts with the chord progression of any old standard or bebop chart. After this progression has been established, the composer then picks a diatonic interval to cycle the progression with. Coltrane usually used the interval of the dominant (fifth) and the subdominant (fourth). By moving the basic chord progression around the circle of keys and ending back at the beginning, cyclic composition gives the listener an intense tension followed by a delicious resolution. Coltrane described the bass line as "looping" (qtd. in Lyons 235). Coltrane worked with this compositional style for the first half of his career as a composer. By the early

Writer combines ideas from two sentences to make clearer connections.

Writer corrects a subject-verb agreement problem.

continued on next page

1960s Coltrane had begun to feel trapped by his own innovations. He felt that the quality of his improvisations was being diminished by the complexity of the chord progressions in his compositions. To remedy this, Coltrane invented what would come to be known as modal improvisation. Modal composition breaks down the compositional process to its bare minimum. The piece starts with a melody and then the composer picks a group of scales or modes for the improviser to use in the piece. The improviser is then left free to explore the tonal and harmonic possibilities of the composer's choice of sounds. He began using this technique in 1960 when he recorded "My Favorite Things" and continued to use this method until his death in 1967 (Porter).

Writer revises consistency problem.

Writer adds more information.

John Coltrane has had an important influence on nearly every major improviser and composer who followed him. The school of free jazz, which was founded in 1959, was started by two Coltrane fans: Eric Dolphy and Ornette Coleman. It is difficult to find a contemporary bebop chart that doesn't cycle. Modern improvisers such as David Sanborn, Branford Marsalis, Sonny Stitt, and Cannonball Adderley all rely on the improvisational techniques invented and mastered

Writer corrects a factual error and changes a word for accuracy.

Writer corrects spelling of "Adderley."

continued on next page

by John Coltrane. In fact, his improvisational style has influenced other musicians such as rock guitarists Carlos Santana and John McLaughlin (Lyons 333) and classical composer Philip Glass (Nisenson 232).

Writer expands the scope of Coltrane's influence.

Many believe that Coltrane did more for modern jazz than any other musician. His technical innovations were many years ahead of their time. His compositional genius is matched only by Thelonius Monk, and his influence on contemporary improvisation is unsurpassed. He is a giant among giants, and certainly, the greatest saxophone player ever.

Writer combines sentences.

Writer eliminates conversational phrases and combines sentences into a more direct restatement of main idea.

Works Cited

Lyons, Len. The 101 Best Jazz Albums: A History of Jazz on Records. New York: Morrow, 1980.

Nisenson, Eric. Ascension: John Coltrane and His Quest. New York: Da Capo, 1993.

Porter, Lewis. "Jazz." Microsoft Encarta. 1993 ed. CD-ROM. Redmond: Microsoft, 1993.

Thomas, J. C. Chasing the Trane. New York: Da Capo, 1975.

Writer adds "Works Cited" to identify fully the sources cited in essay.

This version of the essay shows that the writer has paid some attention to refining language in ways affected by the three shaping influences—self-knowledge, purpose, and audience. Some writers tend to work on the task of refining the language only after the other two tasks have been completed. But that is by no means a requirement. Paying too much attention to this task at the beginning of the process, however, can interfere with generating the content and focusing the ideas.

A large part of the material in this handbook has to do with the task of refining the language, in effect, putting the finishing touches on a work. Some of the details involved in this task have to do with punctuating sentences, revising for matters of usage (e.g., subject-verb agreement, pronoun reference, and use of possessives), checking for appropriate conventions (e.g., spelling, capitalization, and the use of apostrophes), and enhancing style (e.g., combining sentences and making word choices that affect the tone of the work). Some people think this is all there is to writing. They often become obsessed with correctness and style; consequently, they may lose sight of communicating the ideas they have in mind. Although Task 3 is essential, it is not the only thing that needs to happen in writing.

CommonSense Checklist

Refining Language—Task 3

Self-knowledge

Have you created natural and authentic voice, tone, and writing style?

Does your language represent you to your audience as you want?

If you have used language that would offend or alienate your audience, have you done so purposefully?

Purpose

Does your language reflect your purpose?

Is your tone appropriate for your purpose?

Does the layout of your piece of writing clearly define your purpose?

Audience

Have you varied sentence length and sentence patterns in order to engage the reader?

Have you used language that your audience will not understand (e.g., jargon your audience would not be familiar with or undefined terms)?

Have you used language that your audience would not approve of (e.g., sexist language)?

Are there problems with usage (Part VII) or with the use of conventions (Part VIII) that would distract the reader?

The three tasks will allow you to check your progress toward the completion of your project. Completing them will necessarily require that you create multiple drafts (except in those rare instances when the first draft is also the last one) and revise your work as you produce each draft. In essence, the process demands two kinds of action: (1) creating the pieces of the work—either as the original, as replacements for the original, or as additions to the original; and (2) deciding how to order those pieces you retain. Any time you revise any draft of your work, you will be doing one or both of those two things. The tasks will help guide you toward the completion of any writing project.

2

Discovery and Invention

4 TOPIC

How to find ideas . . . see 4A

How to narrow a broad subject . . . see 4B

How to make personal connections as you focus on a topic . . . see 4C

5 PURPOSE

How to write about yourself . . . see 5A

How to entertain other people with language . . . see 5B

How to persuade an audience to agree with your position . . . see 5C

How to inform your readers or interpret information for them . . . see 5D

6 AUDIENCE AND CONTEXT

Making the process of reading easier for the reader . . . see 6A

What to consider when you write for a specific audience . . . see 6B

What to consider when you write for a general audience . . . see 6C

How the situation that has prompted you to write will
affect your work . . . see 6D

7 CONTENT

How to get ideas into written form . . . see 7A

How to show relationships between parts of a topic . . . see 7B

How to use different kinds of questions to help create details . . . see 7C

How to use drafts as stages in the process of writing . . . see 7D

Topic

If you were required to write a thousand-word paper for a sociology class on a topic of your choice, you would immediately be confronted with several problems. One problem would be to decide on something to write about—a topic that could be covered in one thousand words and one that you liked well enough to spend your time on. After exploring several possibilities, you might choose a topic such as status and role in the college environment.

Topic—its content, its scope, its importance to you, its relevance to the reader—affects every phase of writing. As you write, you will constantly refine, reshape, develop, and discover your topic. It does not become frozen at the beginning but will change as you write.

4a
GETTING IDEAS

In school, often your instructor will assign a topic to you. If, however, you have to come up with one on your own, don't despair. Ideas for writing are all around you. Everything you experience and everything you know about can potentially be a subject for writing: pollution, the circus, a football game, studying for a test, making pasta, throwing a party, kinds of houses, rap music, the best kind of pet to have, the issue of gun control, a memorable vacation. The trick is in isolating just the right ideas from the almost endless series of thoughts, memories, and images that stream continuously through your mind.

4a.1 What You Have Experienced

Examining your own experiences is the most obvious way of finding a starting point for your writing because experience is the primary source of ideas for all writers. One good way to start examining your experiences is to think about things you have done, places you have been, or people you have met. You might find it helpful to explore some of the ideas suggested below.

Events

What memorable events have you participated in during your lifetime? No doubt some particular experiences you had in school stand out in your

31

mind. Consider each school you have attended: elementary school, junior high, high school, college. Make a list of events from each of them—for example, reading aloud in class, your first date, a science project, moving away from home.

What experiences with family members, relatives, or close friends stand out in your mind? You might find it helpful to create a list of people and try to recall something important that happened with each of them.

What things have happened to you since you left home and started to live on your own? Are there job experiences that are significant to you? See if you can list them.

Other significant events include things that have annoyed you, frightened you, depressed you, amused you, or thrilled you. You might also recall an achievement that you consider to be your biggest success or a mistake that you consider to be your biggest failure. Has something happened to you that changed the way you look at things? For example, have you taken a trip to Europe, experienced the loss of a loved one, won an award?

Places

You might find it helpful to try to remember all the places you have lived. Think about the details of your homes, dorm rooms, or apartments. What did they look like? How did they make you feel?

Think about the towns and cities you have lived in. Make a list of them. What significant feature do you associate with each one? What was it like to live there? You might also find it helpful to explain how each town or city was similar or different. (See Section 14e, "Comparing and Contrasting.")

What places have you visited? Make a list. Explain why you visited them. How did you like each one? Would you go back? Why or why not?

People

Think about people you have known. What made each one memorable? You might try limiting the list to certain periods of time or to certain groups: high school friends, college roommates, or longtime acquaintances. Describe each person you have listed. (See Section 14a, "Describing.")

Useful techniques for examining your experiences are keeping a journal (Section 2a) and engaging in freewriting (Section 7a.1).

4a.2 What You Know About

Another source of ideas for writing is the wealth of knowledge you already have available to you. Have you ever thought of yourself as an expert? Perhaps not, but you certainly are expert at something. All of us know more about some things than most other people do. Consider how you spend most of your time. Your job, your hobbies, your pastimes—all are activities you know a great deal about. You may have extensive knowledge about how a computer program works, about the number and scope of Star Trek clubs in America, or about the history of a particular rock group or singer. In addition, from your educational experiences or from your reading, you may have accumulated a large body of knowledge on some subject because you have found it to be especially interesting. You may know quite a lot about the dismantling of apartheid in South Africa or about the stats of a particular baseball team or player.

Usually, though, people are unaware of the enormous amount of knowledge they have acquired. Sometimes it helps to let your thoughts range over all the things you have done and read about. Have you recently purchased or assembled a computer? Have you studied one of the martial arts? Have you followed a controversy in the news? Have you trained for a new skill at work?

4a.3 What You Are Interested in Knowing

Often, even though we don't actually know a great deal about a particular subject, we have a desire to know about it. Many people enjoy writing because it allows them to identify subjects they would like to know more about—something they have always found interesting but have never had time to learn. Consider something you have always wanted to do, a subject you have always wanted to study, or a place you have always wanted to visit: ballroom dancing, backpacking, gourmet cooking, the Civil War, calculus, astronomy, Austria, bookbinding, gardening, mountain bikes, flower arranging, England, bonsai plants, computer programming, the Rockies.

Background Reading

Initially, you will want to find out some general information about the topic, information that is outside your own experience and personal knowledge. The best way to get a general background is to go to a general-purpose encyclopedia such as the *Encyclopaedia Britannica* or the *Encyclopedia Americana*. In addition to helping you get some basic information on your topic and helping you narrow your thinking about the topic, encyclopedia articles often include lists of books and articles on the subject you are investigating.

After you've gained a working background, you may want to consult some specialized encyclopedias and dictionaries. A list of a few representative specialized reference works follows; your library will have these or similar works.

Art and Music

Britannica Encyclopaedia of American Art

Encyclopedia of World Art

The New Grove Dictionary of Music and Musicians

The New Oxford History of Music

Business and Economics

A Dictionary of Economics

Encyclopedia of Banking and Finance

The Encyclopedia of Management

The McGraw-Hill Dictionary of Modern Economics

History and Political Science

Dictionary of American History

Dictionary of American Politics

An Encyclopedia of World History

New Cambridge Modern History

Literature and Film

Cassell's Encyclopedia of World Literature

International Encyclopedia of Film

The Oxford Companion to American Literature

The Oxford Companion to English Literature

Philosophy and Religion

The Encyclopedia of Philosophy

Encyclopedia of Religion

The HarperCollins Dictionary of Religion

History of Philosophy

Science and Technology

The Encyclopedia of the Biological Sciences

Handbook of Chemistry and Physics

The McGraw-Hill Encyclopedia of Science and Technology

Van Nostrand's Scientific Encyclopedia

Social Science and Education

Dictionary of Anthropology

Encyclopedia of Education

Encyclopedia of Psychology

International Encyclopedia of the Social Sciences

Browsing the Internet

Just as you might search through a stack of books in a library looking for something you could be interested in writing about, you can also use your computer to browse the Internet. Many people enjoy the freedom of sitting in their offices or in their homes and cruising the telephone lines of the world looking for the next odd and interesting site.

If you can connect to the Internet—that is, you have a computer, a modem, a telephone line, and an account with a service provider—you can browse the Internet. (See Part XI for more about the Internet.)

4a.4 What You Find Disturbing

Most of us are disturbed by certain things that are going on around us. No doubt there is something you find troubling: war, poverty, racism, sexism, pollution, abuse of human rights, age discrimination, governmental intrusiveness, taxation. Whatever it is, by examining your responses, you may find a subject you can use to begin the writing process. If nothing comes to mind immediately, try looking in a newspaper or a newsmagazine for ideas or listening to a call-in talk radio program. Television news or newsmagazine shows, such as *60 Minutes* or *Nightline*, can bring disturbing things to your attention.

4b
NARROWING SUBJECTS AND TOPICS

If you are uncomfortable working on a particular writing assignment, the reason may be that you have only a vague idea of what to say or that you have identified only a broad subject to write about and have not yet focused on a suitable topic. Gathering ideas is a necessary first step toward beginning to discover a topic. But eventually general subjects like "problems in school" or "criminal justice in this state" must become more **focused topics**—for example, "choosing classes" and "the shortcomings of our state parole system."

Whether a subject is too broad depends in part on the number of words you plan to use when you write about it. For instance, if you plan to write a paper of five hundred to a thousand words, then the subject "the future of computers" is certainly too large. How would you adequately discuss computer graphics in film, the paperless library, the use of the *Thomas Legislative Guide*, and the creation of virtual reality games all in one short (or even long) essay? More appropriate topics might be "computers in the twenty-first century kitchen," "computers in the classroom," or "computer games." The first task you face is to make the subject more manageable, to *narrow* it.

The general subjects that follow would probably have to be narrowed, limited in some way before you could develop a paper about that idea. As you read the list, try to change the general subject into a specific topic.

General Subject	Specific Topic
Backpacking	
Music	
Pollution	
Politics	
Computers	
Bicycles	
Energy sources	

Compare your answers with the following suggestions. Then try to narrow the topics even further by making them more specific.

General Subject	Specific Topic	More Specific Topic
Backpacking	Kinds of packs	
Music	Classical music	
Pollution	Air pollution	
Politics	Elections	
Computers	Software	
Bicycles	Road bikes	
Energy sources	Solar energy	

How do your topics compare with those below?

General Subject	Specific Topic	More Specific Topic
Backpacking	Kinds of packs	External-frame pack
Music	Classical music	The symphony
Pollution	Air pollution	Auto emissions
Politics	Elections	Voting fraud
Computers	Software	Computer games
Bicycles	Road bikes	How gears work
Energy sources	Solar energy	Passive solar collectors

As you can see, if you are dealing with a broad, general subject, you will more than likely need to try to narrow it, make it more specific. Trying to write about a general subject often results in a vague, confusing treatment. Even if you have made a broad subject into a narrow topic, you may need to see if you can narrow it further. Shaping the topic initially may save you time and frustration later on as you write.

In Chapter 5, "Purpose," you will find a discussion of how a further narrowing of the topic occurs when you are able to state a specific purpose. For instance, if you were writing a persuasive paper about the topic of solar collectors, you would need to decide what issue to address. You may find that several of the techniques explained in Part II may help you narrow a broad subject by allowing you to explore the subject from a number of perspectives. See especially listing (Section 7a.2) and mapping (Section 7a.3).

4c
CARING ABOUT A TOPIC

If you are writing about a topic you chose yourself, chances are it will address a subject you care about. If, on the other hand, you are working with an assigned topic, you may find it difficult to be very enthusiastic.

Often, we as writers can find a way to care about almost any topic. We simply have to make it our own. Part of the process of making a topic your own may have occurred while you were narrowing it (as you saw in Section 4b). If you are still not satisfied with the topic, look for a more personal perspective, a way of seeing the subject matter that reflects your own special point of view.

Let's say an instructor has assigned an essay about a controversy on campus. Assume that you don't know much about the controversy, nor do you care very much about it. One approach you could use to form an opinion would be to read articles or interview students about the topic; chances are, you would find that your attitudes already cluster on one side of the issue or the other. Or you could write from your dispassionate perspective—why the controversy is unimportant and a distraction from your purposes at school.

Examining your **personal experiences** can be a useful way of gaining insight. If you have had direct contact with the topic, you will be able to use that experience to generate details. Even if you haven't had direct experiences with the topic, something similar may have happened to you. Suppose that one day your boss, Ms. Green, tells you that she needs to inform her staff about a new policy concerning sick leave; however, she is leaving town for a week-long conference, so she asks you to write a memo explaining the policy. Even though this writing assignment must be professional in tone, you can use a personal experience to help you care about it. You remember that when you were new to the company, you had the flu and felt very insecure because you didn't have clear information about sick-leave policies. Your actual experience, while not part of the memo, will encourage you to answer questions that you know will be asked by others.

Purpose

On any given day you may encounter a number of different kinds of communication: billboards, news stories, TV advertising, song lyrics, informal conversations, lectures, textbooks, graffiti, poetry, instructions, political speeches, personal letters. These are all examples of communication using words. Even though they occur in different circumstances and have different audiences, some of them are similar enough to be grouped together. What do the following two have in common?

Personal letter

Graffiti

How about these two?

Song lyric

Poem

And these?

TV advertisement

Political speech

And finally, these?

News story

Instruction booklet

Seeing the examples placed into these four groups, can we begin to perceive another likeness? Don't the examples in each group have a similar **purpose,** the reason the writer created them?

Extending the list of examples in each group reveals more clearly the similarity of purpose. As you consider each group, imagine why a person may write them.

Personal letter

Graffiti

Autobiography

Diary

All the above focus on the writer or speaker and have as their purpose the desire to express the personality and identity of the person creating the message. What about the following?

Song lyric

Poem

Novel

Script for a TV sit-com

Notice that the four examples above all have the purpose of entertaining an audience. The purpose of the next four examples is different.

TV advertisement

Political speech

Editorial

Magazine article about a social issue

All the examples above have the purpose of persuading an audience to take a position on some issue, or perhaps even to take action based on that belief. What is the purpose of the examples below?

News story

Instruction booklet

Encyclopedia

Business letter

The writers of these examples wish to explain a topic so that their readers can understand it.

Now, if you didn't group the types of writing in the same way as the above examples, it is probably because you see something that is almost always true about a piece of writing—it has more than one purpose. A song lyric meant to entertain the listener might also be an expression of the writer's feelings. A billboard meant to persuade us to buy a new candy bar may also entertain us.

So it appears that all forms of communication have one or more purposes and that those purposes determine how we treat a subject. Like filters, they allow into a document only features and content appropriate to the writer's purpose. For example, a chemist writing a lab report would not tell about the joys or frustrations of performing experiments. So, in effect, the purpose (explaining a topic) prevents such a writer from including personal feelings in an objective report.

The four purposes of writing—to express yourself, to entertain others, to persuade an audience, and to explain a topic—may be regarded as the general purposes of your writing. In addition, each time you write, you will have a more specific purpose, a main idea that reflects your approach to the specific content of the paper (see Section 13a). While you are writing, the main idea may continue to be modified as new information is added to the document, even though the general purpose remains unchanged. The main idea of writing may be explicitly stated or it may be implied, but either way it will control the structure and content of the work.

5a
EXPRESSING YOURSELF

Take a few minutes and read the following passage. As you read it, try to recognize the author's purpose, which is to express herself. But how do we recognize that expressing herself is her purpose?

Are there places, for instance, where the writer appears to want anything from the reader other than an understanding of who she is? Does she want the reader to do anything? Or may it be that for her, the act of writing, the act of expressing herself, is her ultimate purpose? Dorothy Wordsworth wrote this journal entry on April 16, 1802.

> We saw a fisherman in the flat meadow on the other side of the water. He came towards us and threw his line over the two arched Bridge. It is a Bridge of a heavy construction, almost bending inwards in the middle, but it is grey and there is a look of ancientry in the architecture of it that pleased me. . . . A Sheep came plunging through the river, stumbled up the Bank and passed close to us, it had been frightened by an insignificant little Dog on the other side, its fleece dropped a glittering shower under its belly. Primroses by the roadside, pile wort that shone like stars of gold in the Sun, violets, strawberries, retired and half buried in among the grass. When we came to the foot of Brothers water I left William sitting on the Bridge and went along the path on the right side of the Lake through the wood. I was delighted with what I

saw. The water under the boughs of the bare old trees, the simplicity of the mountains and the exquisite beauty of the path. There was one grey cottage.
—Dorothy Wordsworth, *The Grasmere Journals*

The author of this passage is defining herself, explaining who she is in relation to her topic. She uses personal language (the first person pronoun *I*) and she reveals her values. When you express yourself, the main idea is a statement of the identity of the writer. In the previous example the main idea is an implied self-definition, "I am a lover of nature." The content of any writing in which you express yourself will reflect facets of your personality—your feelings, your values, your goals, and even your language patterns. This kind of writing can be called writer-centered because it is concerned with the writer's interests. In its purest forms, such as a diary or a personal journal (usually unpublished), the writer pays almost no attention to any potential reader, except, perhaps, an imagined future self. In other forms of personal writing, such as autobiography and personal letters, the writer will usually do his or her best to make sure the reader understands. Although you are basically free from restrictions when you write to express yourself, you may sometimes find it difficult to be spontaneous and self-reflective, especially if you are not used to talking about your feelings. However, this kind of introspective activity can be a valuable thing to do because, as you discovered in Sections 2a, "The Journal," and 4a.1, "What You Have Experienced," keeping a journal is a powerful tool for getting ideas. In addition, the act of exploring your life and your experiences can have other benefits, such as increasing your understanding of your identity and making you more aware of what happens to you from day to day.

5b
ENTERTAINING OTHERS

Now read the following passage by Mark Twain. How does it differ from the example by Dorothy Wordsworth in Section 5a? Since Twain wants to entertain his audience, what has he done that is different from what Wordsworth has done? In particular, how has he focused our attention on the language? How does this focus on language help us feel the emotions ourselves?

Along about an hour after breakfast we saw the first prairie-dog villages, the first antelope, and the first wolf. If I remember rightly, this latter was the regular coyote (pronounced ky-o-te) of the farther deserts. And if it was, he was not a pretty creature, or respectable either, for I got well acquainted with his race afterward, and can speak with confidence. The coyote is a long, slim, sick and sorry-looking skeleton, with a gray wolf-skin stretched over it, a tolerably bushy tail that forever sags down with a despairing expression of forsakenness and misery, a furtive and evil eye, and a long, sharp face, with slightly lifted lip and exposed teeth. He has a general slinking expression all over. . . . He is so spiritless and cowardly that even while his exposed teeth are pretending a threat, the rest of his face is apologizing for it. And he is so homely!—so scrawny, and ribby, and coarse-haired, and pitiful. When he sees you he lifts his lips and lets a flash of his teeth out, and then turns a little out of the course he was pursuing, depresses his head a bit, and strikes a long, soft-footed trot through the sage-brush, glancing over his shoulder at you, from time to time, till he is about out of easy pistol range, and then he stops and takes a deliberate survey of you; he will trot fifty yards and stop again—another fifty and stop again; and finally the gray of his gliding body blends with the gray of the sage-brush, and he disappears. . . . But if you start a swift-footed dog after him, you will enjoy it ever so much—especially if it is a dog that has a good opinion of himself, and has been brought up to think he knows something about speed. The coyote will go swinging gently off on that deceitful trot of his, and every little while he will smile a fraudful smile over his shoulder that will fill that dog entirely full of encouragement and worldly ambition, and make him lay his head still lower to the ground, and stretch his neck further to the front, and pant more fiercely, and stick his tail out straighter behind, and move his furious legs with a yet wilder frenzy, and leave a broader and broader, and higher and denser cloud of desert sand smoking behind, and marking his long wake across the level plain! And all this time the dog is only a short twenty feet behind the coyote, and to save the soul of him he cannot understand why it is that he cannot get perceptibly closer; and he begins to get aggravated, and it makes him madder and madder to see how gently the coyote glides along and never pants or sweats or ceases to smile; and he grows still more and more incensed to see how shamefully he has been taken in by an entire stranger, and what an ignoble swindle that long, calm, soft-footed trot is; and next he notices that he is getting fagged, and that the coyote actually has to slacken speed a little to keep from running away from him—and then that town-dog is mad in earnest, and he begins to strain and weep and swear, and paw the sand higher than ever, and reach for the coyote with concentrated and desperate energy. This "spurt" finds him six feet behind his gliding enemy, and two miles from his friends. And then, in the instant that a wild new hope is lighting up his face, the coyote turns and smiles blandly upon him once more, and with a something about it which seems to say: "Well, I shall have to tear myself away from you, bub—business is business, and it will not do for me to be fooling along this way all day"—and forthwith there is a rushing sound, and the sudden splitting of a long crack through the atmosphere, and behold that dog is solitary and alone in the midst of a vast solitude!

—Mark Twain, *Roughing It*

You may have noticed that you were engaged in the events of the story because of the conflicts revealed in the struggle between the coyote and the dog.

Notice also that writing that entertains others usually focuses our attention on the significance of the work. The implied main idea of this work is that coyotes are crafty and cunning.

When you write to entertain others, you focus the reader's attention on the writing itself by creating tension through conflict and suspense, by using vivid language to describe setting or character, and by using traditional literary devices (or creating new ones). Most cultures throughout history have produced a large body of this kind of writing, the kind of writing we call **literature**. An enormous number of forms have been developed—novels, sonnets, plays, ballads, short stories, epics, and haiku, to name a few. We enjoy these kinds of writing because they appeal to our aesthetic sense in the same way that other forms of art do.

5c
PERSUADING AN AUDIENCE

As you read the next passage by Rachel Carson, notice how she has focused on her audience, in particular by trying to convince readers that children ought to be encouraged to love the beauty of nature instead of being made to learn facts. How does she control the topic, word choice, and content in her attempt to persuade?

> A child's world is fresh and new and beautiful, full of wonder and excitement. It is our misfortune that for most of us that clear-eyed vision, that true instinct for what is beautiful and awe-inspiring, is dimmed and even lost before we reach adulthood. If I had influence with the good fairy who is supposed to preside over the christening of all children I should ask that her gift to each child in the world be a sense of wonder so indestructible that it would last throughout life, as an unfailing antidote against the boredom and disenchantments of later years, the sterile preoccupation with things that are artificial, the alienation from the sources of our strength.
>
> If a child is to keep alive his inborn sense of wonder without any such gift from the fairies, he needs the companionship of at least one adult who can share it, rediscovering with him the joy, excitement and mystery of the world we live in. Parents often have a sense of inadequacy when confronted on the one hand with the eager, sensitive mind of a child and on the other with a world of complex physical nature, inhabited by a life so various and unfamiliar that it seems hopeless to reduce it to order and knowledge. In a mood of self-defeat, they exclaim, "How can I possibly teach my child about nature—why, I don't know one bird from another!"

I sincerely believe that for the child, and for the parent seeking to guide him, it is not half so important to *know* as to feel. If facts are the seeds that later produce knowledge and wisdom, then the emotions and the impressions of the senses are the fertile soil in which the seeds must grow. The years of early childhood are the time to prepare the soil. Once the emotions have been aroused—a sense of the beautiful, the excitement of the new and the unknown, a feeling of sympathy, pity, admiration or love—then we wish for knowledge about the object of our emotional response. Once found, it has lasting meaning. It is more important to pave the way for the child to want to know than to put him on a diet of facts he is not ready to assimilate.

—Rachel Carson, *The Sense of Wonder*

In this example, the writer is trying to get the reader to believe something or to do something. She does this by offering several reasons why she thinks children would benefit from a focus on developing appreciation of the natural world. She also uses emotional appeals to inspire the reader to encourage children to appreciate the natural world.

In writing meant to persuade an audience, the main idea makes a claim about the writer's position. In this example, Carson claims that children will benefit from gaining an appreciation of the natural world rather than being given a "diet of facts" they are "not ready to assimilate."

Writing to persuade requires attention to the practical effects that the ideas have on the audience. Since writing to persuade has to do with a debatable assertion, you will make **appeals** to the readers (Section 9c), trying to convince them that your position is the correct one and that they ought to agree with you and, perhaps, even take some action based on that belief. Of course, there are many ways to persuade. Sometimes we persuade by making an argument based on reason (see Sections 9c.4 and 13e). At other times we argue based on how we feel or what we believe is morally correct.

5d
EXPLAINING A TOPIC

As you read the passage below, you will notice that, in contrast to the previous passages, this writer is primarily concerned with ideas, the information he is communicating. Does the writer want the readers to do anything with the information, as in the example of writing that persuades? Is the writer particularly concerned that the readers enjoy themselves as they read? How do you know?

[Bob] Marshall was legendary as a hiker. His brother and chief biographer, George Marshall, said Bob—who hiked with tennis shoes because they were light and dried fast—made over 200 day hikes of 30 miles each and many 40-mile day hikes. One of his lifetime goals was to walk 30 miles in a day in every state. In 1936, he hiked 70 miles through Arizona's Fort Apache reservation in *one day;* then, after going sleepless for 34 hours, he attended a meeting. Paul Schaefer, past vice president of the Association for the Protection of the Adirondacks, recalled in a 1966 article in *The Living Wilderness* how Marshall decided on returning from an Alaskan trip to see how many high Adirondack peaks he could climb in a single day, and how many vertical feet he could achieve while doing it. Starting at 3:30 a.m. on July 15, 1932, Marshall climbed 14 peaks totaling 13,600 feet by 10:00 at night.

Such peripatetic love of wild places began for Marshall in New York's Adirondacks where his father, Louis (1856–1929), and mother, Florence Lowenstein Marshall (1873–1916), owned a summer home called "Knollwood" on Lower Saranac Lake. Its green and brown buildings overlooked a fleet of islands, while in the southeast were the high peaks of the Adirondacks. There young Bob—following his birth in the family's brownstone house in New York City on January 2, 1902—spent 21 consecutive summers.

—Jim Vickery, *Wilderness Visionaries*

You might have noticed that this passage is more objective than the previous three: Dorothy Wordsworth's in Section 5a, Mark Twain's in Section 5b, and Rachel Carson's in Section 5c. The language seems emotionally neutral and focuses our attention on the subject itself, Bob Marshall, rather than on the writer or on how the writer wants the reader to behave. When we write to explain a topic, we present facts objectively, accurately, and logically. We carefully choose our words to describe the subject objectively.

You can see from the above example that the main idea of writing that explains a topic usually focuses the reader's attention on the conclusion that the explanation warrants. Here the writer explains one part of Bob Marshall's life. From this explanation most readers will conclude that Bob Marshall was obsessed with hiking; this is the main idea of the article.

When you write to explain a topic, you will present facts to the reader without as much of the emotional content usually present in writing that has one of the other three purposes. In some cases, writing that explains will simply inform. In other cases, it will interpret the subject, analyzing its meaning and importance, and present an argument that supports the validity of the interpretation (see Section 9a).

6

Audience and Context

Have you ever wondered why schools separate a subject like calculus into as many as four different courses? There are probably several reasons, but one of them is to simplify the act of communication in the classroom. Arranging classes into levels allows the instructors to predict what their audiences know. Imagine trying to discuss a subject as vast as calculus, Spanish, or chemistry in an informative, interesting, and clear manner in a group that may include both novices and experts. With almost every sentence they speak, effective instructors take into account the ambitions and prior knowledge of the students. Instructors try to use language their **audience** will understand, choose details that are clear and telling, and organize the lecture or activity so that the connections between ideas are apparent.

We can look at pieces of writing as a continuum ranging from writer-centered to reader-centered. **Writer-centered** compositions, such as diaries and personal journals, tend to focus almost exclusively on the needs of the writer. When we write only for ourselves, we don't think about accommodating the needs of an audience. If we want to use foul language, we use it. If we want to make up an abbreviation that only we can understand, we do it. If we want, we can skip from one idea to another without showing any connections (if there are any) and break every rule that every instructor or editor ever warned us about. Anything we do as concession to an audience is incidental. However, as writing becomes more **reader-centered**, we begin to think more about the needs of an audience other than ourselves, to consider what kind of help the reader needs in order to understand what we have written. Like teachers lecturing in class, writers must take into account the background of their audience.

6a
ANTICIPATING READER QUESTIONS AND NEEDS

You may believe that you don't have a clue about how to consider the needs of readers of your writing, but in fact, you do. All you have to do is remember the different ways in which you communicate with people in various social relationships. In other words, think of the various social uses of the language you already speak. Applying concepts you already understand from conversation can help you immensely in writing appropriately for readers.

Our social uses of language occur in different zones determined by social circumstances: intimate communication, friendly communication, exchange communication, and formal communication. By becoming more conscious of the four zones, we can use our intuitive understanding of human communication to enable us to write more effectively for specific readers. After all, whether we are conversing or writing, communication occurs when we are "in sync" with our audience.

6a.1 Intimate Communication

Intimate communication with family members and close friends often occurs through eye contact and facial expressions. When we use words, we feel that we can talk openly about our fears, our desires, and our goals. Usually we don't attempt really intimate communication with strangers. But unless we allow some form of intimacy, strangers may not feel comfortable, so we often make use of some characteristics of intimate communication in order to establish rapport (see Section 6a).

A writer who has an intimate style is often successful in engaging readers because they feel comfortable as they read. The intimacy that a writer can develop with unknown readers is, of course, artificial, yet it can foster common feelings at a level that arguments cannot reach.

6a.2 Friendly Communication

Each of us deals with members of several social groups with whom we maintain a friendly association. We may acknowledge a kind of intimacy with them, but it is an intimacy that grows out of shared experiences, not an intimacy deeply felt; we may be on the same sports team, work at the same kind of job, belong to the same club or church, have children in the same school, come from the same neighborhood, vote for the same political candidate, and so on. Talk among associates tends to keep the channels of **friendly communication** open rather than to transmit substantive information. It often expresses feelings of identification because we have common causes and goals.

Writing classes and office work groups, like sports teams, develop a strong associate level of communication. When a friendly environment is established in the classroom or the workplace, people feel free to open up, even to risk making mistakes, because they feel that they're "all in it together." Problems occur, however, when groups do nothing but maintain community with friendly communication; nothing gets done because no one challenges anyone else to develop and communicate clearly defined ideas.

6a.3 Exchange Communication

When intimates or associates question each other or find themselves in conflict, they move into the communication zone of exchanging ideas. Once questions are answered and conflicts resolved, they can return to the generalized-thinking level of association or to the good-feeling level of intimacy. Since **exchange communication** sounds confrontational to those who have grown complacent at the level of intimate or friendly communication, some people resist being dragged into a conversation that produces an exchange of ideas. Yet those who have come to understand how exciting learning can be are mentally stimulated by the exchanges they have in this third communication zone. Communication in this zone is naturally disorganized, since questions may come intuitively, arising spontaneously out of the context of previous questions.

　　Writing in this zone is often innovative and lively. Its style may have the flair and variety of conversation, and its organization may have the character of a good discussion. Good journalistic style is often of this nature. However, writing in this zone of communication can also be uneven. For instance, writers who use a conversational style may seem glib and insincere to readers who are deeply concerned about a subject. Writing to exchange ideas is thus characterized by conversational give-and-take, but as communication moves into the fourth zone, writing takes on distinctive shape and form.

6a.4 Formal Communication

Formal communication occurs in speech when the speaker has information and wants to deliver it quickly and directly, yet ordinary conversation would be either distracting or ineffective. It also may occur when the speaker is unwilling to tolerate questions from others. Formal writing is most effective when the communicator considers the needs of the reader and imagines what the audience needs to know, making decisions about linguistic, organizational, informational, logical, emotional, and trust requirements. Effective formal communication occurs when the speaker has asked enough questions—either of him- or herself or of the imagined audience—to foster agreement and understanding.

　　In effective formal writing, if the purpose of the writing is to explain a topic, the writer usually tries to use clear statements of main ideas to guide the reader through individual paragraphs and the complete paper (see Section 13a). Since part of the reading process is predicting what comes next, effective writers help their readers by making it easy for them to make those predictions; for instance, a familiar pattern of organization (see Chapter 14) will help the readers feel comfortable with the material and predict what is coming next (see Section 10a.2).

? 6b
WRITING FOR A SPECIFIC AUDIENCE

Have you and your family ever received an annual letter from friends who live out of town, one that begins "Dear Family and Friends, We can't believe another year has passed and it's time to time to wish you another New Year's greeting"? Somewhere in the letter they will tell you what all the children in the family are up to.

> All the kids are busy. Elizabeth is now eight and really enjoying school. We were very proud when she brought home straight A's in math this year. Karl, in middle school, is still charming his teachers. He's become a garage sale junkie and has amassed five shoe boxes of baseball cards. Mary is still busy in basketball and Girl Scouts. Next year, the troop goes to Switzerland, so all her free time is devoted to projects to raise money for the trip. And Eric has left the nest and taken off to the University of North Carolina. We worry sometimes because he gave up soccer and has bought a drum set, but we're grateful he waited until he left the house before starting. He says his room-mates don't mind.

When you write for a **specific audience**, whether it is a single person or a narrowly defined group as above, you are able to make certain assumptions about what that audience will or will not understand. When you write to friends or relatives, you will probably know what they believe, what they value, and what they know about the topic. For instance, the writer of the letter above knows that many of the older adults (the grandparents, uncles, and aunts) live in small towns and have conservative attitudes about raising children, so the writer concentrates on achievements and interests of the children. The writer doesn't mention the fact that Mary, who's fifteen, started dating last year or that Eric has let his hair grow and has joined a heavy metal band.

In the same way, scientists writing to other scientists can use a vocabulary different from the one they would use in writing to nonscientists. They are able to use the **jargon** of their specialized field because they know that their audience will understand it. Knowing the specific characteristics of your readers will shape what you say to them.

Imagine that you are a committed environmentalist writing a persuasive essay defending the legal limitation on logging in Northwestern forests as a way of protecting the spotted owl. An understanding of your specific audience will affect how you present the argument. Take a moment and try to imagine your intended readers. You might be addressing one of the groups listed below.

- Land developers
- Loggers
- Residents of the area
- Biologists and environmentalists
- Nonscientists interested in scientific topics
- Any readers apathetic about the topic
- Students like you
- Family
- Close friends
- Federal bureaucrats
- Legislators considering a bill to restrict logging

As you consider each different possible reader, notice how your thinking about the topic changes. Each group of potential readers will change your strategy about what information to include and exclude, what kind of language you can use, what examples to give, what terms must be defined, and what style you adopt. You will want to consider what the readers already know about the topic, what information they may need to know, and what they hope to learn by reading your work. You will also want to consider other characteristics of the readers: age, level of education, and place of residence.

6c
WRITING FOR THE GENERAL READER

Let's return for a moment to the example about the essay on logging in the Northwest. Imagine that instead of writing to one of the groups mentioned, you are about to write an essay that may be read by all the groups. For instance, your work might be published in a newspaper or general-interest magazine. How can you tell that the following passage was written for a general reader?

> For species on the brink, from birds to fungi, the end can come in two ways. Many are taken out by the metaphorical equivalent of a rifle shot—they are

erased, but the ecosystem from which they are removed is left intact. Others are destroyed by holocaust, in which the entire ecosystem perishes.

The distinction between rifle shot and holocaust has special merit in considering the case of the spotted owl (*Strix occidentalis*) of the United States, an endangered form that has been the object of intense national controversy since 1988. Each pair of owls requires about 3 to 8 square kilometers of coniferous forest more than 250 years old. Only this habitat can provide the birds with both large enough hollow trees for nesting and an expanse of open understory for hunting mice and other small mammals. Within the range of the spotted owl in western Oregon and Washington, the suitable habitat is largely confined to 12 national forests.

—E. 0. Wilson, *The Diversity of Life*

You may have noticed that Wilson is careful to use language most readers would understand. He gives background information about the conflict over the spotted owl and even uses an analogy to illustrate the different kinds of destruction that can cause species to become extinct. Wilson's writing, therefore, appears to be intended for a **general reader**.

When writing to unknown and general readers, we make some assumptions about what those readers are like. We assume that they are educated and literate and that they read a variety of printed material, including newspapers, magazines, and books. We also assume that even though they have a general acquaintance with most subjects, they will not understand complicated technical information no matter what the subject is.

Think about some of the things that you expect to see when you read.

- You want to read something you find interesting and understand its importance to you.
- You like clear, orderly statements.
- You like to see writing that reflects the grammar, spelling, and punctuation you are used to seeing in print.
- You want to learn something.
- You want to think about the topic in a new way.
- You want concrete details.
- You want to hear an honest, natural voice.
- You want some degree of depth of information.
- You prefer fresh insights and information to those you have heard often.

What you prefer in writing is probably what the general reader is going to prefer, too.

6d
UNDERSTANDING CONTEXT

Communication does not occur in a vacuum. Each time we speak or write, we do so in the **context** of a time and a place. In the broadest sense, the historical period and the society we live in provide what is called a **cultural context**. This context will determine in large part what value systems and belief systems an audience is familiar with. For instance, some words once used to refer to women—such as *wenches, dames, gals,* and *chicks*—are now no longer appropriate in most social groups (see Chapter 21). Similarly, an argument for an arms buildup based on a fear of communism, while once powerful, no longer carries much weight. We can also think of context in a narrower sense, one that depends on the specific situation we are in and the events or circumstances that have prompted the writing in the first place. We call this kind of context a **situational context**. For example, a position paper by an anticrime group may change greatly if, during its work, the city experiences some highly publicized murders.

Audience and context are inseparable. When we think about context, we also think about how the audience is affected by cultural values and by the specific situation that has prompted the communication. It is important for you to recognize and be sensitive to those needs in potential readers.

It seems obvious that context determines much of the style and tone of the language we use (see Part V). A letter to the editor requires a kind of language different from a technical report. An accountant may use different words when speaking to a superior than when speaking to a subordinate. The language we use is always influenced by our audience and the context.

CHAPTER

7

Content

How many times have you sat down to write and . . . nothing happened? Maybe you stared at a blank sheet of paper or a blank computer screen awhile and still nothing happened.

What you experienced in those cases is normal. It was simply the action of an internal editor that questions almost everything you write. Fortunately, there are a number of ways to keep the editor at bay when it is not needed. In this chapter you will find techniques that will help you come up with words to express your ideas.

Generating content is closely tied to arrangement: the details you generate must be arranged (see Part IV). Consequently, as soon as you begin to work on a writing project, you will probably be engaging in both activities at the same time. Even though you will read about them separately in this book, remember that most often they occur simultaneously, a fact that makes writing both challenging and satisfying. The kinds of details you create are also affected by your topic, purpose, and audience, concepts discussed in Chapters 4 through 6. Sometimes you will find that the addition of new details changes your purpose somewhat, either the general purpose or the main idea. Each different purpose, each new audience, and each altered context makes it necessary for you to generate different kinds of information. Even changing a single word can open several new avenues of thought.

In the sections that follow, you will find explanations of how to use a variety of techniques to generate content. They have been put into several different groups because of the kinds of details they help you generate. Each technique has its own special uses. Some may be used when you are shaping your topic. Others lead inevitably to certain patterns of arrangement. The one you use may vary depending on what your general purpose is.

7a
FREE ASSOCIATION TECHNIQUES

Don't think about elephants.

If you are like most people, you are thinking about elephants right now, and you will continue to think about elephants—big, gray, lumbering beasts with tusks and tails and trunks, swaying back and forth as they move. Perhaps images from a documentary film about elephants come to mind. Perhaps a memory of a trip to the zoo flashes through your consciousness. This series of associated thoughts is part of the stream of ideas that flow through the mind continuously. This fact about the way our minds work can be a fertile source of ideas, images, and details for writing. The trick is, of course, getting at that wealth of material you always have at your disposal. Untapped, this **stream of consciousness** is simply there. But controlled and directed, it can become a powerful tool that will help you write more effectively. Not only will the free association techniques included in this chapter help you generate details after you have decided on a topic, but they also may help you find topics and subjects to write about (Section 4a).

7a.1 Freewriting

As the name implies, **freewriting** is writing without restriction. You simply put down on paper or on the computer screen whatever comes to mind by **free association** (one idea suggesting another) without worrying about form or content or correctness. This technique will allow you to get words down, words you can work with later. You may end up throwing away half of what you write, or even all of it, but that doesn't matter because what you want to do initially is to start the flow of words. When you are having trouble getting started, you may find it helpful simply to let yourself write without stopping for a period of time (five or ten minutes is usually enough) or until you have filled up a set number of pages. Remember, don't stop writing. Put down whatever pops into your head. Freewriting is a way of getting ideas down without interference from your internal editor.

Freewriting can be used in three different ways—as unstructured or focused freewriting or as looping. Each of these three variations has a slightly different application.

Unstructured Freewriting

First, freewriting can be completely **unstructured**. Simply let your mind wander and record on paper or on a computer any random thoughts that occur to you. This kind of freewriting can help you discover a topic to write about if you use it in conjunction with some of the ideas discussed in Section 4a.l. You may also find the technique useful if you get stuck in the middle of a writing project. An example of this kind of freewriting follows.

> When I was a child the world of nature was a playground and a context for the world of fantasy that was my main preoccupation. I romped with playmates, both real and imaginary, and had imaginary adventures with toys of all kinds, action figures, cars, trucks, construction toys, stuffed animals, etc. I was free and happy. Later I became aware of nature and found that the natural world was as fascinating as the imaginary world I had created. I also discovered that it demanded a more mature attitude.

Unstructured freewriting allows you to explore your thoughts. Even if you don't use any of the material produced in a freewriting activity, you will have gained some momentum, and that in itself is often very helpful.

Focused Freewriting

Freewriting may also be **focused**. This technique allows you to generate ideas once you have decided on a topic. In this kind of freewriting, you can let your writing wander and be spontaneous, but you will try to refocus on your topic anytime you wander too far afield. Here's an example of focused freewriting on the topic of the outdoors.

> I have always been interested in the outdoors. As a child most of my playtime was spent outdoors, weather permitting, and even sometimes when it didn't, much to Mom's dismay. As I grew up, the kind of outdoor activity changed. In contrast to the wild, exuberant unstructured play of childhood, I began as an adolescent to enjoy more purposeful activities like fishing and hunting. Now as an adult I have discovered other outdoor pastimes, less aggressive. These turn out to be both physical and intellectual, like bird watching and hiking. But there is another aspect of nature that is more disturbing—environmental pollution. Pollution is something that demands the attention of everyone who enjoys the outdoors. Pollution, in fact, threatens the quality of life we can live.

This technique of focused freewriting will help you develop a topic when you are in the initial stages of drafting. You may also use focused freewriting to develop parts of a topic if you have reached an impasse in your work on a project.

Looping

Another freewriting technique is called **looping**. With looping, you identify a statement in a previous freewriting activity and use that statement as the beginning for another round of freewriting. You can repeat the looping technique as many times as you want. An example of looping follows. Notice that the sentence "Pollution is something that demands the attention of everyone who enjoys the outdoors" in the previous freewriting exercise is the starting point for the following loop.

> Pollution is something that demands the attention of everyone who enjoys the outdoors. It is startling and sometimes painful to realize

the extent of the destruction of the natural environment around us. Rivers, lakes, and oceans have been polluted by industrial waste and agricultural runoff. The air has been polluted by auto emissions and smoke from factories and power plants. The soil has been damaged by runoff and erosion. We continue to see the effects of our disregard for the environment in acid rain, the greenhouse effect, the depletion of the ozone layer, deforestation, smog, and toxic waste dumps. One of the most disturbing consequences of pollution is the greenhouse effect. We must all take a more active part in trying to reverse the effects of our unthinking destruction of our environment.

To continue looping, you would simply identify a new focus by underlining a sentence and then start writing again. This process can be repeated as many times as you need. At some point you will certainly be able to begin to use some of the material gained from freewriting by arranging it and integrating it into your writing project.

7a.2 Listing

Do you take a list to the grocery store? If you do, is it well organized? Probably not; in all likelihood, you put down items as they occur to you, one image triggering another—bananas, cereal, coffee, coffee filters, dishwashing liquid, bath soap, toothpaste. Using **listing** as a method of invention and discovery is the same kind of activity.

Like freewriting, listing is a technique involving free association. As the name implies, you simply list one word or phrase after another, letting the associations continue as long as you can.

The following is a list generated from the topic "pollution."

acid rain	poisoning of fish	dust storms
air pollution	groundwater	toxic wastes
agricultural runoff	water pollution	scrubbers
erosion	automobile exhaust	smokestacks
toxic waste	greenhouse effect	the Superfund
ocean dumping	CO_2 emissions	oil spills

| cleanup operations | soil pollution | smog |
| sewage in rivers | deforestation | ozone layer |

The list you generate can be used in several different ways. Out of the list, you may find a focus for further idea development through focused freewriting (Section 7a.1), mapping (Section 7a.3), diagramming (Section 7b.1), or outlining (Section 7b.2).

7a.3 Mapping

The technique of **mapping** (also called clustering or webbing) is a bit more structured than listing. Mapping shows relationships among the various aspects of your topic and so begins to create some order out of the relative chaos of the free association techniques—freewriting (Section 7a.1) and listing (Section 7a.2).

Start by writing your subject in the middle of a blank sheet of paper and circling it. (You can also do this activity with some computer programs.) Then put down any related ideas that occur to you, circle them, and draw connecting lines that show how the various ideas are related to each other and to your main subject.

An example of mapping follows. Notice that the mapping exercise includes many of the same items as the listing exercise above. But mapping allows you to begin to move toward a more organized body of information.

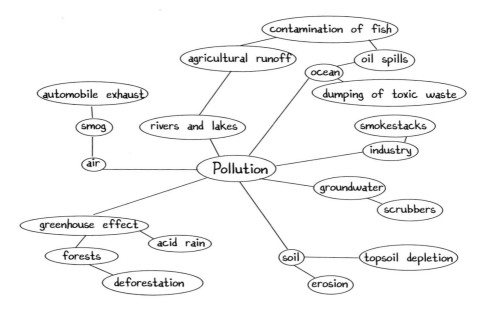

You can use your map as a stimulus for the other techniques of free association (freewriting and listing) to generate more details or as a starting point for the outlining techniques (tree diagrams or outlining—see Section 7b) to organize your ideas. You can also select one of the items identified in your mapping exercise and create a new map around it.

7b
OUTLINING TECHNIQUES

The two techniques that follow are more structured than the techniques of free association. They are used most often when the writer has a fairly clear idea of the nature of the topic. Outlining techniques can be useful if you are dealing with a topic that has a number of discrete parts and requires a fairly formal presentation. In such cases, an outline of some sort can enable you to see the global structure of your work and may help you decide what kind of details you need to include in each part.

7b.1 Using Tree Diagrams

Like mapping, a **tree diagram** allows you to group similar ideas together. You might take a list from a listing exercise (Section 7a.2) and make some of the key items into a tree diagram. You will probably begin to see some connections between items on your list. In addition, tree diagrams enable you to establish hierarchies, to show which details are most important. For example, in the following tree diagram, notice how the relationships between the general category "pollution" and the more specific examples of pollution are shown.

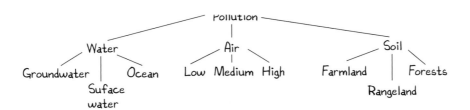

7b.2 Making an Outline

An **outline** helps you establish relationships just as the tree diagram does, but the outline allows you to make more detailed distinctions because you can subdivide the topics in greater detail. For some kinds of writing, especially those that have the purpose of explaining a topic, a working outline created before you begin to write can be a helpful tool for making sure that you have covered all aspects of the subject. For other projects, you may use a working outline after you have already written much of the paper, as a way of checking the material you have included. An explanation of two types of outlines follows.

Preliminary Outlines

Preliminary outlines are only a little more organized than the free association lists shown in Section 7a. They represent an effort to focus on possible areas of investigation. You can develop a preliminary outline in one of three ways: as a **rough outline** (arrangement of lists by categories), as a **question outline** (questions to answer), or as a **developmental outline** (kinds of information needed).

Rough Outline	Question Outline	Developmental Outline
Pollution	What is pollution?	Pollution
Awareness	How prevalent is it?	Definition
Laws	What causes it?	Examples
Sources	What are its effects?	Statistics
Industry	What has been done	Case studies
Agriculture	to stop it?	Causes
Gasoline	What can be done?	Effects
Landfills		Cleanup
Elimination		
Scrubbing		
Prosecution		

Working Outlines

As you continue to shape your topic, your preliminary outline will begin to develop into a **working outline** that has a more definite structure than any of the preliminary outlines. Working outlines are especially helpful when you need to do research to find and organize material on your topic.

Notice how the arrangement of the working outline that follows controls the nature and amount of material gathered on the topic.

I. Water
   A. Groundwater
   B. Surface water
      1. Rivers
      2. Lakes
   C. Oceans

II. Air
   A. Low-level—smog
   B. Midlevel—acid rain
   C. Upper level—ozone depletion

III. Soil
   A. Farmland
   B. Ranchland
   C. Forests

Once you have a working outline, you might consider using some of the other techniques of discovery and invention to generate more detail in each category. Some of the questioning techniques discussed in Section 7c might be helpful. Or you might find it necessary to do some research to find needed information for your topic. (For information on research techniques, see Part IX, "Research and Documentation.")

7c
QUESTIONS

One way to think about writing is to see it as an answer to questions. The different formats for asking questions provided in this section will allow you to look at the topic from a number of perspectives. You may use all of them at various times for different topics, or you may find that you feel comfortable using only a few of them.

7c.1 Journalists' Questions

To make sure that they have thoroughly covered the topic for the reader, journalists frequently ask the following questions.

Who?

What?

When?

Where?

Why?

How?

Like journalists, you can use these questions to explore events comprehensively and accurately. They are especially useful when your purpose is to explain a topic by giving information. Although not every question will be equally important for every topic, questions do give you a method for initial exploration. By answering them, you will be able to ensure that you have a comprehensive base of information to work from. You may then elaborate on one or several of the areas covered by the questions. Notice how the following example covers all the essential points of the Boston Tea Party.

Who?	A group of men disguised as Native Americans.
What?	They threw 342 chests of tea over the sides of ships.
When?	December 16, 1773.
Where?	Boston Harbor.
Why?	To protest the Tea Act.
How?	The men boarded the ships at night.

If you were writing a paper about the Boston Tea Party, you could use these answers in various ways. You might elaborate on each question, giving more information about each answer, or you might elaborate on one of the points, for example, by telling what it was about the Tea Act that so inflamed the colonists. (Section 13d.1 shows how the exercise above can lead to a prose passage.)

7c.2 The Topics

Developed by classical philosophers, the topics allow you to look at relationships implicit in your subject. They force you to look at **definition**, **comparison**, **cause and effect**, and **evidence**. The topics are especially useful when your purpose is to persuade an audience. The following questions arise from the topics.

Definition: What is it?
  Classification: What larger class is it in?
  Division: What are its parts?

Comparison/contrast: What are its similarities and differences?
  Comparison: How is it similar to other things of the same class?
  Contrast: How is it different from other things of the same class?

Cause and effect: What are the reasons and results?

Cause:	What causes it to happen?
Effect:	When it happens, what are the effects?

Evidence: What evidence supports the topic?

Authority:	What do authorities say about it?
Testimony:	What do people say about it who have had experience with it?
Statistics:	What statistics support it?
Maxims:	What famous sayings can be applied to it?
Law:	What laws support or prohibit it?
Precedent:	What previous examples support it?

An Example of Invention Using the Topics

Subject: Water pollution

Definition: Water pollution consists of toxic substances in the water supply.

Classification:	It is a member of the general class of pollution, which also includes air and soil pollution.
Division:	The subject can be divided into groundwater, surface water, and ocean pollution.

Comparison and contrast

Comparison:	It is similar to other forms of pollution in that it is detrimental to the environment and to humans.
Contrast:	It is different from other forms of pollution in that it contaminates a substance that humans consume.

Cause and effect

Cause:	It is caused when industrial and agricultural wastes are emptied directly into water or indirectly into the ground. It can also be caused by natural processes, such as minerals leaching into the water from the soil.
Effect:	It contaminates drinking water and damages the ecosystem.

Evidence

Authority:	According to a study by the Environmental Protection Agency (EPA), two-thirds of the surface water in the United States meets water quality standards, but there is

	a continuing problem with contaminated runoff from farms, streets, and lawns.
Testimony:	I have seen pollution in the rivers I have canoed on.
Statistics:	Agricultural runoff figured prominently in an EPA analysis that found nearly half of the more than 500,000 miles of rivers tested to be too polluted for their intended uses.
Maxims:	Save our springs. Someone always lives downstream.
Law:	The Clean Water Act was extended for eight years in 1987. The goal of the original act was to make freshwater "swimmable and fishable" again.
Precedent:	The act has had some effect on water quality since its inception.

7c.3 General Questions

In this section you will look at a list of general questions covering a number of different kinds of topics, some of which we have already touched on in earlier sections. If your topic fits into one of these categories, these questions may help you generate details for your writing project. Most of the questions that follow are directly related to the organizational patterns discussed in Chapter 14, "Familiar Patterns of Organization."

If you are writing a paper analyzing a work of literature (fiction, drama, or poetry), you should look at the questions in Chapter 12, "Literature."

General Questions

A natural object

  What does it look like?

  What are its characteristics?

  What are some examples of it?

  What class is it a member of?

  How is it similar to something else in its class?

An artificial object

  What makes it work?

  How is it made?

  How is it similar to other members of its class?

How is it different from other members of its class?

Into what categories can it be arranged?

What are its limits?

An event

What happened?

When did it happen?

Where did it happen?

How did it happen?

A process

How does it work?

What steps are included in the process?

How are people affected by the process?

What are the outcomes of the process?

A historical event

What caused it?

What does it cause?

What are its effects?

A concept

What is it?

What are its parts?

How can the parts be arranged?

7d
DRAFTING

When you write, you always have choices about how to put your thoughts into words. Having choices is a good thing because it frees you to be creative in what you say and how you say it. On the other hand, it is possible to become so overwhelmed by the idea of having so many choices that you will be unable to write *anything* at all. Many professional writers solve this problem by thinking of their writing in terms of different **drafts** of the same writing activity: they write, read what they have written, and write again. Each draft will usually reflect a change in their thinking as they gain greater understanding of the topic, the audience, the purpose for writing, and the organization that will best reveal the ideas. Consequently, you should probably expect to write more than one draft, each for a rather specific purpose; don't feel that you have to make all the needed choices all at once.

7d.1 Zero Drafts

Some writers feel pressured by blank pages when they sit down to write. It can seem as if the empty space just dares them to find anything worthwhile to write about. If that happens to you, you may like the idea of writing not what you eventually will write, but rather a draft that discusses what you *probably* will do once you finally settle down and start writing. Just think about it: anything you write when drafting this way is okay, because all you are doing is mulling over and exploring what you might want to do. Writing a **zero draft** is a good way to break the ice: it can take pressure off and give you the freedom to muse, to plan.

7d.2 Discovery Drafts

When you draft with the purpose of discovering what to say, you are making an attempt to filter relevant concepts out of the chaos of ideas and words flowing through your mind. A **discovery draft** allows you to explore what you know and to invent content as you write. Techniques such as freewriting (Section 7a.1) and responding to questions (Section 7c) are useful in creating a discovery draft. They help you start the process of transforming ideas into words. You may also incorporate material from your journal (Section 2a). Even though drafting for discovery will be spontaneous and more or less unstructured, you will want to center it on a topic that unifies your writing and gives you a chance to focus your perspective. You might hope in the process to state your main idea (Section 13a.1), but even if the main idea is never stated formally, the general direction of your writing will probably become apparent. The benefit of discovery drafting is that at the end of the writing, you can hope to have disclosed most of what you know about the topic and most of what you think you can say about it. A discovery draft may help you choose what you can say and may thus accomplish Task 1 of the writing process (Section 3a).

However, discovery drafting is something you can do at any time in the process of writing. Your first attempt at adding details to a nearly completed paper may be drafted in a discovery mode and then later transformed into more appropriate forms. Also, if you find yourself stumped and unable to decide what to do next, break away from the draft you are working on and draft for discovery on the topic you need to discuss.

One more point about writing a discovery draft: you will probably have to relax to do it. Let go of the fear of making mistakes; become so accepting of errors that you don't notice them. Keep in mind that writing something seemingly unrelated to the topic may give you new insight; therefore, accept what seems to be nonsense, as well. If later on you find you have written nonsense, you can remove it. Trust your intuition and your imagination. You may discover that you have something important to say.

Using Speech as a Drafting Tool

Speech can be one of your most useful writing tools. If you are having difficulty trying to decide what to write, consider just *saying* it first. Working this way can give you the freedom to experiment with the way something will sound to your reader before you write it. It can keep you from feeling trapped—even get you "unstuck" when you can't figure out what to write next. Some people use tape recorders and tape what they say, then transcribe the tape as part of their zero or discovery draft.

7d.3 Rough Drafts

Whenever you write a **rough draft**, your purpose is to produce *roughly* what you intend the final work to include, roughly what you intend it to look like. Proficient writers who know a lot about their topic and audience can do a rough draft the first time they write. Whenever you write a rough draft, you already have a good idea what you are going to say; you are thus likely to write from some kind of plan and produce writing that is more cleanly structured than when you are drafting to discover.

This is not to say that a rough draft cannot be spontaneous, or that you cannot discover the design of your paper as you write it, letting the design grow out of what you want to say. In fact, if you are moved by passion or insight to just sit down and write without planning ahead of time, go ahead and do it. You may find that your intuition will reward you with an original and forceful statement. But if spontaneity is not your strong suit, and especially if you are unsure of direction or method, planning ahead may be a good idea for you.

As you write a rough draft, you may choose to leave some parts undeveloped by leaving place markers—words or phrases that tell you what idea or ideas you want to put in a certain place in the work. You may also use the technique of *sufficing*, putting down ideas in a rough form that is sufficient for the moment so you can go back to that material later. These two devices let you make progress on the entire project by allowing you to move on to parts that you feel comfortable with and so let you leave for later more difficult pieces of the puzzle that might slow down or even stop your progress overall. Given a little time and assuming you can develop parts of the work later, you will be able to bypass the more difficult parts until you have discovered the solutions to the problems you had with them. You may even find they were not needed after all.

7d.4 Working Drafts

Any draft that succeeds a discovery draft or a rough draft can be called a **working draft**. Sometimes, you may produce many of them. At other times, your rough draft may become a working draft: you may merely make notes on it and move swiftly to completion. It all depends on how thorough your prior drafts are. Writing working drafts as needed will help you clarify the relationship among the parts of the paper and prepare the paper for a reader to consider.

If you have used place-holding words or phrases in a rough draft, or if you have let a sentence or a short explanation suffice until you can research or think further about a part of your paper, you may want to isolate that part and draft it separately. If your content is rather complete, however, you will probably want to use working drafts to deal with the coherence of your paper (Chapter 16), attending to things like transitional words and phrases and your placement of known and new ideas in the text. If you have given your paper to a member of your writing group for comment and criticism (Section 2c), you will need to address the issues brought up by your colleagues as you work on the next draft of your paper. You will also want to check your writing for clear, logical expression (see Section 9d).

If you find that you are using a succession of working drafts, you may want to number them so that you can tell clearly which is your current draft (especially if you are drafting on a computer). Some writers discard earlier drafts so they do not run the risk of inadvertently putting back into a current draft information that they had edited out of an earlier version; others find it useful to keep the discarded content so they can use it later if they wish without rewriting.

CommonSense Suggestion

Drafting on a Word Processor

The ease with which writers can delete, substitute, or insert words, phrases, sentences, and whole paragraphs in a word processing program is what makes writing on a computer so attractive. Rearranging paragraphs is easy using either a drag-and-drop or cut-and-paste feature. Inserting explanations, specific examples, quotations, or anything else becomes remarkably simple. Putting in transitional words and phrases becomes a breeze; it's only a matter of choosing the right ones, being sure the sequence is right, and avoiding repetition.

7d.5 Final Drafts

You can call any draft a **final draft** when you decide it is ready for your intended audience to read it. A final draft is complete for the intended purpose, fully readable by the intended reader, as error-free as you can make it, and likely to accomplish the goal you set out for yourself when you started to write. If it is ready for the copy machine or some other exact reproduction process such as offset printing, it can be called a *camera-ready draft*, one that you are truly ready to publish. In a draft that is truly final, you will have accomplished all the tasks discussed in Chapter 3.

Sometimes final drafts and first drafts are the same thing. For example, the first draft of a personal letter is often the final draft. The first draft of an essay exam is the final draft if there is not enough time to write another, and some documents at work are both first and final drafts when they are written using a standard form, such as an office memo.

CommonSense Strategies

Taking Essay Exams

Taking an essay exam is like writing a working or final draft in one sitting. You can do excellent work if you are prepared and you work carefully and efficiently. Begin by reading the whole test—all the questions—and deciding how much time and energy each question will require of you. If you can, work on the questions you can give the best answers on. Read the question or topic carefully. Pay attention to key words so that if you are asked to *define, analyze, discuss* causes, or *explain* a process, you will do exactly that and nothing else.

As much as possible, take a process approach to each question, reserving a set amount of time at the end (10–15 minutes) for revising, editing, and proofreading.

For each question, make a list (Section 7a.2) of what you want to write about. Don't try to put the list in any order; just get all your major points and examples on paper.

Create a preliminary outline (Section 7b.2) to work from; put everything on your list in the outline.

Read each question again before you answer it; for each essay answer, write an introduction that restates the question.

$\longrightarrow$

continued from previous page

Be productive; if you get stuck, go on to another question or edit previously written parts; then go back to the difficult question in the remaining time.

Write with clarity, and use enough examples and details to be convincing and to show that you know the material. This kind of writing need not be eloquent, but it must be exact and sufficient.

Sometimes final drafts become working drafts after other people—instructors or editors or colleagues—have responded to them. What we think is final in isolation sometimes looks different in the light of the criticism of others.

3

Critical Thinking and Critical Reading

Manuscripts

Before any written work is published or presented to its intended readers in a final form, it will exist as a **manuscript**. While in manuscript form, it will be read and reread through a number of **drafts** (see Section 7d).

Reading a manuscript, either your own or someone else's, is different from reading a finished work. When reading a work that has been published (such as a book or an article) or a work that has been delivered to its intended audience (such as a letter or a report), the reader will generally accept the work as it is and try to understand it. But the reader of a manuscript will feel an obligation to respond to the writer in some way, to offer suggestions about what could be improved or to comment on what is effective and what is ineffective. The reader of a finished work and the reader of a manuscript have different sets of expectations when they read.

If you are reading someone else's manuscript, you are reading not only to understand the work's content, but also to identify problems that may exist in features such as arrangement, style, usage, and conventions. In addition, the author may have asked you to look at the work with specific things in mind—for example, the relevance of an illustration, the appropriateness of the work's tone, and the suitability of page design. If you are reading your own work, you are trying to read your writing as someone else would read it. Further, you are trying to accomplish each of the tasks discussed in Chapter 3.

What the reader focuses on when reading a manuscript varies, of course, with the nature of the writing project, the relationship between the writer and the reader, and the length of the work. A book-length manuscript may require several readings by different reviewers over a long period of time. The manuscript of an article or a report, on the other hand, may need only one reading before it is finished.

No matter how many times a manuscript has been read, the reader will need to consider four questions: (1) Does the work make sense? (2) Is it polished? (3) Does it have any distracting mistakes? (4) How effective is it? This chapter focuses on strategies the reader can use to identify places in a manuscript where problems may exist. The details of correcting such problems are discussed throughout this handbook. This chapter, then, is an explanation of reading that leads to revision.

?

8a
READING FOR CLARITY

Unclear or confusing writing creates problems that can be distracting and often insurmountable for the reader. It is important, therefore, as you read a manuscript, whether your own or someone else's, that you look for places where the text does not make sense or where it causes confusion.

In writing that has the purpose of explaining a topic (Section 5d), lack of clarity can be especially troublesome because the topic may not be fully understood by the reader. If the purpose of the writing is to persuade the reader to accept the writer's position on some issue (Section 5c), then confusing statements may actually defeat the argument. Although some ambiguity may appear in writing that entertains (Section 5b) as well as writing that expresses the self of the writer (Section 5a), the work as a whole must make sense to the reader.

One technique you can use to help identify parts of a manuscript that may not be clear is to read aloud what you have written. Consider the meaning of the following sentences as you read them aloud.

When Mary and June discussed her project, she became very excited.

On top of the mountain with his back to the sky stood Bill, huge, bright, and blue.

In each of the sentences above, there are problems that the writer may not have noticed while composing the sentence. In the first sentence, it was June who was completing the project and who became excited, but the writer failed to notice the confusion that resulted from this sentence structure. Paying close attention to the connection between nouns and pronouns might have alerted the writer to the possible confusion.

CommonSense Strategies

Identifying Problems with Clarity

Read the manuscript aloud. Listen to the words.

Circle words and phrases that address the same ideas, and connect them with lines. This visual diagram can sometimes let you see whether or not ideas are clearly related to each other.

Check all personal pronouns (*he, him, his, she, her, hers, it, its, they, them, their*) to make sure that the word each one is referring to is clear.

Check the words *this, that,* and *which* to make sure that the word or idea that each refers to is clear.

Often classmates and friends can offer suggestions and advice that will help you as a writer to improve your work. Comments about purpose, organization, content, tone, and voice from a person other than the instructor can be invaluable in clarifying what you want to say.

8b
READING FOR POLISH

The **polish** that finely crafted prose exhibits is certainly a goal that most writers strive for and most readers like to see in what they read. Does the following sentence flow smoothly?

> The chief administrative officer has admitted that the administration of the admission policy is best left to the administrative clerks in each department.

The writer of this sentence, in an effort to be exact, has created some awkward phrasing. Oral reading will make clear the distracting repetition of words and sounds.

Reading your work aloud enables you to hear whether your writing sounds like you, with words and sentences that you would actually use. If you can read your writing out loud, pausing where you mean to pause, emphasizing words and ideas that you want emphasized, taking a breath where you would naturally take a breath, then you know that your words will convey what you want them to convey, smoothly.

CommonSense Strategies

Polishing the Work

Read the manuscript aloud. Listen to the words.

Check for repetitive words. Listen for unnatural phrasings.

If a sentence doesn't sound exactly right, play with it. Remember that any sentence can be rewritten.

8c
READING FOR MECHANICS

Reading for mechanics involves recognizing the obvious problems that mar a manuscript: spelling errors, problems in subject-verb agreement, uncalled-for shifts, and inappropriate punctuation, for example. Strategies for correcting such problems are explained in Part VI, "Sentence Punctuation"; Part VII, "Usage"; and Part VIII, "Conventions." But you don't have to go through this handbook each time you read a manuscript. With practice, you will develop a sense of where such problems occur in your own writing, and perhaps you will be able to develop a list of priorities to attend to while you are reading.

CommonSense Strategies

Identifying Mechanical Problems

Read the manuscript aloud. Listen to the words.

On a word processor, always use your spell checker. It only takes a few minutes. Or read the manuscript backwards, looking for errors in spelling and word formation.

Be aware of words you frequently confuse with other words.

Keep a personal list of words and phrases that you have repeatedly misused.

Focus on one element at a time. For example, first read through the manuscript making sure that subjects and verbs agree, and then read through the manuscript making sure that you have written complete sentences.

8d
READING FOR QUALITY

To some extent, the quality of a manuscript depends on all the elements discussed in the previous sections of this chapter. When we read to evaluate the quality of a work, we pay attention to how clearly the information is communicated, how eloquently the message is expressed, and how well mechanical details have been attended to. It is hard to separate these different aspects of a work from each other because they are interconnected in many ways. In fact, determining the quality of a manuscript requires the reader to evaluate how well these components work together. Even the most highly polished writing can be marred by problems with mechanics and clarity.

Writers are often defensive about their work, so when you evaluate someone else's writing—or even your own—you may be entering difficult and emotional territory. As both writers and readers, we enter this territory with trust and honesty and with more than a little fear. (If grades are involved, then we are all the more fearful and careful.) You need to consider first of all the writer's purpose. Obviously, you would not evaluate a personal letter in the same way that you would evaluate a business letter. You could not evaluate them in the same way because they have very different purposes (see Chapter 5). Knowing what a writer's purpose is will tell you something about the intended audience. And knowing the audience will tell you something about what the style of the writing should be.

Argumentation

From time to time, all of us find ourselves involved in an argument with someone over a debatable issue. Sometimes the argument is over a trivial matter, and sometimes it deals with a question of great importance. But whatever the issue, our purpose is to persuade the other person to accept our position and perhaps even to take some action based on that acceptance. When the term *argument* is used to refer to a discussion of this sort—a disagreement or a debate—the argument will have a persuasive intent.

Argumentation, however, is a course of reasoning that demonstrates the validity of an explanation of some idea or phenomenon. When writers present arguments in scientific or scholarly papers, either they are attempting to prove that a logical explanation is valid or they are testing an idea to see whether it is reasonable. In such objective analytical arguments, writers explain the topic and attempt to demonstrate the soundness of the explanation by showing that the argument is a logical one. For example, a researcher wanting to find out whether exercise reduces the risk of a certain disease would assemble a body of information about people who exercise and try to determine whether in fact the incidence of the disease under consideration is affected. Such a study would involve a logical argument showing the relationship between exercising and the probability of contracting the disease. This kind of argument would be quite different from one designed to persuade people that they should abandon a sedentary life-style and start exercising. So when you listen to or read an argument, you will want to consider whether the writer is trying to persuade you to accept some assertion about a debatable proposition or to explain a topic by using logical analysis. Your critical response to the argument will depend on your understanding of its purpose.

9a
ARGUMENTS THAT EXPLAIN

Arguments that explain (those used in scientific treatises, scholarly articles, and business reports) address questions that can ultimately be answered. These questions of fact require that the writer address the problems in an unbiased way, without any preconceptions that would distort the accumulation of data. Arguments about such questions depend on the relationship between the specific facts available for the argument and a generalization related to those facts (see Section 13e). The following passage illustrates that relationship.

> Can we regard primitive knowledge, which . . . is both empirical and rational, as a rudimentary stage of science, or is it not at all related to it? If by science be understood a body of rules and conceptions, based on experience and derived from it by logical inference, embodied in material achievements and in a fixed form of tradition and carried on by some sort of social organization—then there is no doubt that even the lowest savage communities have the beginnings of science, however rudimentary.
>
> Most epistemologists would not, however, be satisfied with such a "minimum definition" of science, for it might apply to the rules of an art or craft as well. They would maintain that the rules of science must be laid down explicitly, open to control by experiment and critique by reason. They must not only be rules of practical behavior, but theoretical laws of knowledge. Even accepting this stricture, however, there is hardly any doubt that many of the principles of savage knowledge are scientific in this sense. The native shipwright knows not only practically of buoyancy, leverage, equilibrium, he has to obey these laws not only on water, but while making the canoe he must have the principles in mind. He instructs his helpers in them. He gives them the traditional rules, and in a crude and simple manner, using his hand, pieces of wood, and a limited technical vocabulary, he explains some general laws of hydrodynamics and equilibrium. Science is not detached from the craft, that is certainly true, it is only a means to an end, it is crude rudimentary, and inchoate, but with all that it is the matrix from which the higher developments must have sprung.
>
> —Bronislaw Malinowski, *Magic, Science and Religion*

9b
ARGUMENTS THAT PERSUADE

Arguments that persuade deal with debatable propositions, issues that cannot be proved the way questions of a scientific or scholarly nature can be. The debate is usually the result of questions that have to do with political matters and social policy or with ideas related to morals and ethics. The following statements represent two sides of a question having to do with a question of social policy that has also become a matter of political debate.

Nuclear reactors should be dismantled.

Nuclear reactors should be built.

Each statement could be the basis, or the main idea (Section 13a), of a persuasive argument designed to convince an audience that the writer's position is credible. The writer would attempt to support the argument with facts, opinions, and assertions. When you read works that try to persuade, you will find it helpful to determine what the main idea of the argument is.

In the following passage, notice how Joseph Wood Krutch, in arguing that killing animals for sport is evil, appeals to the **rationality** of the reader (Section 9c.4). In addition, notice how Krutch uses appeals to credibility (Section 9c.1), emotion (Section 9c.2), and style (Section 9c.3).

It wouldn't be quite true to say that "some of my best friends are hunters." Still, I do number among my respected acquaintances some who not only kill for the sake of killing but count it among their keenest pleasures. And I can think of no better illustration of the fact that men may be separated at some point by a fathomless abyss yet share elsewhere much common ground. To me, it is inconceivable that anyone can think an animal more interesting dead than alive. I can also easily prove, to my own satisfaction, that killing "for sport" is the perfect type of that pure evil for which metaphysicians have sometimes sought.

Most wicked deeds are done because the doer proposes some good for himself. The liar lies to gain some end; the swindler and the thief want things which, if honestly got, might be good in themselves. Even the murderer is usually removing some impediment to normal desires. Though all of these are selfish or unscrupulous, their deeds are not gratuitously evil. But the killer for sport seems to have no such excusable motive. He seems merely to prefer death to life, darkness to light. He seems to get nothing other than the satisfaction of saying: "Something which wanted to live is dead. Because I can bring terror and agony, I assure myself that I have power. Because of me there is that much less vitality, consciousness and perhaps joy in the universe. I am the spirit that denies." When a man wantonly destroys one of the works of man, we call him "Vandal." When he wantonly destroys one of the works of God, we call him "Sportsman."

The hunter-for-food may be as wicked and as misguided as vegetarians sometimes say, but he does not kill for the sake of killing. The ranchers and farmers who exterminate all living things not immediately profitable to them may sometimes be working against their own best interests; but whether they are or are not, they hope to achieve some supposed good by the exterminations. If to do evil, not in the hope of gain but for evil's sake, involves the deepest guilt by which man can be stained, then killing for killing's sake is a terrifying phenomenon and as strong a proof as we could have of that "reality of evil" with which present-day theologians are again concerned.

—Joseph Wood Krutch, *The Great Chain of Life*

9c
PERSUASIVE APPEALS

Appeals are attempts to affect readers' attitudes toward a claim made in persuasive writing. Writers of persuasion use one or a combination of four appeals in an effort to convince the reader. These appeals are based on four elements: credibility of the writer, emotional response of the reader, style of the presentation, and appearance of rationality.

9c.1 Credibility of the Writer

If you have ever paid close attention to a political campaign, you will have noticed that in their speeches, candidates often attempt to establish their **credibility**. Like a political candidate, a persuasive writer may try to create a positive image so that the reader will be more willing to accept the writer's position on the issue. Very often the writer will try to create the impression that he or she is an expert on the issue or has firsthand knowledge of the subject being argued. Certainly an argument by an expert in the field is more persuasive than an argument by someone who knows little about the subject and is merely expressing an uninformed opinion.

9c.2 Emotional Response of the Reader

Writing that persuades may appeal to the emotions of readers—either their needs or their fears. Television advertising often involves an appeal to the need to belong. Such advertising attempts to convince members of the audience that buying a certain product will make them part of the group—and that not having the product will cause them to be rejected by the group. The need to belong is a powerful appeal. Almost any emotion human beings are capable of can be used as an appeal in persuasion.

9c.3 Style of the Presentation

Occasionally, especially in advertising, the style of the writing itself will appeal to the reader. Pleasing images and clever turns of phrase make it easier for the reader to agree with the claim the writer is making.

9c.4 Rationality

Appeals to rationality are based on assertions that appear to be logical, whether the proof is fully logical or not. (See Section 9d on logical fallacies.) Often such appeals are shortened forms of more complicated logical arguments.

9d
LOGICAL FALLACIES

Logic is a system of reasoning that is used to analyze the validity of relationships between statements. As you saw in Section 9a on arguments that explain, by using logic we are able to show that if one thing or group of things is true, then another thing or group of things must be equally true. Often we can see intuitively that a series of statements is logically valid. The logical connections between them are apparent. As a critical reader, editor, and writer, however, you will want to be aware of the kinds of arguments that are not valid. Some arguments, known as **fallacies**, may appear to be true, but on closer inspection they reveal their logical inconsistencies. These fallacies can be conveniently divided into five groups. They occur because the writer has (1) made generalizations that cannot be substantiated, (2) made inaccurate assumptions, (3) made erroneous connections between causes and effects, (4) introduced irrelevant information into the argument, or (5) used language that is ambiguous.

9d.1 Fallacies Created by Unwarranted Generalizations

Arguments that begin with specific statements are valid if enough information is presented to support the conclusion drawn from them. The conclusion is a general statement that covers all the specific statements being used to support it.

Sweeping Generalizations

Sweeping generalizations occur because statements are too broad.

> All wealthy people are conservatives.

Usually such statements will be more convincing if they are qualified in some way or made more specific. The statement above could be made more convincing by qualifying it.

> Many wealthy people are conservatives.

Hasty Generalizations

Consider the following assertion.

> Gun control is a good idea. I think most people would agree with that. All my friends think it is a good idea.

Obviously, this assertion, whether it can be defended or not, is based on an unrepresentative sample. The friends of the speaker are not representative enough to allow the generalization that most people agree with the idea. A **hasty generalization** is one that is made before enough support has been assembled. Problems occur in making generalizations when the evidence they are based on is (1) insufficient, (2) unrepresentative, (3) unreliable, or (4) irrelevant.

9d.2 Fallacies Created by Inaccurate Assumptions

Some fallacies occur because the writer makes inaccurate assumptions to begin with.

False Analogy

Suppose that an author makes the following argument.

> Studies have shown that when chickadees store food in preparation for the winter, they show an increase in the number of brain cells, apparently so that they can better remember all the different places they store their food. When they are put into captivity and given their food, no extra brain cells appear. So it would seem that chickadees benefit from having to be self-sufficient. In the same way, people who are on welfare lose the ability to fend for themselves. They lose initiative and the will to work. They become dependent on government handouts. Welfare programs should be curtailed drastically.

A **false analogy** is the inaccurate assumption that two things are equivalent. Notice the flaws in the argument above. People are not equivalent to chickadees. Biological traits of animals are rarely analogous to traits found in human beings.

Black-and-White Arguments

Black-and-white arguments present the reader with a false dilemma.

> We must end welfare immediately. If we don't, the country will go broke. We must act now or face certain disaster later.

There are usually other possibilities to consider in such arguments.

Circular Reasoning

In **circular reasoning** the writer assumes in the premise of the argument that the question being argued is true.

> The police officer did not beat the suspect because the job of the police department is to serve and protect.

The argument goes in a circle.

9d.3 Fallacies That May Occur in the Explanation of Causes

Our common sense view of the world is based on the relationship between causes and effects. We need to understand relationships between causes and effects so we can make sense of the events going on around us and make valid predictions about the consequences of actions we take.

"After, Therefore Because Of"

The fallacy of "**after, therefore because of**" is an effort to convince the reader that just because an event follows another, it is caused by the previous event.

> Personal income tax has destroyed American society. Women are forced to work in order to pay the exorbitant and burdensome tax. As a result, children are left to wander the streets without parental supervision. Is it any wonder that crime has increased so dramatically?

This statement lists a series of events as though each one has caused the ones that follow it.

Oversimplification

Cause and effect is rarely simple.

> Crime has increased because of the collapse of the family.

Although the change in family structure may contribute to the increase in crime, it is certainly an **oversimplification** to say it is the only reason.

Slippery Slope

Slippery slope is a prediction that dire consequences will result from certain actions or events.

> If you drop out of school, you will end up on the streets with no job and nobody to care about you.

Obviously, many variables affect what happens to people. To predict such a narrow chain of causation is unreasonable.

9d.4 Fallacies Created When Irrelevant Material Is Introduced

Information Unrelated to the Argument

An argument that brings in unrelated information is often called a **red herring**. The name comes from the practice of dragging a smoked fish across a trail to distract hunting dogs.

> Those people who oppose the new shopping mall would do better spending their time on more important issues, such as what to do about crime in the streets.

In the argument above, the issue of crime is a red herring to divert attention from the issue of building a new shopping mall.

Name-Calling

As the name implies, **name-calling** is an attempt to discredit the opposition.

> Of course Mr. Fagan wants to double our expenditures for day-care workers; he's a bleeding-heart liberal, pot-smoking throwback.

Calling someone names really doesn't advance an argument.

"You Too"

Consider the following statement.

> How can you call me insensitive to the plight of others just because I don't want to increase spending? I recall that you voted against appropriations for day-care workers.

In this case, the argument of "**you too**" is based not on any aspect of the current issue but on the opposition's past behavior.

Poisoning the Well

Poisoning the well means countering the argument by calling into question the veracity of the opposing side.

> Although Senator Polanski will make a compelling argument, you can't believe a word he says—he's a notorious liar.

Attacking the Source

Another fallacy involves an attempt to discredit an argument by discounting its source.

> That argument sounds like it came straight out of *Mein Kampf*.

The response evades the issue by calling into question or **attacking the source** of the argument.

Unqualified Authority

Consider the following statement.

> The invasion is certainly justified. George Patton would have done the same thing.

Although we may admire Patton as a great general during World War II, his supposed opinion certainly cannot be used to defend an event that happened after he died. Further, we cannot be certain that if he were still alive, he would have approved.

Celebrity endorsements of products also represent the fallacy of **unqualified authority**.

"Because Everybody Else Does"

The fact that many people support an idea does not make that idea true.

> You should live in the Lake Shore Apartments. All our classmates live there.

In this appeal, the writer suggests that you as a reader ought to agree with the claim because **everybody else does**.

9d.5 Fallacies Created by Ambiguous Language

Some fallacies are created by the use of misleading words.

Use of Relative Terms

The word *good* is used differently in each of the following sentences and represents the **use of a relative term**.

> Ms. Jones would make a good teacher. She is a good engineer.

> A *good* engineer will not necessarily be a *good* teacher.

What Is True of One Must Be True of All

A writer may make a general statement that is not true.

> Cars made by Mercedes-Benz are expensive. All German cars are expensive.

While it is true that cars made by Mercedes-Benz are expensive, not all cars made in Germany are expensive.

What Is True of a Group Must Be True of Each Member of the Group

> Citibank is an important corporation. Harvey is an important executive because he works there.

That Citibank is an important corporation does not necessarily make Harvey important. Harvey might be either an important executive or a relatively unimportant one.

Textbooks, Newspapers, and Sources of Specialized Information

When you read any work that attempts to explain a topic, like a textbook or a newspaper does, you employ a set of critical strategies different from those you use when you read other kinds of writing. First of all, you may not read such writing from beginning to end. For instance, you might read only those textbook chapters concerned with assignments in your class. And you probably read a newspaper by first scanning the headlines to decide what stories to read. If you find an article you are interested in, you might read only until you find the information you want. Then you might stop and go to another article. When you read reference books and articles in scholarly journals, you might skip around, reading articles or portions of articles relevant to what you are studying or researching (see Sections 4a and 43a).

10a
READING AND STUDYING TEXTBOOKS

Most of the classes taken in school make use of a textbook, so the ability to read and study textbooks effectively is essential to success in school. Of course, you are not necessarily a good student just because you know how to read. However, becoming conscious of the strategies you probably already use as a reader can improve your study skills.

You can think of reading in three ways: what happens before you actually read the work, what happens while you are reading, and what happens after you have finished reading it.

10a.1 Prereading

Prereading involves a number of activities that allow you to read more productively. When you first look at a textbook, it is a good idea to familiarize yourself with the book. Looking at the table of contents, the index, and the chapter introductions can help you to gain information from a source more efficiently.

Scanning and skimming the preface, the introduction, and opening and closing paragraphs of chapters will also give you a better idea of what the book contains. Often when you are reading textbooks and doing research, you will not need to read every page of the work you are studying. Instead, you will need to scan the work, looking for important ideas related to your study or your research.

10a.2 Active Reading

After you have gone through prereading activities and have become familiar with the book, you will be able to read more actively. **Active reading** is more than just looking at the words as you read them. Active reading involves predicting and anticipating what will come next in the book and asking questions about what you are reading based on both your prereading activities and the information you gain as you read.

Prediction

After you read the following sentence, think about what would probably come after it.

> In his work *The Art of Rhetoric*, Aristotle distinguished three kinds of rhetoric: deliberative, forensic, and display.

From the information presented in the passage, you would probably expect the writing that followed to elaborate on each of the three kinds of rhetoric. You would also expect that at least a paragraph would be devoted to each one. You are able to make that kind of prediction because of your prior experience with writing organized by classification. Being able to predict what comes next in material you are reading depends in part on your understanding of typical organizational patterns such as narration, description, classification, and analysis (see Chapter 15; many of these familiar structures are also discussed in Part IV, "Arrangement").

When we read, we constantly predict what will come next. If we did not, reading would be a very slow and painful process, as it certainly is for some people. We can predict because we have had experience with various types of sentences, various patterns of development in paragraphs, and the structures of complete works of different lengths.

For example, when we read a narration, we know that events follow each other to make up the narration. So we expect to see words that indicate relationships between events in time. When we read a physical description, we know that the details of the description will follow a logical pattern of relationships in space.

Asking Questions

If you form questions as you become familiar with a work, you will be able to use your study and reading time more efficiently. You might jot down some questions that will help you focus on important aspects of the work. As you read actively, you will want to make notes and formulate questions that help you understand what you are reading.

10a.3 Reflective Reading

After reading an assignment, reflect on what you have learned. If what you have read is material that you will need to learn for a test, you will need to make an effort to retain it. Trying to remember the main ideas of what you have read and looking back at the text to reinforce what you remember will enable you to gain a greater understanding of the material.

10b
READING NEWS STORIES

Reading news stories is different from reading just about any other kind of written work, primarily because of the organization of the information. News stories are typically organized in one of three ways: the inverted pyramid, the focus structure, or the opinion poll.

The Inverted Pyramid

In a news story, information is usually arranged in the order of most important to least important. The most important material comes at the beginning of the story. As you read, you will notice that information after the first few sentences becomes less and less important. You could stop reading after learning the main points and not miss too much. Subsequent details are elaborations on the important information presented at the beginning.

This **inverted pyramid** structure, used in the vast majority of news stories, is determined by—and perhaps even influences—the way most people read newspapers. Most of us know from experience that we can glean the important information of a news story from the first few sentences, so we use that knowledge to skip around in the paper, finding different headlines we are interested in, reading a paragraph to get the gist of the story (reading more if we are really interested in the information), and then moving on to another story. (The inverted pyramid structure also allows editors to cut stories to fit space requirements.)

The Focus Structure

Not all news stories fit the inverted pyramid structure. For variation, especially if the information presented in the story is not new, writers may use a **focus structure** to concentrate on a person, a scene, an anecdote, or a bit of dialogue; then they move to a larger issue. For example, a reporter might begin a story about a fire by focusing on how a firefighter rescued a person from a burning building and then move on to discuss the larger issue of fire safety.

The focus structure is widely used in newsmagazines because they are usually published weekly rather than daily. As a result, most of the stories have already been reported in newspapers or other media.

Reports of Opinion Polls and Research Studies

Reports of statistical information can sometimes be misleading if you as a reader don't know what to look for. Readers, and sometimes even the reporters themselves, may draw unwarranted conclusions from statistics.

When you read an **opinion poll**, ask yourself the following questions.

- Who sponsored the poll?
- What was the exact wording of the questions?
- What was the nature of the population sampled?
- What is the margin of error?
- How and when was the information collected?

Similarly, when you read a **research study**, ask yourself these questions.

- Are the research methods explained?
- Are the limitations of the study spelled out?
- Who funded the study?
- How large was the study?
- Over how many years was it conducted?
- Does it build on the conclusions of previous studies?

10c
READING SOURCES OF SPECIALIZED INFORMATION

When you read works in any field, from anthropology to zoology, you will inevitably come across new technical terms. As a result, you may have to slow your reading down to compensate for the complication and take a little extra time to look up words you are not sure of. If you are doing research in that area, you will want to keep a list of key words in the field along with their definitions.

When you read in various academic disciplines, you will need to use different strategies.

Humanities

Reading in the humanities (including history) will often involve primary sources like those discussed in Chapters 11 and 12. Frequently, scholarly articles written about primary sources will assume you are familiar with those sources.

Social Sciences

Case studies and field studies reported in scholarly journals in the social sciences often require an understanding of statistics. In addition, a familiarity with the kinds of charts and graphs used to report such information will also be helpful.

Sciences

Articles in scientific journals are often almost unintelligible to nonscientists. If you are doing background reading in some area, you may want to start with articles in periodicals that are not quite so technical. Introductory textbooks will help you gain some grasp of the basic terminology of the field.

Business

Reading business letters, technical reports, memorandums, and business periodicals is a necessity made even more critical by the fast pace of modern life and the immediacy of technology. Anyone working in business will benefit from the ability to analyze the intent of a letter or memo quickly and to interpret a chart or table. Picking up important details from business communications of all kinds may mean the difference between success and failure in a competitive business environment.

Diaries, Letters, Autobiographies, and Biographies

Imagine it's twenty years in the future. You've become famous, and the public is interested in your life story. You find out that a publisher has hired a well-known journalist to write your biography. Will you have confidence that the public will have the opportunity to learn who you really are?

What factors may contribute to a fair or slanted view of your life and achievements? Will you be concerned about which people from your past the journalist interviews? Have others written negative reviews of you and your work? Will the journalist use those sources? Is the book being written at a time when you and your views are accepted and popular? Or might the book be a part of a backlash against you and other people who currently hold your philosophy? Will the journalist have access to letters you have written? Do you think the journalist will understand your relationship with the recipients of those letters? Will you make your unpublished diaries and journals available? Do you trust the journalist to treat your random feelings and observations with fairness and intelligence?

As you can see, there are many factors you would worry about if your life story were written by someone else. These are basically the same factors that you, as a reader, will be concerned with when you look at writing that deals with someone else's life. Whenever you read autobiographical and biographical materials, you will exercise certain critical reading and thinking skills that, while similar to those used with other types of writings, have unique applications to writings about a person's life.

11a
DIARIES

Before you read someone's diary, you probably have certain impressions about the writer, about the person's values, about when and where the passage was written, and about who the people mentioned were. So your first task will be to decide whether your impressions are reliable and accurate. These are matters you can clear up with basic facts.

Still, even after answering factual questions concerning the text of the diary and context in which it was written, you will examine other aspects of the work. For instance, you may need to look at the particular writer's reasons for writing. Did the person write daily; did he or she habitually explore certain themes and ideas and ignore others, or hold particular grudges and bizarre attitudes?

Finally, in reading diaries, you might consider the form of the diary you are reading. Reading an original diary—for instance, a parent's notebooks you have inherited or someone's journal in a library manuscript collection—poses different questions from reading a published and edited diary. Almost invariably, editors of published diaries alter a writer's words, if only to regularize spelling, punctuation, and sentence structure. Editors also affect your reading by shortening passages, omitting passages, and selecting passages that focus on only a narrow range of topics. For various reasons, editors "select" what you read. Sometimes it is to protect the reputations of people mentioned in the diary; sometimes it is to clarify the development of only one concern the diarist had; and sometimes it is even deliberately to tarnish the writer's reputation. It is always a good idea to read the introduction or preface to a published diary to discover the editor's philosophy and practice.

11b LETTERS

Letter writing may be a lost art. The telephone has certainly made us less dependant on mail to stay in touch with other people. But reading letters and their modern transformations, fax and email, is still an important skill.

While reading someone's letters, whether they are private letters never intended for publication or public letters such as those sent to newspapers, you will apply many of the same critical reading and thinking techniques used when reading diaries and journals. Of course, you will need to become familiar with much factual information concerning the contents of the letters. And the historical and biographical context of the letters is vital. However, questions about audience become very important. Unlike people's diaries, which present the writers without concern for how others view them, letters provide glimpses of how the writers present themselves to specific audiences. The writers may hide or disguise information, not only for psychological reasons but also for social ones.

For this reason, you will want to examine who the recipients of the letters are. What is their relationship to the writer, both at the occasion of the current letter and over time? You might also examine how the recipients' philosophies or attitudes differ from the writer's. Why would the writer be writing to this person at this time? Is this letter a singular event or part of an ongoing discussion? Were other people likely to read the letters, such as other friends, family members, or business associates? Also of critical interest is how letters to one recipient differ from letters to other audiences. What qualities of personality and character did the writer display to different audiences?

Then, of course, how you come upon the letters affects the way you examine them. Are you reading an original, handwritten letter that is part of a manuscript collection in a library archive? Or are you reading a letter contained in a book edited by the writer or by an editor? Is the editor a noted scholar or a family member or friend of the writer? Editorial policy is important to your reading and thinking about printed letters.

11c
AUTOBIOGRAPHIES

It can be argued that an autobiography contains two major characters: the writer as he or she is at the moment of writing and the writer at the time being written about. So you will want to understand the context of the autobiographies you read. Why did the writers produce the books at the time they did? Were the writers promoting or defending themselves or their philosophical outlook? Where in their lives are the writers—early, middle, or late career? What tone do they take toward their lives and work? What focus do the writers follow? Do they examine mainly personal and family matters, or do they focus on the work they did? What do they leave out of the work? Why?

Autobiographies are similar to diaries, journals, and letters in that they are all works in which writers express their inner selves. Yet most autobiographies, at least those intended for publication, are addressed to a general and distant audience. As you examine different autobiographies, you will want to reflect on what the writers assume about their audience and its values. These considerations were important to the writers as they chose and organized details from their lives. In addition, the writers' other books are important. Writers whose lives are well known, such as celebrities or novelists who write semiautobiographical works, may write works very different from those of writers whose lives have been relatively private.

11d
BIOGRAPHIES

Whenever you read a biography, you are encountering not only the life of the subject of the biography but also the writer's own intellectual and philosophical limitations. Therefore, reading a biography and thinking critically about it involves understanding the context in which the biography was written. In this light, as a reader you will want to become aware of the sources the biographer uses. Does the biographer primarily employ diaries, letters, and interviews with the subject? Or does the biographer rely on the work of previous biographers and critics? Not only will you be concerned with whether the information is reliable, but also you will want to verify that the sources are appropriate for the biographer's approach.

In addition to the particular approach the biographer takes toward the subject, you will want to examine critically the context of the biography and how the biographer reacts to that context. You will want to notice how the writer reacts to previous biographies. Similarly, you will want to determine whether the biographer had any personal relationship with the subject of the biography. A biography by a family member often offers an intimacy that one by a scholar, distant in time and place, does not. But it may also avoid delicate family topics that relatives want to keep secret.

It may sometimes seem that in a biography your understanding is limited to the intelligence and prejudices of the biographer, but with careful reading, you may discover that important ideas are conspicuous by their absence.

Literature

When we read a literary work, almost inevitably we begin to think about it critically, to try to get at the meaning of the work, to try to understand the significance of what we have read. For example, after reading a poem, we may continue to think about certain rhyming words or images that were particularly appealing. Or after reading a novel, we may continue to think about a powerful scene. Even if we don't do a full-blown interpretive analysis of the work, the process of reading by itself will cause us to begin examining the work with a critical eye. This initial critical response provides a basis for further critical thinking and critical analysis.

12a
FICTION

When you read fiction, you enter into an imaginary world created by the writer, a place where characters are presented in some detail as they go through a series of events involving conflict of some sort. So any work of fiction, whether it is a short story or a novel, will contain these elements: **plot** (what takes place in the story), **character** (who performs the action), **conflict** (what causes the action to occur), and **setting** (where the action takes place).

We discover who the characters are in a number of different ways. That discovery is controlled by the **point of view** of the narrator. Some narrators know everything about the various characters and tell us about their motivations, their desires, and even their thoughts. Other narrators, especially those who are characters in the story, will reveal to us only what the characters do and what they say.

The unity of the plot structure in a work of fiction often reveals its **theme**, its main idea. How that theme is related to other elements will often provide you with clues to an interpretation of the meaning of the work.

Other important elements to consider when you are forming an interpretation are these: What motivates the characters (both major and minor characters)? What kinds of conflict are present (physical, psychological, social, or moral)? And what effect does the language have?

12b
DRAMA

When you were a child, you may have pretended to be another person, or you may have created an imaginary playmate. The same kind of thing happens in drama. People pretending to be other people create dramatic situations on a stage.

As with fiction, when you read or see drama, you will want to pay attention to plot, character, conflict, and setting, including their relationship to theme. However, since most dramas are written to be performed on the stage, **dialogue**—what the actors say onstage—becomes a much more important part of the analysis and interpretation. In addition, if you see the drama performed, staging (the props, scenery, costumes, and lighting) will affect how you respond to the work.

12c
POETRY

Most people find certain patterns of words pleasing—rhyming sounds, for instance. You may have noticed how children play with language, creating games and songs that involve rhymes. They seem to do it almost instinctively. Although some poems, especially long narrative works, may demand that you attend to some of the same elements of analysis as you do in analyzing fiction and drama (plot, character, conflict, setting, and dialogue), you will find that other considerations may be more important: speaker, language, and form.

The speaker's attitude toward the subject of the poem and the speaker's tone will affect the way you hear the poem. For example, if the speaker is sarcastic, sad, ironic, angry, or euphoric, you will no doubt participate in that emotion to some degree as you read the poem.

In many ways, poetry is the most artistic of all literary forms. It is an art created by language. So, when you read poetry, you will want to be sensitive to how language is used. The **imagery**—language that appeals to the senses—and dominant images or patterns of imagery will usually suggest an approach to theme. An understanding of how **figures of speech** are used (most notably, similes, metaphors, and personification) will often deepen your understanding of the poem.

The **form** of the poem, especially the rhyme scheme and metrical pattern, will control the emphasis you put on certain words, phrases, and images. An oral reading of the poem will often reveal such structures. The sounds of the words, the rhythms of the lines, and the pace of the language—all will give you clues to the meaning of the poem.

CommonSense Checklist

Writing About Literature

For the most part, when you write a critical paper about a literary work, you are asked to write an argument—to offer an interpretation of the interrelationship of a work's form and meaning. You should be able to use a process approach to each paper, drafting as needed, so long as you incorporate the following elements into your final draft.

Base your interpretation on your personal, fully informed attitude about the topic you are addressing.

Pay attention to the conventions of the type of literary work you are criticizing.

Make first reference to authors and titles using complete names.

Refer to what an author writes in a story or poem not as if it happened in the past but rather as if it were happening now (for example, "Shakespeare compares his mistress to starkly realistic features of the ordinary world in order to declare his honest affection for her"). Use words that refer to the past only if you are talking about historical information.

→

continued from previous page

Avoid simple plot summary, and be careful not to lapse into summary when you are interpreting a passage or scene.

Make specific references to the work, using examples and quotations to support your interpretation.

Explain *why* you think examples and quotations illustrate what you think they illustrate.

Combine summary, paraphrase, and direct quotation with your own interpretations of the work (see Chapter 44, "Using Sources").

Never say that a character's speech is a quotation; rather, identify parts of a work by referring to scene, passage, and so on. If you consult secondary sources, be sure to give appropriate credit and avoid plagiarism.

If using a formal documentation style, consult guidelines for MLA in-text citations (see Section 45a.1).

4

Arrangement

16 COHERENCE

CHAPTER 13

Unity

Have you ever moved? If you have, you will remember that when you first arrived at your new place, all your furniture and clothing and other possessions were probably not arranged exactly as you wanted them. Boxes of dishes may have been put in the bedroom and books may have been put in the kitchen. You had to go through the process of putting things where they belonged. Writing is like that: when you begin putting your ideas on paper or on a word processor, the words and phrases and sentences may not be exactly where you want them to be. You will need to arrange them so that they communicate clearly what you want to say to your reader.

As you continue to write, you will be involved in a series of decisions about where to put what. These decisions create **unity** in writing. You consider the arrangement of paragraphs, the arrangement of details in the paragraphs, the arrangement of the sentences that make up the paragraphs, and the arrangement of the words that make up each sentence. In each case, you attempt to make every idea focus on the same topic and to unify your writing.

13a
MAIN IDEA

For readers to be able to understand any extended piece of writing, all the ideas and information must be relevant to a central, controlling idea—a **main idea**. When you introduce irrelevant information into your writing, you break the unity, and that break may distract and even confuse the reader. Even if the main idea of the work, or of any paragraph in the work, is unstated, it will control what information is included.

CommonSense Observation

Stated Main Idea

Many writing texts say that the main idea for the whole work and the main ideas for each paragraph should be explicit. However, close examination of many published works by respected writers shows

→

continued from previous page

> that the main idea is not always stated. When you write, be sure you know your audience's expectations. It is often a good practice to state the main idea so that you can be certain your writing is unified.

In Chapter 5 you discovered that the main idea of a work makes the purpose of the writing more specific. As a writer, one of your problems is to make sure the details you add to a work are relevant to the main idea.

13a.1 Main Idea of the Work as a Whole

Suppose you have decided to write about the *topic* of nuclear reactors and that your *purpose* is to *persuade* your audience, perhaps the readers of your local newspaper, that nuclear reactors are too dangerous for countries to continue to use as a source of energy. The statement "Nuclear reactors are dangerous and should be dismantled" is the main idea of what you will be writing. To avoid confusing or distracting your reader, you will want to make sure that everything you include is relevant to that main idea.

Notice how the main ideas that follow reflect a narrowing of a topic (Section 4b) and make us aware of the writer's specific purpose (see Chapter 5).

Bicycles offer convenient transportation for students.

Investing in the stock market can be risky.

You can see that each of the main ideas above is a general statement about a topic. Each one represents a narrowing of a topic and a refinement of the purpose. For instance, the main idea "Bicycles offer convenient transportation for students" is a narrowing of the topic "transportation for students," which is a narrowing of the general subject "transportation." Similarly, the main idea "Investing in the stock market can be risky" is a narrowing of the topic "investing in the stock market," which is in turn a narrowing of the general subject "investing." In both cases, the reader would expect that an essay on the topic would present information relevant to the main idea.

13a.2 Main Idea of Each Paragraph

A **unified paragraph** is one with ideas that are all related to each other. As with the work as a whole, the unity of each paragraph can be summed up in a single statement, a main idea. Sometimes the main idea of the paragraph is stated, and sometimes it is not. If it is not actually stated in so many words and if the paragraph is unified, then the main idea can be inferred by the reader. See if you can identify the main idea in the following paragraph.

There have been a number of nuclear accidents over the last several years. In the United States, the Three Mile Island reactor had a leak in its system and consequently released some radioactivity into the atmosphere. In the former Soviet Union, the reactor at Chernobyl caused catastrophic damage when it malfunctioned.

The main idea in the preceding paragraph is of course presented in the first sentence. The two sentences that follow it add information related to that main idea.

See if you can identify the main idea in the following paragraph.

To develop skill at playing a musical instrument requires daily practice. To achieve proficiency in athletic performance requires diligent workouts. To gain competency in writing requires continued work. The development of any skill depends on constant work and application.

Notice that in the preceding paragraph, the main idea appears in the last sentence rather than in the first. That arrangement has the effect of reinforcing the conclusion the reader may have already come to before reading it at the end of the paragraph.

? 13b
ELABORATION

As you read the following sentence, think about what information you could include in any sentences that would follow it in a paragraph. What kind of information could you add so that the reader would have a better understanding of your idea?

When I was younger, I enjoyed strenuous exercise.

Each of the four sentences that follow illustrates a possible alternative for developing the idea. Consider how each alternative functions.

1. I loved a good, hard workout.
2. Recently, however, I have discovered that heavy-duty exercise programs may have some negative effects.
3. It was this preparation that got me interested in mountain climbing.
4. I enjoyed the exhilaration that came with a hard game of basketball, tennis, or squash.

Each of the numbered sentences illustrates an alternative way of elaborating an idea in a piece of writing. Alternative 1 is a restatement or a repetition of the initial sentence. Alternative 2 is a divergence that moves the information in a different direction. Alternative 3 is a generalization that will need further development and elaboration. Alternative 4 is an example.

Any sentence you write can be elaborated through one of these four kinds of development. In fact, writing is a constant process of elaborating ideas presented in previous sentences.

13b.1 Restatement

Notice how the following passage develops the main idea by using **restatement**.

> Regular exercise may counteract the negative effects of stress. Most people will benefit from a reasonable exercise program that conditions the body to better deal with many of the stressful features of life in an industrial society. Many who exercise regularly feel that their improved health and conditioning is an essential antidote to the ills of modern life.

The two sentences that follow the initial one add very little new information. They simply comment on and emphasize the main idea of the passage. They are essentially a restatement of the first sentence.

Restatement is useful when you want to add emphasis to what you are writing about and to expand the focus of the ideas presented. Sentences that restate are frequently included in either introductory or concluding paragraphs because they call the reader's attention to the main idea by repeating it in several ways.

13b.2 Divergence

Notice how the following passage uses **divergence** to alter the direction of the topic.

> Our society has come to believe that exercise is beneficial—a good thing to do. In some cases, however, exercise can be detrimental.

You will use divergence when you want to add an idea that is a digression or when you want to move the discussion in a different direction. Of course, continuous digressions and changes of the direction can become confusing to the reader, so there are limitations to how much you can develop your writing by using divergence and still maintain unity and coherence.

13b.3 Generalization

Consider how the **generalizations** in the following passage develop from the material that precedes them.

> Do you experience persistent soreness or stiffness? Do you catch colds frequently? Are you sometimes nervous and irritable? Do you frequently have an upset stomach? If you have any of these symptoms, you may be a victim of stress. It will be important for you to reduce your overall level of stress.

The last two sentences of the passage are more general than the first four. These generalizations at the end of the passage make the earlier comments more understandable by offering a generalized explanation.

You may find that you need to summarize specific details and examples that you have presented at the beginning of a paper, a passage, or a paragraph. If so, then generalization will be an appropriate and effective way of elaborating a topic. But generalizations have limitations. To present material only in general statements will create difficulties for most readers. Our natural tendency is to follow a generalization with specific details, particulars, and examples that comment on the general idea presented.

13b.4 Example

Consider how the following passage illustrates the use of **example**.

> We sometimes think of stress as coming from internal, emotional sources, but some kinds of stress come from external sources. For example, inadequate recovery from hard work or sleep deprivation can exacerbate stressful situations. Too much food, too little food, or the wrong type of food may make it difficult to cope with stress. Also, environmental sources such as noise pollution, hot weather, or cold weather may increase the level of stress.

Example is the most common and the most effective method for developing a topic. By adding specific details that elaborate the main idea, you enable the reader to better understand what you have written. This principle applies to both the main idea of the work as a whole and to the main idea of a paragraph. The other methods of development discussed above—restatement (Section 13b.1), divergence (Section 13b.2), and generalization (Section 13b.3)—have limited uses. When you make use of them, exercise some care and make sure that you are using the most appropriate method for the material. You will find that giving examples is generally the most effective method of elaboration.

13c
LOGICAL SEQUENCES

The main idea of a paragraph and the details that are related to that main idea are connected to each other by **logical sequences**. The main idea is the most general of all the statements that appear in a paragraph. If the main idea does not actually appear in the paragraph, it can be stated as a generalization about the content of the paragraph. The content of the paragraph is developed as a series of ideas related to the main idea.

13c.1 Parallel Ideas

Notice how the following paragraph develops a series of ideas that are at the same level of generalization.

> Bicycles are the ideal form of transportation for students. They are economical. They cost less to purchase and maintain than a car. They don't take up a lot of space. That makes them easy to park and easy to store in an apartment or a dorm.

The main idea is stated in the first sentence. It is also the most general statement in the paragraph. Each sentence that follows is more specific than the first sentence, but all the sentences are at the same level, so we see them as having a parallel structure.

This kind of logical sequence can be represented by numbering the sentences at each level. For example:

1. Bicycles are the ideal form of transportation for students.
    2. They are economical.
    2. They cost less to purchase and maintain than a car.
    2. They don't take up a lot of space.
    2. That makes them easy to park and easy to store in an apartment or a dorm.

13c.2 Subordinate Ideas

As you read the following paragraph, pay attention to the logical sequence of the sentences.

> Investing in the stock market can be risky because there is nothing to insure the value of any particular stock on any given day. A person's invest-

ment can easily decline. If a stock's price drops, everyone who owns that stock loses money. For example, the fact that IBM stock is selling for $125 a share today doesn't mean that it will be selling for $125 a share tomorrow. So, if you had bought it for $127 a share yesterday and it went down to $125 a share today, you would have lost $2 for every share you owned.

Each sentence is at a more specific level than the one that precedes it. The paragraph could be represented as follows.

1. Investing in the stock market can be risky because there is nothing to insure the value of any particular stock on any given day.

   2. A person's investment can easily decline.

      3. If a stock's price drops, everyone who owns that stock loses money.

         4. For example, the fact that IBM stock is selling for $125 a share today doesn't mean that it will be selling for $125 a share tomorrow.

            5. So, if you had bought it for $127 a share yesterday and it went down to $125 a share today, you would have lost $2 for every share you owned.

This kind of **subordinate** arrangement shows clearly the relationship between the various sentences of the paragraph.

13c.3 Combination of Parallel and Subordinate Ideas

Using a combination of parallel and subordinate ideas enables you to present a complex body of information to the reader in a logical, unified way.

> Pollution affects us in several different ways. As we breathe, we may be inhaling particulate matter, ozone, and carbon monoxide, all of which can cause respiratory irritation. Many cities issue warnings if the pollution in the air exceeds safe levels. When we eat food, we may be ingesting pesticides and other pollutants that have been introduced into the food chain by human beings. For example, a chemical that makes apples redder was used for years before the growers were forced to stop using it.

You will be able to see from the following representation how parallel and subordinate sequences fit together.

1. Pollution affects us in several different ways.

   2. As we breathe, we may be inhaling particulate matter, ozone, and carbon monoxide, all of which can cause respiratory irritation.

      3. Many cities issue warnings if the pollution in the air exceeds safe levels.

   2. When we eat food, we may be ingesting pesticides and other pollutants that have been introduced into the food chain by human beings.

      3. For example, a chemical that makes apples redder was used for years before growers were forced to stop using it.

13d
EMPHATIC SEQUENCES

Emphatic sequences create unity by arranging details in order of importance. Accordingly, the details presented are either more important or less important than those they follow. Two patterns of emphatic sequence—most important to least important and least important to most important—allow you to emphasize important information either by putting it first or by delaying it until the end of a paragraph or passage.

13d.1 Most Important to Least Important

The pattern of most important to least important is frequently used to present details in news stories. Notice how the following passage illustrates the pattern.

> During the evening of December 16, 1773, a group of Bostonians disguised as Native Americans boarded three British ships and threw 342 chests of teas into Boston Harbor. The act was an apparent protest against the British tax on tea imported to the colonies. Even though the duties imposed on glass, lead, paper, and paints by the Townshend Revenue Acts of 1767 had been repealed in 1770, the tax on tea remained. It was reduced in May 1773, but the colonists still resented taxation without representation and the monopoly given to the East India Company to sell tea in the Americas.
>
> It was rumored that Samuel Adams, a distant cousin of John Adams, had organized the Tea Party. The British Parliament enacted the Coercive Acts (called the Intolerable Acts in America) to punish Boston. As a result, the other colonies came to the aid of Boston, and the resistance that eventually led to the Revolution began.

The most important information, that the Boston Tea Party occurred, appears first in the article. Each subsequent piece of information is less and less important. You could stop reading almost anywhere during the article and still have the feeling that you knew most of the important facts being reported.

13d.2 Least Important to Most Important

The pattern of least important to most important creates another kind of emphasis because the information builds to a **climax**. Notice how the following passage illustrates that pattern.

> A person who cleans houses or mows lawns for a living is not likely to need to be very skilled at operating a computer. Even someone who works in a restaurant or in a retail store may need only minimal skills to perform a few basic operations on a computer, such as recording sales or entering items for inventory. But people who work in offices—either in the public sector or in the private sector—will certainly need more than a nodding acquaintance with computers. Increasingly, offices, both large and small, depend on computers, not only for word processing but also to store information, to perform complicated bookkeeping and accounting functions, and to transfer messages. Computer skills are rapidly becoming a requirement for employees in the modern workplace.

The information at the beginning of the passage is not as important to the main idea as the information at the end. The passage builds gradually to an emphatic statement about the importance of computer skills.

13e PATTERNS OF ARGUMENTATION

Some arguments are based on a general principle and show how that principle explains certain observable facts about our world. These arguments can be called **arguments from principle** since the relationship between the generalizations and specific facts depends on first establishing the general principle and then showing how specific facts fit that principle.

Other arguments are based on specific facts. The argument then explains how those facts support a general principle. Arguments of this type can be called **arguments from fact** because the relationship between the generalizations and specific facts depends on first presenting the details and then showing how a general principle can be derived from them.

Furthermore, each of these two patterns of argumentation can be used either to explain a topic, as in scientific and scholarly works, or to persuade an audience, as in debates over public policy issues. These four patterns are discussed in the following subsections.

13e.1 Argument from Principle

The two passages that follow illustrate how argument from a general principle to specific detail can have a purpose of either explaining a topic or persuading an audience about the validity of an author's position on an issue.

Argument from Principle That Explains

This passage from a book by a scientist who studies animal and human behavior illustrates an argument that explains how a scientific principle underlies altruism in human beings.

> Since selfishness is genetic rather than personal, we will have a natural tendency to help our blood relatives and hence our whole tribe. Since our tribes have swollen into nations, our helpfulness becomes stretched further and further, aided and abetted by our tendency towards accepting symbolic substitutes for the real thing. Altogether this means that we are now, by nature, a remarkably helpful species. If there are break-downs in this helpfulness, they are probably due, not to our "savage nature" reasserting itself, but to the unbearable tensions under which people so often find themselves in the strained and over-crowded world of today.
>
> —Desmond Morris, *Manwatching*

Beginning with the general principle that "selfishness is genetic," Morris argues that helpfulness is really an outgrowth of selfishness extended to the family and the tribe. He further argues that "break-downs in this helpfulness" occur because of "unbearable tensions."

Argument from Principle That Persuades

The following passage illustrates an argument that persuades by moving from a general principle to specific details.

> "We measure ourselves by many standards," said the great American psychologist William James, nearly a century ago. "Our strength and our intelligence, our wealth and even our good luck, are things which warm our heart and make us feel ourselves a match for life. But deeper than all such things, and able to suffice unto itself without them, is the sense of the amount of effort which we can put forth."

If women do not put forth, finally, that effort to become, they will forfeit their own humanity. A woman today who has no goal, no purpose, no ambition patterning her days into the future, making her stretch and grow beyond that small score of years in which her body can fill its biological function, is committing a kind of suicide. For that future half a century after the childbearing years are over is a fact that an American woman cannot deny. Nor can she deny that as a housewife, the world is indeed rushing past her door while she just sits and watches. The terror she feels is real, if she has no place in that world.

The feminine mystique has succeeded in burying millions of American women alive. There is no way for these women to break out of their comfortable concentration camps except by finally putting forth an effort—that human effort which reaches beyond biology, beyond the narrow walls of home, to help shape the future. Only by such a personal commitment to the future can American women break out of the housewife trap and truly find fulfillment as wives and mothers—by fulfilling their own unique possibilities as separate human beings.

—Betty Friedan, *The Feminine Mystique*

Asserting the principle that fulfillment comes from "putting forth an effort," Friedan argues that to find that fulfillment, housewives must put forth effort to break out of the trap they are in.

13e.2 Argument from Fact

The two passages that follow illustrate how arguments from fact can be used to explain a topic or to persuade an audience.

Argument from Fact That Explains

Notice how this passage illustrates an argument from fact that explains a topic.

Many cognitive psychologists have concluded that long-term memory is based on the apprehension of meaning rather than on precise verbal or visual content. For example, when people were asked to recall pictures or sentences as part of a psychological experiment, it was discovered that what they had stored in their memory was really an abstract representation that captured its meaning, rather than the actual details of how the picture or sentence was constructed. [Two researchers] discovered a similar pattern when they studied chess masters. They found that what made these people so skillful was that they had learned the array of action possibilities associated with distinct patterns of chess pieces. These patterns were stored in memory as "chunks" that defined "meaningful game relations among the pieces." In other words, the pattern, once understood, could become part of a tacit store of knowledge. When the chess master recognized the pattern on the chessboard, it triggered an immediate knowledge of the relevant action possibilities. While other players have to consciously think through the available courses of actions, the chess master's attention is freed to deal with the more sophisticated problem of overall game strategy.

What might this imply for the human being at the data interface? Over the long term, intellective mastery will depend upon being able to develop a tacit knowledge that facilitates the recognition of decision alternatives and frees the mind for the kind of insight that could result in innovation and improvement. Such tacit recognition depends upon being able to explicitly construct the significance of patterns and relationships of data.

—Shoshana Zuboff, *In the Age of the Smart Machine*

Zuboff's argument—that effective action occurs because of the ability to recognize patterns and relationships—is based on the factual results of studies by cognitive psychologists about long-term memory.

Argument from Fact That Persuades

Notice how this passage illustrates a persuasive argument from fact.

. . . I acknowledge that the world, the weather, and the life cycle have caused me no end of trouble, and yet I look forward to putting in another forty or so years with them because they have also given me no end of pleasure and instruction. They interest me. I want to see them thrive on their own terms. I hate to see them abused and interfered with for the comfort and convenience of a lot of spoiled people who presume to "hate" the more necessary kinds of work and all the natural consequences of working outdoors.

When people begin to "hate" the life cycle and to try to live outside it and to escape its responsibilities, then the corpses begin to pile up and to get into the wrong places. One of the laws that the world imposes on us is that everything must be returned to its source to be used again. But one of the first principles of the haters is to violate this law in the name of convenience or efficiency. Because it is "inconvenient" to return bottles to the beverage manufacturers, "dead soldiers" pile up in the road ditches and in the waterways. Because it is "inconvenient" to be responsible for wastes, the rivers are polluted with everything from human excrement to various carcinogens and poisons. Because it is "efficient" (by what standard?) to mass-produce meat and milk in food "factories," the animal manures that once would have fertilized the fields have instead become wastes and pollutants. And so to be "free" of "inconvenience" and "inefficiency" we are paying a high price—which the haters among us are happy to charge to posterity.

—Wendell Berry, *The Gift of Good Land*

Berry uses facts—examples of litter and pollution—to support his argument that efficiency is not free.

13e.3 Traditional Patterns

A pattern of arrangement that was first developed in the ancient civilizations of Greece and Rome is still an effective way to present arguments that persuade an audience. The following outline identifies the kinds of information you would need to include in an argument using this traditional pattern of arrangement. Consider how such an arrangement would increase the persuasive effect of an argument.

I. Introduction
   A. Create interest in the topic.
   B. Establish your credibility as an authority.
   C. Establish a common ground for both you and the reader.
   D. Show fairmindedness on your part.
   E. State or imply the main idea of the entire argument.

II. Background

III. Lines of Argument
   A. Present rational and/or emotional appeals.
   B. Present reasons in order of importance.
   C. Show that your position is in readers' best interest.

IV. Refutation of Any Opposing Arguments
   A. Consider any opposing views.
   B. Note advantages and disadvantages of any opposing views.

V. Conclusion
   A. Summarize the argument.
   B. Elaborate on the implications of the argument.
   C. Make clear what you want readers to think or do.
   D. Make a final emotional appeal.

You can see from this outline that an argument arranged in this way would be used for writing that has as its purpose to persuade a reader. Although some parts of the argument do explain the topic, overall the material included would address an issue or a debatable question.

Familiar Patterns of Organization

Some patterns of organization are familiar to us because they reflect basic patterns of perceiving reality. Notice what is around you. What do you see and hear and smell? Are you in a room? What does it look like? If you are outdoors or in a public place, what details can you observe? What events are going on around you? As you observe your environment, what kinds of things do you see? Tables, desks, chairs, trees?

If you were to write down your responses to these questions, you might find yourself using a pattern of organization. You might tell a story or attempt to explain how some object looks. You might show how two things are similar or different. You might show how a process works or what causes an event to occur. All these responses correspond to patterns of organization discussed in this chapter.

An essay, a report, or any other large piece of writing may have several patterns of organization. The essay as a whole may follow one pattern while different parts of the essay may be developed by other patterns. Single paragraphs, however, tend to follow a single pattern of organization.

The sections that follow explain many of the principles of organization. Each example treats the same topic, "jeans." As a result, you will be able to see how almost any pattern of organization can be used to develop a topic.

14a
DESCRIBING

The following passage describes the appearance of a pair of well-worn jeans, developing details about the appearance and coloration.

> A pair of well-worn jeans hardly resembles the pants originally purchased. The seat is shiny and threadbare from much sitting and sliding around. The knees have horizontal tears that expose bare threads. The cuffs are quite ragged. Overall, they have lost their uniform blue color. Instead they are faded, almost white, especially around every seam, pocket, and snap and even the zipper. But for many people, that is a condition long sought after, and even expedited on occasion with bleach and razor blades.

Description tells what a person, place, or thing looks like. The details of a description are arranged according to their relationships between each other in space. As you can see from the description of the jeans, the gen-

110

eral appearance of a pair of pants is assumed, but other details that distinguish jeans from other pants are presented in a spatial arrangement. The main idea of a paragraph developed by description will give a general overall impression of the thing described. The main idea of the paragraph above is "Well-worn jeans have a distinctive appearance."

14b
NARRATING

Events are arranged in time order in the following narrative.

> Shopping for a new pair of jeans is a serious activity. At least I take it seriously. Last Saturday I decided to replenish my dwindling stock of jeans. I got up early, in an effort to beat the other shoppers, but it didn't seem to make any difference. By the time I got to the mall, it seemed that everybody else in town was there too. Since almost every store in the mall was having a sale, many of the sizes were picked over, and, unfortunately, I wear an average size. But eventually, through perseverance and luck, I found four new pairs, in assorted colors. Needless to say, I am very happy.

Narration is telling a story. The organizing principle is the relationship of events in time. Notice that the sentences in the paragraph record the passage of time. "Last Saturday" and "I got up early" communicate the time sequence.

14c
EXPLAINING A PROCESS

The following paragraph reveals steps that could be followed over and over.

> If you want your new pair of jeans to stay roughly the same size and the same color as they were when you bought them, you will need to take a few simple precautions. First, before you wash them, turn them inside out. This will prevent them from fading excessively, especially around seams and pockets. Second, set the water temperature on cold, again a precaution against fading as well as shrinking. Third, after the washing is completed, line-dry them, or at least dry them for only ten minutes or so in a dryer to prevent them from becoming too hot.

Organization by **process analysis** is similar to narration in that it involves the ordering of events in time. The difference is that a process explains events that occur over and over. Notice how the paragraph above identifies the steps in the process as *first*, *second*, and *third*.

14d
CLASSIFYING

The following example tells what kinds of methods are used to make jeans look worn.

> Manufacturers have used three methods of producing jeans that were already faded: stonewashing, enzyme washing, and acid washing. Stonewashing involves putting pumice stones into the prewashing cycle. The stones cause the fabric to wear and some of the color to fade. Enzyme washing (sometimes combined with stonewashing) uses cellulase enzymes to "eat" the fabric, softening it and lightening the color. Finally, acid washing uses pumice stones soaked in bleach to fade and distress the fabric.

Classifying is arranging elements of the topic according to logical categories. Writing that organizes by classification answers the implied question "What kinds of the topic are there?" The subject of the paragraph above is organized into three categories: stonewashing, enzyme washing, and acid washing. This kind of organization is common with scientific topics.

14e
COMPARING AND CONTRASTING

Notice how the following two paragraphs show the differences between two items.

> In the 1950s, practically the only style of jeans available was the traditional regular fit. Now, because so many designers and manufacturers are producing jeans, other styles have emerged. Many people still feel comfortable with the traditional cut, but as the baby boomers, who popularized jeans in the 1950s, have gotten older, so has the popularity of a style that fits more loosely, called, among other names, easy fit, loose fit, and relaxed fit.
>
> Regular-style jeans fit the wearer relatively tightly, especially after they've been washed a couple of times; they have straight legs and are narrow at the ankle. They are usually the attire of working people. The looser-fitting styles are fuller through the seat and thigh and so are more comfortable. Some retain the look of the traditional style while others may tend to look baggy. What-

ever the demands, and physique, of the modern jeans wearer, chances are that some designer has already produced, or will soon produce, a style that will accommodate.

Comparing and contrasting is the arrangement of similarities and differences between two ideas, objects, people, or places. Comparing and contrasting depends on a classification system. The two things to be compared or contrasted must be at the same level in the classification system. In the passage above, the two things being compared are in the same general system of classification: styles of jeans.

14f
MAKING ANALOGIES

The following paragraph reveals unexpected connections between the two things being compared.

> Sometimes, when I'm wearing jeans on campus, I feel like a chameleon, not because I blend in with the scenery, tree limbs or rocks or foliage, but I do blend in with other people—everybody wears jeans. Jeans have become such a fixture in American culture that it is possible to wear them practically anywhere, in practically any circumstance. When I go to a concert, I wear my faded jeans and a baggy sweater. When I work outside in the yard, I wear old, stained jeans like everyone else in the neighborhood. When I go out to eat, I wear designer jeans with a tailored shirt and maybe even a jacket. No matter where I go and what I do, I can wear jeans.

Analogies are comparisons of two things that are not alike, that is, that come out of different classification systems. In the passage above, "people wearing jeans" and "chameleons" are entirely different, but the writer has shown points of similarity that help the reader understand that the prevalence of jeans has made them socially acceptable for almost any occasion.

14g
DEFINING

The following extended definition uses synonyms as well as other methods of definition.

> Jeans are casual pants made from a coarse denim dyed an indigo blue. The word *jean* itself was derived from the name given to the heavy cotton

cloth used to make the pants. Since the cloth had originally been imported from Genoa, Italy, it was called *jene fustian*, meaning "Genoan fustian" (Genoan cloth). Traditionally, the pants have been cut so that they fit snugly, with the front pockets set at an angle a couple of inches under the waistband and the back pockets sewed on as patches. The more traditional styles also have a watch pocket.

Definitions explain what something is or is not. A definition can simply be a synonym for the word, but it usually also makes reference to the classification system in which the idea is located. An extended definition will elaborate by using description, examples, and perhaps even narration to aid the reader in understanding the idea.

14h
ANALYZING

The following paragraph breaks the topic into its component parts.

> Jeans have been an obvious part of American culture for several generations. In the 1950s, clean-cut young men wore blue tapered-leg jeans. In the 1960s, free-spirited, antiestablishment hippies wore hip-hugging, bell-bottomed, faded jeans. In the 1970s and 1980s, yuppies wore designer jeans that had been swept up into the world of high fashion and had become the modern symbol of a culture so affluent it could afford to relax.

In this passage the concept being **analyzed**—broken into parts—is American culture as it is represented by jeans. The "jeans culture" is explained by showing how some of the parts—the changing styles of jeans—fit together.

14i
SHOWING CAUSE AND EFFECT

The following paragraph shows how events cause others that follow them and are the effect of still others that have gone before.

> A man named Levi Strauss designed the first pair of jeans during the California Gold Rush. Because of their sturdy durability and comfortable fit, jeans became popular work pants throughout the United States in the decades that followed. Today, jeans are worn by all types of people for every occasion, from working in a mine to spending an evening out on the town. Jeans, the great social equalizer, have become America's revenge on the world of foreign

fashion design. This single item of clothing continues to define the trendy, sexy look sought after by everyone.

Showing **cause and effect** is an attempt to explain why certain events have taken place. Such an organization is a central feature of writing about historical events. The passage above examines some of the events that may account for the popularity of jeans.

CommonSense Guide

Be aware of how your ideas relate to each other. Do they tell a story? Do they show similarities? Do they explain causes? Structure your writing to clarify that relationship.

Conventional Structures

"Once upon a time . . ." ". . . and they lived happily ever after." If you have ever heard or read fairy tales, you will recognize each of those phrases, the traditional beginning and ending for many of the fanciful stories told to children. What is true of fairy tales is also true of other communications: anything you write will have a beginning, a middle, and an end. That seems obvious enough. But the options available for developing those parts of what you write are not quite so obvious.

In this chapter you will find examples of many possible variations for beginnings and endings as well as suggestions for developing transitional paragraphs and content paragraphs.

15a
BEGINNINGS

If you were taking a new friend to a party, you would probably want to introduce that person to a number of other people. The same thing happens when you write. You will want to introduce your topic to your readers. An **introduction** will help the reader understand the rest of what you have written. Without an introduction, the reader may spend some time trying to figure out what you are getting at. Of course, exactly what you put in the introduction will depend on the topic, the purpose, the audience, and the context (see Part II, "Discovery and Invention"). But most introductions include three parts: first is a lead sentence that defines a general topic and/or grabs the readers' interest; second is general background information that often narrows the topic; and third is a statement that defines the topic for the rest of the piece of writing.

This doesn't mean that all introductions look alike—far from it. You can use a number of strategies to begin your writing. A sampling of the possibilities follows.

Story

Begin your writing with a short, humorous story.

> In the early 1850s, a twenty-year-old Bavarian named Leob Strauss devised a plan to make his fortune in America. His plan was simple. He would travel to San Francisco, a town booming with gold and miners, and sell brown canvas cloth strong enough for tents and wagons. When he arrived, he discovered the miners needed something else more than they needed tent cloth; they were desperate for pants that could withstand the rigors of their hard labor. Not missing his own opportunity to strike it rich, Leob, better known as Levi, cut up his tent cloth and designed a special kind of trousers. Though in subsequent years the cloth would change and so would the color, Levi's jeans were born. Now, almost 150 years later, the one indispensable article of clothing for almost anyone, from miners to CEOs, is a pair of jeans.

Startling Statement

Open your essay with a shocking or surprising sentence.

> Levi's jeans are so traditional that it took a hot rivet in the private parts of the president of the company to change one design flaw. Although we tend to associate jeans with cowboys, Levi Strauss created his trousers for hardworking California miners in the 1850s. So Strauss added metal rivets at the

pants' stress points, including the crotch. As the pants became more popular, the company received many complaints about the crotch rivet, including complaints from cowboys, who had to ride long hours on that rivet. But Levi Strauss and Company remained loyal to its basic design until 1941, when Levi's president Walter Hass, Jr., went on a fishing trip, stood too close to a campfire, and felt how hot a metal rivet could become. In subsequent years, other features have changed and other manufacturers have offered new variations, but jeans have remained basically the same for almost 150 years. It is just this sort of dedication to tradition that has made jeans an indispensable part of the American wardrobe.

Summary

Introduce your topic by summarizing a piece of writing or an event associated with your topic.

> In a recent article in *Consumer Reports*, the editors described the results of their tests on over forty brands of jeans. They examined a wide variety of jeans, from the classic Levi's 501s to Calvin Klein UDO2111s, with plenty of Lees, Wranglers, Sears, and L.L. Bean jeans in the middle. The article details their criteria: price, fit and appearance, durability, and construction quality. The editors were also careful to examine jeans for both men and women and for people with different body shapes. The top three brands for men are Levi's 509s, Guess/George Marciano 10001, and Wrangler Rustlers (Wrangler American Heros for fuller sized men). For women, the top brands are Chic Heavenly Blues, Levi's 501s, and PS Gitanos. But what the article says more than anything else is that no matter who you are, if you wear clothes, jeans are probably an indispensable part of your wardrobe.

Question

Grab your readers' interest by raising questions. The questions could be ones that the readers can answer from their experience or ones that you will provide answers to in the essay.

> How many pairs of jeans do you own? This is a question you almost could ask a new acquaintance to test whether you are compatible. No other article of clothing defines a philosophy of life as well as jeans do. Relaxed, untamed, democratic, friendly, ready for adventure, people who wear jeans don't need expensive fabrics tailored in exotic locations. They can meet anyone eye to eye, free of fashion's power statements. For anyone who wants to be quintessentially American, jeans are the one indispensable article of clothing.

Quotation

Open your essay using the authority of someone your reader may respect or find compelling.

> Harry Call, executive vice president of Goody's Family Clothing in Knoxville, Tennessee, knows the value of blue jeans. "Denim works for us like tuna fish works for a grocery store," he says. In recent years, Goody's has become an important source for high-quality, yet affordable clothing in the southeastern United States. In a recent five-year period, the company's sales and earnings tripled and the number of stores doubled. What is Goody's secret? Jeans. Goody's sells jeans at lower prices than all its competitors, and when Goody's customers are picking up a deal on jeans, they also purchase a couple of other more expensive items. Goody's is building a business on one belief: the one indispensable piece of clothing for most people is a pair of jeans.

Description

Grab your readers' interest by making them feel, hear, taste, smell, and see your topic.

> When I am folding clothes just out of the dryer, I like first to gather up my blue jeans. I stretch them out on the table and run my hand down the full length of the legs. The heat of the dryer seems to have permeated so deeply into the jeans that I feel as if I am stroking something alive, like an animal. If it's one of my old trusty pairs that I have had for a year or more, the denim is as soft and smooth as velvet. But what I like most is arranging my folded jeans on the table, side by side, newest pair to oldest. Each pair is a different shade of blue, from the deep indigo of the quarry "blue hole" swimming pool to the washed-out pale blue sky of the hottest summer's day. I don't know what I would do without my favorite blue jeans—the one indispensable piece of clothing I own.

General Statement

Begin your essay with a broad statement so that almost any reader will have some knowledge of the topic.

> Jeans, especially blue jeans, are the United States' one indisputable contribution to fashion. The French give us dresses only models can wear, and the Italians design suits only thin actors can fit into (or afford). While the Japanese may wear kimonos, the Ghanians, kentes, and the Arabs, burnooses, nothing crosses borders—geographic, gender-based, economic—as well as a

pair of jeans. For comfort, price, and personal philosophy, all across the world, jeans are the one indispensable article of clothing.

Statement of Purpose

Most effective in essays describing how to do a process ("When buying jeans, there are several steps to follow"), this technique also works well with some kinds of persuasion.

> I want you to purchase more jeans. I don't care what kind you buy. Buy traditional Levi's 501s, straight-legged with button flies, or go out and drop a fifty-dollar bill on the latest designer brand. Get them at Sears or Mervyn's, from L.L. Bean or St. Vincent de Paul. I don't care. Wear them brand-spanking-blue new; wear them faded and ripped; wear them cut off so short your parents blush; or wear Oshkosh-by-Gosh coveralls. I don't care. But I do want you buying jeans, because jeans are the indispensable foundation of the American wardrobe. I want you out there in the streets and in the fields, in the factories and in the executive suites, saying, "I'm proud to be an American."

Analogy

Introduce your topic by comparing it to something familiar to the reader.

> Owning a pair of jeans is like developing a great friendship. When you first purchase a pair of jeans, they are rigid, scratchy, and difficult to move around in. In the same way, when you meet someone new, your conversation is stiff, full of abrasive starts and stops. Later, after you've worn the pair of jeans many times, they become almost a part of you. They fit perfectly and make you look great. The jeans have become like your friend. And if you are lucky, you have some jeans that bring back memories, like your best friends; you just have to look at them to remember any number of great experiences and milestones in your life. Even when your jeans become torn and stained through random events and carelessness, you just can't throw them away. You might not wear them anymore, but just as it's impossible to say goodbye to friends who've grown apart from you, it's impossible to toss a good pair of jeans in the trash. Jeans, like friends, are an indispensable part of our lives.

Personal Experience

Begin by telling your reader about your own experience with the topic.

> My mother took a picture on my first day of school. We arrived at McEll-wan Elementary School early. The sun was bright on this morning in late August. Kids of all sizes stood around talking on the school steps, and they

frightened me with their confidence. Would I fit in? Would they like me? But I didn't have time to indulge my fears. My older sister, Barbara, escorted me up the stairs to the front doors and began yelling at the other students: "Move out of the way! This is my brother's first day at school, and we want a picture." I instantly felt confident. I look at the picture often. I'm wearing a plaid shirt and brand new blue jeans with the bottoms rolled up four inches— "There's room to grow into," my mom said. I look at myself now attending college, and except for the fact that my jeans are faded and the correct length, I haven't changed that much. I still feel confident in my jeans—ever since I was a kid, they've been my one indispensable article of clothing.

15b
ENDINGS

When you are having a conversation with someone, usually you don't just stop talking and walk away or abruptly hang up the phone. That kind of behavior would be rude and would perplex the person you were talking with.

Although a reader probably wouldn't feel offended by an abrupt ending, the effect of what you have written would probably be weakened. A well-crafted ending signals that you are coming to the conclusion of what you want to say. It tells your reader that the concluding information will refer to significant parts of the writing. Just how the ending works will depend on what the purpose of your writing is (see Chapter 5). If you are trying to persuade someone, the conclusion gives you a chance to remind the reader of your main arguments and perhaps recommend a future action. If you are trying to explain a topic, the conclusion will allow you to summarize the main points of the information so that the reader can more easily understand what you are explaining.

Several possible options for ending your writing follow.

Restatement

Remind your reader of your main point by restating it. However, try to do so without repeating the idea word for word.

> So look around you. For durability, practicality, price, and style, jeans can't be beat. If everyone from President Ronald Reagan and actor James Dean to Playmate Anna Nicole Smith and TV character Beaver Cleaver has worn them, you can't go wrong. They are truly an indispensable part of everyone's wardrobe.

Statement of Importance or Implications

Show your readers that what you have said will be important to them in the future.

> In 1964 the Smithsonian Institution in Washington, D.C., recognized the importance of jeans by adding a pair of Levi's 501s to its permanent collection. Since then jeans have become collector's items. A Lee cowboy jacket sold for $15,000, and one pair of Levi's from the 1920s sold for $25,000 in France. So remember, your jeans may be more than a friend. They might be an investment.

Appeal or Warning

Close the essay by trying to guide the reader to particular action by showing its benefits or by showing the difficulties of another action.

> Each year Levi's sells something like 90 million pairs of its riveted jeans. These jeans are the basics—stiff denim, dark blue, five pockets, button flies, and rivets. You can buy other brands. You can buy other styles. But why would you want to? Put on some of the others, and you're wearing a pair of jeans. But put on a pair of Levi's, and you're wearing a tradition.

Clever Statement or Quotation

End the piece of writing by entertaining your readers, either by making them smile or by making them nod in agreement with someone they respect.

> Buying jeans really isn't as difficult as you might at first believe. By considering the factors discussed above, you'll always be able to find the jeans that are right for you. Remember, being cool isn't in the genes; it's in the jeans.

You want your ending paragraph to leave your reader with your main idea clearly in mind.

CommonSense Guide

You can create unity by ending your essay with a reference to a key idea from your beginning.

?
15c
DEVELOPING THE MIDDLE

Content paragraphs form the substance of what you are writing. As you work with them, you will want to check to see that they are tied directly to the main idea you are trying to develop. You may find it helpful to work in the middle first. Sometimes developing an introduction first will limit you. Starting in the middle can allow you to be more flexible in your approach to the topic.

CommonSense Observation

The Five-Paragraph Essay

Many traditional writing texts recommend that essays be written in five paragraphs: a beginning paragraph, three middle paragraphs, and an ending paragraph. They point out that this structure is effective because it reinforces the unity of the essay. Others disagree, stating that the recommendation is too rigid, that it creates boring and predictable essays, and that the subject and purpose of the essay should determine the number of paragraphs. Even if you choose not to adhere rigidly to the five-paragraph format, you should pay attention to creating a clear, accurate, and unified presentation.

The familiar organizational patterns discussed in Chapter 14 are all options for developing the middle of the work. You may use more than one, or you may find that for your topic, one or two dominant patterns would be most effective. For example, if you were writing a paper discussing the process of cleaning up pollution in the environment, you could develop it by explaining the process involved in the cleanup. You could also develop the topic by classifying the methods used in cleaning up toxic dumps or making industry cleaner. Within each category of the classification system, you could examine the processes used. In addition, you might want, or need, to describe the equipment used in the process. Your choice of organizational patterns will depend on the scope and nature of your topic (Chapter 4), your purpose (Chapter 5), and the information you have available to you (Chapter 43, "Collecting Information").

15d
TRANSITIONAL PARAGRAPHS

It is often important to connect one paragraph to another. Transitions give important clues that enable the reader to follow the content of your work more easily. Read the passage that follows and consider how the second paragraph allows the reader to move easily from the first paragraph to the third paragraph.

Jeans are made of denim, a coarse cotton fabric. The name *denim* is a shortened form of the term *serge de Nîmes,* so called because it was originally produced in Nimes, France. The indigo color, which gave blue jeans their name, was first used by Levi Strauss and has been the traditional color of jeans since. However, as most of us know, the dark blue color eventually fades. The faded look became a part of the jeans culture in the 1960s.

When the faded look became popular, manufacturers were ready to meet the demand ahead of time. Rather than having to wait for the jeans to fade, buyers could purchase them prefaded.

Manufacturers have used three methods for producing faded jeans: stonewashing, enzyme washing, and acid washing. Stonewashing involves putting pumice stones into the prewashing cycle. The stones abrade the fabric and cause some of the color to fade. Enzyme washing (sometimes combined with stonewashing) uses enzymes to "eat" the fabric, softening the fabric and lightening the color. Finally, acid washing uses pumice stones soaked in bleach to fade and distress the fabric.

As you can see, the second paragraph enables the reader to see the connections between the first and third paragraphs. Note particularly the use of the terms *faded* and *prefaded.*

Coherence

Consider the details communicated by the following series of sentences.

Animals struggle to avoid change.

Physiological constancy is the first biological commandment.

Animals strive to avoid enemies.

Animals strive to keep warm, well fed, and internally moist.

Animals strive to stay supplied with essential substances.

Too great an internal change means death.

Maintaining the internal status quo is called homeostasis.

The preceding series of statements has **unity** (see Chapter 13). They all refer to the same topic: birds' ability to maintain homeostasis. But notice how the paragraph that follows changes your perception of the topic.

> The great struggle in most animals' lives is to avoid change. Physiolog-
> ical constancy is the first biological commandment. All animals must strive
> eternally to avoid enemies, to keep warm, well fed, internally moist, and sup-
> plied with oxygen, minerals, vitamins, and other substances, often within
> precise limits. Too great a change, especially in the internal economy of an
> animal, means death. If, for example, the concentration of salt in the blood of
> a man or a bird is increased or decreased by only one-half of one per cent, the
> animal dies. A Chickadee clinging to a piece of suet on a bitter winter day is
> doing its unconscious best to maintain the internal status quo—to maintain
> what the physiologists call homeostasis.
>
> —Joel Carl Welty, *The Life of Birds*

The passage has **coherence,** a connectedness that the list lacks. Four useful techniques—the placement of known and new information, the repetition of key words, the use of transitions, and the use of parallel sentence elements—that will help you achieve coherence are discussed in the following sections.

16a
KNOWN AND NEW INFORMATION

Which of the following passages presents the information most clearly?

> A very fine hiking boot for both men and women is the Cyclone by Mer-
> rell. Its weight is only about twenty-five ounces. Yet it gives enough support
> for rugged hiking and backpacking with a strong, cleated rubber sole. The
> boot has an AirCushion midsole that creates excellent stability and maintains

proper heel alignment. Even in wet conditions, the Cyclone will keep you dry because of its Aqua Shield liner and Watershed leather. For a more comfortable fit, it has a bellows tongue, a reinforced toe box, and a padded collar. Despite all these features, the boot has a surprisingly affordable price.

The Cyclone by Merrell is a very fine hiking boot for both men and women. Only about twenty-five ounces is its weight. Yet a strong, cleated rubber sole gives support for rugged hiking and backpacking. Excellent stability is created and proper heel alignment is maintained by an AirCushion midsole. The Aqua Shield liner and Watershed leather will keep you dry even in wet conditions. A padded collar, a reinforced toe box, and a bellows tongue make the boot fit more comfortably. Despite all these features, the price makes the boot affordable.

Most people who read these two passages seem to think that the first one presents the information more effectively. The reason for the effectiveness of the first paragraph is that **known information** (information that is already part of a reader's knowledge about the topic or that can be inferred from the context) appears in the first part of each sentence and **new information** (information that the reader has never seen before) is presented in the second part of the sentence. In the second passage, the reverse is true.

Information at the end of a sentence receives greater stress than information at the beginning of a sentence, and as a result, readers pay more attention to it. Usually, the information we want to emphasize is new information; it is also usually the most important information in a sentence. Putting known information at the beginning of a sentence lets the reader connect with something familiar. A sentence with known information at the beginning is usually easier to read and more effective than a sentence with new information at the beginning.

16b
REPETITION OF KEY WORDS

As you read the following passage, pay attention to the words that are repeated.

All **fiction** is **metaphor**. **Science fiction** is **metaphor**. What sets it apart from older forms of **fiction** seems to be its use of new **metaphors**, drawn from certain great dominants of our contemporary life—**science**, all the **sciences**, and technology, and the relativistic and the historical outlook, among them. Space travel is one of these **metaphors**; so is an **alternative** society, an **alternative** biology; the **future** is another. The **future**, in **fiction**, is a **metaphor**.

—Ursula K. Le Guin, *The Left Hand of Darkness*

The key term *metaphor* is repeated five times. That repetition serves as a connecting link throughout the passage and also reinforces the main idea: fiction is a metaphor.

16c
TRANSITIONS

As you read the following sentences, see if you can imagine what sentence might have preceded it.

This was **in spite of** the fact that he said he wouldn't interfere in the hiring process.

He is **also** something of a fashion plate.

As a result, production has slowed down.

On the other hand, it hardly seems fair that the workers pay the price for management's ineptitude.

In the sentences above, the **transitions** *in spite of, also, as a result*, and *on the other hand* show the reader how the information is connected to previous information. Transitions create coherence by indicating relationships between ideas. There are a great many transition words and phrases at your disposal. They can be grouped by what they indicate.

Addition   *again, also, and, and then, besides, finally, first, further, furthermore, in addition, last, likewise, moreover, next, second, similarly, third*

Contrast or alternative   *after all, although, and yet, at the same time, but, conversely, however, in contrast, in spite of, nevertheless, nor, notwithstanding, on the contrary, on the other hand, or, still, yet*

Conclusion   *accordingly, as a result, consequently, hence, in brief, in conclusion, in general, in other words, in short, on the whole, otherwise, overall, then, therefore, thus, to conclude, to summarize, to sum up*

Example   *for example, for instance, incidentally, indeed, in fact, in other words, in particular, namely, specifically, that is, to illustrate, to sum up*

Even though transitions make clear the connections between ideas, they can clutter writing as well. Therefore, you may want to use them sparingly.

16d
PARALLEL STRUCTURE

Consider how similar patterns of words in the sentences of the following paragraph create coherence.

The popularity of jeans seems to be linked in many ways to the popularity of rock music. Jeans, although they had been popular work clothes since the late nineteenth century, became the fashion of choice for teenagers in the 1950s. Rock music, although it had been around in an incipient form as country and blues since the 1930s, became the music of choice for the same group at about the same time. Jeans and rock seem to have been made for each other. Both jeans and rock music have endured as the group that popularized Levi Strauss's work clothes and Elvis's music has grown older.

Notice that the second and third sentences have similar structures, and both contain the word *although*.

5

Style

17 CLARITY AND PROFESSIONALISM

How to make your language more accurate... see 17A

How to balance your use of concrete and abstract language... see 17B

How to use verbs to make your writing clearer... see 17C

How to make your writing clearer by separating and combining sentences... see 17D

How to use lists to make your writing clearer... see 17E

How to use typographical techniques for emphasis and clarity... see 17F

18 CONCISENESS AND COMPLETENESS

How to add depth to your writing with description and modification ... see 18A

How to make your writing more concise by eliminating empty language ... see 18B

How to make your writing more concise by eliminating unnecessary word groups ... see 18C

How to make your writing more concise by eliminating repetitive or unnecessary sentences ... see 18D

How to make your writing more concise by editing sentences that begin with *There* or *It* ... see 18E

19 LIVELINESS AND APPROPRIATENESS

How to make your writing lively by emphasizing strong actions and actors ... see 19A

How to make your writing lively by focusing on the level of your vocabulary ... see 19B

How to make your writing lively through figurative language ... see 19C

How to accommodate for the tone of your word choice ... see 19D

How to strengthen your writing by using short sentences ... see 19E

How to strengthen your writing by using sentence interrupters ... see 19F

20 VARIETY AND REPETITION

How to improve your writing by varying the beginnings of your sentences . . . **see 20A**

How to improve your writing by varying the endings of your sentences . . . **see 20B**

How to emphasize ideas by using parallelism . . . **see 20C**

How to vary your writing by combining ideas with coordination . . . **see 20D**

How to vary your writing by combining ideas with subordination . . . **see 20E**

How to emphasize through repetition of sounds and words . . . **see 20F**

21 TONE AND SEXIST LANGUAGE

What words to use instead of *man, mankind, man-hours,* etc. . . . **see 21A**

How to avoid inaccurate stereotyping of men and women . . . **see 21B**

How to avoid words that end with a gender reference . . . **see 21C**

How to avoid inappropriate use of *he, him,* and *his* . . . **see 21D**

Why you should avoid using potentially insulting language. . . **see 21E**

CHAPTER 17

Clarity and Professionalism

The writing of professionals, such as doctors, lawyers, scientists, and educators, often confuses the general public—so much so that newspapers and magazines regularly feature articles about how to talk to your doctor, how to understand bureaucratic "doublespeak," and how to speak like a lawyer. Some states have even passed laws requiring that legal contracts be written in "plain English."

No doubt, many of these complaints are warranted. However, there are good reasons why prestigious professional journals publish this kind of writing: the topic may require such language, and the audience for much professional writing is not the general public. For instance, if for no other reason, lawyers write the way they do because lawyers have traditionally written that way. Good writers use the language style their readers understand.

17a
ACCURATE AND PRECISE LANGUAGE

Most of us would not accept a job if our contract said we would be paid "a lot of money." We would say, "How much?" and ask the employer to fill in the amount with a precise number. Similarly, in almost all situations, writers strive to be as accurate as possible. The only exceptions might occur in some writing that entertains. In poetry, for example, authors often want to emphasize a multiplicity of meanings through ambiguous language.

Of the examples below, which is clearest to a general audience?

Do your taxes carefully.

Be sure, when you fill out your 1040, to follow the instructions regarding IRA investments carefully.

Enter the smaller of line 1 or line 2. Enter on Form 1040, line 23a, the amount from line 3, column (a), you choose to deduct. Enter on Form 1040, line 23b, the amount, if any, from line 3, column (b), you choose to deduct. If filing a joint return and contributions were made to your nonworking spouse's IRA, go to line 4.

You probably feel that the second example communicates the most to the general audience. It is both precise and clear. In contrast, the first example fails to be accurate; it uses words such as *do* and *well* that do not convey exact meanings. But inexact meaning has its place: since these words are not specific enough to offend anyone, some people use them to establish rapport with the audience. For example, you can begin a conversation about a movie you know others like by saying that the camera work was "interesting." Once you have the audience's ear, you can go on to identify specific faults in the director's technique.

The third example above also fails to be accurate for some people. It uses words that a specialized audience expects but which a general audience cannot understand. This kind of language is called **jargon**. When writing for a general audience, you will most often avoid using jargon, or, at least, define the words for the reader.

Vague language and jargon identify two ends of a continuum. Language on one end is difficult to understand because the words contain so little meaning and on the other because they carry so much. The box "Types of Inaccurate Language" identifies other ways writers fail to be accurate.

CommonSense Guide

Types of Inaccurate Language

If your writing contains many of the following words, it may be confusing for a general audience.

Empty words   Words whose meanings are so general that they can mean almost anything: *interesting, nice, great, special, very, do, have,* and so on.

Fudge words   Words whose sweet meanings soften the harsher realities they smooth over: *passed away* for "died," *let go* for "fired," *put to sleep* for "killed," *visiting the rest room* for "urinating," and so on.

Fancy words   Words whose purpose is to impress rather than to communicate meaning—often words from a foreign language: *raison d'etre, chef d'oeuvre, modus operandi,* and so on.

Doublespeak   Words whose purpose is to lie or distort the truth, often for political reasons: *bombs* become *incendiary devices, killing* becomes *deprivation of life,* and so on.

Bureaucratic language   Words whose purpose is to impress or to avoid responsibility: *prioritize, impact, input, customer representative, intake specialist, downsizing,* and so on.

⟶

continued from previous page

Sexist language Words whose purpose or effect is to stereotype people of a particular gender: *chairman, male nurse, gals, deadbeat dads,* and so on. (Chapter 19 focuses on this and other difficulties in dealing with gender in writing.)

17b
CONCRETE AND ABSTRACT LANGUAGE

Sometimes we find that our writing lacks precision because we focus on abstract words that convey broad meanings. **Abstract language** represents ideas that exist only in our minds. For instance, abstract words such as *religion, democracy, socialization, relationships,* and *cognition* do not refer to anything we can see, taste, feel, hear, or smell. Abstract words often make up language of professions and specialties because they indicate the way a group of people think about a subject. **Concrete language** represents objects, actions, and qualities we can see, hear, taste, smell, and touch. The game Monopoly is a concrete reality, while the ideas *competition* and *capitalism* are abstractions.

One way to recognize abstract words is look at word endings. The following endings, among others, often indicate that a word is abstract.

-tion	condition, prevention, cognition
-ment	employment, government, agreement
-ness	kindness, weariness, worthlessness
-ism	communism, criticism, empiricism
-ive	appreciative, affirmative, excessive
-ence	difference, negligence, reverence
-ship	citizenship, relationship, showmanship
-ology	psychology, sociology, zoology

Although abstract language is sometimes derided, it has important uses. Abstract language is often necessary for clarity. This kind of general language allows us to make an overall point and to set up wide-ranging observations and arguments.

Compare the two sentences below.

Motivation is an important factor in the success of students.

My son got straight A's after I promised to buy a new video game system if he made the honor roll.

Certainly both sentences are clear statements and are of a sort needed in all kinds of writing. The first sentence contains instances of abstract language; the second primarily employs concrete language. By themselves they pose no difficulties for a reader. However, problems arise when a piece of writing is dominated by a single type.

Beginning writers often are afraid of saying too much; they don't want to bore their readers, or they feel they don't have anything to say about the topic. So teachers and editors often encourage them to incorporate more and more details. However, it is certainly possible to be too specific, to tire readers with too many details. It is also possible to confuse readers by including details without generalizations that guide readers through the material.

Your goal in writing is to provide enough general information so that your readers can understand the significance of the examples and to provide enough specifics so that readers can understand the meaning of the generalities.

17c
ACTIVE, VIVID VERBS

Verbs create energy and power in our sentences. When we tell stories, we naturally use active, vivid verbs. But when we write on the job or when we write about ideas, we often produce static sentences that focus on defining our topic. For instance, an attempt to "nail down" an idea by telling what something *is* instead of what it *does* sometimes backfires and produces a wordy, cluttered sentence. Sentences like this may "sound" professional, but they lose clarity. To make our writing clearer, we can rewrite, focusing on action verbs. Since unclear sentences often hide action verbs in nouns that end in *-ment, -ion, -ance, -ence,* and *-al,* look for these word endings and turn the nouns back into verbs.

CommonSense Guide

Verbs That Show Action and Verbs That Link

English sentences have one of two qualities: they are either **dynamic** or **static**. A dynamic sentence establishes a topic and then names what that topic does, how it acts. This dynamic quality is created by **action verbs**, words such as *run, duplicate, remember, electrify,* and *think.* A static sentence establishes a topic and then either renames, defines, or

→

continued from previous page

describes it. Usually, this kind of sentence employs **linking verbs**, words such as *is, was, been, appear, seem,* and *taste.* In developing your style, you will write both dynamic and static sentences often, but depending on your purposes, you will need to employ a mix of the two types. Here's a general guideline: If your writing seems boring and static, as though nothing is happening, you probably have not used enough action verbs. If you feel that your writing is breathless, that you are on a roller coaster of actions and twists and turns, then you may want to use linking verbs to slow things down and make your writing less dynamic.

As you read the following passage, notice the weak static verbs and try to identify nouns that disguise the real actions.

There **is** a resistance among some of us toward the establishment of a group that **will have** the task of deciding the most effective prioritizing of next year's goals. This course of action **is** counterproductive in the short run and **is having** the long-term effect of hampering the desire that others **have** to suggest new marketing strategies for our services in the future.

Now read the following passage. Notice that ideas are clear because the verbs are active and precise.

Some of us **resist** establishing a decision group to prioritize next year's goals. Besides being counterproductive in the short run, prioritizing goals **discourages** others from suggesting future marketing strategies.

17d
ONE SENTENCE OR TWO?

Has your desk ever become so cluttered that you can't find the pen you were just writing with? To locate it, you have to clean up the entire desk, putting all the paper in one place, all the pencils in a container, and all the books back on the shelves. Sentences are sometimes like that. They get so cluttered with so many ideas that you can't make sense of them. An effective strategy for coping with clutter is to break the sentence into smaller units and reorganize. As you read the sentence below, try to identify the most important ideas.

Since most women prefer to settle disputes without direct confrontation, they think that conflict is a threat to connection, to be avoided at all costs, all of which is very different for men, who accept conflict and may even seek, embrace, and enjoy it because conflict is the necessary means by which status is negotiated.

There are four important points in the sentence: two about women and two about men. You might also notice that each pair cites a cause-and-effect relationship: the way men and women view conflict affects how they react to it. The passage below rearranges the ideas to reflect this relationship and separates the ideas into three sentences.

To most women, conflict is a threat to connection, to be avoided at all costs. Disputes are preferably settled without direct confrontation. But to many men, conflict is the necessary means by which status is negotiated, so it is to be accepted and may even be sought, embraced, and enjoyed.
—Deborah Tannen, *You Just Don't Understand*

Note that although short, direct sentences often create a clear prose style, sometimes they can produce confusion because they do not provide logical connections between the ideas they contain (see Sections 17b, 18a, 19e, 19f, 20d, and 20e).

17e
LISTS

Sometimes writers need to express ideas that either are very complicated or require many connecting and explanatory words to indicate how the ideas relate. In these situations, usually in academic and professional writing, prose can become so dull and slow that readers can't locate important information quickly enough to stay interested. One way to simplify the writing is to highlight information in lists. In the passage below, notice how clearly the act of writing is defined through listing.

The subject of how writers work, where and how they get their ideas, how they nurse them into form . . . is important to the beginning writer. It reveals the mess and privacy of the behavior called writing, and beneath that, a sequence of concentrations that seem implicit in the act of writing:

1. Getting the thought—recognizing it, first, and then exploring it enough to estimate one's resources (motivational and informational) for writing about it.

2. Getting the thought down—proceeding, that is, into the thick of the idea, holding on to it even as the act of articulation refines and changes it.

3. Readying the written statement for other eyes, a matter of teaching whatever in the content or form is likely to deflect the reader's attention from the writer's meaning.

—Mina P. Shaughnessy, *Errors and Expectations*

For the most part, it doesn't matter whether numbers, indentations, spaces, dots, or bullets are used to indicate separate items in a list. However, it does seem that numbers indicate an ordered sequence more than other techniques, while bullets and other graphic elements tend to stress the individual items.

17f
TYPOGRAPHICAL TECHNIQUES

Notice the differences in sound when you read the following three sentences.

I did not ask you to bring that book.

I did not ask *you* to bring that book.

I did not ask you to bring *that* book.

Did you read the first sentence in a natural, normal tone? And then did you stress the italicized words in the next two sentences? You probably did so because you understand that writers sometimes italicize words to give them **emphasis**. It is one of the ways that writers highlight particular words and thus make their meaning more clear. In general, you will want to include typographical elements sparingly.

Other typographical techniques for indicating emphasis include exclamation marks, quotation marks, underlining, and boldface type. In almost all instances, you will want to follow the conventions for each of these elements (see Chapter 41).

Conciseness and Completeness

Very often we hear people complain about the predominance of the sound bite in television news. Complicated issues such as health care, racism, values in education, and the like are often presented only in two-minute segments. However, we have also listened to experts drone on in lengthy, tiring disputations concerning the complexity of some public policy issue.

In presenting almost any kind of information, writers struggle between saying enough to be clear and accurate and saying so much as to be ponderous and confusing. Certainly a writer's audience and purpose will determine how complete a presentation must be. For instance, when you purchase a friend's CD collection, you do not need much more than a few spoken words; but when you purchase this friend's house, you will need a complicated, detailed legal contract. Balancing conciseness and completeness, then, is often a product of understanding the reader's needs.

18a
MODIFICATION AND DESCRIPTIVE LANGUAGE

One method of making your writing more complete is to add words and phrases that modify or describe. By the time most writers reach college or a job that requires writing, they have long passed the time when they wrote without modifiers. Few adults can say what they need to say in simple sentences like "See Dick run" or "Sam I am."

Modifiers add so much to our writing that sentences stripped of them become almost meaningless. Read the following paragraph taken from liner notes to a jazz CD. It has been rewritten to exclude almost all single words and groups that modify and describe. Do you think the passage is clear and interesting?

> Jazz is something. Jazz twists your brain, but leaves your body. Jazz appears as a form.

Now compare the passage above to the one below, which is the original paragraph with all the modifiers intact. For convenience in comparing, the descriptive language and modifiers have been boldfaced.

> **According to popular notion,** jazz is something **which you research and study, inspect and dissect, scrutinize and analyze.** Jazz twists your brain

like an algebraic equation, but leaves your body **lifeless and limp. In the eyes of the general public,** jazz appears as an **elite art** form. . . .

—Joshua Redman, liner notes, *Moodswing*

Do you see how depth is added to the basic ideas? As depth is added, so are precision, clarity, liveliness, and emphasis. First, Redman focuses his readers on his point of view. He isn't discussing the way all people view jazz, so he adds the **modifiers** "According to popular notion" and "In the eyes of the general public." Second, he clarifies a number of ideas: how the brain is twisted ("like an algebraic equation"), how jazz leaves your body ("lifeless and limp"), and what kind of form jazz is ("elite art").

CommonSense Guide

Words and Word Groups That Modify and Describe

Single Words

Descriptive words indicating number, color, size, quality, speed, quantity, location, and time: *six, red, large, perfect, quick, much, there, soon*

Words that end in *-ly*: *quickly, friendly, jointly, basically, accurately*

Words that end in *-ive, -ate, -less, -al, -some, -ic*: *automotive, accurate, breathless, classical, lonesome, majestic*

Groups of Words

Those that end with *-ing*:

   examining the evidence for accuracy

   discussing the information over dinner

   typing the appropriate keystrokes

Those ending with *-ed* and comparable verb forms:

   appreciated by her colleagues

   understood without formal training

   torn between two lovers

Those beginning with words like *at, on, near, in, with*:

   at the conference

   on whatever topic she likes

   with a clear explanation of existentialism

→

continued from previous page

Those beginning with the word *to* and a verb:

to speak quickly

to populate an area the size of Rhode Island

to frequent establishments that serve alcohol

Those beginning with *who, whom, which, that, whose*:

who is the force behind total quality management

which stood in the corner

that he told us about

Those beginning with *although, before, if, when*:

Although he told us about it

Before you frequent establishments that serve alcohol

Whenever a disgruntled employee wants to complain

Those beginning with a noun that are not complete sentences:

an environmentalist who supports business interests

bridges built in the 1920s

love springing from a religious faith

You will enhance the power of your communication if you ask yourself whether you have achieved an appropriate depth in your writing. The key is to think of your audience: ask yourself whether you have explained everything in enough detail for your reader to

1. Understand the exact nature of your topic,

2. See everything you want seen,

3. Know precisely the who, what, when, where, and how of your topic, and

4. Make all the correct connections between your ideas.

18b
EMPTY LANGUAGE

Can you follow the instructions in the sentence below?

At the present moment, would you read this passage for the purpose of looking for words and phrases that are examples of places where it would seem to be easy to edit in order to make the writing more concise?

If you took out the empty language, would your edited sentence look something like the following?

Would you now read the following passage, identifying words and phrases to edit for conciseness?

As these two sentences show, sometimes you can improve the power of your writing simply by shortening or eliminating lengthy and unimportant groups of words.

CommonSense Guide

Empty Word Groups and Their Substitutes

Empty Word Group	Shortened Counterpart
accompanied by	with
as a matter of fact	[omit]
at the present time	now
at the time that	when
due to the fact that	because
experience has indicated that	I have found
for the purposes of	for
in order to	to
in the eventuality that	if
in this modern world of today	today
in this time and age	today
in the process of	in
in view of the fact that	since
it is obvious that	obviously
it is our opinion that	we think
it is to be assumed that	I suppose
on the part of	on
that is to say	[omit]
the point I'm trying to make	[omit]
the question of whether	whether
type of	[omit]
what I mean to say is	[omit]

18c
UNNECESSARY WORD GROUPS

A simple but effective way to make your writing more concise without making it incomplete is to eliminate word groups that begin with *at, by, from*, and so on. Often these word groups can be turned into single-word modifiers, actors, and actions.

Read the following passage from respected science writer Howard Gardner. The word groups beginning with *about, in, to*, and *with* are bold-faced.

> **In contrast to linguistic and musical capacities**, the competence that I am terming "logical-mathematical intelligence" does not have its origins **in the auditory-oral sphere**. Instead, this form of thought can be traced **to a confrontation with the world of objects**. For it is **in confronting objects, in ordering and reordering them, and in assessing their quantity**, that the young child gains his or her initial and most fundamental knowledge **about the logical-mathematical realm**.
>
> —Howard Gardner, *Frames of Mind*

The length of this passage is 76 words, and 38 of them are in this kind of word group—over half of the total. Simply by concentrating on these word groups, eliminating them, shortening them, and rephrasing them, you can reduce the paragraph to 48 words.

> Unlike linguistic and musical capacities, "logical-mathematical intelligence" does not have an aural or oral source. Instead, this form of thought can be traced to confrontations with objects. Confronting objects—ordering and reordering them and assessing their quantity—teaches the young child the most fundamental logical-mathematical knowledge.

To make your writing more concise, you may want to eliminate groups of words beginning with *at, on*, and so on, while emphasizing liveliness and clarity by using single-word modifiers.

18d
REPETITIVE AND UNNECESSARY SENTENCES

Every person who survives high school and college learns the trick of writing what he or she knows in two, three, or four different ways. Sometimes, it seems, it is the only way to find enough words to write an essay with as many words as the teacher assigns. The practice, however, creates a very bad habit that, once learned, is hard to break. Repetitive and unnecessary sentences often indicate that writers can think of nothing else to include. Either they do not know the subject well enough to provide more detail, or they have committed to a method of organization that highlights unimportant aspects of the topic.

What statements in the following passage are repetitive or unnecessary?

> I have been teaching Plato's *Symposium* for many years, and I have always enjoyed it. Up until a few years ago, class discussion was very lively and provocative. However, I have discovered in recent years that the feast to which the *Symposium* invites us is less appealing to students than it once was. Students do not like to have to justify their sexual tastes or practices. They do not want to talk about certain subjects that matter to them the most. These subjects usually have to do with topics that are sexual in nature. Sexual topics nowadays make students become reticent in the classroom. So I have found it difficult to discuss Plato's *Symposium* with them recently.

The writer of this paragraph repeats ideas, almost as if he had only one observation to make. Now read the next paragraph, in which the writer avoids repetition, yet slowly deepens his observations of his students.

> I have discovered in recent years that the feast to which the *Symposium* invites us is less appealing to students than it once was. They do not like to have to justify their sexual tastes or practices. Whenever they are asked to make a judgment about the quality of Phaedrus' or Eryximachus' statements, they are inclined to say, "Men and women have a right to do whatever they want in the privacy of their own bedrooms, provided, of course, one's partner or partners consent." This is probably true, but it is not sufficient. It bespeaks an unwillingness to think about one's experience and its relationship to the whole of life and the moral order. Today's students hesitate to articulate their reasons for loving—they must certainly have such reasons somewhere within them—for fear that they may come up with negative judgments about someone else's tastes or practices. This would be illiberal and might lead to persecution. Liberal society guarantees the right to privacy, even when nobody wants to keep anything private. A *de facto* equality among all preferences and practices is declared in order to avoid criticism and comparison. "You let me do what I want, and I'll let you do what you want."
>
> —Allan Bloom, *Love and Friendship*

In the passage above, the writer tells how his own students reacted to specific passages from Plato's *Symposium*. And then he hypothesizes about the causes of their reactions. Throughout, he substantiates his thoughts thoroughly.

18e
SENTENCES BEGINNING WITH *THERE* AND *IT*

Do you see a difference in the meaning of *there* in these two sentences?

There walks the dog we've been looking for.

There exist three conditions under which economic growth is rapid.

In the first sentence, *There* tells us where to look. It refers to an actual place. In the second sentence, *There* means nothing. The word is a kind of filler, a word that gets the sentence going while the speaker thinks about what really needs to be said. In most instances, revising sentences beginning with *There* strengthens the writing. Notice how the sentence below says the same thing as the second sentence above, but in fewer words.

Three conditions foster rapid economic growth.

This sentence does not have to sacrifice *completeness* to achieve *conciseness*.

In addition, sentences that begin with *It* sometimes suffer from the same problem. Do you see the difference between these sentences?

It came flying through the window.

It has come to our attention that prices have risen five percent.

The *It* in the first sentence, of course, refers to something from a previous sentence, such as a baseball, a rock, or a Molotov cocktail. The *It* in the second sentence, however, does not refer to something previously stated, but to the group of words that follows: "that prices have risen five percent." The sentence is easily revised to a more concise form.

Prices have risen five percent.

We have observed that prices have risen five percent.

Liveliness and Appropriateness

Which of the following sentences seems appropriate for a review of a dance club? Assume the article will be published in your local newspaper.

1. A number of people, principally of the female gender, perambulated to the location in the dinner and dance establishment where one can indulge a desire to trip the light fantastic.
2. Several women stepped onto the nightclub floor and danced.
3. A pack of chicks scurried onto the hot slab in a writhing frenzy.
4. A series of bouncing, gyrating motions were indulged in by a group of women on the dance floor.

Probably you would say that sentence 2 is perfectly acceptable, even though it lacks excitement. And you might tolerate sentence 3 if it were written by a male columnist known for his slightly offensive, yet colorful, manner.

One quality of an effective style is its lively word choice. Yet what is lively and energetic to some members of the general reading audience may be inappropriate and offensive to others. As you develop your writing style, you will find a balance that accommodates the tones and character of your voice. But remember that your voice, like that of the male columnist, may alienate some members of the general reading public, even while it attracts others.

Of course, there is always a middle ground, sometimes difficult to find, where your language is lively and appropriate for any audience. Does the following sentence accomplish this?

Several women nudged each other into a sudden clearing amid the swirling dancers.

This chapter examines practices that will help you find this middle ground.

? 19a
ACTORS AND ACTIONS

Which sentence will best grab the interest of most audiences?

1. A series of bouncing, swaying motions were indulged in by a group of men on the dance floor.
2. A group of men indulged in a series of bouncing, swaying motions on the dance floor.
3. A group of men bounced and swayed on the dance floor.

Even though each sentence contains several lively words and phrases, only sentence 3 begins to live. In sentence 1, the inverted word order and extra words do nothing to enhance communication. Therefore, a reader will have trouble knowing who the actors are and what the action is. The sentence uses **passive voice** rather than active voice, obscuring the meaning. (See Section 21d.8.)

Sentence 2 corrects the word order, but the active verb *indulge* distracts us from seeing what really is occurring—bouncing and swaying.

Sentence 3 improves on the preceding sentence by focusing the reader's attention on the real actors and their liveliest actions.

Although many instructors and editors often denounce passive voice, it does have its appropriate uses. Sometimes you won't know who the actor is, and sometimes you will want to emphasize the subject's helplessness. (For instance, consider this sentence: "Tiptoeing through the dark room, the police officer was stuck on the back of the head.") And to encourage friendly relationships, you will sometimes use passive voice in a formal piece of writing, as in a contract, to disguise the power of one of the parties. The sentence "The lessee will be fined five dollars per day for late payments" illustrates this practice. (Here, a lively active voice is not appropriate: "The lessor will fine the lessee five dollars a day for late payments.") And finally, the passive is often used to maintain focus on the topic (as in this sentence).

19b
LEVELS OF VOCABULARY

One of the examples below is from a telephone company pamphlet. Can you recognize it?

1. Would it peeve you if some joker rang you up, but wouldn't fork over his number? If so, here's a trick to stop him dead in his tracks.

2. Would it bother you if someone called, but wouldn't willingly give you a phone number? If so, here's a way to make sure those calls won't even get through.

3. Would it irritate you if second parties telephoned, but refused to provide voluntarily their own telephone exchanges? If so, here's a method to circumvent their attempts and impede their ability to disturb you.

Example 2 appeared in a telephone company's letter to its customers. While all three examples communicate the same general ideas, example 1 is too whimsical for business communication with the general public, and example 3 is too dense. You'll notice that the differences are merely the words themselves. Example 1 includes a low-level, informal vocabulary, while example 3 has a higher level, formal vocabulary.

For almost every word in English, there are several other words that mean more or less the same thing. These **synonyms** offer you a large and varied palette of words. Some of these words—those that are slang, colloquial, descriptive, evocative, or specific to a dialect—offer you ways to enliven your prose. Other words, such as technical terms or words derived from Latin and Greek, are less lively but are more appropriate for particular audiences and purposes.

In an essay about capital punishment, columnist Anna Quindlen wrote the following sentence.

> I have always been governed by my gut, and my gut says I am hypocritical about the death penalty.

Part of the power of Quindlen's sentence derives from her use of the informal word *gut*; but note how she balances informal language with more formal choices such as *governed* and *hypocritical*. By varying the level of vocabulary in your writing for a general audience, you, too, will most likely find a style and tone that is both lively and appropriate.

19c
FIGURATIVE LANGUAGE

Below is the concluding sentence of "Letter from the Birmingham Jail" by Dr. Martin Luther King, Jr.

> Let us hope that the dark clouds of racial prejudice will soon pass away and the deep fog of misunderstanding will be lifted, . . . and in some not too distant tomorrow the radiant stars of love and brotherhood will shine over our great nation with all their scintillating beauty.
> —Martin Luther King, Jr., "Letter from the Birmingham Jail"

The sentence is long, but it is still completely understandable. In the letter, Dr. King wants to inspire well-meaning but fearful whites to join in the struggle for racial equality. He hopes he can inspire his readers to join him, and he tries to inspire them through the power of his language, using figures of speech that enliven and clarify his meaning.

Figures of speech are words or phrases that provide meaning and grace to our writing through comparisons that we do not intend to be taken literally or viewed as factual. When Dr. King describes racial prejudice as "dark clouds" and misunderstanding as a "deep fog," he does not expect readers to envision the ideas as literally floating in the air. But he does intend that we *feel* prejudice and misunderstanding as things that prevent our seeing reality clearly. He does, however, intend that we *feel* racial tension as we would feel a storm ready to unleash itself.

Figures of speech are very useful when explaining professional or academic matters to general readers. Compare the following pairs of sentences.

1. An essay is an author's arrangement of sentences and paragraphs designed to have an effect on a reader.
2. An essay is like a conversation.

1. Our new automobile has a solid design and great power.
2. Our new automobile is the fullback of sports coupes.

1. Our profit margin has changed from fifteen to two percent in only one quarter.
2. Our profit margin has taken a nosedive, but we have several people watching the controls.

In each pair, sentence 2 creates a picture in the reader's mind. These pictures aid the reader by providing an emotional context for the information being presented ("Help! Our company is crashing!") and an organizational context for the information ("Any new information I learn might be the source of a new understanding for our company's growth").

CommonSense Guide

Figurative Language

Enliven your style by practicing the following techniques. All these techniques have special uses and effects; you will need to determine whether they are appropriate for your particular topic, purpose, and audience.

Compare two unlike things using *like* or *as*.

He was as nervous as a long-tailed cat in a room full of rocking chairs.

My job has gotten so complicated I feel like a juggler on icy steps.

Define or describe one idea using words related to a second idea.

Love is a rose boiling in acid.

With my new job, I'm having trouble keeping everything in the air.

The new movie zoomed to the top of the charts, leaving the competition in the dust.

$\longrightarrow$

continued from previous page

Substitute a part to represent the whole.

Our band will have someone on skins, someone on the ivories, and someone on the reeds.

Customer service is the art of always greeting the customer with a smile.

Use words that sound like their meaning.

Their coins jangled in their pockets.

In the waiting room, time tic-toc, tic-tocs without end.

Pair words that have contradictory meanings.

Committees are exercises in enlightened stupidity.

History is the study of the ever-present past.

The painfully kind driver's education teacher coaxed the young driver off the freeway.

Overstate and understate.

You have to be a millionaire now to take a vacation.

After eight double espressos, I got a little nervous.

Attribute human characteristics to abstract ideas or inanimate objects.

The dirty car cried out, "Wash me! Somebody, please, wash me!"

It seems as if Marxism has packed its bags and returned home to the nineteenth century.

19d
WORDS AND TONE

Let's say four people have sent you email with the following messages.

I've eyeballed things, and the project looks peachy.

I've jotted down some numbers, and I think we can OK the project.

I've added up the figures and am certain we can continue safely.

I've computed the costs and projected revenues, and I recommend we proceed with the project.

All four people are communicating the same message—or are they? Their sentence structure is similar, but the words they use differ. What would you say is the difference between *eyeballing, jotting, adding,* and *computing*?

The words we use have histories and current usages that affect the tones, feelings, or moods of the words. Often the pictures we see in our minds indicate these moods. *Eyeballing*, for instance, might call to mind a big, cartoonish eye gazing at a sheet of paper, but we do not see the speaker's hands doing anything. *Jotting* might call up an image of a hand moving quickly, perhaps without much evidence of the writer concentrating. *Adding* makes us see an orderly line of numbers or maybe even fingers tapping a calculator or adding machine. Finally, *calculating* forces us to see a more complicated set of numbers; somebody has started to do some really hard work. *Calculating* feels more difficult than *adding*, doesn't it? So in the above examples, the pictures we see in our minds reflect the **tones** the words have.

Another feature of words that affects their tone is their sound, how we pronounce them. For instance, the word *jot* has a quicker, lighter sound than *calculate*. In revising your writing, read your words aloud to listen to their sounds. Are they scary-sounding, sexy, dull, rough, tender?

Also affecting the tone of words are our associations about the people who most often use the words. In a business meeting, we would never speak like parents of a one-year-old: "We've looky-wooked at the number-wumbers, and they don't scare us one itty-little-bit." Nor would we speak like jazz musicians from the 1950s: "We've been eyeing the bread, man, and everything's cool."

Finally, the history of usage creates specific tones to certain words. Certainly this is why people find offensive many words that describe race, gender, political or religious persuasion, and sexual orientation. One way to enliven your writing is to vary the tone of the words that you use, but you should be very careful. While you may think you are enlivening your writing with ethnic humor and references to gender politics, you may be offending a potentially friendly audience.

19e
SHORT SENTENCES

Following is a passage from the essay "Remembering Richard Wright" by Ralph Ellison. As you read it, notice how Ellison makes you vary your reading speed and especially how he emphasizes a couple of key ideas with short sentences.

> I read most of [Richard Wright's novel] *Native Son* as it came off the type-
> writer, and I didn't know what to think of it except that it was wonderful. I
> was not responding critically. . . . Such opportunities are rare, and being
> young, I was impressed beyond all critical words. And I am still impressed.
> —Ralph Ellison, "Remembering Richard Wright"

In this passage, Ellison twice slowed down his readers to emphasize "I
was not responding critically" and "I am still impressed." These short sentences change the speed with which we read the paragraph, and with their
abruptness they focus our attention more sharply. The passage below indicates how the emphasis can be lost if the ideas blend into the flow of the
other sentences. The ideas haven't disappeared. They just aren't stressed.

> I read most of [Richard Wright's novel] *Native Son* as it came off the type-
> writer, and since I was not responding critically, I didn't know what to think
> of it except that it was wonderful. Such opportunities are rare, and being
> young, I was impressed, and I am still impressed beyond all critical words.

19f
SENTENCE INTERRUPTIONS

As you consider the following passage, notice the pace at which you read.
Where do you read with your usual pace? Where is that pace interrupted
and slowed down? Where do the words flow smoothly and with relative
speed? Where does the flow stop?

> That many emotions activate us alike—joy often looks like pain—caused sci-
> entists to think that all brain and bodily emotion signs are alike. But emotions
> are not binary computers, merely off/on, good/bad, stop/go systems.
>   I grew up, intellectually, in the cognitive tradition and began work on
> information-processing studies of the mind. I chose time as the subject and
> later on studied consciousness. But, like most of my colleagues, I tended to
> overlook how basic emotions were to the mind, because I didn't look at mind
> in an evolutionary perspective. Mental processes, I have come to believe, are
> not organized around thought or reason but around emotional ideals: how we
> feel we want something to be.
> —Robert Ornstein, *The Evolution of Consciousness*

You probably noticed that only the second and fourth sentences flow
smoothly. In the other sentences, the speed is interrupted by phrases
designed, it would seem, to slow the reading down and thus to point up
stylistically the change of mind that the writer experienced.

CHAPTER 20

Variety and Repetition

As you read the following excerpt from Booker T. Washington's book *Up from Slavery*, think about the momentum that builds throughout the paragraph.

> I cannot recall how long I lived with Mrs. Ruffner before going to Hampton, but I think it must have been a year and a half. At any rate, I here repeat what I have said more than once before, that the lessons that I learned in the home of Mrs. Ruffner were as valuable to me as any education I have ever gotten anywhere since. Even to this day I never see bits of paper scattered around a house or in the street that I do not want to pick them up at once. I never see a filthy yard that I do not want to clean it, a paling off a fence that I do not want to put it on, an unpainted or unwhitewashed house that I do not want to paint or whitewash it, or a button off one's clothing or a grease spot on them or on a floor, that I do not want to call attention to it.
>
> —Booker T. Washington, *Up from Slavery*

By the time you reach the end of his paragraph, aren't you ready to go to work, too? His statement "that I do not want to," spoken five times, indicates the kind of power you can add to your writing through **repetition**. Now compare this to a different kind of power that he creates in his very next paragraph.

> From fearing Mrs. Ruffner I soon learned to look upon her as one of my best friends. When she found that she could trust me she did so explicitly. During the one or two winters that I was with her she gave me the opportunity to go to school for an hour in the day, during a portion of the winter months, but most of my studying was done at night, sometimes alone, sometimes under someone whom I could hire to teach me. Mrs. Ruffner always encouraged and sympathized with me in all my efforts to get an education. It was while living with her that I began to get together my first library. I secured a dry goods box, knocked out one side of it, put some shelves in it, and began putting into it every kind of book that I could get my hands upon, and called it my "library."
>
> —Booker T. Washington, *Up from Slavery*

Although this paragraph includes instances of repetition, you probably noticed more how each sentence begins slightly differently and that the sentences are of various lengths. This paragraph lacks the urgency of

150

the previous one; it settles into a more contemplative tone because Washington appears to be thinking and remembering rather than urging us all to get to work.

As you develop your writing style, you will begin to see how you can vary momentum from sentence to sentence by relying on four basic rhythmic patterns. (See the box "Four Rhythmic Patterns for Sentences.") These four basic patterns are built on the relationship of the subject and verb groups to descriptive words and word groups.

CommonSense Guide

Four Rhythmic Patterns for Sentences

Focusing on the Subject and Verb Group

> The **project** *required* our time, energy, and resources.

Building to the Subject and Verb Group

> Whenever you have the time, energy, and resources to complete a project before the deadline, **you** *should*.

Flowing from the Subject and Verb

> The **project** *confused* us, presenting too many options too early, eliminating too few of the options later on, and focusing, as the project ended, on a single option we weren't prepared for.

Balancing Subject and Verb Groups

> Whenever Clarita wrote essays, **she** *used* her computer; whenever she wrote poetry, **she** *turned* to pen and paper.

As you develop your style, watch for places where you have repeated words or sentence structures, and determine whether the repetition is effective.

20a
SENTENCE BEGINNINGS

Sometimes we have an interesting story to tell or some compelling information to communicate, but we weaken the power of our work because we use the same sentence structure repeatedly. Over the years, critics and editors have developed many ways to respond to such writing. They call it "boring," "lazy," "unimaginative," and "repetitious." However, a more accurate way of describing this kind of writing is to look at it as a stage of development and drafting. The writer has done something important—gotten all the ideas down on paper. Now the writer needs to attend to style by varying the sentence openings.

Read the passage below and notice the many ways the writer has begun his sentences.

> For every present-day species, there have been thousands in the past. The mammals of today are a shadow of former glories, even though they include some of the most beautiful and extraordinary creatures that have ever lived. Thus, the fossil record suggests that throughout the Cenozoic each species of mammal has lasted for an average of around a million years before going extinct or evolving into something else. Since the Cenozoic has lasted 65 million years, then commonsensical but slightly esoteric math suggests that for every species that exists at present, there must have been 30 or more in the past. Add the mammals of the Mesozoic, which shared the planet with the dinosaurs, and we may reasonably guess that for each mammalian species of today there have been as least 50 in times gone by. Now there are about 4,300 mammalian species on Earth, but the total that have lived since the group began can hardly be less than 200,000—not as many, but in the same league, as the known inventory of present-day beetles.
>
> —Colin Tudge, *The Time Before History*

20b
SENTENCE ENDINGS

Both of the sentences below contain the same information, but their emphasis is different.

The prices of our biomedical stocks plummeted after two years of steady growth.

After two years of steady growth, the prices of our biomedical stocks plummeted.

Did you notice that in the first sentence, you concentrate on the "steady growth" of the stocks, while in the second sentence, you focused on the fact that the stocks "plummeted"? The reason for this shift of focus is that the ends of sentences are naturally emphatic. So if you want to be sure a particular idea in a sentence is emphasized, place it at the end.

CommonSense Guide

Highlighting Sentence Endings

You can highlight your ideas by focusing on the natural emphasis of sentence endings.

Cut unimportant information. Cutting unnecessary words helps emphasize the important ones.

Original

> During the sales meeting, I marveled at the high level of my colleagues' speaking skills when they stood before the crowd, being entertaining and informative.

Rewritten

> During the sales meeting, I marveled at the high level of my colleagues' speaking skills.

Move less important information to the beginning of the sentence. The beginning of a sentence is less emphatic, so less important material should appear there.

Original

> Randall lost himself in thoughts about his first marriage while watching wrens building a nest.

Rewritten

> Watching wrens building a nest, Randall lost himself in thoughts about his first marriage.

Invert sentences. Subjects and verbs carry their own natural emphasis, and when the subject is moved to the end of a sentence, it is more emphatic. This technique, however, should be used sparingly.

Original

> The snake slithered over the rough stones and into the warm, still pond.

Rewritten

> Over the rough stones and into the warm, still pond slithered the snake.

→

continued from previous page

Begin the sentence with *There, What,* or *It*. Sentences beginning with these words delay the appearance of the important ideas of the sentences. The delay creates an emphasis. Because this technique creates wordiness, use it only when necessary.

Original

While in Boston, we can do many things.

Rewritten

There are many things to do in Boston.

Original

That it should take so long to negotiate the contract irritated every one of the lawyers.

Rewritten

It irritated every one of the lawyers that the contract should take so long to negotiate.

20c
PARALLELISM

As you read the following passage by linguist and archeologist Elizabeth Wayland Barber, notice how her style emphasizes the relationships of her ideas. How does she use **parallelism** (the expression of ideas in similar structures) to indicate the equal importance she places on these ideas?

What did the ancient people try to accomplish when they deliberately made cloth bear meaning? A good look at folk customs and costumes recently in use reveals three main purposes. For one thing, it can be used to mark or announce information. It can also be used as a mnemonic device to record events and other data. Third, it can be used to invoke "magic"—to protect, to secure fertility and riches, to divine the future, perhaps even to curse. Today clothing is also used as an indicator of fashion, but the subtleties of that expression, which change so very rapidly, are largely beyond our ability to reconstruct in the ancient world.

—Elizabeth Wayland Barber, *Women's Work: The First 2000 Years*

Did you notice that she repeats several words from one sentence to the next to show us that the ideas are parallel, or equal in value? "It can be used," or a variation, is stated four times. (For more information about the uses of parallelism for coherence in writing, see Sections 16b and 16d.) And did you also see her repetition of another structure to clarify the many uses of magic in clothing? Her fifth sentence includes the following:

> *to protect,*
>
> *to secure fertility and riches,*
>
> *to divine the future, perhaps even*
>
> *to curse.*

(For more information on how to develop effective parallel structures, see Section 34d. For information on how to punctuate parallel structures, see Section 24c.)

Dr. Barber's primary purpose most likely is to convey information clearly and not to dazzle readers with her style. Yet she manages to communicate with a style that builds in this paragraph like waves rolling in on a beach, each idea rising through parallelism until the waves crest with the next use of parallelism. Finally, she indicates the contemporary implications of her ideas and concludes her paragraph.

20d
SENTENCES WITH COORDINATION

Coordination is related to parallelism (Section 20c), but coordination is different in that usually it refers to showing the equal relationship between two parts of a sentence. Coordination between sentences, then, often creates a smooth, rocking rhythm. Ideas flow from one sentence to the next, and they keep moving until the coordination stops. There are three ways to create coordination between sentences.

> *By using the words* and, but, or, nor, for, so, *and* yet;
>
> *By using words like* however, consequently, then, *and* for example
>
> *By using a semicolon, dash, or colon*

Coordination with **and, but, or, nor, for, so, yet**

Read the following passage and notice the boldfaced words.

> Evolution, as usually depicted in textbooks and reported in the popular press, is a process of inexorable improvement in form: animals are delicately "fine

tuned" to their environment through constant selection of better-adapted shapes. **But** several kinds of environments do not call forth such evolutionary response. Suppose that a species lives in an environment that imposes irregular, catastrophic mortality upon it (ponds that dry up, for example, or shallow seas ripped up by severe storms). **Or** suppose that food sources are ephemeral and hard to find, but superabundant once located. Organisms cannot fine tune themselves to such environments **for** there is nothing sufficiently stable to adjust to. Better in such a situation to invest as much energy as possible into reproduction—make as many offspring as you can, as quickly as possible, so that some will survive the catastrophe. Reproduce like hell while you have the ephemeral resource **for** it will not last long and some of your progeny must survive to find the next one.

—Stephen Jay Gould, Ever Since Darwin

Coordination with words like **however, consequently, thus,** *and* **for example**

All the artifices of flattery are used to harness the fears and hatred, prejudices, and biases, convictions and ideals common to the group; **thus** emotion is made to push and pull the group on to the Band Wagon.

—Institute for Propaganda Analysis, "How to Detect Propaganda"

Coordination with only a semicolon, dash, or colon

The following passage illustrates coordination with the dash and a colon.

A take-no-prisoners style of logging is used on . . . six-hundred-year-old trees: all life, from ferns and huckleberry bushes on the ground, to eagles' nests on the tree crowns, is cut down, bulldozed into garbage heaps, stripped of commercial wood, and then burned.

—Timothy Egan, The Good Rain

20e
SENTENCES WITH SUBORDINATION

When people arrange ideas in sentences, sometimes they string the sentences together as if they were simply listing them. They write something like this: "This happened; then that happened; then the next thing and then the next thing." After a while, the reader gets tired of reading because the sentences become tedious and predictable. In addition, the sentences probably fail to reflect accurately the true relationships between the ideas. Look at the following sentences.

I want to go to Spain, and I read a book about the country.

The stock crept toward seventy dollars a share, and fewer buyers expressed interest in purchasing it.

The President made a valid case for reforming the health care system, and Congress was equally convincing in its reasons for hesitating.

Each sentence clearly presents two ideas that have some relationship to each other. The relationships are reflected in the word *and*. But does *and* accurately reflect the relationships, and will readers enjoy reading paragraphs full of *and*, *and*, *and*? Probably not. Now consider the sentences below. Are the relationships between the ideas more clearly stated?

I want to go to Spain because I read a book about the country.

As the stock crept toward seventy dollars a share, fewer buyers expressed interest in purchasing it.

Although the President made a valid case for reforming the health care system, Congress was equally convincing in its reasons for hesitating.

One way to create variety in your writing and more accurately present the relationships between your ideas is to join the parts of a sentence with words that subordinate one idea to the other. Words that reflect and create this kind of relationship between ideas include *although, if, unless, when, after,* and *because*.

CommonSense Guide

Words That Create Subordinate Relationships

The following words can create variety in your writing and help you more accurately reflect the relationships between your ideas.

after	before	once
although	even if	since
as	even though	so that
as long as	however	than
as soon as	if	that
as though	in case	though
because	in order that	unless

→

continued from previous page		
until	where	which
what	whereas	who
when	wherever	whom
whenever	while	whose

In the passage below, the subordinating words are boldfaced.

When I was a psychotherapist in practice, I sometimes adopted an approach derived from this technique [active imagination] with middle-aged patients suffering from depression. Such patients are often people **who**, because of the demands of their careers and families, have neglected or abandoned pursuits and interests **which**, at an earlier point in time, gave life zest and meaning. **If** the patient is encouraged to recall **what** made life meaningful to him in adolescence, he will begin to rediscover neglected sides of himself, and perhaps turn once again to music, or to painting, or to some other cultural or intellectual pursuit **which** once enthralled him, but **which** the pressure of life's business had made him abandon.

—Anthony Storr, *Solitude*

20f
ECHOES

Consider the two short passages below.

Rather than drive around to Seattle, you may want to take the ferry. The ferry leaves for Seattle often during the day.

Efficient managers have well-established daily routines. Some routinely begin their morning work schedules by turning on their computer screens. Their assistants, who screen all incoming telephone calls, schedule all calls that need to be returned that morning. So managers turn to scheduled appointments, or, if emergencies have turned up, appoint their assistants to reschedule those appointments.

Then consider the next two passages.

We have nothing to fear but fear itself.

Supporters of bilingual education today imply that students like me miss a great deal by not being taught in their family's language. What they seem not to recognize is that, as a socially disadvantaged child, I considered Spanish to be a private language. What I needed to learn in school was that I had the right—and the obligation—to speak the public language of *los gringos*. The odd truth is that my first-grade classmates could have become bilingual, in the conventional sense of that word, more easily than I. Had they been taught (as upper-middle-class children are often taught early) a second language like Spanish or French, they could have regarded it simply as that: another public language. In my case bilingualism could not have been so quickly achieved. What I did not believe was that I could speak a single public language.

—Richard Rodriguez, *Hunger of Memory*

All four passages contain repetitions and echoes. But only the second pair use them effectively. **Echoes** are repetitions of forms of words or sounds from words. Repetitions and echoes can enhance your style in two ways. First, they help your reader focus on your ideas, providing guideposts and markers as ideas develop. This quality is evident in the passage by Richard Rodriguez as he repeats the words *language, public, bilingual,* and *taught*. Second, repetitions and echoes can make your writing *sound* good. Readers, even those reading silently, will hear the consonants and vowels of your words forming patterns similar to music. Often this quality is discussed in terms of its relation to poetry, but prose has its music, too. Reread the last two sentences in Rodriguez's passage, quoted again below. Listen for the repetition of vowel and consonant sounds, particularly the sounds of *e, i, k, c, gu,* and the nasals *m* and *n*.

In my case bilingualism could not have been so quickly achieved. What I did not believe was that I could speak a single public language.

However, repetitions and echoes can become tiresome and distracting for the reader, as they are in the two examples at the beginning of this section. One reason to read your work out loud is to *hear* the repetitions that interfere with communication.

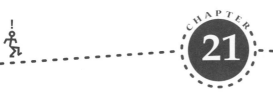

CHAPTER 21

Tone and Sexist Language

Imagine that for one week you could live your life as a member of the other gender. You would dress as the other gender does and perform the social roles of the other gender. More important, people would behave toward you as they usually behave toward individuals of that gender. Although social roles are certainly not as strict as they once might have been, you would no doubt be surprised by how people would treat you.

These reactions would occur no matter whether you are a man or a woman and no matter how "politically aware" your friends and co-workers are. One of the most important manifestations of **gender roles** is language, not only the language you use yourself but also the language you hear others use. You would become very aware of how the history of English sometimes collides with our changing society. As communicators, we inherit a language with its own meanings woven into the history of its users. However, as the current culture changes, as it inevitably must, certain words acquire new meanings and connotations.

In this chapter you will learn how our language is changing to adapt to contemporary awareness of gender.

21a
THE GENERIC *MAN*

One of the major reasons to become aware of **gender bias** in your language is that sometimes words are just plain inaccurate. One example is the word *man*. For many years, in certain situations, *man* referred to both men and women; some people still defend the word as being genderless. However, nowadays *man* ordinarily means someone of the male gender. For example, if someone said, "What a man!" or described another person as "manly," wouldn't you rely on a gender-specific definition? Probably. So, although women can be manly, the very definition of *manly* indicates that the word *man* can refer only with great difficulty to both men and women.

Do you see any problems in the following sentences?

Man is destructive and violent.

Man naturally cares for his offspring.

When Eliza escaped from the prison, we organized a manhunt.

Dorothy and Mary have worked 96 man-hours.

Rather than using the word *man* to represent both men and women, a more accurate practice is to substitute a term that is non-gender specific.

Instead of	Use
man	people
mankind	humanity, humankind
the common man	the average person
manmade	artificial
manhunt	search party
man-hours	hours, worker-hours

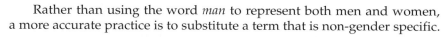

21b
GENDER STEREOTYPING

In the nineteenth century, often nurses and secretaries were men. It would have been accurate and sensible to say, "The secretary performed his duties efficiently." Then, for a period in the twentieth century, women filled most of those positions, so it was sensible and accurate to say, "The secretary performed her duties efficiently." These sentences may have reflected stereotypes, but the stereotypes were mostly accurate.

Currently, it would be difficult to name any profession that is performed by one gender exclusively. Therefore, when writing about people in general, it is usually more accurate to avoid any references to gender. The following sections illustrate how inaccurate stereotyping occurs and how to revise it.

21b.1 Stereotyping with Modifiers

Gender stereotyping occurs when writers overcompensate and use certain words and phrases to indicate that a role or occupation is almost exclusively for men or exclusively for women.

Instead of	Use
male nurse	nurse
lady lawyer	lawyer
woman doctor	doctor

Also notice that the terms *male nurse* and *woman doctor* are ambiguous. You could be speaking, for instance, of a nurse who has specialized in working with male patients.

21b.2 Stereotyping with Pronoun Reference

Gender stereotyping also occurs when writers use the pronoun *she* (and its other forms) to refer to roles that were traditionally female but now are actually mixed. And it occurs when writers use the pronoun *he* (and its other forms) to refer to roles that were once predominately male.

You can avoid this problem by using plural forms, speaking of several typical workers instead of one typical worker. As you read the following sentences, do you notice the unnecessary stereotyping?

A secretary has **her** hands full working in a busy office.

An accountant works steadily and carefully on **his** client's behalf.

The following sentences convey the same information without stereotyping.

Secretaries have **their** hands full working in a busy office.

Accountants work steadily and carefully on **their** clients' behalf.

If you are writing about an individual secretary or accountant, name the person. Then the pronoun *she* or *he* will make sense, and you will avoid inaccurate statements and false stereotypes.

Sandra Weaver, the secretary, has her hands full working in our busy office.

As our accountant, Tomas Perez works steadily and carefully in everything he does for us.

21c
TROUBLESOME WORD ENDINGS

If someone told you the chairman of the finance committee was entering the room and you turned toward the door and saw two people, a man and a woman, would you know which of them was the head of the committee? Could anyone blame you if you assumed it was the man, since it was, after all, a chair*man* you were looking for? But since these jobs are performed by men and women alike, a word ending that indicates gender seems confusing.

21c.1 Words Ending in *-man*

The use of *-man* at the end of a word has the same effect as the generic use of *man* (see Section 21a) and should be avoided.

Instead of	Use
chairman	chair, head
foreman	presiding juror
policeman	police officer
workman	worker

21c.2 Words Ending in *-ix* and *-ess*

The suffixes *-ix* and *-ess* have generally been discarded in favor of non-gender specific language.

Instead of	Use
executrix	executor
poetess	poet
sculptress	sculptor
waitress	server, wait staff
stewardess	flight attendant

21d
THE GENERIC *HE*

Traditionally, writers used the masculine personal pronoun *he* to indicate people of either sex. For centuries this practice went unchallenged, but now many readers are offended by this distortion of reality.

Eliminating the generic *he* may be difficult at first because some of the solutions carry with them certain stylistic disadvantages. However, by using a combination of the following strategies, you can craft prose that is both effective stylistically and free of the gender bias that the generic *he* communicates.

21d.1 Pronouns

Sometimes you can simply delete the pronoun without losing clarity. Is the first sentence below clearer than the second?

Original

A journalist must consider all facts revealed to **him** by a source.

Rewritten

A journalist must consider all facts revealed by a source.

21d.2 Noun Plurals

When speaking about people in general, a writer can often use plural nouns. Is the first sentence any clearer than the second?

Original

A journalist must consider all facts revealed to **him** by **his** sources.

Rewritten

Journalists must consider all facts revealed to **them** by **their** sources.

21d.3 Repeated Nouns

There are occasions when you can repeat the noun rather than using a pronoun.

Original

At the uncontested docket, the judge hears a few minutes of testimony from one of the parties. If the pleadings are in order and the court has jurisdiction, **he** grants the divorce.

Rewritten

At the uncontested docket, the judge hears a few minutes of testimony from one of the parties. If the pleadings are in order and the court has jurisdiction, **the judge** grants the divorce.

21d.4 *A, An*, or *The*

Look for instances when the singular is not needed and can be replaced by *a, an,* or *the*. Is anything lost in the second sentence?

Original

A journalist must consider all facts revealed by **his** source.

Rewritten

A journalist must consider all facts revealed by **a** source.

21d.5 *He* or *She*

One substitute for the generic use of *he* to refer to singular nouns is the use of *he or she*. While this practice is accurate and useful, it can create a wordy style.

Original

A journalist must consider all facts revealed by a source. **He** must listen carefully to everything the person says.

Rewritten

A journalist must consider all facts revealed by a source. **He or she** must listen carefully to everything the person says.

21d.6 *Who*

Sometimes instead of using a pronoun that refers to the gender of the noun, you might rewrite the sentence using the word *who*.

Original

If a journalist does not pay attention to details, **he** cannot expect to be successful.

Rewritten

A journalist **who** does not pay attention to details cannot expect to be successful.

21d.7 Reworded Sentences

On some occasions the best alternative to using *he* is a complete rewrite of the sentence to avoid a situation needing the pronoun.

Original

The original lawyer knows **his** case well by the time of the trial, but that doesn't mean that **he** is the **man** to handle the case through appeal.

Rewritten

The original lawyer, **who** knows the case well by the time of the trial, *may not be the best* **one** to handle the case through appeal.

21d.8 Passive Voice

While the use of passive voice brings with it its own set of stylistic problems, you may find passive voice a useful alternative to the generic *he*.

Original

The lawyer represented **his** client adequately.

Rewritten

The client was represented adequately.

21e
INSULTING TERMS AND CONNOTATIONS

The tone of a communication is always an important consideration. As discussed in Section 19d, writers often avoid language that the audience will find offensive. Some words are simply so inflammatory that they must be avoided unless, of course, your purpose is to insult members of your audience. It should be noted, though, that insult is rarely effective as a rhetorical strategy.

You will want to use the following words with care.

male chauvinist pig	girls, gals
femi-Nazis	chicks
old boys' network	ladies
old hens	boys
dead white European males	guys

6

Sentence Punctuation

22 MARKS OF PUNCTUATION

23 SENTENCES

24 COORDINATE ELEMENTS

25 INTRODUCTORY ELEMENTS

26 INTERRUPTING ELEMENTS

22

Marks of Punctuation

Read the following passage.

> Bruce stood at the hill's crest where a small outcrop of rock interrupted the gentle slope he looked at his watch over two hours ago he and his hiking partner tired of the day's trek had dropped their heavy packs rested awhile and then gone off in different directions for some time alone beyond the hills and over the distant mountains a glowing orange sun barely hung in the sky waiting in the fading light seemed foolish so he started to set up camp by himself

Notice how much easier it is to read the same passage when it includes punctuation marks.

> Bruce stood at the hill's crest where a small outcrop of rock interrupted the gentle slope. He looked at his watch. Over two hours ago, he and his hiking partner, tired of the day's trek, had dropped their heavy packs, rested awhile, and then gone off in different directions for some time alone. Beyond the hills and over the distant mountains, a glowing orange sun barely hung in the sky. Waiting in the fading light seemed foolish, so he started to set up camp by himself.

Punctuation marks show you how the writer wants you to read a passage; they are signals to readers about the meaning of written language. It is important to your readers, therefore, that you use punctuation when you write.

It is sometimes said that punctuation marks are used to *join* parts of sentences, but a more accurate statement would be that punctuation marks are always used in writing to *separate* language in print, to keep it all from running together. Writers who listen to the ways punctuation can signal these separations will find that punctuating is simply a part of their style, just like word choice and sentence structure. They will begin to see that punctuation is a way to indicate the extent of the separations in their writing because each mark indicates a certain length of pause in the oral reading of a text. They will also understand that punctuation marks indicate some of the attitudes present in the speaking voice and that they imply changes in pitch and volume. In other words, the silences that punctuation marks identify in print serve to guide readers to a better understanding of meaning.

The reason that silences can guide you to punctuate effectively is this:

> The modern English sentence moves along without pause when all sentence elements are in their naturally occurring places. In speech (and in writing), we alter these natural patterns to make what we want to say more effective or more clear, inserting pauses to guide our listeners to understand what we mean.

These two statements illustrate the point they make. In the first statement, the words follow a natural sequence that grammarians would identify as the basic phrase structure of the English language. But the second statement contains ideas complex enough that breaks and pauses are essential if the concepts are to be expressed in a single sentence. If we try to create a "pauseless" version of the second statement, we have to use two sentences.

> We alter these natural patterns in speech and in writing to make what we want to say more effective or more clear. We do this by inserting pauses to guide our listeners to understand what we mean.

Notice that these two sentences require more words and are less emphatic and less clear than the single, more complex sentence. Using a conventional set of pauses in speech (and punctuation marks in print) allows us to move ideas around—even to combine sentences—for emphasis and clarity. All punctuation within sentences can be accounted for by some kind of restructuring of pauseless statements to focus or clarify content. In the first set of sentences, a speaker would give both sound and silence signals to focus the listener's attention; what the punctuation does is to give these signals to a reader.

CommonSense Guide

Reasons for Punctuating

There are only seven reasons for using punctuation marks.

1. To keep sentences from running together (using the period, the question mark, or the exclamation mark)
2. To separate two statements in a single sentence (using the colon, the semicolon, or the comma)
3. To signal that parts of a sentence are not in their natural order (using the comma and, sometimes, the dash)

→

continued from previous page

4. To single out items in a list or series (using the comma and, sometimes, the semicolon or the dash)

5. To signal interruptions in the flow of a sentence (using commas, dashes, parentheses, and brackets)

6. To signal a logical reversal (using the comma or the dash)

7. To prevent misreading (using the comma)

22a
END PUNCTUATION

Consider the way end punctuation changes how you would say the following sentences.

You think I'm really surprised to see you here.

You think I'm really surprised to see you here?

You think I'm really surprised to see you here!

Obviously, the words used in the three sentences are the same, but the meaning of the sentences is different. What is it that signals these differences to you? Clearly, it is the punctuation marks, but just looking at the marks will not reveal the differences in meaning. It is what the marks imply about how the sentences would be spoken that makes the meaning clear.

This is how the end punctuation marks work: a period signals a drop in pitch and in volume; a question mark usually signals a dramatic rise in pitch at some point in the sentence; and an exclamation mark signals a strong emphasis on one of the words before the pitch and volume drop at the end.

22a.1 The Period

The use of a period makes the following sentence read as a simple *declaration*.

You think I'm really surprised to see you here.

This sentence does not so much inform the reader as simply declare what its writer observes. If you read the sentence in a speaking voice, the pitch of your voice naturally rises and falls depending on what you mean; most people drop both pitch and volume as they say the word *here* and then stop. This example illustrates the role of a period in punctuation. It absolutely separates matter-of-fact utterances from each other. Anytime your voice drops in both pitch and volume at the end of a statement, resulting in a stop before continuing, a period can be used.

The appropriate use of the period at the end of sentences is further addressed in Section 23a. The propriety—and impropriety—of using a period to form a sentence fragment is discussed in Section 23b.

22a.2 The Question Mark

In the following sentence, a question mark signals that the pitch at which the sentence is spoken will rise at the end.

You think I'm really surprised to see you here?

Questions that sound like this one are true inquiry questions; the rise in pitch is a natural sound that English speakers make when they are genuinely curious. We all recognize these statements as true inquiries, regardless of how they are phrased. However, sometimes sentences that are worded as questions drop in pitch at the end and are spoken as declarations. For example, statements that seek agreement or affirmation by having questions tacked onto the end do not rise in pitch.

You're really hungry, aren't you?

Some kinds of questions do not require question marks, especially indirect questions. Notice, for example, where question marks are used and not used in the examples below.

Direct question

Where did she go?

Indirect question

I wonder where she went.

22a.3 The Exclamation Mark

When you speak the following sentence, the exclamation mark encourages you to give considerable stress to some word (probably *surprised*), then to decrease both volume and pitch as you approach the end of the sentence and stop.

You think I'm really surprised to see you here!

An exclamation usually expresses strong emotion, and some part of the statement is always spoken with vigor. Though writers find this mark useful when recording the speech of others or when writing dialogue, they use the exclamation mark sparingly—perhaps because shouting in print is neither formal nor polite.

22b
THE COLON AND THE SEMICOLON

Other punctuation marks also have corresponding influences on the way sentences sound; conversely, the way a sentence reads calls for specific marks of punctuation. Though they are not used to end sentences, the colon and the semicolon are both strong marks of punctuation—the strongest of the internal marks of punctuation. They signal more significant pauses than the other internal punctuation marks.

22b.1 The Colon

A colon always sounds like a period—except that it always means that what follows will further explain what was just said. Read the following sentences and note that both of these conditions apply in each case, whether what follows is a complete sentence or not.

Suddenly his demeanor changed: a smile broke through the gloom like a shaft of sunlight through clouds.

The expense of repairing the car would be enormous: $2500 for body work, $1200 for new parts, and $600 for a paint job.

The colon is not used very often because it slows reading speed significantly. When it is used, it emphasizes formality.

22b.2 The Semicolon

Two conditions apply to the semicolon: it always comes between grammatically identical elements, and it always implies balance. Thus, use of a semicolon tends to impose a distinctive structure on the writer's ideas, in that it tends to place similar items side by side for the purposes of comparison. It also imposes a particular arching sound to a sentence, so that the pitch of the voice is rather elevated just prior to the mark. Look at (and listen to) the following sentence.

Sylvia looked wistfully at the horizon beyond the breakers; she leaned earnestly into the strong, salty breeze.

The silence that is signaled by a semicolon is not at all like the one signaled by a period; it causes a hesitation that makes the first part "lean toward" the second. When writers want to separate two complete statements that are uttered in the same sentence, the semicolon is the preferred punctuation mark (see Section 24c, "Balanced Sentences").

The semicolon is also used to signal strong pauses between sentence elements that themselves contain pauses indicated by weaker marks of internal punctuation.

Wing-Lin's recipe for chicken-and-hominy soup calls for cumin, a spice often used in Mexican cooking; cilantro, sometimes called Mexican parsley; and poblanos (mild green chilis)—as well as the expected onions and garlic.

Even when used in this way, the semicolon signals balance between like kinds of sentence components (see Section 24d, "Series").

22c
THE COMMA

The punctuation mark that seems omnipresent is the comma: if there is a short pause in any sentence, chances are good that the pause can be signaled by a comma. Some people will wince at this statement, but the truth of the matter is that most of the time when an internal punctuation mark is needed, a comma is indeed the right choice. Though commas have various uses, they always signal slight breaks in speech, and they never cause problems for writers who are aware of the special-case uses of the other punctuation marks. Both of the following sentences need a comma to signal the slight breaks that occur when you speak them aloud.

Shauna grudgingly got in the car, though really she'd have preferred to walk.

Hermann twirled the flattened dough high over his head, then felt it falling down over his fist, wrapping around his arm like a pleated dress around a dancer.

Neither of these sentences can be spoken without internal pauses, and both can be conventionally punctuated with commas. However, a writer might want to use parentheses in the first example or a dash for the first comma in the second. How to make such decisions is discussed fully in

Chapter 25, which deals with introductory elements; Chapter 26, which deals with interrupting elements; and Chapter 27, which deals with concluding elements.

There are, however, conventional uses of the comma that are not subject to the writer's choice. These include separating coordinate elements such as the principal parts of compound sentences (Section 24a), separating items in a series (Section 24d), and separating coordinate modifiers (Section 24e).

22d
THE DASH, PARENTHESES, AND BRACKETS

It was noted in Section 22c that the sentence beginning "Hermann . . ." might make use of a dash instead of a comma and that the sentence beginning "Shauna . . ." might make use of parentheses. *Whether* to use one of these marks to punctuate is seldom open to interpretation, but *which* of these marks to use at a given time is determined by circumstance and purpose. The three marks have quite specific uses.

22d.1 The Dash

While a phrase set off with a comma would probably be said in an ordinary voice, a phrase following a dash would be uttered loudly, or said with special emphasis, or spoken with a different attitude. For example, read the following sentence aloud in a straightforward manner, simply relating the information.

> The third house from the corner, the one without a fence, is the one our letter carrier always hated to pass.

What is placed inside commas is merely set off from the sentence with pauses and spoken in ordinary tones. Now read the same sentence again, with dashes substituted for commas.

> The third house from the corner—the one without a fence—is the one our letter carrier always hated to pass.

Commas setting off an interrupting phrase impart a matter-of-fact sense to the content. In contrast, dashes are generally used to make an interruption stand out—to emphasize a phrase the way the dash does in this sentence. What is placed inside dashes is highlighted and is usually spoken with emphasis or vigor.

22d.2 Parentheses and Brackets

Two other marks of punctuation—the parenthesis and the bracket—operate in the same way as paired commas and paired dashes.

What is inside parentheses is usually spoken softly, either as an aside or under the breath (if it is spoken at all); it is as if the writer were hiding what is in parentheses, allowing the reader to decide whether to look or not. As you read the sentence below, say what is in parentheses in a low voice, using almost a confiding tone, and you'll understand why parentheses can be useful.

> The third house from the corner (the one without a fence) is the one our letter carrier always hated to pass.

Writers also include information within parentheses that may be useful to the reader but would interrupt the flow of ideas if placed in the text itself. For example, in research papers, sources are cited in parentheses (see Section 45a).

What is inside brackets is actually never spoken, because it is usually added by someone other than the writer (or, in dialogue, other than the speaker). Brackets give the reader additional information about how to read or think about what has been written. Here is the same sentence with both a parenthetical addition and an editorial comment.

> The third house from the corner (the one without a fence) is the one our letter carrier always hated to pass. [The family occupying this house raised pit bulls.—Ed.]

CommonSense Guide

Punctuation Marks

Period   Follows a declaration, with decrease in volume, drop in pitch, and complete stop.

> This is a sentence ending with a period.

Question mark   Follows a question, with decrease in volume, rise in pitch (inquiry) or drop in pitch (demand), and complete stop.

> Can you think of a better example for the question mark?
>
> If so, what is it?

⟶

continued from previous page

Exclamation mark Follows a loud or intense declaration, with increase in volume, drop in pitch, and complete stop.

Always, always signal exclamations appropriately!

Colon Like the period, marked by decrease in volume, drop in pitch, and complete stop; always precedes a further explanation of a previous statement, phrase, or word.

The colon: a signal that something of added significance is coming.

Use the colon effectively: add further explanation when it is needed.

Semicolon Follows a declaration in which pitch and volume are maintained, as if the statement were not yet complete; indicates more than a brief pause, imparting to the statement a sense of balance.

A semicolon is not as strong as a period; it is, however, stronger than a comma.

Semicolons are useful when items in a series contain commas, which set off ordinary explanations or examples; dashes, which set off remarkable explanations or examples; or combinations of these two marks.

Comma Follows slight decreases in volume and pitch, with only a brief pause; language that follows is spoken at regular volume.

To signal a short pause, use a comma.

Dash Follows slight decreases in volume and pitch, with only a brief pause; emphasizes language that follows, which is spoken at a louder volume.

Surprising information—when set off with dashes—shows up very well.

→

continued from previous page

Parenthesis Signals slight decreases in volume and pitch, with only a brief pause; emphasizes language that follows, which is spoken at a softer volume (if it is spoken at all).

Place highly interruptive or insignificant information, or asides (such as this), inside parentheses.

Bracket Signals editorial insertion into a text, enclosing language which would be neither spoken nor heard.

Brackets [like those that enclose this statement—Ed.] supply editorial information.

Sentences

When we write formally, we usually employ complete sentences in our attempt to say fully what we want to say. When we use fragments, it may seem to our readers that we are relinquishing our responsibility as writers, and when we use fused sentences, it may seem that we are blocking out reasonable responses from our readers. Thus, it is important that we not accidentally create fused sentences by erratic punctuation, and just as important that we not unintentionally punctuate fragments as sentences. The key way to maintain the proper kind of alertness is to pay attention to the way our sentences sound in speech—and to punctuate or rephrase our statements accordingly.

23a
COMPLETE SENTENCES

How can we tell that a statement is complete?

One way to make sure we are writing complete sentences is to check their grammatical components: a **complete sentence** contains a complete (or implied) subject and a complete verb. But since we speak in complete sentences all the time without consciously checking grammatical functions, there is no reason why we cannot do the same thing in writing. All it takes to assure that our sentences are complete is for us to read our statements aloud.

There are three basic types of complete sentence statements, each of which has a typical utterance pattern or sound in speech and a typical end mark of punctuation in writing. A full discussion of the sound patterns these statements and punctuation marks make can be found in Section 22a. In brief, however, these are the key points.

- A declaration typically drops in pitch at the end when spoken and is punctuated with a period when written.
- A question typically rises in pitch at the end when spoken and is punctuated with a question mark when written.
- An exclamation typically rises in volume when spoken and is punctuated with an exclamation point when written.

Read the following statements aloud and listen to pitch.

What's new? He keeps getting minor injuries to his back. He really ought to start an exercise program. But do you think he will ever really start managing his own health? I don't!

23b
SENTENCE FRAGMENTS

If all sentences were simple ones, punctuation would be easy. It's not difficult to put in punctuation marks at the ends of simple statements. However, read the following passage.

I slowed the car as I approached the crossroads. It was then that I saw him. A man standing alone by the side of the road.

The third statement is incomplete. Although it is quite understandable if taken in context, taken by itself it doesn't communicate a complete thought. It would probably be spoken as part of the previous statement with only a brief pause between the two: "It was then that I saw him, a man standing alone by the side of the road." It could be rephrased, of course, as "A man was standing alone by the side of the road." But as written above, it is only a part of a sentence, or a partial sentence; we call it a **sentence fragment**.

Most sentence fragments in writing are accidental; writers seldom compose fragments on purpose. Here are some examples of fragments accidentally punctuated as complete sentences or written in dialect.

Omitted verb

> She working in her garden.

Complete sentence

> She **has been** working in her garden.

Missing verb

> The concert he looked forward to since Christmas.

Complete sentence

> The concert he looked forward to since Christmas **was postponed**.

Part of a previous sentence

> Since the Fourth of July.

Complete sentence

> **I haven't seen Rick** since the Fourth of July.

Part of a following sentence

> Because he really didn't want to tell Erika he didn't want to go out with her.

Complete sentence

> Because he really didn't want to tell Erika he didn't want to go out with her, **Justin feigned illness**.

In every case above, the fragments could have been avoided if the writer had spoken the statement aloud. In every case, the fragments spoken *as punctuated* do not sound like sentences, and both native speakers and new speakers of the language can easily hear the discrepancy.

CommonSense Guide

The Complete Sentence

In spite of all that teachers and grammarians can do to get everyone to use complete sentences, sentence fragments are often used in public writing. Novelists use them. Journalists sprinkle them

$\longrightarrow$

continued from previous page

around. Ad agencies use them as a staple in ad copy. Judicious use of an occasional fragment can make writing more conversational, more interactive with the reader.

You should, however, exercise some caution. If you use many fragments—especially if they seem to be accidental or unintentional—readers may think you do not know what a complete sentence is; as a result, some may think less of you as a writer, to the point that they ignore part of what you say. And if it seems to a reader that a fragment *should have been* written as a complete sentence, it will not be effective even if you wrote it intentionally.

23c
FUSED SENTENCES

Consider the following statement.

He drove through the town he had no idea where he was.

This statement presents the reader with a problem. There would clearly be a break after the word *town* if the statement were spoken aloud. But there is no punctuation to indicate that a reader should pause or stop at that point. As a result, most readers would find the statement somewhat confusing. We might read all the way through to the end before figuring out that "He drove through the town" and "He had no idea where he was" are fused into the same statement.

Readers invariably feel that **fused sentences** are errors. There is probably nothing in writing except misspelling that stands out to readers more than a fused (or run-on) sentence. Student writers are often urged to look over their papers and see whether they have written any fused sentences. But *looking* will not help you find fused statements nearly as quickly as *listening* will. Writers who read their work aloud can easily find fused sentences because they can hear them.

When you read a manuscript aloud, read it *as punctuated*—or as *not* punctuated—exactly as you have written it. When you correct your writing to avoid fused sentences, be sure to follow the suggestions for punctuating found in Section 24a. In particular, however, you should be alert to the misuse of the comma known as a comma splice (see Section 24b); in academic writing as well as in legal, business, and social writing, it is considered a major error.

Coordinate Elements

Notice how the marks of punctuation are used in the following sentences.

I read his paper; I thoroughly enjoyed it.

Not only was her paper interesting to read, but it was also most informative.

His paper was interesting, but it contained many awkward sentences.

His paper was easy to read: it was well organized.

Let me tell you, it wasn't fun.

Her exotic, colorful hat was outrageous.

She packed her toothbrush, her swimsuit, and some suntan lotion.

He likes semisweet; she, milk chocolate.

In the preceding sentences, the marks of punctuation are used to guide readers to give certain sentence elements equal emphasis. We call these **coordinate elements**; we signal their presence in speech with the subtle use of pauses of various lengths, and we signal their presence in writing through a systematic use of commas, semicolons, and colons. In the following sections of this chapter, you will learn to use these marks to punctuate coordinate elements conventionally.

24a
COMPOUND SENTENCES

As you read the following sentences, notice how the paired statements are treated.

1. He loomed dramatically over his notes; he looked deliberately from one side of the room to the other.
2. His face bore a puzzled expression, and he stared out the window for what felt like several minutes.
3. He looked agitatedly at his watch: he was evidently trying to decide what to do.
4. Either he would begin his lecture, or he would dismiss class.
5. The students were confused and angered by his indecision.
6. They grew restless in their chairs; however, there was much to cover before the coming test.

180

You can see that the sentences above have been created by combining statements that could also be punctuated separately as two independent sentences. Such **compound sentences** are used in writing when the writer wants to show a close connection between two complete ideas. Often such statements are joined with some kind of connector; regardless, they are always separated within the same sentence by standardized punctuation.

The most common kind of compound sentence is formed through the use of a comma and a single-syllable connecting word called a **coordinator**—*and*, *but*, *or*, *nor*, *for*, *so*, *yet*. Statements joined by these connectors into a single sentence (see sentence 2 above) are typically spoken with a very brief pause before the connecting word, as the use of a comma signals. Note, however, that sentence 5 contains the connector *and* but has no comma. In this case the connector does not join complete statements, only phrases, and the sentence generally would be spoken without a pause before the connector.

Some connecting words typically used with a comma are employed in pairs: *either . . . or*, *neither . . . nor*, and *not only . . . but also*, for example. These, too, make use of a comma before the one-syllable connecting word, as in sentence 4, which records the break that naturally occurs when the sentence is spoken.

In other cases, a semicolon or a colon is used in the writing of a compound sentence, as in sentences 1, 3, and 6. In sentence 1, the semicolon is used to signal the balance that exists between the two statements. Notice that when you speak this sentence, you naturally make use of a longer pause than a comma would signal, all the while suggesting through tone of voice that you still have more to say in the same sentence. When two independent statements are not joined by a connecting word, they typically point up a comparison or contrast between two statements. Sentence 6, on the other hand, makes use of the semicolon along with a connecting word. When **connectives** like *however*, *therefore*, *nevertheless*, *moreover*, and *furthermore* are used following a semicolon, they are set off from the rest of the sentence by a comma; the connective literally states the relationship between paired statements in a compound sentence.

24b
COMMA SPLICES

Consider the following sentences.

1. I question the practice, I think it is wrong.
2. He has very strong feelings about the rule, he does not think it is justified.

3. Even though he hasn't expressed his opinion on the matter, he has very strong feelings about the rule, he does not think it is justified.

Each of the sentences above contains a **comma splice**, the inappropriate use of a comma between two independent statements in the same sentence. (In sentence 3, the comma splice is the second comma, not the first.) Although English teachers would tell you to avoid comma splices in formal writing, most would also admit that some comma splices are acceptable—especially those that combine short, closely related sentences. Sentence 1 above is such a sentence. While many English teachers would probably allow a sentence like that, they would perhaps balk at sentence 2. Most writers, English teachers or not, would likely agree that sentence 3 creates such a problem in reading that it should be rewritten.

A comma splice can be corrected in several ways. Notice the following statement that contains a comma splice.

Farm life follows the seasons, winter is a time of relative inactivity.

You can divide the statement into two separate sentences.

Farm life follows the seasons. Winter is a time of relative inactivity.

You can make it into a compound sentence by inserting a coordinator like *and, but, or, nor, for, so,* or *yet.*

Farm life follows the seasons, **so** winter is a time of relative inactivity.

You can make it into a compound sentence by changing the comma to a semicolon to signify balance between the two statements.

Farm life follows the seasons**;** winter is a time of relative inactivity.

You can make it into a compound by changing the comma to a colon. The colon usually indicates that the second part of the sentence is an explanation of or a comment on the first part.

Farm life follows the seasons**:** winter is a time of relative inactivity.

You can combine the two statements in the sentence with a word like *if, because, when, although,* or *since,* making the part that begins with the connective dependent on the other part.

Since farm life follows the seasons, winter is a time of relative inactivity.

Though this is an effective correction method, it does not produce a compound sentence.

24c
BALANCED SENTENCES

Sentences that have similar structures on either side of a central pause are usually called **balanced sentences**. When writing them, you will want to give careful consideration to the way you punctuate them. Look at the following:

> He poured it up, he quaffed it down.

> Our knowledge separates us as well as it unites; our orders disintegrate us as well as bind; our art brings us together and sets us apart.
> —J. Robert Oppenheimer, *The Open Mind*

In general, longer sentences employ a semicolon between the parallel statements, while shorter sentences make use of a comma. However, using a comma even in the shortest of balanced sentences can create what seems like a comma splice to some readers.

A word can be omitted in the following example because of the structure of the sentence.

> To err is human; to forgive, divine.

The sentence is balanced, having the same structure on both sides of the connecting semicolon, with the exception that the writer has omitted the second verb, since it is the same as the first. The omission, signaled by a pause in speech, is marked by a comma, and the balancing mark of punctuation is necessarily a semicolon. If you read the sentence aloud in a conversational manner, you will hear a balancing pause after *human* and another pause after *forgive*.

24d
SERIES

Notice how commas are used in the following sentences.

> They wanted popcorn, peanuts, and candy.

> Jane smiled coyly, nodded her head, and walked away.

> We all knew that she would be infuriated at the report, that she would identify us as the responsible parties, and that she would certainly take action to avenge what she considered to be an unwarranted attack on her good name.

The commas in the sentences above separate elements in a **series**. In the first sentence, three nouns appear in series. In the second sentence, three verb phrases are in series.

CommonSense Guide

The Final Comma in Items in a Series

Some authorities contend that the second comma can be deleted in a short series of items, as in the following example.

> They wanted peanuts, popcorn and candy.

Whether you place a comma after *popcorn* will probably be determined by the style required by the situation: if your teacher or your office style manual requires the comma, you will put it in. If you are free to do as you please, here is a good general rule to use: If you would pause before the connector, place a comma there; if you would not pause, don't use one. For example, you probably would not pause before *and* in the sentence above. However, in the following sentence, you would probably pause naturally before *and* and would therefore want to use a comma in that place.

> They wanted six bags of peanuts, four big tubs of popcorn, and about a dozen candy bars.

The use of commas elsewhere in a sentence may require a semicolon to separate coordinate elements. Consider the punctuation in the following sentence.

> Before he left, he made certain that the cattle, which had been herded into the corral earlier in the day, had been fed; that they were not overly agitated by the disruption; and that all of them, at least as far as he could tell, were accounted for.

You can see that each of the series of elements, in this case the word groups beginning with the word *that*, require commas to set off nonessential interrupting modifiers and explanations (Sections 26a–26b), just as speaking the sentence would require us to pause before the word groups. Since separating the series with commas could cause confusion because of the other commas in the sentence, writers usually choose to separate them with semicolons.

24e
COORDINATE MODIFIERS

Consider the punctuation in the following sentences.

Her short, happy life had been filled with love.

His cheerful, smiling face was a mask.

In each sentence there is a pause between the two modifiers. Each one modifies the noun that follows the pair. Both *short* and *happy* modify *life*. They are **coordinate**; they have equal weight. When speaking, we have a clear method of showing that coordination: we pause between the words to show that the first word does not modify or relate to the second. When writing, we place a comma between them to signal the same thing to the reader. If we replaced the comma with *and*, the meaning would not change, but the connecting word would indicate the coordinate relationship. We could even reverse the words without changing the meaning.

Her short and happy life had been filled with love.

Her happy, short life had been filled with love.

The same is true of the second sentence.

His cheerful and smiling face was a mask.

His smiling, cheerful face was a mask.

Notice, however, that what is apparently the same kind of sentence structure in the following sentence does not require a comma.

The soft flannel shirt was very warm.

To say "The soft and flannel shirt" would sound odd. "The flannel soft shirt" carries a meaning different from "The soft flannel shirt." In both cases, neither a pause in speech nor a comma in writing would be appropriate.

Introductory Elements

Consider how the commas are used in the following sentences.

1. In the first place, I object to his being here at all.
2. If we are to make any progress on this project, we must all work together.
3. Well, the obvious reason is its complexity.
4. Fred, would you come over here?

As you can see, in each sentence above, an **introductory element** delays the appearance of the main part of the sentence. In sentence 1, the main part is delayed by the transition "In the first place." In sentence 2, the main part is delayed by the introductory modifier "If we are to make any progress on this project." In sentence 3, the main part is delayed by the introductory tag "Well." In sentence 4, the main part is delayed by the initial direct address "Fred." When an introductory element delays the appearance of the main part of the sentence, you will hear a pause between them.

In the following sections you will discover how introductory elements are punctuated.

CommonSense Guide

The Effect of Most Introductory Words

Except as noted in Section 25e, "Lists," there is *one* primary effect of sentence introductions: they establish a framework of meaning for the main part of the sentence. In each of the examples in this chapter, a particular frame set up by the introduction requires the reader to consider the rest of the sentence only in a certain way.

Eventually, the basement filled up with water. [sequence frame]

Beside the lake, the new hotel rose on concrete stilts. [location frame]

After the fire had cooled, the renters were allowed to sift through the charred timbers for personal effects. [time frame]

Therefore, no one expected any less of him. [logical frame]

$\longrightarrow$

continued from previous page

Writers often find sentence introductions useful devices to shape the thinking of their readers. In each of these examples, the introduction is set apart from the rest of the sentence by a pause in speech and a comma in writing. The varieties of this kind of sentence introduction are explained in Sections 25a through 25d.

25a
MODIFIERS

Notice the difference between the following sentences.

1. I did not go to work because of the icy roads.
2. Because of the icy roads, I did not go to work.

The phrase "because of the icy roads" appears at the end of sentence 1 and at the beginning of sentence 2. As a result, we read the two sentences differently. As you read sentence 1, you will notice that you read from beginning to end without a pause. However, as you read sentence 2, you will notice that you naturally pause after "roads." The pause is there because the phrase "Because of the icy roads" is out of the normal word order for an English sentence. It delays the appearance of the main part of the sentence, "I did not go to work." Consequently, you naturally pause after the introductory element before you begin to read the main part of the sentence. You do not pause when the explanatory element comes after the main part of the sentence, as it does in sentence 1.

Notice how the comma is used in each of the following sentences.

Across the street from the store, Harvey crouched behind a bush in a vacant lot.

According to Harvey, the incident was inconsequential.

Because I was sick, I did not go to work.

Running through the woods, I tripped over a root.

Dirty and hungry, the hordes scavenged the fields.

In each example, the main part of the sentence follows the comma. Each introductory element preceding the comma modifies all or part of the information contained in the main part of the sentence. The introductory elements could not stand on their own because they do not express complete thoughts.

25b
TRANSITIONAL EXPRESSIONS

Now look at the following sentence.

Consequently, you will have to clean up the mess.

The sentence has an introductory element used as a **transition**. The purpose of a transitional word or phrase is to bridge the gap between what has been said and what is about to be said. We naturally pause after *consequently* and other multisyllable transitions, so a comma is appropriate at that point when such sentences are written.

However, notice how you would say the following sentence, which has a one-syllable introductory transition.

Thus you can expect to find plenty of nuts under the tree.

You would probably not pause after the introductory transition in this sentence. Depending on the length of the transition and the amount of emphasis you want to give it, you may choose not to use a comma after one-syllable and other short introductory transitions.

25c
TAGS

Notice how the following sentences are punctuated.

Yes, you can be sure of it.

Hey! Get away from my bicycle!

In each case, the introductory "tag" precedes the main part of the sentence. There is an obvious pause afterward. Pauses, and requisite commas, are typically used after such initial tag statements regardless of their length. Of course, if the main sentence is an exclamation, then an exclamation mark may be in order after the tag.

25d
DIRECT ADDRESS

Consider how the following direct address sounds.

Jack, the mail has come.

Since the direct address "Jack" is not grammatically connected to the rest of the sentence, we pause after it when speaking; to say the sentence with no pause would sound odd. Therefore, a comma after a direct address is always appropriate.

25e
LISTS

Consider the following sentence.

> A comfortable pack, sturdy boots, and a healthy respect for the power of nature—all are essential ingredients for a successful hike.

In the sentence above, the introductory list is summed up by the word *all*. After the list and before the main part of the sentence begins, we notice a distinct pause. A dash in this case appropriately reflects that pause. No other mark of punctuation would work in this sentence.

Interrupting Elements

Consider the following sentences.

> The officer, **who was in full-dress uniform,** saluted.

> I don't think that ethical questions **(whether religious or legal)** can be disregarded in this matter.

> Santa Fe—**the oldest capital city in the United States**—was founded in 1609.

> A few novels, **such as *Pride and Prejudice*,** are popular with all groups of readers.

> His car, **a convertible with racing stripes and a hood ornament,** looked out of place in our driveway.

> Owen Flanagan notes that to modern human beings, "the consensus is that the answer to the first question **[What is truth?]** is: truth is a property of sentences."

> The red sports car was, **in fact,** the least expensive car on the lot.

You will notice that some kind of **interruption** is present in all these sentences. As you can see, such an interruption can be punctuated in several different ways, depending on the nature of the pause intended by the writer and based on what the sentence is intended to say. Punctuation—or lack of it—sometimes determines whether a word or phrase actually is an interruption and thus quite literally changes the meaning of the sentence.

Interrupters cause a disruption in the natural flow of the sentence. Effective punctuation signals the extent and nature of the interruption for the benefit of the reader.

26a
NONESSENTIAL MODIFIERS

When a modifier is *not essential* to the meaning of the sentence, as in the sentences below, it is always spoken with a pause, and when the sentence is written, the modifier is set off by commas.

> George, **who was dressed in a gray-and-black uniform,** was almost invisible in the crowd.

> The beach, **its white sand glistening in the afternoon sun,** was deserted.

> Harvey, **an intensely inquisitive person,** will never give up until he knows the answers to all his questions.

In the following sentences, however, the interruptions "who was wearing a red shirt" and "who carry heavy packs" are *essential* to the reader's understanding. When you read the two sentences aloud, there are no pauses, as there are in the three sentences above.

> The man **who was wearing a red shirt** threw the tomato.

> Hikers **who carry heavy packs** walk very slowly.

Now look at the difference between the two sentences below.

1. My oldest brother, **Harvey,** is a pathological liar.
2. My brother **Harvey** is a pathological liar.

In sentence 1, the subject has already been identified specifically as "my oldest brother"; therefore, the name "Harvey" is not really essential to the meaning of the sentence. In sentence 2, however, since the subject is identified only as "my brother," we don't know for sure which brother the writer is referring to. As a result, the name "Harvey" is essential to the meaning of the sentence. Note, however, that if the writer had only one brother, then "Harvey" would be set off by commas since the name would be nonessential information. In other words, when you are deciding whether a modifier is essential and should be written as part of the main sentence, or nonessential and should be separated from the main sentence with punctuation, the determining factor is *meaning*: what the sentence *means* is what allows you to decide how to punctuate it.

CommonSense Guide

The Word *That*

The word *that* usually indicates that a modifier is essential and should not be set off by commas. In the sentence "I like apples that have green skins," the modifier "that have green skins" is essential to the meaning of the sentence. It is read aloud without a pause.

26b
NONESSENTIAL EXPLANATIONS AND COMMENTS

Consider the following sentences.

Education, **I'm sure you will agree,** is essential for career advancement.

Schools, **both elementary and secondary,** affect all of us profoundly.

In Anglo-Saxon society, *wergild* **(meaning literally "manprice")** was a payment exacted from someone who had killed another person.

In each of the preceding sentences, the comment set off by commas or parentheses is *not essential* to the meaning of the sentence. Each comment creates a slight break, a pause at the beginning and end of the element, that disrupts the flow of the sentence. The writer must decide which mark best signals the intent of the sentence.

26c
DRAMATIC BREAKS

Consider the effect the dashes have on the following sentences.

Spotted owls—**the unobtrusive birds that have caused such an uproar**—need old-growth forests for survival.

All bicycles—**road bikes, mountain bikes, and hybrids**—are great for exercise.

Education can empower—**and ennoble**—students who are serious.

As you can tell as you read, dashes highlight dramatic breaks in the flow of the sentence. The pause at each dash is about the same as the pause created by a comma, but the dash signals an emphasis in volume and dramatic presentation that a comma would not. Note that in the last example, the interruption is punctuated only because the writer chooses to highlight the phrase "and ennoble"; in some cases, the meaning the writer imparts to a phrase will determine whether to highlight it as an interruption or simply leave it unpunctuated as an integral part of the sentence.

26d
EXAMPLES AND ILLUSTRATIONS

Read the following sentences aloud.

My two passions, running and bicycling, take up quite a lot of time.

Many people—especially city dwellers—have had little contact with wilderness areas.

Many areas of electronics (for example, computer programming) have attracted large numbers of students recently.

In each example, the interrupting illustration or example causes us to pause as we read the sentence. The punctuation marks reflect the pauses as well as whether the writer thinks of the interruption as matter-of-fact, dramatic, or not of great consequence. (For a more complete discussion of the difference between commas, dashes, and parentheses, see Chapter 22.)

26e
REPETITIONS

Notice how the repeated word and its modifiers interrupt the flow of the following sentence.

His **beard**, a **beard** with gold and brown highlights, was certainly impressive.

Notice the following sentence, in contrast.

His beard with gold and brown highlights was certainly impressive.

Though we do not need to pause in the second sentence above, the inserted repetition "a beard" in the first sentence caused us to pause both before the repetition and after "with gold and brown highlights" as we read. In cases such as this, the interruption should be set off with punctuation.

26f
EDITORIAL INSERTIONS INTO QUOTED MATERIAL

Look at the following sentence.

> According to Margaret Mead, "She **[Ruth Benedict]** had written poetry and under a pseudonym began to publish some poems, but no one was allowed to see her writing."

The information inserted editorially in brackets clarifies the meaning of the quotation. The information contained in brackets is there only to clarify the information for the reader; it is not essential to the meaning of the sentence. Note that it is also permissible simply to omit the pronoun and replace it with the bracketed name that clarifies it—without using the ellipsis marks explained in Section 26g.

26g
OMISSIONS FROM QUOTED MATERIAL

Look at the two quotations that follow.

> Owen Flanagan writes, "Our kind of mental life must have appeared initially as a biological accident . . . and subsequently became a species characteristic because it conferred a survival advantage, and therefore a reproductive advantage, on those individuals who possessed it."

> Margaret Mead observes, "The whole method had developed out of the study of the broken cultures of tribes which had long since given up hunting buffalo. . . ."

Each **ellipsis** (three spaced periods) in these two sentences indicates that some words have been omitted from the quotation. If the omission occurs in the middle of the quotation, use three spaced periods. If the omission occurs at the end of the sentence, add a period immediately after the final word of the quotation, then three spaced periods. If you omit a line or more of poetry or a paragraph or more of prose, you may insert a single typed line of spaced periods.

26h
UNUSUAL WORD ORDER

Note the word order in the following sentence.

> The students, **in an effort to improve their test scores,** studied very diligently.

The element "in an effort to improve their test scores" causes an interruption in the normal flow of the sentence. You can hear the pause before "in" and after "scores."

There would have been no interruption had the sentence been written as follows.

> The students studied diligently **in an effort to improve their test scores.**

26i
TRANSITIONS

As you read the following sentences, notice how the transitions interrupt.

> She knows, **however,** that it will do no good.

> He regards this task, **nevertheless,** as an important part of the whole project.

> He thinks, **for example,** that we all owe him money.

The **transitional words** in the sentences above are set off by commas because they interrupt the flow and cause us to pause as we read. (When transitional connectives like *therefore, however, nevertheless, consequently, accordingly, moreover, furthermore, hence, thus, besides, indeed,* and *in fact* are used to create a compound sentence, you normally use a semicolon before the transitional word or phrase and a comma after it (see Section 24a).

26j
DIRECT ADDRESS

Consider how the commas are used in the following sentences.

> No, **George,** I don't want to do it that way.

> Good schools, **my friends,** are essential for the health of the community.

The words "George" and "my friends" interrupt the flow of the sentence. The commas setting off the direct address tell the reader that there is a pause before and after the direct address.

Concluding Elements

Some of the following sentences use internal punctuation.

Many poems contain graphic images that increase the reader's interest.

Well-conditioned athletes share several important characteristics: **dedication, perseverance, and discipline.**

She likes powerful cars—**cars that can pass anything else on the road.**

He likes her; he no longer sees her, **however.**

It's not going to freeze tonight, **is it?**

You can't do this to me, **Sylvan!**

Each example except the first has a **concluding element** that is set off from the rest of the sentence. The marks of punctuation (the comma, the dash, and the colon) indicate the natural pauses a reader makes before finishing the sentence.

27a
MODIFIERS

Look at the following sentences.

1. The store handled clothing sold on consignment.
2. The store handled used clothing, sold without regard for the current fashion.
3. They approached a river too wide to cross.
4. They approached the river, wide and turbulent.
5. A backpacker is wise to choose a campsite that is protected from the wind.
6. Joe loves to fish, which his family tolerates.

In sentence 1, the modifier "sold on consignment" is necessary so that the reader can understand the kind of clothing that is meant. As a result, the modifier is not set off by commas. In sentence 2, the word "used" modifies "clothing" enough so that the modifier "sold without regard for current fashion" is *not essential* to the meaning of the sentence.

In sentences 3 and 4, the word "river" is modified by the phrase following it. In sentence 3, "too wide to cross" adds *essential* information by specifying which river. In sentence 4, "wide and turbulent" is not essential to the meaning of the sentence because the river has already been identified. Consequently, the comma is necessary to set the modifier off from the rest of the sentence. Notice that the words *the* and *an* preceding the word *river* tell the reader how specific the reference is.

In sentence 5, the final modifier "that is protected from the wind" is *essential* to the main idea of the sentence since it limits the number of possible campsites to those that are protected by the wind. The modifier cannot be left out, so the comma is not needed. To say "A backpacker is wise to choose a campsite" has an entirely different meaning. In sentence 6, the final modifier "which his family tolerates" is not essential to the main idea of the sentence, so "Joe loves to fish" is followed by a comma.

What is the general principle to be derived from these examples? Simply this: When you are unsure about whether to set off a final modifier from the rest of the sentence, read the sentence aloud in a speaking voice. Punctuate pauses, and do not use internal punctuation in sentences without pauses.

27b
EXPLANATIONS, LISTS, AND EXAMPLES

The following sentences include short examples or lists.

He had one overwhelming obsession: **to make the dean's list**.

A diligent writer uses several kinds of desk references: **a dictionary, a handbook, and a thesaurus**.

It is beneficial to engage in an aerobic activity**, such as jogging.**

In the first two sentences, the explanation and the list follow a colon. In the last sentence, an example follows the comma. You probably noticed, if you read the sentences aloud, that the colons required a longer pause than the commas did.

When you have questions about punctuating final lists, decide whether you want a long pause before the list or just a slight break (usually if there are only a few examples). If you are trying to set off the list dramatically, use a dash as the separating mark of punctuation.

27c
REPETITIONS

A word repeated at the end of the sentence is typically set off by a comma, along with any modifiers, as in the following example.

She felt panicky in the **crowd**, a large **crowd** of discourteous shoppers.

27d
TRANSITIONS

In the following sentence, the final transition "after all" seems to be almost an afterthought.

> We expect immediate results, **after all.**

Notice the definite pause after "results." We would not read the sentence without the pause: "We expect immediate results after all."

27e
ECHO QUESTIONS

In the next sentence, notice the natural pause following the initial statement and before the echo question at the end of the sentence.

> They are going, **aren't they?**

Echo questions are always set off from the main part of the sentence.

27f
DIRECT ADDRESS

Notice how direct address is punctuated in the following sentences.

> You can't go in there, **Fran.**

> Is this your car, **sir?**

Like direct addresses that introduce and interrupt, these concluding direct addresses need a comma to indicate the pause.

CHAPTER
28

Clarifying Elements

In the following sentences, commas are needed to clarify meaning.

> I want a double espresso, not a single.

> Beagles are howlers, whereas collies are barkers.

I could go play bridge, though I'd rather not.

Dogs that can, run loose in the neighborhood.

The commas either signal contrasts or separate sentence parts to prevent misreading.

28a
CONTRASTS

Each of the following sentences has a contrast indicated by a comma.

The tailpipe, not the muffler, is the problem.

The green peppers are mild, the red ones hot.

He has the skill, although he never uses it.

We naturally pause in speaking when we use a construction that contradicts what we just said; it is conventional to punctuate written sentences to reflect those pauses.

28a.1 Contrasts with and without *Not*

In the sentences below, the commas indicate a pause because a contrast has been introduced.

His brother, not his wife, is more concerned.

The summers are mild, the winters harsh.

In the first sentence, the contrast is indicated by the use of the word *not*. In the second, the contrast is created by the elements themselves. Note that if the last sentence were longer, the comma might be considered a comma splice; always use the balanced contrast structure sparingly.

28a.2 Contrasts with *Though, Although, Whereas, Whether, No Matter How*

Notice the following sentences.

He enjoyed the work, **though** it was difficult.

She was cold, **whereas** everyone else was comfortable.

She could not complete the project, **however** hard she tried.

In each sentence, a pause, indicated by a comma, precedes the word that sets up the contrast: *though, whereas,* or *however*. Notice that *however* in this case means "no matter how." When *however* serves as a connective in a compound construction or as a transition, it is punctuated differently (see Sections 24a, 26i, and 27d).

28b NECESSARY SEPARATIONS

Take a look at the commas in the following sentences.

Hikers who want to see birds, walk very slowly.

Years before, he had begun a journal.

"Who want to see birds" adds essential information to the first sentence. Based on the principles discussed in Section 26a, a comma would seem to be unnecessary; however, because a reader could conceivably think, at least momentarily, that the sentence means "Birds walk very slowly," a comma is necessary to prevent misreading. The second sentence illustrates a similar case. In general, you should insert commas to prevent misreading.

28c UNNECESSARY SEPARATIONS

Note the incorrect punctuation in the following sentences.

1. The cowboy dressed in boots and chaps, was ready for work rounding up cattle.
2. She smiled as she looked at him, and then turned to leave.
3. He said that he would show up on time tomorrow, and that he would make up everything he does not finish today.
4. We were pleased to have him join us, because we felt that he would fit into the organization well.
5. The mayor's car is more expensive, than either mine or his.
6. Celebrities such as, actors enjoy special privileges.
7. She confronted the problem in a way, she had never confronted anything before.

8. He asked the question "What do I do?", before he left.

9. The birds, (jays and sparrows) flocked to the feeder.

10. They locked the car, and, then went in the store.

11. His main objectives were: to finish the marathon and to have fun doing it.

Internal punctuation is unnecessary in the preceding sentences. You may have an inclination to pause where some of these marks are when reading the sentences aloud (for instance, at the colon in sentence 11 and at the comma after "such as" in sentence 6). However, these are places where it is not conventional to punctuate.

7

Usage

29

Verb Forms

You may have noticed that when you write, some words change form. Look at each of the following sentences. Notice how related ideas are communicated by different forms of the verb *blow*.

Storms often **blow** boats off course.

The wind **blows** many boats off course.

The wind is **blowing** our boat off course.

The wind **blew** her boat off course.

The wind has **blown** her boat off course.

The wind will **blow** her boat off course.

The basic form of the word is *blow*. It tells us about an *action*, what is happening to something or what something is doing at the present time. These words, called **verbs**, change *form* (that is, sound and spelling) to indicate that the action is taking place at a different time. For an action that has taken place in the past, we change the form of *blow* to *blew*. For an action that has already been completed, we change *blow* to *blown* and combine it with either *have*, *has*, or *had*. To show that an action is a continuing one, we add *-ing* to the basic form of the verb and combine it with a form of the verb *be* (*am*, *is*, *are*, *was*, *were*). To indicate that the action will take place in the future, we combine the basic form of *blow* with *shall* or *will*.

CommonSense Observation

The Word *Shall*

Except in legal writing and when it appears at the beginning of a question (as in "Shall I go with you?"), *shall* is hardly ever used in American English.

29a
REGULAR VERB FORMS

How would you change the forms of the following verbs to show that action took place in the past?

talk, ask, walk, enter, smile, frown, laugh

You would indicate that action took place in the past by adding *-d* or *-ed* to each word.

talked, asked, walked, entered, smiled, frowned, laughed

A great many verbs change form from present to past in this way. The word *talk* can be used as a verb to show the action of speaking in the present time. To indicate that the action occurred in the past, we simply add *-ed* to the end of the word to create *talked*. To show a completed action, we add to *talked* the helping verb *has* or *had* to create *has talked* or *had talked*.

29b
IRREGULAR VERB FORMS

With other verbs we show a change in the time of action by changing the form of the entire word, as in *drink, drank, drunk*. *Drink* indicates that the action takes place in the present as in the sentence "I drink milk every day." To show that the action has taken place in the past, we change the spelling of the word to *drank*, as in the sentence "I drank three glasses of milk yesterday." To indicate that an action has been completed, we change the spelling to *drunk*, as in the sentence "I had drunk more milk than usual."

Most of us readily recognize and use, without really thinking about it, many irregular verb forms like *fly, flew, flown* or *go, went, gone*. But a few of them create problems, especially the verbs *lie* (*lie, lay, lain*) and *lay* (*lay, laid, laid*); *sit* (*sit, sat, sat*) and *set* (*set, set, set*); and *rise* (*rise, rose, risen*) and *raise* (*raise, raised, raised*). The following explanations illustrate the verbs' forms in standard English. Read carefully to see if your own language usages coincide with the generally used standard forms.

29b.1 *Lie* and *Lay*

Look at how the various forms of the two verbs *lie* and *lay* are used below.

I **lie** in the sun every day.

I always **lay** the mail on the table.

She **lay** in the sun.

She **laid** the mail on the table.

She has **lain** in the sun every day since we arrived.

She has **laid** the mail on the table.

In the first sentence of each pair above, you can see that *lie, lay,* and *lain* mean that somebody or something is situated somewhere, that somebody or something was situated somewhere, or that somebody or something has been situated somewhere, respectively. In the second sentence of each pair, the words *lay, laid,* and *laid* mean that somebody is putting or placing an object somewhere, that somebody put or placed an object somewhere, or that somebody has put or placed an object somewhere.

29b.2 *Sit* and *Set*

Consider how the various forms of *sit* and *set* are used in the following sentences.

I **sit** on the porch every day.

I always **set** the drink on the table.

I **sat** on the porch yesterday.

I **set** the drink on the table yesterday.

I have **sat** on the porch before.

I have **set** the drink there before.

In the first sentence of each pair above, the words *sit, sat,* and *sat* mean that someone is seated, that someone was seated, or someone has been seated, respectively. In the second sentence of each pair, the words *set, set,* and *set* mean that something is being put or placed, that something was put or placed, or that something has been put or placed.

29b.3 *Rise* and *Raise*

Notice how the various forms of *rise* and *raise* are used in the following sentences.

I **rise** at five every morning.

I **raise** the flag at six.

I **rose** today at four.

I **raised** the flag at six.

I have **risen** every day at five for ten years.

I have **raised** that window often.

In the first sentence of each pair above, the words *rise, rose,* and *risen* mean that someone or something gets up or goes up, that someone or something got up or went up, or that someone or something has gotten up or has gone up, respectively. In the second sentence of each pair, the words *raise, raised,* and *raised* mean that someone lifts something or makes it go up, that someone lifted something or made it go up, or that someone has lifted something or has made it go up.

29b.4 Other Troublesome Irregular Verbs

Most other irregular verbs are not nearly as confusing, although some of the standard forms may seem odd enough so that most people avoid using them. Take for instance *swim, swam, swum.* Instead of saying "I have swum all day," most people would say "I have been swimming all day" or "I swam all day."

Other verbs sometimes create questions when they are used to indicate that the action has taken place in the past. For example, most people would say "The balloon burst." Although some might say "The balloon bursted" or "The balloon busted," most would think of those usages as nonstandard. The construction "I seen the airplane crash," though used by some people, would also be considered nonstandard.

Some verbs have two generally accepted forms when they are used to show that action has taken place in the past.

dived *or* dove	sank *or* sunk
dreamed *or* dreamt	thrived *or* throve
lighted *or* lit	waked *or* woke

The verbs *drag, drown,* and *spoke* create problems for some speakers when they are used with the helping verbs *have* or *had.*

have dragged	*not*	have drug
have drowned	*not*	have drownded
have spoken	*not*	have spoke

The verbs *got* and *prove* can be written two ways when they are used with the helping verbs *have* and *had.*

have gotten	*or*	have got
have proved	*or*	have proven

Some verbs have two different forms that have two different meanings.

We **hung** the picture.

Antigone **hanged** herself.

The crystal **shone** in the sunlight.

We **shined** our shoes.

29c
VERB FORMS INDICATING SOMETHING CONJECTURAL OR DESIRABLE

Notice how the boldfaced verbs function in the following sentences.

If I **were** you, I would make an effort to change.

I wish I **were** on vacation now.

He requested that everyone **be** quiet.

He asked that we **explain** what we mean.

In each case, the verb indicates an action contrary to fact or something desirable. In such instances, we use the basic form of the verb (without the -s): *have* instead of *has*, *be* or *were* instead of *am*, *is*, *are*, or *was*.

29c.1 Something Contrary to Fact

The following sentences express an idea that is contrary to fact.

If Jennifer **were** feeling well, she would be playing outside. [Jennifer is not feeling well.]

Last year, the lawn looked as if it **weren't** going to survive. [But it did survive.]

If Harvey **were** here, he would create a disturbance. [But he isn't here.]

In each sentence the selection of the verb form *were* indicates that we are saying something contrary to fact. The word *if* is usually an indicator that we need a different form of the verb. However, not all word groups beginning with *if* express a condition contrary to fact. Consider the following sentence.

> If the test flight **is** successful, it will be a great achievement.

The sentence does not imply that the test flight is going to be unsuccessful. It merely states that the condition, if met, will indicate success.

29c.2 Something Desirable

When we are expressing something desirable, we use the word *were* instead of *was* after the word *wish*. Instead of writing "I wish I was on vacation now," we write "I wish I were on vacation now" to indicate something desirable that is not a fact.

After words such as *ask, demand, insist, order, recommend, request, require, suggest,* and *urge,* we use the basic form of the verb (*be, have, make, explain*) rather than the form ending in *-s* (*is, has, makes, explains*). We would write "He requested that everyone be quiet," rather than "He requested that everyone is quiet." The sense of the sentence is "Everyone should be quiet" (something desirable), so if the word *should* is omitted, the basic form of the verb *be* carries that meaning.

CommonSense Observation

"If I Be ..."

Except in obvious cases, like those cited above, this verb form used to indicate matters contrary to fact or something desirable has all but disappeared from speech and is diminishing in written works. No one today would consider using an older, outdated construction like this: "If I be a brute for suggesting it, she should object now." Rather, modern speakers of English would replace the verb *be* with *am* and write, "If I am a brute for suggesting it, she should object now."

29d
VERB FORMS USED WITH HELPING VERBS

In English we often change the meanings of verbs by combining them with **helping verbs**, forms of the verbs *be, have, can, may, shall, will,* and *do.* Depending on the meaning you want to convey, you will need to pay attention to the form of the main verb you use with these helping verbs.

29d.1 To Show Continuing Action

To show continuing action, use forms of the verb *be* (*am, is, are, was, were, be,* or *been*) followed by a main verb with the ending *-ing*. Notice how the forms of the main verb are combined with the helping verbs in the following sentences.

> I **am writing** a paper for my history class.
>
> > *not*
>
> I *am write* a paper for my history class.

> He **was working** diligently on the project.
>
> > *not*
>
> He *was work* diligently on the project.

When the helping verb *be* is used with a main verb ending in *-ing*, it must be preceded by *can, could, may, might, must, shall, should, will,* or *would,* as in the sentence "Frederick will be going to the library tomorrow." When the helping verb *been* is used with a main verb ending in *-ing*, it must be preceded by *have, has,* or *have,* as in the sentence "Gillian has been making progress on her paper."

Some verbs, especially those that express a condition or a mental activity rather than an action, cannot be used as a main verb in the *-ing* form. For example, we would not write "The box is containing a present for her" or "The student is belonging to the club." Other verbs of this type are *appear, believe, hear, know, like, need, see, seem, taste, understand,* and *want.*

29d.2 To Show Completed Action

To show a completed action, use forms of the verb *have* (*have, has,* and *had*) followed by a main verb ending in *-ed, -d, -en, -n,* or *-t.* Notice how the main verbs are combined with the helping verbs in the following sentences.

> I **have talked** to him.
>
> > *not*
>
> I *have talk* to him.

> He **had left** the room before we got there.
>
> > *not*
>
> He *had leave* the room before we got there.

29d.3 To Show That the Subject Receives the Action of the Verb

To show that the subject, rather than an object, receives the action of the verb, use forms of the verb *be* (*am, is, are, was, were, be,* or *been*) followed by a main verb with the ending *-ed, -d, -en, -n,* or *-t.* Notice how the main verbs are combined with the helping verbs in the following sentences.

The laws of motion **were formulated** by Sir Isaac Newton.

not

The laws of motion *were formulate* by Sir Isaac Newton.

Radium **was discovered** by Marie Curie.

not

Radium *was discover* by Marie Curie.

He **was conditioned** to respond in that way.

not

He *was condition* to respond in that way.

When the helping verbs *be, being,* or *been* are used, they must be preceded by another helping verb. *Be* must be preceded by some form of the helping verbs *can, may, shall,* or *will,* as in the sentence "They should be helped by the government." *Being* must be preceded by a form of the verb *be,* as in the sentence "They were being helped by some friends." *Been* must be preceded by a form of the verb *have,* as in the sentence "They have been sick for a month."

Some verbs, including *die, fall, happen, occur,* and *sleep,* cannot be written with *-ed, -d, -en, -n,* or *-t* endings when they are used with any form of the helping verb *be.* You cannot write a sentence such as "The wreck was happened in front of the school."

29d.4 To Show Future Action

To show a future action, use the verb *shall, will, should,* or *would* followed by the basic form of the main verb. Notice how the main verb is combined with the helping verb in the following sentences.

My brother **will arrive** at nine o'clock.

not

My brother *will arrives* at nine o'clock.

The concert **could begin** at ten.

> *not*

The concert *could began* at ten.

The airplane **should arrive** on time.

> *not*

The airplane *should arriving* on time.

29d.5 To Show Potential Action

To show a potential action, use the verb *may, might, can,* or *could* followed by the basic form of the main verb. Notice how the main verb is combined with the helping verb in the following sentences.

He **could buy** a new printer.

> *not*

He *could bought* a new printer.

He **might take** a trip next week.

> *not*

He *might takes* a trip next week.

29d.6 To Create an Emphatic Form

To show that an action is emphatic, use the verb *do, does,* or *did* followed by the basic form of the main verb. Notice how the main verb is combined with the helping verb in each of the following sentences.

Did he **make** a good grade on the test?

> *not*

Did he *makes* a good grade on the test?

She **does** not **want** to take the chance.

> *not*

She *does* not *wants* to take the chance.

He **does think** he can do it.

> *not*

He *does thinks* he can do it.

29e
TWO- AND THREE-WORD VERBS

Some verbs combine with other words such as *across, after, away, forward, in, into, on, off, up,* and *with*. When that happens, the meaning of the verb changes. Such combinations can create problems in placing objects and modifiers. Some of the combinations can be separated and others cannot.

> While hiking in the woods, they **came across** a dead horse. [not *came* a dead horse *across*]
>
> He **ran into** a post. [not *ran* a post *into*]
>
> The dog **ran into** the store. [not *ran* the store *into*]
>
> She **took off** her shoes. [also **took** her shoes **off**]
>
> The plane **took off** in a snowstorm. [not *took* in a snowstorm *off*]
>
> He will **put up with** anything. [not *put* anything *up with* or *put up* anything *with*]

29f
USES OF THE BASIC FORM OF VERBS

In each sentence below, the verb indicates that the action is taking place at the present time.

> They **live** together in a very nice house.
>
> Harvey **lives** in a tent on the outskirts of town.

Because of the principle of subject-verb agreement (see Chapter 30), you will need to add an *-s* to the basic form of the verb when a single person, place, thing, or idea is the subject, as in the second sentence.

There are other kinds of actions that require the basic form of the verb, even though they do not occur at the present time. Notice the verbs in the following sentences.

1. In *Out of Africa*, Isak Dinesen **tells** of her struggles to understand Africa and its inhabitants.
2. In the movie *Out of Africa*, Meryl Streep **plays** the part of Isak Dinesen.
3. The problem with waste from nuclear reactors **is** that it **is** radioactive and **remains** that way for years.
4. She **takes** a two-mile walk every morning.

Even though the events referred to in these four sentences do not take place in the present, they are written with the basic verb form. Sentences 1 and 2 suggest that the action of a written or recorded work is taking place in the present. Sentence 3 shows that information accepted as true according to current science or popular wisdom is thought of in the present. Sentence 4 illustrates that habitual actions are thought of in the present.

Subject-Verb Agreement

As you read the following sentences, notice how the boldfaced words are spelled.

The **bird sings** every day.

The **birds sing** every day.

In these two examples, nothing differs but the spelling of four words: *bird*, *birds*, *sing*, *sings*. You will notice that when the word *bird* changes to *birds*, the word *sings* changes to *sing*. This principle of language use is called **subject-verb agreement**—subjects and verbs agree in number. In the first sentence, the subject *bird* is singular and must have a singular verb, *sings*. Similarly, in the second sentence, the plural subject *birds*, must have a plural verb, *sing*. For verbs in the present tense, we add an *-s* when they must agree with a singular subject and delete the *-s* when they must agree with a plural subject.

Social dialects in many parts of the country do not follow this general rule. In some dialects, final consonant sounds remain unspoken; for example, *road* and *row* are pronounced almost identically. In particular, these dialects drop final *s* sounds, so that such words as *student* and *students*, *computer* and *computers* sound alike. So do *drive* and *drives*, *help* and *helps*. Therefore, in these dialects, the following pairs of sentences sound alike.

The **student drives** to school.

The **students drive** to school.

The **computer builds** academic skills.

The **computers build** academic skills.

Read these pairs of sentences out loud, the way you would speak them to friends. Do you pronounce them alike? If you do—or if you have to remember to sound out each final *-s*—then you are not likely to make subjects and verbs agree easily when you write because you do not naturally do so when you speak. To write standard English, you will have to treat this issue as if you were learning a foreign language, for in fact you will have to learn a *new* dialect.

Of course, doing this remains a matter of choice; people using regional and social dialects communicate well within their own language communities. But when you want to reach out to the broader community, it may be wisest to shift dialects.

Those whose native dialect closely resembles Standard American English almost always make subjects and verbs agree without even thinking about it. But confusion can occur when plural nouns do not end in *-s*, when singular subjects do, and when the relationship between subject and verb is unclear.

30a
WHEN THE SUBJECT IS OBSCURED BY OTHER WORDS OR PHRASES

The following sentences illustrate constructions that can be confusing because other words and phrases obscure the real subject.

1. A **street** that winds through several different neighborhoods and subdivisions **is** hard to find sometimes.
2. **Jane**, along with her friends, **is** going to the beach.
3. **That** he has delayed his departure **solves** the problem for the present.

In sentence 1, the subject *street* is singular and so requires the singular verb *is*. In writing a sentence like that, you might be tempted to use the plural verb *are* because it follows immediately after the plural noun *subdivisions*.

In sentence 2, the phrase "along with her friends" seems to be part of the subject, but it is not. It is simply an intervening expression. The words *accompanied by*, *along with*, *as well as*, *in addition to*, *including*, and *together with* introduce such phrases.

In sentence 3, the entire word group "That he has delayed his departure" is the subject of the verb. When an entire word group is the subject, it is singular.

30b
WITH TWO OR MORE WORDS JOINED BY *AND*, *OR*, OR *NOR*

In the following sentences, notice the difference in how subjects and verbs agree.

Jane *and* Martha **ride** to work together.

Either Jane *or* Martha **picks** Mary up every day.

In the first sentence, the plural verb *ride,* agrees with the plural compound subject, *Jane and Martha*. A subject of two words connected by *and* requires a plural verb. In the second sentence, the singular verb *picks* agrees with the singular subject, *Jane or Martha*. A subject of two words connected by *or* requires a singular verb if both words are singular. If one of the words in the subject is singular and one is plural, then the verb should agree with the word closest to it, as in the example below.

Either **traffic** *or* some unexpected **interruptions have** caused him to be late.

Traffic is singular and *interruptions* is plural. Since *interruptions* is the word closest, a plural verb, *have*, is required.

Notice the following example.

My friend and collaborator **has** helped me solve many difficult questions.

Even though the subject is connected by *and*, it is still considered singular and so takes a singular verb because the friend and the collaborator are the same person.

30c
WHEN SUBJECTS REFER TO GROUPS AND TOTAL UNITS

Notice the boldfaced verbs in the following sentences.

The **team is** warming up before the game starts.

The **number** of happy customers **is** a positive sign.

Forty **dollars is** all I have.

Even though each of the nouns *team, number,* and *dollars* refers to more than one item, they are treated as singular subjects. In such sentences, these subjects are singular because they refer to the group as a single unit rather than to the members of the group. You will discover just how this particular concept of subject-verb agreement works as you read the following sections.

30c.1 When Subjects Refer to Groups

Consider the way the boldfaced words are used in the following sentences.

The **jury is** deliberating.

The **jury were** seated around the table.

In the first sentence, we think of the jury as a group, and so *jury* is singular. In the second sentence, we are thinking of the individual members of the group, and so *jury* is plural. The following words require that you make the same kind of determination when you use them in a sentence: *administration, army, audience, class, committee, crowd, family, group, orchestra, team,* and *faculty.*

30c.2 When the Subject Is the Word *Number*

The word *number* is sometimes singular and sometimes plural.

The **number** of unclaimed strays **is** increasing.

A **number** like seven **is** sometimes seen as a symbol.

A **number** of students **are** waiting in the lab.

Number is always singular if the word *the* precedes it. When *number* is preceded by the word *a,* however, it is singular if it refers to the total unit and plural if it refers to the individual parts of the group.

30c.3 When the Subject Is an Expression of Money, Time, or Measurement

Expressions of time, money, and measurement are usually considered to be singular even though they have plural forms. They can be either singular or plural, however, depending on whether they refer to the total unit or to the individual members of the group.

Three hundred dollars **is** a lot of money to me.

Three hundred-dollar bills **are** missing.

Three years **is** a long time to wait.

Three years **have** passed.

Three hundred miles **is** a long way to go.

Three hundred miles **are** still ahead of us.

30d
WITH SINGULAR NOUNS ENDING IN -*S*

In the three examples below, the words *economics*, *mumps*, and *news* end in -*s*, but they are actually singular and require the singular verb *is*.

Economics **is** sometimes a depressing study.

Mumps **is** more serious for adults than it is for children.

The news **is** good.

Other nouns that are usually singular include *aerobics*, *aeronautics*, *mathematics*, and *physics*.

When words like *acoustics*, *politics*, and *statistics* are used as subjects, whether they are singular or plural will depend on the sense of the sentence.

1. Acoustics **is** an interesting area of study.
2. The acoustics in this place **are** terrible.
3. Politics **is** a complex subject.
4. His politics **are** off the wall.
5. Statistics **is** more difficult than algebra.
6. These statistics **are** unreliable.

In sentences 1, 3, and 5, the words are singular because they refer to a field of study. In sentence 2, *acoustics* refers to the effect of sound in a closed place and so is plural. In sentence 4, *politics* refers to beliefs and is consequently plural. Finally, in sentence 6, *statistics* refers to statistical data and is plural.

30e
WITH WORDS LIKE *ALL, EVERYONE, FEW, MANY, NOBODY,* AND *SOMEONE*

The subjects in the following sentences agree with their verbs.

Another is going instead.

Many are interested in the subject.

Each of the members **is** here.

Anyone is welcome to come along.

Several are interested in attending.

Some of these pronouns are singular and others are plural.

Singular

> another, any, anybody, anything, anyone, each, each one, either, everybody, everything, everyone, much, neither, nobody, no one, nothing, none, one, somebody, something, someone, such, whoever, whatever, whichever

Plural

> all, both, few, many, most, others, several, some

The words that are singular always take a singular verb. The words that are plural always take a plural verb.

30f
AFTER *WHO, WHICH,* AND *THAT*

Who, which, and *that* are neither singular nor plural. Notice in the following sentences how the number of these words is determined.

He knows the **man** *who* **is** following him.

He knows the **men** *who* **are** following him.

The **conclusion,** *which* **is** now being challenged, **is** controversial.

The **conclusions,** *which* **are** now being challenged, **are** controversial.

The **car** *that* **is** parked in the driveway **is** mine.

The **cars** *that* **are** parked in the driveway **are** mine.

In the first sentence of each pair, *who, which,* and *that* are singular because they are referring to the singular words *man, conclusion,* and *car* and so require the singular verb *is.* In the second sentence of each pair, *who, which,* and *that* are plural because they refer to the plural words *men, conclusions,* and *cars* and so require the plural verb *are.*

30g
WHEN THE SUBJECT FOLLOWS THE VERB

The subjects of the following sentences do not appear in the normal position. Notice how word order affects agreement between subjects and verbs.

There **are** three **birds** sitting on the fence.

There **is** a **bird** sitting on the fence.

Here **come members** of the band.

Here **comes** the **band**.

In the sentences above, even though *there* and *here* are in a position normally occupied by a subject, they are not the subjects of the sentences. The subjects—*birds, bird, members,* and *band*—actually come after the verb.

30h
WITH TITLES AND WORDS USED AS WORDS

Consider how subject-verb agreement works in the following sentences.

Riders of the Purple Sage **is** a novel by Zane Grey.

Rats **is** an expression of disgust.

Titles and words used as words are regarded as singular and so take singular verbs.

Pronoun Reference

As you read the following sentences, notice what the boldfaced words refer to.

If Jim comes, you'll have to give **him** a ride.

Jane said that **she** would consider the proposal.

In the first sentence, the pronoun *him* refers to the noun *Jim*, and in the second sentence, the pronoun *she* refers to the noun *Jane*. Pronouns always refer to some other word, usually a word in the same sentence or in a previous, closely related sentence. They do not refer to general ideas or to whole sentences.

31a
CONFUSING REFERENCE

In the sentence below, notice how the italicized word is used. Which person is it referring to?

When Jack took Bill to school, I had to give *him* directions.

You can see that there is confusion about which person *him* refers to, Jack or Bill. The sentence could have either of the following two meanings.

I gave Jack directions when he took Bill to school.

or

I gave Bill directions when Jack took him to school.

We can't know for sure. When you are editing your work, it is important that you make sure the reader can tell what word the pronoun refers to.

31b
REFERENCE TO MODIFIERS

In the following sentence, what does the word *it* refer to?

I was late getting to the bus station, but I caught *it* anyway.

It appears to refer to the bus station, but if that is so, the statement means "I caught the bus station." Obviously, the writer didn't mean to say that. The writer meant to say that he or she caught the bus, not the bus station. The word *bus* is not the name of a vehicle you can catch, but a modifier of the word *station*, telling us what kind of station. The sentence should be reworded to make the reference clear.

I was late getting to the bus station, but I caught the bus anyway.

or

I caught the bus even though I was late getting to the station.

31c
VAGUE *THIS*, *THAT*, AND *WHICH*

As you read the following examples, pay special attention to the use of the words *this*, *that*, and *which*.

1. I knew he was not doing his job, but my supervisor seemed to be unaware of *this*.
2. Juan was late and didn't even apologize. *That* makes me angry.
3. George was late in returning the manuscript to me and now some of the pages are missing, *which* creates a huge problem.

In sentence 1, we cannot be sure whether the word *this* refers to the fact that the writer knew that a co-worker was not doing his job or to the fact that the co-worker was not doing his job. In sentence 2, it is not clear whether the word *that* refers to the fact that Juan was late or to the fact that Juan didn't apologize. Finally, in sentence 3, it is not clear whether the word *which* refers to George's returning the manuscript late or to the fact that some of the pages were missing. When you use *this*, *that*, and *which*, you will want to check to see that the reference is clear.

Sentence 1 could be reworded in one of the following ways.

I knew that he was not doing his job, but my supervisor seemed to be unaware of his behavior.

or

I knew that he was not doing his job, but my supervisor seemed to be unaware that I knew.

Sentence 2 could be reworded in one of the following ways.

That Juan was late makes me angry. He didn't even apologize.

or

Juan was late. It makes me angry that he didn't even apologize.

Sentence 3 could be reworded in one of the following ways.

That George was late in returning the manuscript to me creates a huge problem. Some of the pages were even missing.

or

George was late in returning the manuscript to me. That some of the pages were missing creates a huge problem.

? 31d
USE OF *WHO*, *WHICH*, AND *THAT*

Notice how the words *who, which,* and *that* are used in the following sentences.

1. Students **who** budget their time wisely will do well in school.
2. My watch, **which** I bought while on vacation, reminds me of all the places we visited.
3. The watch **that** I really want is too expensive.
4. The man **that** I met at church is very nice.
5. Aesop's fable about the tortoise and the hare is a story **whose** moral we all know very well.

You will notice that the choice of *who, which,* or *that* in a sentence depends on the person or thing being referred to. *Who* refers to people; *which* refers to things; and *that* refers either to people or to things.

In sentence 1, you will notice that *who* refers to *students*. In sentence 2, *which* refers to *watch,* a thing. It would certainly sound odd to use *which* to refer to a person: "The man which owns the house is not very nice." In sentences 3 and 4, you can see that the word *that* can be used to refer to either a thing or a person. Finally, even though the word *whose,* the possessive form of *who,* is normally used to refer to a person, you can see that in sentences it is used to refer to a thing. The use of *which* in the sentence would be a bit awkward: "Aesop's fable of the tortoise and the hare is a story the moral of which we all know very well."

? 31e
VAGUE *THEY*, *IT*, AND *YOU*

Notice how the words *they, it,* and *you* are used in the following sentences.

They say we'll have rain this week.

It says on the sign that we will have to wait here.

You couldn't change your social status very much in the Middle Ages.

In the sentences above, you can see that *they, it,* and *you* are not referring to anybody or anything in particular. In sentences like these, such vagueness can create a moment of uncertainty in the reader. A better strategy would be to replace the vague pronouns with more exact nouns, as in the following sentences.

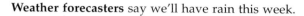

Weather forecasters say we'll have rain this week.

The sign says that we will have to wait here.

People couldn't change their social status very much in the Middle Ages.

Note: The word *you* is most appropriately used to mean "you, the reader."

31f
WHEN *IT* IS USED IN TWO DIFFERENT WAYS IN THE SAME SENTENCE

As you read the following sentence, notice that the word *it* is used in two different ways.

> Her bicycle is her most valuable possession, and she always chains *it* up when she leaves *it* because *it* is wise to be careful.

The first two times, *it* refers to the bicycle, and the third time, it does not. Although the expression "it is wise to be careful" is certainly a clear statement, the switch in the usage of *it* creates some confusion. The sentence would be clearer if it were worded as follows:

> Her bicycle is her most valuable possession, and she always chains **it** up when she leaves **it** because she is a very careful person.

31g
AGREEMENT OF PRONOUNS WITH WORDS THEY REFER TO

Notice the connection between the two boldfaced words in the following sentence.

> **Mary** went to **her** room.

Her refers to *Mary*. Notice that the use of *her* is consistent with how *Mary* is used. Both *her* and *Mary* are singular, and both words refer to females.

31g.1 When Referring to a Word That Names a Group

In the following sentences, observe how singular and plural references are used.

The **faculty** voiced **its** opinion.

The **faculty** worked in **their** offices.

The **team** worked hard at **their** tasks.

The **team** prepared for **its** ultimate test.

When pronouns refer to words like *faculty* and *team* that indicate a group, the sense of the sentence will determine whether the pronoun should be singular or plural. If the word indicates a group, the pronoun will be singular. If the word indicates the individual members of the group, the pronoun will be plural.

31g.2 When Referring to Words Joined by *And*, *Or*, or *Nor*

Notice what the pronouns *their*, *her*, and *his* are referring to in the following sentences.

1. Both Jane *and* Mary are taking **their** cars.
2. Either Jane *or* Mary is taking **her** car.
3. Neither the members of the team *nor* the coach has made **his** opinions known.
4. Neither the coach *nor* the members of the team have made **their** opinions known.

In sentence 1, *their*, a plural pronoun, is used because it refers to two people, Jane and Mary. In sentence 2, *her*, a singular pronoun, is used because the word *or* indicates that *her* is referring to either one of the two people, not both. In sentence 3, *his*, a singular pronoun, is used because it refers to the part of the compound subject closest to the pronoun. The same principle holds for sentence 4, but in this case the part of the compound subject closest to the pronoun is the word *members*, so a plural pronoun is required.

31g.3 When Referring to Words Like *All*, *Everyone*, *Few*, *Many*, *Nobody*, and *Someone*

Notice what the pronouns *their*, *his*, and *her* refer to in the following sentences.

1. **Few** will bring **their** own equipment.
2. **All** should bring **their** own equipment.

3. **Each** should make up **his or her** own mind.

4. **Anyone** who will bring **his or her** own equipment is welcome.

Some of these indefinite pronouns are plural and some are singular.

Singular

> another, any, anybody, anyone, anything, each, each one, either, everybody, everyone, everything, much, neither, nobody, no one, nothing, none, one, somebody, something, someone, such, whatever, whichever, whoever, whomever

Plural

> all, both, few, many, most, others, several, some

Traditional usage required that the singular, masculine personal pronoun *he* be used to refer to indefinite pronouns such as *everyone, everybody,* and *anybody.* So the "generic *he*" was, for many years, the accepted standard. Because of objections that using *he* to refer to all people is sexist, some writers in recent decades have advocated substituting the phrase *he or she* for the word *he* in such cases. (See Chapter 21 for additional discussion of the problem of sexist language.)

CommonSense Observation

Singular *They*

For centuries, most people have used the pronoun *they* in speech to refer to indefinite pronouns and to nouns like *person* and *student.* As a result, some authorities have suggested that this "singular *they*" be used instead of the "generic *he*" or the combination *he or she* (because the phrase is unwieldy after an initial use). Writers have done the same thing as speakers have, using the singular *they* with some regularity—except when teachers and editors have objected. It is clear that this singular *they* is an easy way to avoid sexist language and a reasonable alternative to the more cumbersome *he or she.* Whether this usage will ever be accepted as standard is debatable.

Noun and Pronoun Case

In the following sentences, you can see that the form of the pronouns used as subjects is *he* and *they*, while the form of the pronouns that follow the word *to* changes to *him* and *them*.

> **He** sent an extremely nasty letter to **them**.

> **They** sent a very cordial letter to **him**.

Pronouns have one form when they are used as the subject of a sentence and when they follow a verb like *is*. They use another form when they are used as the object of a verb; when they follow words like *at*, *by*, *of*, *on*, *to*, and *with*; and when they appear either immediately before or after the combination of *to* and a verb. They have yet a third form when they show possession. Nouns change form only when they show possession and when they are plural; they have the same form whether they are used as subjects or objects.

32a
WHEN USED AS A SUBJECT

Notice the form of the pronoun used as the subject of a verb in each of the following sentences.

> **She** wrote a wonderful report.

> **He** read the report very carefully.

> **They** read the report in its entirety.

> **Who** wrote that report?

> So Harvey is the one **who** wrote the report.

> Sarah will recommend **whoever** wrote that report.

The pronouns *I*, *we*, *you*, *he*, *she*, *it*, *they*, *who*, and *whoever* are used as subjects of sentences. The principle governing the choice of *who* in the sentences above is this: Ask what other pronouns would substitute for *who*. In each case above, the answer would be *he*, *she*, or *they* rather than *him*, *her*, or *them*. *Who* wrote the report? *He* wrote it.

32b
AFTER FORMS OF THE VERB *BE*

Which one of the following sentences sounds right to you?

It is I.

It is me.

According to traditional usage, "It is I" would be preferred. But in speech, we would usually opt for "It is me." The dilemma presented here illustrates the power of word order in English. Since we almost always expect the object form of a pronoun to come after a verb, "It is me" actually sounds more natural, although the sense of the sentence, because of the verb *is*, equates *I* with the subject of the sentence. To solve the problem, many writers avoid that construction in writing altogether. When you are confronted with such situations, it is perfectly acceptable simply to reword the sentence.

The following sentence actually sounds natural and conforms to the rules of traditional grammar.

Is this **who** I think it is?

32c
WHEN USED AS THE OBJECT OF A VERB

Notice the form of the pronouns used in the following examples.

She *recommended* **him** for the job.

She *congratulated* **them** on a job well done.

She *will recommend* **whomever** she wants to recommend.

Whom do you *prefer*?

The other speakers, **whom** John will introduce, are also well qualified to address this subject.

The words *me, us, you, him, her, it, them, whom,* and *whomever* are used as objects of verbs. What principle governs the choice of the word *whom* in these cases? Actually it's quite simple. Ask what person the *whom* is referring to. If the answer is *he, she,* or *they,* then *who* is appropriate. If the answer is *him, her,* or *them,* then *whom* is the appropriate word.

32d
AFTER WORDS LIKE *AT, BY, FROM, IN, OF, ON, TO,* AND *WITH*

Notice the form of the pronouns in the following examples.

He gave the report *to* **her**.

He made an impassioned plea *to* **them**.

To **whom** do you want this sent?

The words *me, us, him, her, them, whom,* and *whomever* are used after words like *at, by, from, in, of, on, to,* and *with*. When *whom* follows a word like *to*, it is clear that *whom* is the correct choice. *Who* would sound odd. We would not write "To who do you want this sent?"

32e
BEFORE AND AFTER THE COMBINATION OF *TO* AND A VERB

Notice the form of the boldfaced pronouns in the following sentences.

She thought **him** *to be* a good employee.

She planned *to see* **him**.

She thought the speaker *to be* **whom**?

When personal pronouns are used before or after the combination of *to* and a verb, they take the form *me, us, him, her, them, whom,* or *whomever*—the same form used when the pronoun is the object of a verb or when it follows a word like *to, from, of,* or *with*.

32f
AFTER *THAN* AND *AS*

Notice the form of the personal pronouns used in the following sentences.

She is more diligent *than* **he**.

He is not as industrious *as* **she**.

The meaning of the first sentence is "She is more diligent than he is." The pronoun *he* is being used as the subject of the implied verb *is*. The meaning of the second sentence is "He is not as industrious as she is." The pronoun *she* is being used as the subject of the implied verb *is*.

32g
WHEN USED TO SHOW POSSESSION

Consider the forms of the boldfaced words in the following sentences.

1. **Their** house was spacious.
2. **Its** house was cramped.
3. **His** house was modest.
4. **Her** house was enormous.
5. The **dogs'** house was tiny.
6. The **dog's** house was very large.
7. **James** and **Babette's** house was embarrassingly small.
8. **Fred's** and **Jane's** houses were both expensive.
9. **Dickens's** novels are widely admired.
10. My **boss's** house is surprisingly small.

In each case the spelling of the boldfaced noun or pronoun shows ownership. In sentences 1 through 4 you can see that the pronouns change form to show possession.

Sentences 5 through 10 illustrate the number of variables you will need to consider when you make nouns possessive. You show that a noun is possessive by adding an apostrophe plus -*s* to singular nouns and an apostrophe after the -*s* for plural nouns. In sentences 5 and 6, the placement of the apostrophe and the -*s* is critical to the meaning of the sentence, to let readers know how many dogs are involved. In sentence 5, the fact that the apostrophe is after the -*s* means that the house belongs to more than one dog. In sentence 6, the placement of the apostrophe before the -*s* indicates that the house belongs to one dog.

In sentence 7, the apostrophe plus -*s* after the second name in the compound indicates that James and Babette own the house together. In sentence 8, the apostrophe plus -*s* after each name shows that Fred owns one house and Jane owns another house.

Usage varies when a singular noun ends in -*s*. Sentence 9 could have been written with the word *Dickens'* instead of *Dickens's*. In sentence 10, the word *boss* seems to call for an extra syllable and so is written *boss's*. When a singular noun ends in -*s*, you can use an apostrophe plus -*s* or an apostrophe after the -*s*.

32h
BEFORE WORDS ENDING IN *-ING*

Notice the form of the boldfaced words in the following sentences.

His *leaving* town created a problem.

George's *leaving* town created a problem.

When a noun or a pronoun is positioned immediately before a word ending in *-ing*, it takes the same form as words that show ownership (see Section 32g).

32i
PRONOUNS ENDING IN *-SELF*

Notice how the italicized words are used in the following sentences.

Fred and *myself* went to town.

He asked Fred and *myself* to go with him.

Using pronouns that end in *-self* as either subjects or objects serves no particular function. People who create sentences like those above may do so because they are unsure whether to use *I* or *me*. The sentences would sound more normal if they were written as follows.

Fred and **I** went to town.

He asked Fred and **me** to go with him.

Words like *myself, himself, herself,* and *themselves* are used to emphasize or to refer back to a previously used pronoun. The following sentences illustrate their use.

I **myself** have never done that.

He injured **himself**.

In the first sentence, *myself* emphasizes the pronoun *I*. In the second sentence, *himself* is used as the object of the verb and refers back to the subject *he*.

33

Modifiers

Words used as **modifiers** change the meaning of other words or groups of words.

1. The **black** cat crossed the street.
2. The **careful** writer composed a balanced sentence.
3. **Three** birds sat on the fence.
4. The cat crossed the street **immediately**.
5. The writer composed the sentence **carefully**.

In sentence 1, the modifier *black* tells us which cat. In sentence 2, the modifier *careful* tells us what kind of writer. In sentence 3, the modifier *three* tells us how many birds. In sentence 4, the modifier *immediately* tells us when the cat crossed the street. In sentence 5, the modifier *carefully* tells us how the writer composed the sentence.

In the following sections, you will discover how to avoid problems with forms of modifiers and with the position of modifiers.

33a
PROBLEMS WITH FORMS OF MODIFIERS

Sometimes we have problems knowing when it is appropriate to use modifiers that end in *-ly*, *-er*, or *-est* and the modifiers *good* and *well*.

33a.1 Using *-ly* Forms

Notice the form of the italicized words in the following sentences.

This is *awful* kind of you.

She is *terrible* impatient.

That computer is *considerable* more expensive than mine.

That would *sure* be a big help.

I slept *fitful* last night.

In each of the preceding sentences, the modifier is in a form not generally used. Each one would sound better if the modifier ended with *-ly*.

This is **awfully** kind of you.

She is **terribly** impatient.

That computer is **considerably** more expensive than mine.

That would **surely** be a big help.

I slept **fitfully** last night.

33a.2 *Good* and *Well, Bad* and *Badly*

The following sentences make inappropriate use of the words *good, well, bad,* and *badly.*

He doesn't see *good.*

She plays the guitar *good.*

She feels *well.*

He plays the piano *bad.*

He feels *badly.*

The room smelled *badly.*

It is general practice to use *good* and *bad* to refer to a physical condition or to a quality, *well* and *badly* to refer to how something is done.

He doesn't see **well**.

She plays the guitar **well**.

She feels **good**. [Feeling *well* would suggest that her sense of touch is good.]

He plays the piano **badly**.

He feels **bad**. [Feeling *badly* would suggest that his sense of touch is defective.]

The room smelled **bad**. [Saying that the room smelled *badly* would imply that the room had a sense of smell.]

33a.3 Words Ending in *-er* and *-est*

Look at the italicized words in the following sentences.

He is *more good* than I am.

He is the *most laziest* person I have ever met.

In these sentences, a different form of the modifier would be preferred to avoid double modification.

He is **better** than I am.

He is the **laziest** person I have ever met.

Using *more* with a word that ends in *-er* and *most* with a word that ends in *-est* is redundant.

33b
PROBLEMS WITH NEGATIVES

Except in some spoken rural dialects of English (and in country and western music), we would not expect to see the following sentences.

I *don't* have *no* money.

I *can't never* find *nothing*.

To avoid double negatives, the sentences could be rewritten as follows.

I **don't** have **any** money.

I **can't ever** find **anything**.

Some constructions are considered to be double negatives even when there is only one negative word in the sentence. The words *hardly* and *scarcely* suggest a negative idea, so the word *not* is not used with them.

I *can't hardly* believe she is finally here.

I *can't scarcely* imagine what that would be like.

To avoid the double negatives, the sentences could be rewritten as follows.

I **can hardly** believe she is finally here.

I **can scarcely** imagine what that would be like.

33c
MISPLACED MODIFIERS

Notice how placement of the italicized modifiers affect meaning in the following sentences.

He *almost* watched the entire movie.

She read the entire letter from her friend *in the bathroom.*

He left his car on the side of the road *which had a flat tire.*

In each case, the italicized modifier is misplaced. It appears to modify a word that it cannot logically modify. Most readers will be able to figure out the intent of the writer in these cases, but the misplacement causes some initial confusion and can be avoided easily.

In the following sections you will discover how to avoid problems with misplaced modifiers. You will find how to avoid misplacing single-word modifiers (Section 33c.1), misplacing groups of words as modifiers (Section 33c.2), and separating sentence elements unnecessarily (Section 33c.3).

33c.1 Single-Word Modifiers

Placement of the word *only* affects meaning in the following sentences.

Only Jane had permission to ask Mary to make those changes in that document.

Jane **only** had permission to ask Mary to make those changes in that document.

Jane had permission **only** to ask Mary to make those changes in that document.

Jane had permission to ask **only** Mary to make those changes in that document.

Jane had permission to ask Mary to make **only** those changes in that document.

Jane had permission to ask Mary to make those changes **only** in that document.

The placement of modifiers like the word *only* can change the meaning of the entire sentence. The following modifiers usually appear immediately before the words they modify: *almost, even, hardly, just, only, nearly.*

33c.2 Groups of Words as Modifiers

The italicized modifiers in the sentences below are misplaced in relation to the words they modify.

I bought a truck from that man *with mud flaps and a running board.*

When I was in high school, I dated a boy with a Buick *named Fred.*

She wore a medallion around her neck *that was made of silver*.

The misplaced modifiers need to be moved so that the sentences will make sense.

In the first sentence, the modifier "with mud flaps and a running board" is placed so that it modifies *man* rather than *truck*. Rewording makes the connection between noun and modifier clear.

I bought a truck **with mud flaps and a running board** from that man.

In the second sentence, the modifier "named Fred" appears to modify the word *Buick* rather than *boy* as it should. The reworded sentence is clearer.

When I was in high school, I dated a boy **named Fred** who had a Buick.

In the third sentence, the placement of the modifier "that was made of silver" make it appear to modify *neck*. The reworded sentence correctly positions the modifier so that it modifies the word *medallion*.

Around her neck she wore a medallion **that was made of silver**.

33c.3 Separation of Sentence Parts

Consider how the italicized words function in the following sentences.

They had, *in the middle of the night*, remembered that the lights were on.

She found, *after they had all left the party*, the earring she had lost.

The modifier "in the middle of the night" separates the verb *had remembered* unnecessarily. The modifier "after they had all left the party" separates the verb *located* from the receiver of the action, *earring*. Both sentences would be clearer if they were reworded.

In the middle of the night, they had remembered that the lights were on.

After they had all left the party, she found the earring she had lost.

As you read the next two sentences, you will notice that the first one is much less awkward than the second.

It is important to *fairly* make the decision.

We will seek to *permanently and irrevocably to the extent that it is within our power* repair the damage.

In each sentence, modifiers separate the word *to* from the verb. In the first sentence, the separation of *to* and *make* by *fairly* is not especially confusing, although the sentence would probably read better if it were reworded as follows.

It is important **to make** the decision fairly.

The separation of *to* and *repair* in the second sentence creates a serious problem for the reader. The sentence would certainly be improved if it were rewritten as follows.

We will seek **to repair** the damage permanently and irrevocably to the extent that it is within our power.

CommonSense Observation

Not Separating *To* and a Verb

Traditionalists would say never to separate *to* from the verb (never to split an infinitive), but separating *to* from a verb is not always a problem. Consider the familiar phrase "to boldly go where no one has gone before." In that case, the word *to* is separated from the verb *go* by the modifier *boldly*, but the separation does not seem to interrupt the flow of the sentence; in fact, it makes the rhythm of the sentence more pleasing.

33d
DANGLING MODIFIERS

As you read the four sentences that follow, you will notice that what they say is not quite what was intended.

1. *Running through the woods*, a root tripped him.
2. *After typing my paper*, the disk crashed.
3. *To get a high grade in school*, good study habits are necessary.
4. *When a child*, my father gave me his pocketknife.

In each case the italicized part of the sentence has nothing to modify or seems to be modifying the wrong element. Introductory elements like those above usually modify the first word that follows them.

For instance, the structure of sentence 1 above makes us think that the word *running* should modify *root*. Of course, *running* cannot modify *root* because a root can't run. The only word in the sentence that *running* could logically modify is *him*. But *him* is in the wrong place for *running* to modify it. Rewritten as follows, the sentence makes sense.

Running through the woods, **he** tripped on a root.

Sentence 2 suggests that the disk typed the paper. Properly rewritten, it would read as follows.

After **I had finished** typing my paper, the disk crashed.

In sentence 3, "To get a high grade in school" has nothing to modify. The noun *student* should be in the second part of the sentence.

To get a high grade in school, **a student** must have good study habits.

Finally, in sentence 4, the position of the modifier "When a child" makes it appear that the father gave the son the pocketknife when the father was a child. Obviously, that cannot be true. The sentence should be reworded.

When **I was** a child, my father gave me his pocketknife.

33e
CHOOSING *A*, *AN*, AND *THE*

The use of *a, an,* and *the* is rarely a problem for native speakers of English. But for people whose native language is not English, the use of these **signal words** may cause some problems. The words *a, an,* and *the* signal that a noun is about to appear in the sentence. The kind of noun being used determines which of the three signal words is chosen.

33e.1 With Singular Nouns That Can Be Counted

The following sentences need a signal word.

Harvey lives in tent.

Babette lives in apartment.

Since tents and apartments can be counted, the first sentence should be rewritten with the word *a* preceding the word *tent*, and the second sentence should be rewritten with the word *an* preceding the word *apartment*. The word *a* is used with words beginning with a consonant (*a* banana, *a* car, *a* mouse), and the word *an* is used with words beginning with a vowel (*an* apple, *an* auto, *an* orangutan) or vowel sound (*an* honest politician).

33e.2 With Nouns That Cannot Be Counted

The following sentences do not need signal words.

An honesty is the best policy.

Remember to pick up *a* soap.

Since the nouns in these two sentences cannot be counted, *an* is unnecessary before *honesty*, and so is *a* before *soap*. *A* would be necessary if the second sentence read "Remember to pick up a bar of soap."

33e.3 With Nouns Whose Identity Is Known to the Reader

Look at the way *a*, *an*, and *the* are used in the passage below.

Yesterday **a** bus stalled at **a** railroad crossing with its back wheels still on **the** track. There was **an** accident, but fortunately, **the** bus was empty and **the** driver escaped before **a** train demolished **the** bus.

The is required before *track* because we know what track it is from the context of the passage. In the second sentence, *bus* requires *the* because the bus has been identified in the first sentence. In addition, *the* is required when the noun is identified by an *-est* word: *the* best driver, *the* most gifted person. *The* is also required if the noun describes a unique person, place, or thing: *The* moon is full tonight.

33e.4 With Nouns That Mean "All" or "In General"

Consider the following sentence.

Men are often irrational creatures.

The two nouns, *men* and *creatures*, don't require *the* because they refer to men and creatures in general.

33f CHOOSING BETWEEN MODIFIERS ENDING IN *-ED*, *-D*, *-EN*, *-N*, OR *-T* AND *-ING*

Verbs ending in *-ed*, *-d*, *-en*, *-n*, or *-t* and those ending in *-ing* can be used as modifiers. These forms can cause some confusion for nonnative speakers of English because they cannot be used interchangeably.

He sat through the whole **boring** lecture.

He sat through the whole **bored** lecture.

Both *boring* and *bored* are forms of the verb *bore* and function as modifiers of the noun *lecture*, but the phrase *bored lecture* in the second sentence doesn't make sense because a lecture cannot be bored. Words such as *annoy, confuse, excite,* and *surprise,* which describe mental states, can be particularly confusing.

Consistency

Have you ever been concentrating on a task when suddenly the phone rang? Your attention probably shifted to the phone call, and, as a result, you may have found it difficult to focus when you went back to the original task. The same kind of thing can happen to your reader if your writing is not consistent.

I *was working* on my computer and suddenly the electricity *goes* off.

If *a person* wants to stay fit, *you* should exercise regularly.

We want *happiness, good health,* and *to make money.*

Each of the preceding sentences creates a problem with consistency. You will discover in the following sections how to work with shifts, problems with parallelism, and problems with inaccurate sentence construction.

34a
SHIFTS IN THE KIND OF VERB USED

Notice how the following sentence shifts from a verb indicating one time to a verb indicating another time.

We *sat* on the porch and before we *know* what *is* happening the storm clouds *begin* to gather.

The sentence starts out in the past with the verb *sat* and shifts to the present with the verbs *know, is*, and *begin*. There is no reason for the shift. The sentence could be rewritten one of two ways.

> We **are** sitting on the porch and before we **know** what **is** happening the storm clouds **begin** to gather.

> We **sat** on the porch and before we **knew** what **was** happening the storm clouds **began** to gather.

Shifts from a verb form indicating one time (when something took place in the past, for example) to a verb form indicating another time (when something took place in the present, for example) can be troublesome.

34b
SHIFTS IN POINT OF VIEW

Notice how the following sentences change point of view.

> *I* have made a mistake, and *you* should admit it when *you* make a mistake.

> When a *person* makes a mistake, *you* should admit it.

Shifting from the person speaking (*I, me, my, mine*) to the person being addressed (*you, your*) can create a problem for the reader. Similarly, shifting from the person spoken about (a noun or the pronoun *he, she, they*, or *their*) to the person spoken to (*you, your*) can create problems.

Although the first sentence may not cause as much of a problem as the second, both could benefit from being rewritten.

> **I** have made a mistake, and **I** should admit it.

> When a **person** makes a mistake, **he** or **she** should admit it.

34c
SHIFTS IN FOCUS

The focus shifts in the following sentence.

> As *you* cook pasta, a large amount of *sauce* is made.

The sentence creates a problem by beginning with the person (*you*) doing the cooking and shifting to the statement that the *sauce is made*. Nobody is making the sauce. The shift in focus in midsentence means the reader suddenly has to reorient to a different kind of action.

Rewording the sentence eliminates the troublesome shift.

As **you** cook pasta, **you** also make a large amount of sauce.

34d
PROBLEMS WITH PARALLELISM

The following sentences repeat the same kind of sentence element on both sides of the italicized word.

He is **a writer, a teacher,** *and* **a scholar.**

She neither **knows** *nor* **cares** what will happen.

He knows **that the project will fail** *and* **that he will have to find** another job.

Certain sentence patterns set up expectations that a similar construction will follow. These sentence patterns are said to be parallel. In the following sections you will discover how problems in parallelism can be corrected.

34d.1 When Two Elements Are Connected by *And, But, Or,* or *Nor*

Notice how the following sentence defeats the expectation that the constructions on either side of the connective will be similar.

The two things he wanted to do most were **to build** a cabin in the mountains *and* **fishing** every day.

The two elements are parallel in the following revision.

The two things he wanted to do most were **to build** a cabin in the mountains *and* **to go** fishing every day.

34d.2 Paired Connectives

The italicized words in the sentences below create the expectation that the same structure will be used following each connective.

You must *either* **make** a decision *or* **you must** leave school.

Neither **James has** made any contribution *nor* **Babette.**

The following revisions would solve the problems.

You must *either* **make** a decision *or* **leave** school.

Neither **James** *nor* **Babette** has made any contribution.

34d.3 Series of Three or More Elements

The series in the following sentences create expectations that related elements will be similarly constructed.

1. He loves *burgers, pizza,* and *to cook spaghetti.*
2. She likes *sailing, rafting,* and *going canoeing.*
3. She likes *to hunt, to fish,* and *going hiking.*
4. She knows when *to speak up, to say nothing,* and *act.*

In sentence 1, *to cook spaghetti* focuses on the act of cooking, while the other two elements focus on the food. In sentence 2, *going canoeing* keeps the elements from being similar in structure. In sentence 3, *going hiking* is not the same structure as *to hunt* and *to fish.* In sentence 4, the writer may choose from three possible revised constructions.

He loves **pasta, pizza,** and **spaghetti.**

She likes **sailing, rafting,** and **canoeing.**

She likes **to hunt, to fish,** and **to hike.**

She knows **when to speak up, when to say nothing,** and **when to act.**

She knows when **to speak up, to say nothing,** and **to act.**

She know when to **speak up, say nothing,** and **act.**

34d.4 Comparison of Similar Terms

Notice the problem with the following comparisons.

An apartment in Manhattan is more convenient than *the suburbs.*

William James's philosophy is easier to understand than *Immanuel Kant.*

The two things being compared in the sentences are not really comparable. An apartment cannot be compared to the suburbs; a philosophy cannot be compared to a person. If the sentences were reworded as follows, the comparisons would be complete.

An apartment in Manhattan is more convenient than **a place** in the suburbs.

William James's philosophy is easier to understand than **Immanuel Kant's.**

34e
PROBLEMS WITH AGREEMENT OF SENTENCE ELEMENTS

Notice the problem with the italicized sentence elements.

Most *people* make *their life* more complicated than necessary.

Both *people* and *their* are plural. *Life* is singular. The words should be consistent, as they are in the following revision.

Most **people** make **their lives** more complicated than necessary.

Some verb forms (for example, a verb ending in *-ing*, such as *running*, or a verb form preceded by *to*, such as *to run*) can be used as objects of a verb. Sometimes the two forms can be interchanged, but often they cannot.

He hates **to fly**.

He hates **flying**.

Both of these sentences mean roughly the same thing. The two that follow do not.

She remembered **visiting** her grandmother.

She remembered **to visit** her grandmother.

In some cases only one of the forms can be used, as in the two pairs of sentences that follow.

He thinks about **playing** football.

> *not*

He thinks about *to play* football.

He has decided **to work** all weekend.

> *not*

He has decided *working* all weekend.

34f
INACCURATE SENTENCE CONSTRUCTIONS

The following sentences don't quite make sense.

1. The *choice* of a color for the room *was selected* by the painter.
2. His *profession* is a *teacher*.

3. The *dog* with inadequate nutrition *causes* health problems.

4. Public *schools are* problems.

In sentence 1, the *choice* was not selected by the painter; the *color* was selected. When the sentence is rewritten as follows, there is no confusion.

The **color** for the room **was selected** by the painter.

In sentence 2, *his profession* is not a teacher; *he* is a teacher. That problem is eliminated by the following revision.

His **profession** is **teaching**.

Sentence 3 suggests that the *dog* causes health problems. The following revision corrects the problem.

Inadequate nutrition causes health problems in dogs.

In sentence 4, *schools* are not problems. The following revision corrects the inaccurate statement.

Public **schools have** problems.

Similarly, the phrases *is when*, *is where*, and *is by* cause problems in the following sentences.

1. Pollution *is when* we put toxic chemicals in the water.

2. Commuting *is where* people drive a long distance to work or school.

3. His job *is by* cutting down trees.

Sentence 1 is inaccurate because pollution is not a time, and *when* is used to denote a time. The idea would be clearer if it were rewritten.

Pollution **is** the **dumping** of toxic chemicals in the water.

or

Pollution **occurs when** we put toxic chemicals in the water.

Sentence 2 is inaccurate because commuting is not a place, and *where* is used to indicate a place. The idea would be clearer if it were rewritten.

Commuting **is** the **practice** of driving long distances to work.

Sentence 3 is inaccurate because the phrase *by cutting down trees* does not equal the word *job*. The sentence would be made clearer by simply leaving out the word *by*.

His job **is** cutting down trees.

34g
MIXED CONSTRUCTIONS

Each of the following sentences starts out with one kind of construction and ends with another.

1. *By* every excuse he made got him deeper into trouble.
2. The building construction was canceled because *of* not enough money.
3. *Because* he wants to do well does not mean he will.

Each example can be rewritten so that the sentence structure is consistent. We can make sentence 1 consistent by simply deleting the word *by*.

Every excuse he made got him deeper in trouble.

To revise sentence 2, we need to delete the word *of* and add more information.

The building construction was canceled because **the contractor did not have** enough money.

In sentence 3, we could simply change *because* to *that*.

That he wants to do well does not mean he will.

34h
PROBLEMS WITH WORDS THAT RENAME

The following sentences are confusing.

Chang has received only one letter, *his wife*.

Harvey has a health condition, *his liver*.

The first sentence appears to say that the letter is Chang's wife. The sentence could be rewritten to read

Chang has received only one letter, **from** his wife.

The second sentence is inaccurate because it says something that is untrue. Harvey's health condition cannot be his liver. It could be rewritten in the following way.

Harvey has a health condition, **a problem with** his liver.

Completeness

In conversations with somebody you know very well, you may notice that you tend to leave out some words and phrases because you assume that the other person will know what you mean. And even if that person doesn't understand, he or she will ask you to clarify your meaning. Sometimes when you write, the same thing may happen. Unfortunately, you don't always know whether or not your reader will be able to fill in the blanks. And certainly a reader would have no opportunity to ask questions. So you will want to be sure that all your statements are complete and are not confusing.

The sections that follow cover various problems you may have in making your writing complete.

35a
OMISSIONS

As you read the following sentences, note that some necessary words have been left out.

1. We will go *to movie* tomorrow.
2. She was *fascinated and adept at* painting.
3. Jim's notions were *outlandish and rejected* without comment.
4. She *felt aggressive and belligerent behavior* was unacceptable.

The word *a* or *the* was omitted from sentence 1; the word *with*, from sentence 2; the word *were*, from sentence 3; and the word *that*, from sentence 4.

35a.1 Omission of Minor Sentence Elements

Notice how leaving out even a minor word can affect how a sentence sounds. When words that connect are left out, confusion results.

We had a test last class.

The words *during the* were left out of the previous sentence. The sentence would be clearer if it were reworded.

We had a test **during the** last class.

35a.2 Omission of Words Such as *At, By, From, In, Of, On, To,* or *With*

The omissions in the following sentences affects their meaning.

He was both *suspicious and intrigued by* her behavior.

Babette was *attracted and fascinated with* the works of Henry Miller.

In the first sentence, the word *of* should follow the word *suspicious*. Otherwise, the sentence appears to read "He was both suspicious by and intrigued by her behavior." Notice that the reworded sentence is clearer.

He was both suspicious **of** and intrigued **by** her behavior.

In the second sentence, the word *to* should follow the word *attracted*. Otherwise, the sentence appears to read "Babette was attracted with and fascinated with the works of Henry Miller." The reworded sentence is clearer.

Babette was attracted **to** and fascinated **with** the works of Henry Miller.

35a.3 Omission of a Verb

As you read the following sentences, consider how the omissions affect each one.

To err **is** human; to forgive, divine.

The dogs **were** barking and the cat yowling.

In the first sentence, the omission of the verb *is* from the second half of the sentence is perfectly acceptable. The reader supplies the missing verb *is* because the structure of the word groups on each side of the semicolon is the same. In the second sentence, the omission of the verb *was* following *cat* makes the sentence appear to read "The dogs were barking and the cat were yowling." Omitting a verb in a balanced sentence is acceptable as long as the same verb would be repeated. Notice how the reworded sentence makes the meaning clearer.

The dogs **were** barking and the cat **was** yowling.

Some languages permit a verb to be omitted entirely when the meaning is clear. English does not, except in sentences with compound elements like those above. Nonnative speakers of English will need to make sure that verbs are present, especially forms of the verb *be*. The following sentence would make sense in many languages.

The school very large.

In English, this sentence should be rewritten as follows.

The school **is** very large.

35a.4 Omission of *That*

Notice how the omission of the word *that* affects the meaning of the following sentence.

The Justice Department revealed a cover-up was not likely.

The word *that* has been omitted following the word *revealed*. The omission causes a misreading because we think at first that the Justice Department has revealed a cover-up.

35b
INCOMPLETE COMPARISONS

The following sentences illustrate incomplete comparisons.

1. The roller coaster is the *most* exciting ride.
2. That girl has *more* bad luck.
3. My computer is *as good* if not better than his.
4. I like Fred *better than* Jim.

In sentence 1, the word *most* implies that the roller coaster is being compared to other rides. Notice how the reworded sentence makes the comparison clearer.

The roller coaster is the **most** exciting ride **at the amusement park**.

In sentence 2, the word *more* suggests that a comparison is being made. But we are not told what or who the girl is being compared to. The sentence could be reworded to make the comparison complete.

That girl has **more** bad luck **than any other person I know**.

Sentence 3 fails to make the comparison complete because it says *as good* rather than *as good as*. The addition of the word *as* to the sentence makes the comparison complete.

My computer is **as good as** if not better than his.

Sentence 4 is unclear because we cannot tell whether the sentence means "I like Fred better than I like Jim" or "I like Fred better than Jim likes him."

35c
OVERLAPPING COMPARISONS

Think about the logic of these comparisons.

New York City is larger than *any* city in the United States.

She was faster than *any* sprinter in the race.

New York City cannot be larger than itself. The sentence would be better if it were reworded as follows.

New York City is larger than **any other** city in the United States.

Similarly, the sprinter cannot be faster than *any* sprinter, including herself. The sentence would be complete if it were rewritten.

She was faster than **any other** sprinter in the race.

35d
UNNECESSARY REPETITION

The subject of a sentence should not be repeated unnecessarily.

The lawyer she advised me not to sue.

The lawyer who advised me *she* was sensitive to my fears.

In these two sentences, the subject is repeated for no reason. The sentences should be rewritten as follows.

The lawyer advised me not to sue.

The lawyer who advised me was sensitive to my fears.

Conventions

Spelling

Look at the spelling of the words *through, though, rough, cough,* and *bough.* All five words end in *-ough,* but no two of them are pronounced the same way. This illustration suggests just how complicated English spelling can be. Because of the complex history of the development of the English language, spelling is a problem for many people. In other languages—for example, Spanish and German—knowing how a word is pronounced is a sure guide to spelling it. Not so in English. As a result, you may need to memorize the spellings of many words.

Although some people have suggested ways to make English spelling easier by using phonetic spellings, such a solution is not likely to occur in the near future. However, the widespread use of computers will certainly reduce the number of spelling errors. If your word processing program has a spell checker (and most do), the only spelling errors you should have to pay attention to in your writing are typographical errors that actually spell a word (even though it's the wrong word) and errors like those covered in following sections. All other spelling errors should be caught by the spell checker.

36a
WORDS COMMONLY CONFUSED

Notice how *to, too,* and *two* are used in the following sentence.

I want you *to too* come, *two.*

The sentence should have been written in this way.

I want you **two to** come, **too.**

Misuses like those in the first sentence will cause some confusion for the reader. These three words are among many that create problems in spelling because they are similar: they either sound alike or look alike. When you use any words like these, a computerized spell checker will not be able to determine which meaning you intend, so you will want to become familiar with the differences between them. Five of the most frequently confused groups of words are discussed in this section. The following 39 groups are covered in the glossary of usage: *accept, except; advice, advise; affect, effect; all ready, already; all together, altogether; allusion, illusion; bare, bear; brake, break; breadth, breath, breathe; capital, capitol, Capitol; cite, sight, site; coarse, course; conscience, conscious; council, counsel; desert, dessert; dyeing, dying; emigrate, immigrate; formally, formerly; hear, here; hole, whole; later, latter; lead, led; loose, lose; moral, morale; passed, past; patience, patients; peace, piece; precede, proceed; presence, presents; principal, principle; quiet, quite; sense, since; than, then; their, there, they're; to, too, two; weather, whether; which, witch; who's, whose;* and *your, you're.*

No doubt you are already familiar with many of the words in the following list, but chances are that you will find a few you are not absolutely sure about.

Frequently Confused Words

affect ("to influence," "a feeling"—used usually in psychology)

His failure may **affect** his self-concept.

The **affect** is a part of his psychological response.

effect ("to bring about," "a result")

The protest may **effect** a change in policy.

The **effect** of the speech was startling.

its (possessive form of *it*)

The car lost **its** wheel.

it's (contraction of *it is*)

It's going to be a long winter.

their ("belonging to them")

Their belongings had been stolen.

there ("that place"; used to begin a sentence)

The car is parked over **there**.

There are three birds sitting on the wire.

they're (contraction of *they are*)

They're coming as soon as they can.

to ("toward")

We went **to** town.

too ("also," "excessively")

We want to go, **too**.

He cared **too** much.

two (the number 2)

There were **two** ducks on the pond.

your ("belong to you")

> **Your** order is ready.

you're (contraction of *you are*)

> **You're** not going to get away with this.

36b
WORD SUBSTITUTIONS

Other words, besides the ones listed in the previous section, may be mis-spelled because one word is substituted for another. In the following cases, words are substituted because of inaccurate pronunciation.

36b.1 Words Ending in an -*s*, -*sk*, or -*st* Sound

In the following sentence, *prejudiced* is misspelled; the -*d* has been left off.

> She was not *prejudice* against anyone.

Some words are misspelled because we tend to leave the final -*ed* or -*s* unpronounced when the word ends in an -*s*, -*sk*, or -*st* sound.

Some speakers write	When they actually mean
ask	ask**s** or ask**ed**
risk	risk**s** or risk**ed**
desk	desk**s**
bias	bias**ed**
prejudice	prejudic**ed**
suppose	suppos**ed**
use	us**ed**
consist	consist**s**
insist	insist**s**
suggest	suggest**s**
psychiatrist	psychiatrist**s**

He **asks** [not *ask*] too many questions.

He **asked** [not *ask*] the wrong question.

He **risks** [not *risk*] everything.

He **risked** [not *risk*] all he had.

Three **desks** [not *desk*] clutter her room.

He is **biased** [not *bias*].

She is **prejudiced** [not *prejudice*].

He was **supposed** [not *suppose*] to do it.

She **used** [not *use*] to be my friend.

My team **consists** [not *consist*] of players with diverse skills.

The **psychiatrists** [not *psychiatrist*] were at a convention.

36b.2 *Have* and *Of*

When some people intend to say "You should *have* been there," they actually say something that sounds more like, "You should *of* been there." That pronunciation of *have* as *of* may carry over into writing, and so they end up writing "You should *of* been there." Not only do some speakers substitute the word *of* for *have* after *should*, but they also substitute *of* for *have* after *could* and *might*. If you have this tendency, it would be a good idea for you to proofread with that in mind.

could **have** been	*not*	could *of* been
should **have** known	*not*	should *of* known
might **have** seen	*not*	might *of* seen

The confusion is natural since *could've* (a contraction of *could have*) and *could of* are pronounced the same.

36c
COMPOUND WORDS

Note the different ways compounds appear in the following examples.

The attorney **cross-examined** the witness.

The **high school** was crowded.

The car ran into the **lamppost**.

A compound word consists of two or more words expressing a single idea. Compounds start out as two words used together. After some time they may be hyphenated. Eventually, after long usage, the hyphen may be dropped and the two words joined to make one word. Unfortunately, spell checkers are not very useful with compound words.

36c.1 Fixed Compounds

Some compounds are fixed by convention: they are either always hyphenated, always written as two or more words, or always written as one word. It is sometimes difficult to remember which form a compound takes, so you will simply need to look it up in a dictionary if you are not sure.

Hyphenated

cross-reference

flag-waving

heavy-duty

mother-in-law

Written as Separate Words

editor in chief

jump rope

heart failure

martial law

Written as One Word

crossbow

driveshaft

driveway

flagpole

heartthrob

hotcake

36c.2 Compound Modifiers

Notice the different ways the following compounds are used.

The **part-time** teacher worked very hard.

He taught **part time**.

In each case the two words function together to express a single idea. In the first sentence, the compound is hyphenated because it comes before the modified term, *teacher*. In the second sentence, it is not hyphenated because it comes after the modified term, *taught*.

Before Modified Term

When a compound modifier appears before a term it modifies, it is hyphenated. You can tell whether you need a hyphen in such cases by asking if deleting one of the hyphenated terms changes the meaning of the phrase. In the following examples, deleting one of the terms clearly creates a different meaning.

> **twentieth-century artist**
>
> **good-looking man**
>
> **matter-of-fact attitude**

After Modified Term

When the compound appears after the term, the hyphen is usually omitted.

> The athlete was **well conditioned**.
>
> He was a **well-conditioned** athlete.

When the Compound Contains an -ly Form

When the compound contains -*ly*, the words are not hyphenated.

> This is an **easily** learned lesson.
>
> This **easy-to-learn** lesson can be useful.

When Two Words Begin a Compound

Sometimes you add a hyphen at the end of a word.

> Both **part-** and **full-time** teachers deserve respect.

> The presence of the hyphen after *part* communicates to the reader that the compound has not yet been completed.

36c.3 Compound Numbers

Numbers

Spelled-out numbers from twenty-one to ninety-nine are hyphenated.

Forty-six men were with him.

Fractions

Usage of hyphens with fractions varies. Some authorities recommend always hyphenating fractions. Others say fractions should be hyphenated only when used as modifiers. Whichever style you choose, be consistent. If you are not consistent, the changes may distract the reader from what you are saying.

The glass was **three-fourths** full.

The place was **two-thirds** empty.

Three fourths [or **Three-fourths**] were excluded.

36d
PLURALS

In English, words that name something (nouns) can be either singular or plural. We form the plural of nouns in several different ways.

36d.1 Most Nouns

We form the plural of most nouns by adding an *-s* to the end of the word. The plural of *dog* is *dogs*; the plural of *hat* is *hats*. To form the plurals of names, we follow the same conventions. Note that no apostrophe is used to form the plural of a name. We write the plural of *Smith* as *Smiths*, not *Smith's*. Words ending in *-ch, -s, -sh, -x,* or *-z* require *-es* to form the plural. We write the plural of *Jones* by adding *-es* (*Joneses*) to signal the pronunciation of the additional syllable.

36d.2 Nouns That Change Spelling

We change the spelling of some nouns to form plurals. Some words borrowed from Greek, Latin, and French form the plural by changing the final *-um, -on,* or *-us* to *-a* or *-i*.

Singular	Plural
criterion	criteria
curriculum	curricula
datum	data
medium	media

Singular	Plural
phenomenon	phenomena
alumnus	alumni
stimulus	stimuli
syllabus	syllabi
analysis	analyses
basis	bases
crisis	crises
hypothesis	hypotheses

Writers now have a tendency to form the plurals of foreign words as if they were English words, so for the following words, plurals may be formed in both ways. Usually the anglicized version is preferred.

Singular	Preferred	Rather Than
appendix	appendixes	appendices
focus	focuses	foci
index	indexes	indices
radius	radiuses	radii
chateau	chateaus	chateaux
memorandum	memorandums	memoranda
sanatorium	sanatoriums	sanatoria
stadium	stadiums	stadia

36d.3 Nouns That Are the Same for Both Singular and Plural

The singular and plural forms of some words may be the same.

Singular	Plural
bear	bear *or* bears
deer	deer
elk	elk
fish	fish *or* fishes
moose	moose
sheep	sheep
species	species

36d.4 Compound Nouns

When a compound noun is written as one word, the plural is formed just as any other noun would be.

earring	earring**s**
mailbox	mailbox**es**
housewife	housewi**ves**

When a compound noun is hyphenated or written as two words, then the plural is formed by making the most important word of the compound plural.

mother-in-law	mother**s**-in-law
attorney general	attorney**s** general
fifty-year-old	fifty-year-old**s**

Words that end in *-ful* form the plural by adding an *-s* to the end of the word.

spoonful**s**   *not*   spoonsful

36d.5 Letters, Numbers, and Abbreviations

Plurals of letters, numbers, and abbreviations are formed by adding an *s* or an apostrophe plus *s*.

An *s* (without an apostrophe) is added to capitalized abbreviations and acronyms without periods, written-out numbers, and figures.

The RSVP**s** are expected shortly.

How many five**s** go into twenty-five?

The temperature was in the seventie**s**.

The 1960**s** were exciting years.

Some authorities advocate using an apostrophe with plural letters and figures.

She always makes *A***'s**.

Use of the apostrophe prevents confusion with the preposition *as*.

An apostrophe plus *-s* is used to form the plural of a letter, an abbreviation ending in a period, or a lowercase abbreviation.

The *s***'s** on the ends of nouns make them plural.

M.D.**'s** exert a great deal of influence on public opinion.

The rpm**'s** of the engine increased.

36e
ADDING ON TO THE BEGINNING OF A WORD

When you add a **prefix** to the beginning of a word, you will be faced with the question of whether to use a hyphen. The following guidelines will help you, but as with compounds, if you are not sure, consult a dictionary.

In most cases the following prefixes are not hyphenated. Note the examples and exceptions.

Prefix	Examples	Exceptions
ante-	antediluvian, antedate	
anti-	antibiotic, anticlimax	anti-intellectual
by-	bylaw, bypass	by-product
post-	postgraduate, postnasal	post-paleolithic
pre-	prearrange, preexist	pre-owned
ultra-	ultramodern, ultraviolet	
up-	upstage, upstate, uptown	up-tempo

In most cases the following prefixes are hyphenated. Note the examples and exceptions.

Prefix	Examples	Exceptions
all-	all-around, all-time	allspice
co-	co-author, co-pilot	coexist
ex-	ex-wife, ex-convict	excommunicate
like-	like-minded, like-natured	likewise
off-	off-color, off-load	offbeat
one-	one-sided, one-way	oneself
pro-	pro-labor, pro-life, pro-war	pronoun
self-	self-confident, self-image	selfish
well-	well-being, well-born	wellspring
wide-	wide-angle, wide-open	widespread

Words beginning with *half-* are sometimes hyphenated. You will have to rely on a dictionary for these compounds.

The word *vice* is always a separate word (unhyphenated): *vice president.*

When the main part of the word is a figure or begins with a capital letter, the word is hyphenated.

anti-American

mid-1960s

mid-Victorian

pan-Arabic

pre-Columbian

When a prefix is added to a word that starts with the same letter the prefix ends with, the word is usually hyphenated.

anti-inflammatory

semi-independent

However, in words that are very common, the hyphen may be omitted.

cooperate

coordinate

preempt

preexist

reentry

Some words that begin with the prefix *re-* are hyphenated and others are not. Hyphenated and unhyphenated words with the same spelling may have different meanings.

Recover means "to get back or to regain"; *re-cover* means "to cover anew."

Recreation means "refreshment of one's mind and body"; *re-creation* means "a new creation."

Reform means "to improve by alteration"; *re-form* means "to form again."

36f ADDING ON TO THE END OF A WORD

Some endings (**suffixes**) are hyphenated when they are added to a word.

When *elect* is added to the end of a word, it is always hyphenated: *president-elect*.

When *like* is added to the end of a word, it is hyphenated if a triple *l* would result: *bell-like, fall-like*.

The word *childlike* is not hyphenated.

36g CONTRACTIONS AND CLIPPED FORMS

When you use shortened word forms in your writing, you will need to consider the appropriateness of the following conventions.

36g.1 Contractions

Contractions are words formed by combining two or more words into a shortened form and leaving out letters. Convention requires an apostrophe to indicate the missing letter or letters.

can't	can not, cannot
didn't	did not
haven't	have not
they're	they are
it's	it is
o'clock	of the clock

36g.2 Clipped Forms

Clipped forms are shortened spellings of a longer word. They are generally avoided in formal writing.

Use	Do Not Use
though	tho
through	thru
dormitory	dorm
laboratory	lab
professor	prof
telephone	phone
veteran	vet
sales representative	sales rep

The audience of your paper will dictate whether a clipped form is appropriate. Most general readers will find clipped forms a little too "slangy" and informal for the majority of writing situations. Some words may be more acceptable than others. Clipped forms are accepted as part of the jargon in certain fields (*dorm* or *sales rep*, for example), so they might be appropriate in writing addressed to people in that field.

36h
WORD DIVISION

With a word processor, questions about hyphenation at the end of a line rarely occur because word processing programs automatically shift to the next line if a word will not fit on the current one. In those few instances when you decide that you must divide a word at the end of a line, you will make the division less confusing for the reader if you divide the word between syllables and use a hyphen to indicate the break. The hyphen is always positioned at the end of the line after the first part of the divided word rather than at the beginning of the next line. When you must use a hyphen to divide a word at the end of a line, keep the following conventions in mind.

- Words are divided at the syllable breaks as marked in a dictionary. Centered dots usually indicate where a word can be divided (e.g., *dic•tion•ary*).
- Avoid dividing a word if you would leave only one or two letters at the end of a line or shift only one or two letters to the beginning of the next line. Divisions like these—*explain-ed* or *Californi-a*—would only confuse the reader.
- One-syllable words should not be divided (*height, though, rhythm*).
- Hyphenating the last word on a page creates unnecessary difficulties for the reader.
- If a word is already hyphenated (*all-conference*), hyphenating it at a place other than the fixed hyphen is awkward because it creates a word with two hyphens (*all-con-ference*).
- Avoid dividing contractions (*couldn't, didn't*), abbreviations (*atty., CPA, POW*), or numbers (*1492*).

Numbers and Symbols

When you use numbers and concepts that can be expressed as symbols in your writing, you will need to decide whether to spell them out or not. Your decision depends primarily on what kind of writing you are doing: technical (including scientific, business, and news writing) or nontechnical (general writing). Conventions vary for each kind.

37a
NUMBERS

Numbers are spelled out more often in general nontechnical prose than they are in technical and scientific writing. The sections that follow will help you decide how to represent numbers in your writing. (For an explanation of how to form plurals of numbers, see Section 36d.5.)

37a.1 One- or Two-Word Numbers and Round Numbers

In nontechnical writing, most writers follow the convention of spelling out one- and two-word numbers. This convention includes the numbers one through one hundred and other round numbers higher than one hundred that can be expressed as two words.

Numbers Spelled Out

one

twenty-seven

two hundred

five thousand

six million

Figures

203

1052

6750

10,001

62,000

If you are writing for technical, scientific, business, or mass media audiences, then you will want to use figures for most numbers over ten. You may find that you will want to simplify extremely long numbers by using both figures and words.

25 million

34 billion

15 trillion

37a.2 Numbers at the Beginning of a Sentence

Look at the following sentence.

103 students participated in the festival.

Sentences that begin with a figure look awkward. It is usually better to either write out the number or rephrase the sentence.

One hundred three students participated in the festival.

or

A total of **103** students participated in the festival.

The following sentence begins with a number, and according to the convention discussed above, we would want to change the sentence.

4,765 enthusiastic fans attended the concert.

But look what happens when we try to write out the number.

Four thousand seven hundred sixty-five enthusiastic fans attended the concert.

The resulting sentence is difficult to read. In this instance it would definitely be advisable to rewrite the sentence.

The concert was attended by **4,765** enthusiastic fans.

37a.3 Numbers to Indicate Time

Figures indicating time are ordinarily used with the abbreviations *a.m.* and *p.m.*

The crime occurred at **2:15 a.m.**

Words are used with *o'clock.*

He left the scene at about **two o'clock**.

37a.4 Exact Numbers

Try to read the following sentence.

During this year alone *five hundred twenty-two thousand four hundred eighty-three* people have visited the site.

Obviously, the sentence is unwieldy. When numbers refer to exact counts, addresses, exact sums, technical measurements, decimals, percentages, and the like, figures make the information much clearer to the reader.

Addresses

1024 South 18th St.

1425A 12th Ave.

Dates

July 4, 1776

July 14, 1789

Money

$5.26

$102.76

Identification Numbers

SS# 987-00-1111

690.89 J35i (call number for a library book)

107.1 FM

Channel 7

Measurements

55 mph

98°F

5' 9"

3" x 5"

Statistics and Scores

98%

28–7 (Score)

37a.5 Consistency in Using Figures and Written-Out Numbers

Notice how the numbers are used in the following sentence.

> On interstate highways the speed limit is *70 mph* except where the highway goes through a city. At those places the speed limit is *sixty miles per hour*.

Readers may find it irritating if figures and spelled-out numbers are mixed together in a sentence or passage. Both numbers in the preceding passage should be represented as figures.

However, notice the use of numbers in the following sentence.

> For **two months** after the speed limit changed from **65 mph** to **55 mph**, police were giving tickets at the rate of **one thousand** a week.

Mixing written-out numbers and figures in this sentence is acceptable because the spelled-out numbers are referring to a measure of time and to a number of items, while the figures refer to a rates of speed.

37a.6 Numbers Indicating a Position in a Series

Numbers like *first* (*1st*), *second* (*2nd*), and *third* (*3rd*) indicate a position in a series. The choice between spelled-out numbers and figures is the same as it would be for other numbers: *one* (*1*), *two* (*2*), and *three* (*3*).

But there are a few differences between spoken and written conventions.

In Speech	In Writing
George the First	George I
July fourth, nineteen ninety-four	July 4, 1994
July fourth (no year)	July 4 or July fourth

37a.7 Range or Series of Numbers

Notice how the numbers are used in the following examples.

pp. 1–19
pp. 2, 16
July 1–July 4
July 1, 4
1973–1984

A dash is typically used to indicate a range of numbers. A comma is used to indicate separate days or separate pages.

37a.8 Omission of Digits

An apostrophe is sometimes used to show the omission of one or more digits from a number.

He graduated in the spring of '94.

An apostrophe is not used if the deletion covers a range of numbers.

1973–84
pp. 301–04

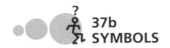

37b
SYMBOLS

As a general rule, concepts that are expressed as symbols in technical and scientific writing are written out in nontechnical writing. In nontechnical writing, we would normally spell out *and* for *&*, *percent* for *%*, *dollar* for *$*, *cent* for *¢*, *pound* for *#* or *lb.*, *degrees* for *°*, *equals* for *=*, *plus* for *+*, *less than* for *<*, and *greater than* for *>*.

The ampersand (&), the percent sign (%), the degree symbol (°), and the dollar sign ($) deserve special consideration.

The ampersand (&) is rarely used in formal writing unless it appears in a title or a name: *Standard & Poor's.*

Percent is most usually spelled out in most formal writing. The symbol % is used in some instances.

> The teacher noticed that **25 percent** of the class had dropped out.

> The stock registered a **15%** decline in the first ten minutes of trading.

If temperatures are mentioned once or twice in a document, you should spell out the word *degrees*. However, if temperatures are mentioned throughout, then the degree sign would be more appropriate.

The dollar sign ($) is called for when exact sums are given.

> He has owed me **$15.83** for a long time.

You could use either the symbol or the word to refer to a sum that is a round number. However, it would be inappropriate to use both; one of them would be redundant.

> The loan is for *$2000 dollars.*

You would write either

> The loan is for **$2000.**

>   *or*

> The loan is for **two thousand dollars.**

Names

Notice the use of capital letters and italic type in the following list of words.

flower, mountain, Tom Jones, Father, Louisiana, Fred, Mr. Smith, AT&T, 8th Avenue, Grand Canyon, Pacific Ocean, gravitation, *Spirit of St. Louis*, Venus, Mars, atom, Dow-Jones Industrial Average, CIA, daisy, evolution, sparrow, Mississippi River, blood, Halley's comet, Wars of the Roses, Super Bowl, metric system, Poland, *Hibiscus syriacus*

These words are names of people, places, things, concepts, and events which use a variety of conventions: some are capitalized; some are italicized; some are abbreviated. When we use words that name people, places, things, concepts, and events, we follow certain conventions in the use of capital letters, lowercase letters, italics (or underlining if the work is handwritten or typed), abbreviations, periods, and commas.

38a
PEOPLE

Different conventions govern how the names of particular people, their titles, their nationalities, their races, and their languages are written.

38a.1 People's Names

Capitalize the names and initials of a particular person or group, modifiers derived from a person's name, and the personal pronoun *I*.

Sally Holt	a woman
Sir Isaac Newton	a man
the Beatles	a rock group
Newtonian physics	a body of physical laws
Shakespearean sonnet	a kind of sonnet
I	the person speaking

If a person uses initials instead of a given name, leave a space between the initials.

T. S. Eliot	a poet

Ordinarily it is not acceptable in any but the most informal writing (handwritten notes, diaries, journals, and signs) to abbreviate a person's name. For example, we would not substitute *Geo.* for *George* or *Chas.* for *Charles.*

38a.2 People's Titles

The titles of courtesy most frequently put before people's names are *Mr.*, *Mrs.*, *Miss*, and *Ms.* (also *Ms*). They are capitalized and abbreviated. Many women prefer *Ms.* instead of *Miss* or *Mrs.* because it is used without regard for the woman's marital status and is therefore comparable to the title *Mr.* used for men.

> Mr. George Jones
>
> Miss Jean Jones
>
> Ms. Jennifer Jones

Other titles are used to indicate professional status.

> Dr. Garcia   a doctor
>
> Rev. King   the reverend

Abbreviations for academic and medical degrees may follow a name and are set off by a comma.

> Fred Black, **Ph.D.**
>
> Joan Fry, **M.D.**
>
> Oliver Atkins, **D.D.S.**
>
> Mary Hendricks, **D.V.M.**

Note that we do not skip a space between parts of the abbreviation of titles.

It is redundant and therefore inappropriate to use titles both before and after a person's name. So you would write

> **Dr.** George Smith
>
> *or*
>
> George Smith, **M.D.**
>
> *but not*
>
> *Dr.* George Smith, *M.D.*

When a relative's title is used as part of a name, it is capitalized.

Uncle Jim   my uncle

Father   my father

(See Section 36d.5 for an explanation of how to form plurals of abbreviations.)

38a.3 Nationalities, Races, Languages, and Religious Groups

When we make references to groups of people or their languages, we must consider the conventions governing capitalization and the use of hyphens.

Brazilian, Dutch   a citizen

Lutheran, Baptist   a church member

Protestant, Buddhist   a believer

English, French   a language

African American   a member of an ethnic group

black, white   a member of an ethnic group

Some words are offensive to various groups in our society because they are considered racist and so should be avoided. Words such as *colored* to refer to African Americans or *redskins* to refer to Native Americans are not acceptable.

Adjectives derived from nationalities, races, or languages are also capitalized and sometimes hyphenated. The conventions for forming compound words are discussed in Section 36c.

Anglophile

Anglo-Saxon

Indo-European

38b PLACES

The names of places include areas, cities, lakes, oceans, mountains, buildings, parks, monuments, addresses, regions, and directions.

38b.1 Geographical Names

Names of particular geographical areas and places are capitalized.

the Mississippi River   a river

New York City   a city

Texas	a state
Lake Huron	a lake
Pacific Ocean	an ocean
Brazil	a country
United States	a country

Some parts of geographical names are always abbreviated.

St. Louis	a city
Mt. Everest	a mountain

The names of some countries may be abbreviated. Note that there are no spaces left between the letters of the abbreviations.

United States	a country
U.S. Congress	a house of government

38b.2 Buildings, Parks, and Monuments

The names of buildings, parks, and monuments are capitalized.

Sears Tower	a building in Chicago
Kennedy Center	a performing arts center
Yankee Stadium	a ballpark
Central Park	a city park
Yellowstone National Park	a national park
the Pecos Wilderness	a wilderness
the Statue of Liberty	a statue
the Golden Gate Bridge	a bridge

38b.3 Addresses

The names of states and roadways may be abbreviated in addresses but are normally spelled out when used in regular prose.

Austin Community College
1212 Rio Grande
Austin, TX 78701

Abbreviations are commonly used for names of roadways.

St.	Front Street	**Blvd.**	Martin Luther King Boulevard

Ave.	Jackson Avenue	La.	Maiden Lane
Ct.	James Court	Dr.	Ten-Mile Drive

38b.4 Regions and Directions

The names of particular regions and continents begin with capital letters. The names of directions are written in lowercase letters.

the East Coast	a region
Asia	a continent
I live in the South.	a region
He lives in the Northwest.	a region
Drive south on First Street.	a direction
We were driving southeast.	a direction

38c
THINGS

In addition to people and places, we also name things: plants, animals, recreational activities, ships, trains, airplanes, spacecraft, products, organizations, school subjects, classes, and religions.

38c.1 Animals and Plants

Common names of flowers, trees, and animals are written in lowercase letters. Scientific names are put in italics. The genus name is capitalized but the species is not.

mockingbird	*Mimus polyglottos*
pansy	*Viola tricolor*
white elm	*Ulmus americana*

Proper names of breeds of dogs, cats, and other domesticated animals are capitalized.

West Highland terrier

Siamese cat

Holstein cattle

Names given to particular animals are capitalized.

Bossy

Silver

Rover

38c.2 Recreational Activities

The names of games, sports, and other recreational activities are not capitalized unless they are the names of products.

Monopoly	basketball
Scrabble	baseball
Nintendo	backpacking
football	mountain climbing

38c.3 Ships, Trains, Airplanes, and Spacecraft

All the important words in the names of such vessels begin with capital letters. The names are italicized (underlined if handwritten or typed).

Titanic	a ship, ocean liner, or tugboat
Orient Express	a train
Spirit of St. Louis	an airplane
Challenger	a space shuttle
Sputnik	a satellite
Boeing 747	a class of airplanes

Boeing 747 is capitalized but not italicized because it refers to a class of airplanes, not one specific airplane.

38c.4 Products

Brand names are capitalized; names that refer to the general group are not.

Compaq LTE	a computer
Ford Mustang	a car
Pirelli RoadHandler	a tire

38c.5 Organizations

The names of particular businesses, agencies, schools, and other organizations are capitalized.

Austin Community College	a college
Roosevelt High School	a high school
First Presbyterian Church	a church
General Motors	an automobile manufacturer
Wal-Mart	a discount store

Acronyms, initialisms, and abbreviations are capitalized. No space is left between the letters.

FEMA	Federal Emergency Management Agency, an agency
NFL	National Football League, a football league
Co.	Ford Motor Company, a company

38c.6 School Subjects and Classes

The titles of specific courses are capitalized. The name of the subject is not unless it is a proper noun.

Introduction to Literature	a literature class
History 1613	a history class
English 101	an English class

School subjects are written out rather than abbreviated. Except in the most informal writing (diaries and journals), it would not be proper to write *econ.* for *economics*, *psych.* for *psychology*, or *lit.* for *literature*.

38c.7 Religions

The names of religions are capitalized.

Judaism, Hinduism, Christianity	religious beliefs
Protestantism, Catholicism	types of Christianity
Methodism, Presbyterianism	Protestant denominations

38d
CONCEPTS AND EVENTS

In addition to people, places, and things, we also name ideas, concepts, and events, including units of measurement, technical terms, scientific terms, seasons, holidays, months, days of the week, dates, historical events, and beliefs.

38d.1 Units of Measurement

Units of measurement may be written as abbreviations according to the following conventions. The following terms may be written in lowercase or capital letters. They are always abbreviated.

> a.m. *or* A.M.
>
> p.m. *or* P.M.

The following abbreviations may be written with or without periods. Notice that there is no space between the letters. They may appear as abbreviations in regular prose.

> mph *or* m.p.h.
>
> rpm *or* r.p.m.

The following abbreviations are written in lowercase letters and usually are not followed by a period. They are ordinarily spelled out in nontechnical prose.

g	gram
lb	pound
ft	foot *or* feet
kg	kilogram
qt	quart
hr	hour

An exception is *in.* (*inch*); to avoid confusion with the word *in*, the abbreviation is followed by a period.

38d.2 Technical and Scientific Terms

Particular scientific terms are capitalized; general terms are written in lowercase letters.

Mars	a planet
Sol	the sun
the Milky Way	the galaxy

Initialisms are capitalized and do not need periods. There is no space between the letters.

DNA	deoxyribonucleic acid
VHF	very high frequency
GDP	gross domestic product

EEG	electroencephalogram
FM	frequency modulation

Most **acronyms** (abbreviations formed by the initial letters of a name and pronounced as a word) are capitalized and do not need periods.

MADD	Mothers Against Drunk Driving
NATO	North Atlantic Treaty Organization
WAC	Women's Army Corps

Those acronyms that have become accepted as words are written in lowercase letters.

laser	*l*ight *a*mplification by *s*timulated *e*mission of *r*adiation
radar	*r*adio *d*etecting *a*nd *r*anging
scuba	*s*elf-*c*ontained *u*nderwater *b*reathing *a*pparatus

38d.3 Seasons and Holidays

Names of holidays are capitalized, and names of seasons are written in lowercase letters.

Christmas	winter
Memorial Day	spring
the Fourth of July	summer
Thanksgiving	fall

38d.4 Months, Days of the Week, and Dates

Months and days of the week are capitalized. Commas are used to separate the day and year. If the day comes before the month or no day is given, no comma is necessary.

January	a month
Monday	a day of the week
September 1, 1993	a date
1 September 1993	
September 1993	

B.C. (before Christ) and *A.D.* (anno Domini) are always capitalized and always abbreviated. *B.C.E* (before common era) and *C.E.* (common era) are the secular equivalents of *B.C.* and *A.D.*

38d.5 Historical Events and Periods

The names of historical events and periods are capitalized.

Revolutionary War	a revolutionary war
Civil War	a civil war
Boston Tea Party	a protest
Russian Revolution	a revolution
World War II	a war
Vietnam War	a war
Middle Ages	a period of history
post-Victorian	a period of history

(See Section 36e for an explanation of the conventions that govern adding on to the beginning of a word.)

38d.6 Beliefs

A reference to the deity of Judeo-Christian belief is capitalized.

Genesis 1:1 tells us, "In the beginning God created the heaven and the earth."

The gods are against us.

The names of philosophical systems are capitalized.

Jean-Paul Sartre was one of the leading explicators of Existentialism.

The philosophical system developed by Hegel, known as Hegelianism, makes extensive use of the concept of the dialectic.

Titles of Written or Recorded Works

The titles of written or recorded works (books, magazines, newspapers, essays, articles, short stories, poems, plays, movies, TV shows, songs, radio programs, musicals, operas, documents, and recordings) are indicated within a text by using several different conventions that identify the kind of work. (Conventions for handling manuscript titles and titles of unpublished papers are covered in Part X, "Document Design.")

39a
WORKS PUBLISHED SINGLY

We use italics (underlining if handwritten or typed) for all titles published as single works: books, magazines, newspapers, plays, movies, computer software, and recordings. Capitalize the first and last words and all other important words in the title. Use lowercase letters for the words *the, a,* and *an* and for connecting words of four letters or fewer.

The Scarlet Letter	a novel
New Yorker	a magazine
New York Times	a newspaper
Hamlet	a play
The Iliad	an epic poem
Star Trek	a television series
the *White Album*	a recording
The Wrath of Khan	a movie
The Shadow	a radio program
My Fair Lady	a musical
Madame Butterfly	an opera
WordPerfect 6.0	software

Even though the word *the* may be a part of the title of some newspapers and magazines, omit the word. Instead of writing *The New York Times* or *The New Yorker*, write the *New York Times* and the *New Yorker*.

39b
SHORT WORKS

Titles of short works that are included in a longer work are enclosed in quotation marks.

"The Raven"	a poem
"Araby"	a short story
"Hey Jude"	a song
"Space Seed"	an episode of *Star Trek*

When titles of short works appear in sentences, periods and commas *always* go inside the quotation marks.

>   I just finished reading Poe's short story "The Pit and the Pendulum."

39c
WELL-KNOWN WORKS

The titles of well-known documents are neither italicized nor placed in quotation marks. The important words are capitalized.

>   the Declaration of Independence
>
>   the Constitution
>
>   the Emancipation Proclamation
>
>   the Bible

Note that the adjective *biblical* is not capitalized.

Quotations and Dialogue

When we write, sometimes we want to use someone else's words or ideas. We may also record dialogue. When we do that, we are using quotations.

40a
DIRECT QUOTATIONS

Direct quotations are the exact words of a speaker or writer and occur in ordinary quoted material and dialogue.

40a.1 Short Quotations

Short quotations are direct quotations from speech, from prose sources of four lines or fewer, and from poetry of one to three lines.

Speech

> "Stop where you are," he said.

> He said, "Stop where you are."

Both of these quotations indicate the exact words of a speaker. They are enclosed in double quotation marks, as are short direct quotations from a written source.

Prose (four lines or fewer)

> Emerson once wrote, "Your genuine action will explain itself and will explain your other genuine actions. Your conformity explains nothing."

One line of poetry is enclosed in double quotation marks, just as short prose quotations are.

Poetry (one line)

> In the line "And all is seared with trade; bleared, smeared with toil," we can see Hopkins's use of internal rhyme.

When you quote two or three lines of poetry, enclose them in double quotation marks with a slash (/) between the lines and with a space before and after the slash.

Poetry (two or three lines)

> In the lines "Generations have trod, have trod, have trod; / And all is seared with trade; bleared, smeared with toil," Hopkins uses both repetition and internal rhyme.

40a.2 Long Quotations

Long quotations of both prose and poetry are set off from the rest of the text without the use of quotation marks. What is considered to be a long quotation depends on the style of documentation being used. (See Chapter 46 for more information about documentation styles.) The examples below reflect MLA (Modern Language Association) style.

Prose (more than four lines)

> Ralph Waldo Emerson once noted this about age:
>> Old age brings along with its ugliness the comfort that you will soon be out of it,—which ought to be a substanital relief to such discontented pendulums as we are. To be out of the war, out of

> debt, out of the drouth, out of the blues, out of the dentist's
> hands, out of the second thoughts, mortifications, and remorses
> that inflict such twinges and shooting pains;—out of the next
> winter, and the high prices, and company below your
> ambition,—surely these are soothing limits.

Some readers might be more disturbed than comforted by Emerson's
remarks.

As shown above, the MLA manuscript form requires that prose quotations of more than four lines be double spaced and indented ten spaces from the left-hand margin. The APA (American Psychological Association) manuscript form requires that prose quotations longer than forty words be double spaced and indented five to seven spaces from the left-hand margin. The CBE (Council of Biology Editors) manuscript form gives no specific length for quotations that should be indented, but it suggests indentation if the quotation cannot be incorporated conveniently into the paper. The CMS (*The Chicago Manual Style*) manuscript form requires that a quotation of eight or more lines be single spaced and indented four spaces from the left-hand margin.

Poetry (more than three lines)

> In "To the Virgins, to Make Much of Time" Robert Herrick works with
> the theme of carpe diem in these lines:
>> Gather ye rosebuds while ye may,
>> Old Time is still a-flying;
>> And this same flower that smiles today
>> Tomorrow will be dying.

MLA manuscript form requires that quotations of more than three lines of poetry be double spaced and indented ten spaces from the left-hand margin. Quotations from poetry are not often included in papers using the APA or CBE manuscript form. The CMS manuscript form requires that quotations of two or more lines of poetry be indented four spaces from the left-hand margin, either single or double spaced.

40a.3 Quotations Within Quotations

When quotations occur within the quotation you are using, you will need to make a clear distinction between the two. To use double quotation marks within double quotation marks would be confusing.

Short Quotation

> In *The Primal Mind* Jamake Highwater writes, "Among the languages of
> American Indians there is no word for 'art.' For Indians everything is
> art . . . therefore it needs no name."

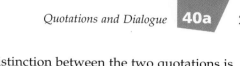

In the quotation above, the distinction between the two quotations is clear. The single quotation marks indicate that double quotation marks were used to enclose the word *art* in the original work. When you use a short quotation that has quotation marks in it, change the double quotation marks to single quotation marks.

Long Quotation

> In "The American Scholar" Emerson called for a revolution based on culture:
>> Men, such as they are, very naturally seek money or power; and power because it is as good as money,—the "spoils," so called, "of office." And why not? for they aspire to the highest, and this in their sleep-walking. . . . Wake them and they shall quit the false good and leap to the true, and leave governments to clerks and desks. This revolution is to be wrought by the gradual domestication of the idea of Culture.

In the long quotation above, the quotation marks are used as they were used in the original: double for double.

40a.4 Dialogue

Dialogue is conversation between two or more people. It is enclosed in double quotation marks just as direct quotations are. The conventions for representing dialogue serve to tell us who is speaking.

Change of Speakers

Notice how quotation marks and paragraphing are handled in the following conversation.

> "I wanted to be there," Babette said.
> "I know," Harvey responded. "It's all right. Everything worked out."
> "But I wanted to be there. I just couldn't make myself get out of bed. I'm so . . . Oh, I don't know, I just feel like I can't . . . you know . . . function."

The bit of dialogue above has two speakers, Babette and Harvey. You will notice that each time the speakers change, a new paragraph begins. In addition, the words of each speaker are enclosed in double quotation marks.

More Than One Paragraph

Now notice the use of quotation marks and paragraphing in the following dialogue.

She looked at him and said, "I don't want to be like this, not with the kids depending on me the way they do. That makes me even more depressed, knowing that they're being neglected. They're little angels, really. They don't ask that much of me. Not as much as he did, really. You know what I mean? It's just that I haven't gotten over it.

"But that's not it either, really. You know? It really doesn't matter to me anymore. I just want to sleep. He doesn't matter. He's not worth it. I get so angry sometimes, I could just scream."

"It's OK," he said as he watched her sob, her shoulders shaking, hugging herself, and rocking slowly back and forth.

The conventions for this bit of dialogue are slightly different. Notice that at the end of the first paragraph above, there are no quotation marks. This convention indicates that the speaker in the second paragraph is the same as the speaker in the first paragraph, the woman. At the end of the second paragraph, the quotation marks indicate that the woman has finished speaking. In the third paragraph, the man begins speaking.

40b
EXPLANATORY WORDS

Explanatory words may precede a quotation, interrupt the quotation, or follow the quotation. Depending on the relationship between the explanatory material and the quotation, you may want to use a comma or a colon, or you may choose to use no punctuation. The punctuation mark used most often with explanatory words is the comma.

40b.1 Preceding the Quotation

In the following examples, the explanatory material introduces the quotation. Notice how the introductory explanations are related to the quotations that follow.

1. She yelled out the door "Don't leave yet."
2. Keats's "Ode to a Nightingale" ends with the question "Do I wake or sleep?"
3. She said to him quietly, "You don't have to go yet—it's still early."
4. In a letter to a friend, Keats defined the poet: "A Poet is the most unpoetical of any thing in existence; because he has no identity. . . ."

In the first two examples, the explanatory words are closely related to the quotation, so no punctuation is used. In the third example, the normal pattern of using a comma is observed. In the last example, the explanatory words are a little more formal, so a colon is used.

40b.2 Interrupting the Quotation

In the following examples, the explanatory material interrupts the quotation. Notice what punctuation follows the explanatory words.

"I prefer," she said, "to do this alone."

"I'll make it some way," she said. "I may have to do it alone, but I'll make it."

The comma following the explanatory words in the first example is there because "I prefer to do this alone" is a single sentence. The period follows the explanatory words in the second example because "I'll make it some way" and "I may have to do it alone, but I'll make it" are two separate sentences.

40b.3 Following the Quotation

The explanatory material follows the quotation in the next examples. Notice the difference in the punctuation.

"I don't understand this question," she said.

"What don't you understand about it?" he asked.

In the first example, the comma separates the quotation from the explanatory words. In the second example, the quotation is a question and ends with a question mark, so a comma is not used.

40c
OTHER MARKS OF PUNCTUATION

The conventions for using other marks of punctuation (commas, periods, semicolons, colons, question marks, and exclamation points) with quotation marks are not complicated.

40c.1 Commas and Periods

As you read the following sentences, notice how commas and periods are placed in relation to the quotation marks.

"The clouds look very strange," he remarked.

He said, "This does not look encouraging."

Periods and commas always go *inside* quotation marks.

40c.2 Semicolons and Colons

The following sentences show how semicolons and colons are used with quotation marks.

She said, "I don't think so"; he turned and walked away.

In the Gettysburg Address, Lincoln repeated the axiom that "all men are created equal": he understood the power of tradition.

Semicolons and colons always go *outside* quotation marks.

40c.3 Dashes, Question Marks, and Exclamation Points

The following sentences illustrate how dashes, question marks, and exclamation points are used with quotation marks.

"The weather is bad"—he looked up at the sky—"and getting worse."

He asked, "What will you be wearing?"

Didn't he say, "I'll be wearing a suit"?

He screamed, "I hate apple pie!"

Don't tell me, "I don't know"!

As you can see, the question marks, dashes, and exclamation points have been placed according to whether they apply to the quotation itself or the sentence as a whole.

40d
INDIRECT QUOTATIONS

Notice the differences between the two sentences that follow.

John Milton once wrote that books are not dead, but contain the life of the person who wrote them.

John Milton wrote, "Books are not absolutely dead things, but do contain a potency of life in them to be as active as that soul was whose progeny they are."

The first example is an indirect quotation that paraphrases the second example. (Paraphrasing is also discussed in Chapters 43 and 44.) You will notice that the indirect quotation is not enclosed in quotation marks and is introduced by the word *that*.

Sometimes you will want to keep part of the original wording in an indirect quotation. Quotation marks are used to indicate the exact words from the original that are retained. Notice the following example.

John Milton wrote that books are not dead, but "contain a potency of life" so that they will be "as active as" the person who wrote them.

Emphasis

When we speak, we use a variety of methods to emphasize particular words: changing the tone of voice or making a physical gesture. But when we write, we don't have the luxury of being able to add such subtleties to our communications. Instead we add emphasis by using one of several graphical devices: capital letters, bold letters, italics (underlining if hand-written or typed), quotation marks, and hyphens. Foreign terms may be translated in the same sentence by using single or double quotation marks to enclose the English equivalent.

41a
FOREIGN WORDS, PHRASES, AND ABBREVIATIONS

When we write foreign words and phrases that have not yet become a part of English, we give them special emphasis by putting them in *italics* (underlining if handwritten or typed).

Pollock's work possesses a certain *je ne sais quoi.*

The German term *Weltanschauung,* meaning "worldview," expresses a philosophical view of the universe.

Some Latin abbreviations in the past have been italicized, but they tend to appear now without italics.

e.g.	*exempli gratia*	for example
i.e.	*id est*	that is
etc.	*et cetera*	and so forth
et al.	*et alii*	and others

41b
WORDS AND LETTERS USED AS SUCH

Words used as words and letters used as letters are ordinarily put in italics.

The word *set* causes some confusion.

When you write, your *a*'s and *o*'s sometimes look the same.

41c
SPECIAL EMPHASIS

Occasionally when we write, we may want to call attention to a word because we want the readers to give the word a special emphasis as they read. You can emphasize words in your writing in several ways.

This is *not* a debatable point.

They said the building had been "newly" renovated.

In the examples above the emphasis is created by the use of italics and quotation marks.

I want you to LEARN this lesson!

Obviously, writing a word in capital letters makes it stand out. Adding an exclamation point also calls attention to what we are saying. But these two techniques should be used sparingly if at all. Certainly there is never a need for more than one exclamation point.

CHAPTER 42

Sentences and Paragraphs

Sentences and paragraphs are the basic building blocks of all writing. Readers expect sentences and paragraphs to look similar to other sentences and paragraphs they have read before. Because of this, you will want to keep in mind certain basic conventions when you write.

42a
SENTENCES

A sentence always begins with a capital letter and ends with one of three marks of punctuation (a period, a question mark, or an exclamation point).

How long has it been since you've had rain?

We have had no rain for a month.

It's raining!

Sentences following a colon may or may not begin with a capital letter. Use the same style consistently throughout a document.

I have one request: you must meet your deadline.

I have one request: You must meet your deadline.

42b
PARAGRAPHS

When we write, we ordinarily create paragraphs by indenting, usually five spaces. How long paragraphs need to be is sometimes difficult to decide. They can range from one sentence to twenty or more sentences. Part of your decision will be based on how the text will appear to the reader. Newspapers, for instance, indent new paragraphs every two to five sentences because columns are so narrow. In typed manuscripts, most paragraphs are between eight and twelve sentences long.

Since much writing is organized in a general-to-specific pattern, with main ideas stated and several examples and explanatory sentences following, let your main ideas guide your paragraphing. A set of sentences focusing on a single idea will ordinarily be grouped together as a single paragraph. Other principles involved in structuring paragraphs are the concepts of unity and coherence (see Chapters 13 and 16).

9

Research and Documentation

Collecting Information

Suppose you wanted to understand the effects of water pollution where you live. What would you do? You could gather some equipment, inspect nearby lakes and rivers, even take samples of the water and try to analyze them. But unless you were a biologist or a chemist who already knew quite a lot about water quality, your activities would most likely be unproductive. Instead, as an interested amateur you would probably go talk with a specialist in the field or visit the library and look up information about water pollution in encyclopedias, books, magazines, newspapers, and electronic sources. The information found in technical articles dealing with water pollution would provide more detailed information about such things as toxic chemicals, particulates, and microorganisms than you could gather on your own.

Collecting information through research is an extension of the activities discussed in Part II, "Discovery and Invention." After you have completed some preliminary reading (Section 4a.3), begun to focus on a topic (Section 4b), and created a preliminary outline (Section 7b.2), you will want to consult a variety of sources that contain information about your topic. As you work, you may wonder how many and what kinds of sources you need to consult. That will depend on what topic you have chosen and what resources you have available to work with, but for many topics you will be able to identify those sources that are absolutely essential. As you are doing your background reading, you will find that some works and authorities are referred to over and over. An encyclopedia article, in either a general or specialized encyclopedia (Section 4a.3), will often list important works related to the topic. You will certainly want to consult those references.

43a
FINDING SOURCES

If you don't know much about the topic you have decided to write about, you may wonder how to begin. Well, you don't actually have to start writing until you know more about your topic. You can locate sources that will give you the information you need. Magazines, journals, and books offer the widest range of source material on most topics. That realization in itself may seem overwhelming at first. Luckily, professional librarians have anticipated this problem and have prepared sources to help. The two best places to look initially for sources are indexes of periodicals and catalogs of books. Later, you may also want to consult newspapers, pamphlets, and electronic sources for further information.

43a.1 Magazines, Journals, and Newspapers

If you have little time to complete your research or if you need the most current information, start by looking in magazines, journals, and newspapers.

Magazines

Articles on various subjects that can be found in magazines written for the general reader are listed in the *Reader's Guide to Periodical Literature*. If, for instance, you are writing about electric cars, you will be able to find articles written for the nonspecialist under that subject heading. If you know the name of a particular author who has written on the subject, you can look under the author's name as well.

Journals

Scholarly journals exist in all academic areas. In them, scholars publish the results of their research. Collectively, these publications form a record of the ongoing development of knowledge in academia.

Various specialized indexes list the articles that have appeared in these scholarly journals. If your topic is in such an area, you will want to consult one of the following specialized indexes.

> *Applied Science and Technology Index*
> *Biological and Agricultural Index*
> *Business Periodicals Index*
> *Education Index*
> *Engineering Index*
> *General Science Index*
> *Humanities Index*
> *Social Sciences Index*

For many fields of study, you will find **abstracts** of articles. Reading these short summaries carefully will help you decide whether you want to use the articles and so save you time, energy, and possibly frustration.

> *Biological Abstracts*
> *Chemical Abstracts*

Historical Abstracts

Linguistics and Language Behavior Abstracts

Physics Abstracts

Psychological Abstracts

Sociological Abstracts

Dissertation Abstracts International

Newspapers

How many years a newspaper has been indexed will vary. Many local newspaper indexes go back only a few years. The *New York Times*, in contrast, has been indexed since 1913. Some small newspapers may not even have indexes, and if you need the information from that particular paper you will have no choice but to thumb through back issues to find what you need.

You will want to evaluate whether the newspaper will give you the kind of information you need and whether it is the kind of information other sources can't provide. Newspapers provide timely articles—everything from up-to-the-minute coverage of famous trials and editorials on current controversies to reviews of books, concerts, films, and the like. But seldom do they contain articles with long-term perspectives or in-depth analysis, though there are always exceptions. Before you begin searching on your own, see if your library maintains articles of importance in a vertical file or pamphlet file (see Section 43a.5).

Microforms

Both indexes and the full text of many magazines, journals, and newspapers are available in microfilm, microfiche, and microcard formats. Because of storage problems, many libraries don't keep back copies of periodicals for very long. Microfilm, microfiche, and microcard copies of the original documents are more easily stored. Your search strategies are the same for these forms of information as for their original form, except that you will need to use special magnifying equipment that the library provides.

Online and CD Sources

Locating sources on online databases and databases stored on CDs has some advantages over print versions. Much more information is available to you, and searching for information can be faster than looking for it in a book. Deciding on the right word for finding a subject may require some creativity. If your search doesn't turn up sources when you use one word, you may have to use another related term or look in another database. (See Part XI, "The Internet," for additional information on searching electronic databases.)

43a.2 Books

If your project requires an extensive range of material, you will certainly want to explore books on your subject. And while you are researching in periodicals, you may find that the names of certain authorities and the names of particular books are frequently mentioned. You will then want to turn to these book-length works.

In the past, catalogs of books were kept on cards arranged alphabetically by author, title, and subject. Now the vast majority of libraries have their catalogs on computers. In either form, the catalog will enable you to find what books are available in your library. You will be able to find the call number of a book if you know either the author or the title. Often when you are doing research, you may not know what books you will need on the subject. In most cases, you will begin your search by looking for the books available on different subjects.

If you need a book that your library doesn't have, it may be available through interlibrary loan. Most libraries can locate the book you want through the OCLC (Online Computer Library Center) system. When ordering a book through interlibrary loan, you will need to wait a few days or as long as several months to receive the book.

Once you have a book related to your topic, the easiest way to find specific information is to look in the book's index or table of contents for your topic or related topics. You may also want to search for key terms by looking at section headings and subheadings.

43a.3 Electronic Sources

The Internet gives researchers access to an enormous variety of sources. As its name suggests, the Internet consists of millions of computers connected to each other. Some information is available only through the Internet.

The easiest and most versatile electronic resource for you to use is the World Wide Web. (See Part XI, "The Internet," for a discussion of that resource as well as others.)

43a.4 Reference Works

As you search for information about your topic, remember that your library has several specialized reference works on almost every subject. Besides general encyclopedias like the *Encyclopedia Americana* and the *Encyclopaedia Britannica* and specialized encyclopedias (discussed in Section 4a.3), the following reference books may be helpful.

Information Please Almanac

Facts on File Yearbook

Guinness Book of World Records

Statistical Abstract of the United States

United Nations Statistical Yearbook

The Americana Annual

Britannica Book of the Year

The Europa World Year Book

43a.5 Pamphlets

Some libraries have collections of pamphlets, brochures, government documents, and even clippings from newspapers and periodicals. These collections may be called either vertical files or pamphlet files. The first time you use these sources, it is best to ask for help from the librarian. Unlike books and periodicals, which are cataloged using the standard Library of Congress system, vertical files are created and maintained by the local librarians, based on their evaluations of the needs of their clientele. Usually these materials are the best source for information concerning local topics.

Vertical files are often arranged alphabetically in file cabinets and are open to use by the general public. Often you will find a booklet near the files that lists the subject headings, and sometimes the headings are written on the file drawers.

43a.6 Interviews and Surveys

Some information you need may not be available in published sources at all. Occasionally, you may need to talk to a knowledgeable authority on the subject. For instance, if you were taking a kung fu class, you might want to write about the current philosophy of martial arts teachers and students. In that case, you would probably want to interview your instructor. And who would know more about the price of Queen Anne-style furniture than the owner of a local antique store? You do not need to be shy about asking to interview such local experts; they are usually eager to share their knowledge. A telephone call is often all you need to introduce yourself and your needs. Similarly, most scholars are more than willing to help earnest researchers, especially student researchers. Even scholars in institutions other than yours will often be happy to help.

We are all familiar with the use of surveys. They are used extensively in the public media. You may find them helpful for some topics you encounter. Suppose you wanted to know the attitudes of your fellow students about the problem of homelessness in your city. You could get that kind of information by doing a survey.

Questions asked in questionnaires are of two types: objective and open-ended.

Objective   How many times in the past month have you been asked for money on the streets?

Open-ended   What has been your experience with people asking you for money on the streets?

Each type has advantages and disadvantages. A series of objective questions can readily be reduced to statistics, but there is always the danger of not getting all the relevant information if the questions are limited in scope, like the question above. Open-ended questions allow the respondent to include important information that would be missed by objective questions, but if there is no consistency in the responses, the information may be of little value.

Because of these potential problems, it is a good idea to test questionnaires before using them. A trial run will allow you to work out some of the difficulties that might decrease the value of the information.

43b
EVALUATING SOURCES

As you continue your research, you will find some sources more compelling than others. You will also find sources that contradict each other, sometimes in fact and often in opinion. How will you decide which sources to rely on and which to discard? As you look through your sources, you will develop a set of criteria for evaluating them. Though your criteria may differ with each research project, you will often begin looking for sources that are *reliable, relevant, current,* and *unbiased.*

A work is **reliable** if it has been written by a scholar or researcher who is known in the field. We tend to give more credence to research and interpretations by writers who have contributed significantly to their fields. As you accumulate information, you may run across repeated references to particular writers. A scholar who is mentioned frequently by other writers is likely to be a reliable source. In addition, articles from scholarly journals are generally considered to be more reliable than articles from newsmagazines.

However, there is another kind of reliability and authority. Firsthand accounts can be reliable if the source does not have a vested interest in some issue related to the events in question. For instance, on the topic of racial relationships in the twentieth-century American South, reliable sources are the much praised book and film *Their Eyes on the Prize* and Richard Wright's autobiography, *Black Boy*—all firsthand accounts.

A work is **relevant** if it contains information that bears directly on your topic. Be wary of using information that is only marginally connected to your topic and purpose. If your topic is the nature of the game of baseball in the 1920s, almost any discussion of Mickey Mantle, a New York Yankee in the 1950s, will be irrelevant. (Perhaps some information about the current game is relevant to help define the old game by contrast.)

Obviously, a work is **current** if it has been recently published. In some fields, especially the physical and social sciences, works that are current are generally more highly valued. Earlier works may be completely out of date. In the arts and humanities, however, standard works and traditional authorities may be used for many years. Aristotle's *Poetics*, for example, is still highly regarded by literary critics as a valuable explanation of literary art.

A work is **unbiased** if it does not reflect a particular political philosophy and strives for a fair and impartial treatment of topics. Most readers familiar with business issues recognize that *Entrepreneur* magazine has a bias toward small business owners, while *Forbes* is usually concerned with larger corporations. This is not to say that you should never use biased sources, for it can be said that every work reflects, at least partially, one bias or another. But you do need to evaluate the usefulness of your source, given your topic, your audience, and your purpose.

If you were researching the effect of gun control laws, you might read *The Spectator* (a conservative magazine) and documents written and distributed by the National Rifle Association. But you should not feel you have fully examined your topic until you read information from, say, *Mother Jones* (a liberal magazine) and gun control advocates. Bias is not wrong; we just need to recognize it.

43c
CREATING A WORKING LIST OF SOURCES

As you identify sources to use in your paper, you will need to record essential information about them. Eventually you will organize this information in a reference list at the end of the paper. You will add to the list as you continue to discover sources.

Some word processing programs allow you to enter bibliographical information while you write your paper. If yours does not, you can simply set up a file that includes the following information. You can also create your own templates with a database program.

For a Book

Author's full name

Title of the book, including edition and volume numbers

Place of publication

Publisher

Date of publication

For a Periodical

Author's full name

Title of the article

Name of the magazine or journal

Volume, issue, number, and date

The pages covered by the article

Similar information should be included for nonprint sources. (See Section 45b for the kind of information needed.)

If you need to record information when you are away from your computer, you may find it convenient to use 3" x 5" cards. Keep updating the master list on your computer to save time as you near the end of your project.

? 43d
TAKING NOTES

As you research your topic, you will quickly begin to learn things that are important to the development of your essay. Begin taking notes, jotting down ideas that you want to remember. Although there are many ways to take notes, ranging from highly systematized schemes with color coding to random scribblings on the backs of envelopes, you will find that no matter what system you use, it will have to accommodate certain information. When you begin taking notes about your topic, be sure to record the following information.

- Facts, ideas, and opinions
- Sources of the information so you can refer to the appropriate entry on the working list of sources

You can record notes in many ways, but most people will end up using one or a combination of the following four ways: templates on a word processor, templates on a database, photocopies, and handwritten notes.

43d.1 Format of Notes

No matter what method you use, you will want to include only one idea per note (75–100 words maximum). If you put too much information in a single note, particularly information of different kinds—say a fact and quotation by an authority—then your task will be complicated. You don't want to put yourself in the position of having to use information from a single note in more than one place in the paper.

Word Processor

Setting up a template on a word processor has the advantage of allowing you, when writing your paper, to transfer your notes directly by cutting and pasting. In addition, with the search feature of most word processors, you can find almost any piece of information easily and quickly.

Sample Template

Topic	Speech encoding and decoding
Text	Encoding of speech is the most recent development in the evolution of human language.
Author	Lieberman
Title	On the Origin of Language
Page	6

Database

Entering notes in a database is much like entering them on a word processor, but it has the advantage that you can automatically alphabetize your notes and reorganize them by identifying key words. Cross-referencing is consequently simplified on a database.

Sample Note on a Database

Topic	Speech encoding and decoding
Text	Encoding of speech is the most recent development in the evolution of human language.
Author	Lieberman
Title	On the Origin of Language
Page	6
Keyword	Encoding
Keyword	Decoding
Keyword	Evolution

Photocopies and Handwritten Notes

Occasionally you may need to take notes when you are away from your computer. You may photocopy pages from books or periodicals so that you can incorporate them into your notes later on. You may also find that you need to record information in handwriting. If so, it may be convenient to have note cards handy. Cards are portable; you can take them with you to the library or the park or any other place you happen to be doing research. When the time comes to transfer the notes you have recorded by hand to your word processor, you can stack and arrange the cards easily.

43d.2 Kinds of Information Recorded in Notes

As you begin taking notes, you will find that you want to include all sorts of information and ideas. You can simplify note taking if you remember that you usually record five kinds of information in notes: *direct quotation* (the exact words of a writer), *paraphrase* (a rewording of a writer's ideas in your own words), *summary* (an abbreviated version of a writer's ideas), *common knowledge* (information that is generally known in the field and can be found in several sources), and *personal observations* (your own reactions to the topic). Each kind of information has its uses when you are collecting research material.

In all likelihood, you will use all these kinds of notes. A paper that contains only quotations will not be much different from reading the original sources. Simply stringing quotations together does not communicate what you have discovered in your research, and your paper will probably be difficult for your reader to understand. On the other hand, an essay full of personal observations, though prompted by research, may sound incomplete and insubstantial.

Quotation

Quotations can be used to give support for what you say and to reflect the actual words of the writer. When you are quoting well-known writers, their exact words are also important because they give the reader an idea of the style of the writer. Notice that in the following note, the information is enclosed in quotation marks to indicate that it is a direct quotation. If you use the exact words of the writer in a paper, you must give credit to the source or you will be guilty of **plagiarism** (taking the words of another writer and presenting them as your own).

SAMPLE NOTE—QUOTATION

```
Evolutionary origin

     "Language was neither invented, nor was it a gift. It

was ground out of the evolutionary mill and suffered the

tests of survival. These tests were passed, the species

'saw that it was good,' and so we are blessed with

language."

Fromkin and Rodman, An Introduction to Language 27
```

Paraphrase

Most of your notes will take the form of **paraphrase**—that is, putting the ideas expressed by another person in your own words in a passage of approximately the same length as the original. A paraphrase allows you to communicate the ideas gained from sources when the exact words of the source are not important. You will want to find synonyms for most words and put quotation marks around quotations of three or more words (or any significant, unusual single words) copied exactly from the original source. If you fail to paraphrase accurately, you will be guilty of plagiarism. Be especially careful when paraphrasing; you may inadvertently plagiarize if your paraphrase is too similar to the original source.

SAMPLE NOTE—PARAPHRASE

```
Vocal tract

     The presence of a vocal tract that could produce a

variety of sounds, along with the development of the

physical ability to hear them, was one of the steps in

the evolutionary development of language. But this step by

itself cannot account for how language originated since

other animals, like mynah birds and parrots, have the same

capacity to produce sounds. Of course, these birds can

only imitate sounds.

Fromkin and Rodman, An Introduction to Language 27
```

The sample note above is a paraphrase of the following passage.

Certainly one evolutionary step must have resulted in the development of a vocal tract capable of producing the wide variety of sounds utilized by human language, as well as the mechanism for perceiving and distinguishing them. That this step is insufficient to explain the origin of language is evidenced by the existence of mynah birds and parrots, which have this ability. The imitations, however, are merely patterned repetitions.

You will notice that the paraphrase is about the same length as the original, but most of the information has been put into different words. Changing the words in a paraphrase is a way of reshaping the information so that it fits the overall style of the paper. You will want to use direct quotations only when the exact language of the original source is especially important to an understanding of the topic. Otherwise paraphrase will be more effective.

Summary

Often you will be able to summarize information. In a **summary** you reproduce the ideas of another writer in a much briefer form than the original. In these cases, you will not need the number and kinds of details the author has used, so you do not need to paraphrase. Nor do you need the exact words. All you need is the author's general idea and major supporting ideas. Remember that if you take a writer's original ideas in a summary form and present them as your own, you will be guilty of plagiarism.

SAMPLE NOTE—SUMMARY

```
Brain--specialized functions

        Since "tool-using and language-using abilities" are

both located in the same area of the brain, there may be

a connection between the development of these two

analytical functions and human brain development. Even

though naming objects may have been a first step in

language development, as other theories suggest, all

languages require the ability to manipulate words. The

ability to organize and combine seems to be analogous with
```

```
tool-making and thus represents another crucial step

toward language development.

Yule, The Study of Language 5
```

The note above is a summary of the following passage.

> The human brain is lateralized, that is, it has specialized functions in each of the two hemispheres. Those functions which are analytic, such as tool-making and language, are largely confined to the left hemisphere of the brain for most humans. It may be that there is an evolutionary connection between the tool-using and language-using abilities of humans, and that both are related to the development of the human brain. Most of the other theories of the origin of speech have humans producing single noises or gestures to indicate objects in their environment. This activity may indeed have been a crucial stage in the development of language, but what it lacks is any "manipulative element." All languages, including sign language, require organizing and combining sounds or signs in specific constructions. This does seem to require a specialization of some part of the brain. . . .
>
> In the analogy with tool-making, it is not enough to be able to grasp one rock (make one sound); the human must also be able to bring another rock (other sounds) into proper contact with the first. In terms of linguistic structure, the human may have first developed the naming ability, producing a specific noise for a specific object.

As you can see, the original is much longer than the summary.

Common Knowledge

Most of us know that George Washington was the first President of the United States, that Abraham Lincoln issued the Emancipation Proclamation, that Neil Armstrong was the first person to walk on the moon, that Yellowstone National Park has a number of geysers, that Mother Teresa was a nun who worked among the poor in India.

Common knowledge is information that you would find in a number of sources and which therefore does not need to be cited. Much common knowledge you know from memory; however, some information that you run across in your reading, even though it is unfamiliar to you, may be considered common knowledge as well. A rule of thumb for determining whether information is common knowledge is to note the number of sources in which you find the same information. If you can find the same information in several sources, you can feel fairly certain that it is common knowledge. Another rule of thumb is that if you find the information in a general encyclopedia, it is most likely common knowledge. If you think your credibility could be called into question, you might want to document material that you consider to be common knowledge. And even if information is common knowledge, you cannot use the exact words of another writer without enclosing them in quotation marks and crediting the source. (If you use the exact words of the writer without giving credit, you have committed plagiarism.) When in doubt, cite your source.

If the validity of the information is important to your topic, you may want to document it even though it is common knowledge. In the example below, the outdated theories of the origin of language are considered to be common knowledge. Even though most general readers would not be aware of these theories, they are commonly known to linguists and appear undocumented in many linguistics textbooks. However, if you were discussing the historical development of a particular theory, you would need to document the sources.

Sooner or later you will develop a feel for what common knowledge is, especially as you become more familiar with certain areas of study. Experience with documentation will help you make such discriminations.

SAMPLE NOTE—COMMON KNOWLEDGE

```
Outdated theories

     A number of theories have been offered over the

centuries and subsequently discarded. Many of them have

picturesque names. For instance, the onomatopoeic theory,

that language was created because people imitated sounds

around them, is called the bow-wow theory. The harmonious

response theory, suggesting that there was a harmonious

connection between language and reality, is called the

ding-dong theory. Other theories are the love song theory

(the woo-woo theory) and the emotional response theory

(the pooh-pooh theory).

Common knowledge
```

Personal Observations

Notes recording your own personal observations about a topic are extremely useful in helping you avoid simply stringing together information taken entirely from other sources. Personal observations allow you to make the work your own. They are useful for another important reason: they allow you to remember insights you had while you were gathering information. This way you won't find yourself scratching your head and saying, "Yesterday I noticed a powerful connection between these two ideas, but what was it?"

Personal observation notes have three basic functions.

1. To interpret information
2. To create transitions
3. To draw conclusions and make summations

You must remember, however, that you cannot represent someone else's ideas as a personal observation. If you do, you will be guilty of plagiarism. You will want to be sure that what you think is a personal observation is not actually an idea picked up from your research.

Notice how the sample note below interprets and draws conclusions.

SAMPLE NOTE—PERSONAL OBSERVATION

```
Reason for fascination with theories

     Even though it is impossible to know for sure just

exactly how and when language originated, most people are

intrigued by the question. Perhaps the reason is that

language is something we are all intimately familiar with,

yet we often find it difficult, illusive, and sometimes

even magical.

Personal observation
```

Using Sources

The strategies used to collect information and take notes will differ for each writer, of course. Sooner or later, however, you will begin to feel that you have collected as much information as you can use in your paper. Then your task becomes the same as it is with all writing projects—organizing and developing your topic—except that now you have an additional task. You will need to look for ways to integrate the information you gained from your research into the actual text of your work.

44a
FROM NOTES TO MANUSCRIPT

Arranging Notes

Integrating information from notes into your work is not just a matter of copying a series of notes. You will want to pay attention to arranging the information in a coherent sequence. Such an arrangement can be accomplished in part by putting similar concepts together. Notice how the following notes are related to each other.

SAMPLE NOTE—PERSONAL OBSERVATION

    Modern evolutionary theories

        Most modern theories that try to explain the origin

    of language are based on the assumption that at some

    point, primitive humans had attained the cognitive ability

    to manipulate language.

    Personal observation

SAMPLE NOTE—PARAPHRASE

    Blending

        The movement of human speech beyond the closed system

    of more primitive primates to a system that is open and

productive can be explained by the process of blending, that is, the ability of humans to recombine discrete meaningful units into new combinations.

Hockett, "The Origin of Speech" 10

SAMPLE NOTE—PARAPHRASE

Call modification

Early humans may have modified the call system by adding an intensified ending to an established call. These intensified endings would have been the first modifiers, indicating for example that danger (suggested by a particular call) was either far away or nearby. After a time the modifiers could have been separated from that call and attached to another to indicate the same kind of modification.

Jaynes, The Origin of Consciousness 132

SAMPLE NOTE—QUOTATION

Call modification

Jaynes's theory is persuasive because it "is based on emotional distinction and the call system at that stage was . . . a completely limbic affair." Further, it suggests "that hearing the difference in cries preceded the intentional changes of the cries made." Finally, "it argues for syntax, especially the manipulation of morphemes . . . right from the beginning of human language."

Maxwell, Human Evolution 270—71

SAMPLE NOTE—QUOTATION

Intermediate languages

"Evolution proceeds in small steps, and the only
reason that human language appears to be so disjoint from
human communication systems is that the hominids who
possessed 'intermediate' languages are all dead."

Lieberman, On the Origin of Language 5

Certainly there are many ways of combining the information from the notes above. The first task facing you would be to decide what general point you want to make and then what information supports your generality. You will search for the logical relationships among the ideas. (See Chapter 13.) Observe how the following passage accomplishes that goal. (The following passage follows to the MLA style of parenthetical documentation, so the numbers in parentheses are the numbers of the pages from which the information was taken.)

Combining Information Taken from Notes

Here is one way to integrate the material from the preceding notes into a paper.

Most modern theories of the origin of language are
explained in terms of human evolution. Such theories
assume that language emerged in the evolutionary process
when primitive humans developed the cognitive ability to
manipulate words. Charles F. Hockett has suggested that
the change from the limited system of primitive calls used
by other animals to the open and productive system of the
language used by humans can be explained by the process
of blending, which means recombining discrete meaningful
[sound] units into new combinations (10). In an
elaboration of Hockett's theory, Julian Jaynes has
explained that the blending may have occurred when early
humans modified the call system by adding to established

calls intensified endings that would have functioned as modifiers. Eventually, the endings could have been separated from the original and added to another call to indicate the same kind of modification (132). Commenting on Jaynes's theory, Mary Maxwell notes that it is persuasive because it "is based on <u>emotional</u> distinction," because "<u>hearing</u> the difference in cries preceded the intentional changes of the cries made," and, finally, because "it argues for syntax, especially the manipulation of morphemes . . . right from the beginning of human language" (270–71).

Of course, none of these theories, no matter how persuasive they are, can be proved, for as Philip Lieberman observes:

> Evolution proceeds in small steps, and the only reason that human language appears to be so disjoint from human communication systems is that the hominids who possessed "intermediate" languages are all dead. (5)

In the preceding example, the writer elects to make use of notes that are all related to the main idea—that human language evolved as new physical and cognitive skills developed. The information selected for use explains Hockett's theory of blending and two elaborations of it, but concludes with a general comment that places such theories in perspective.

44b
INCORPORATING INFORMATION INTO YOUR WRITING

After you have collected and arranged your notes, they may seem like stacked bricks without mortar to hold them together. Your task then becomes finding ways to lead from one piece of information to another

with transitions and introductory phrases. Depending on the kind of information you are using, you will want to employ different strategies for
integrating it into your writing.

44b.1 Introducing Quotations, Paraphrases, and Summaries

As you read the following passage, see if you can determine why it is less
effective than the last passage in Section 44a.

> The change from the limited system of primitive calls
> used by other animals to the open and productive system
> of the language used by humans can be explained by the
> process of blending, which means recombining discrete
> meaningful [sound] units into new combinations (Hockett
> 10). The blending may have occurred when early humans
> modified the call system by adding to established calls
> intensified endings that would have functioned as
> modifiers. Eventually, the endings could have been
> separated from the original and added to another call to
> indicate the same kind of modification (Jaynes 132).
> Jaynes's theory is persuasive because it "is based on
> emotional distinction," because "hearing the difference in
> cries preceded the intentional changes of the cries made,"
> and, finally, because "it argues for syntax, especially
> the manipulation of morphemes . . . right from the
> beginning of human language" (Maxwell 270—71).
>
> > Evolution proceeds in small steps, and the only
> > reason that human language appears to be so
> > disjoint from human communication systems is
> > that the hominids who possessed "intermediate"
> > languages are all dead. (Lieberman 5)

This version of the passage is less effective than the one in Section 44a because it lacks the transitions, introductory phrases, and explanations that make the information more understandable and readable.

The following sentences and phrases that were present in the version in Section 44a were deleted from this version.

> Most modern theories of the origin of language are explained in terms of human evolution. Such theories assume that language emerged in the evolutionary process when primitive humans developed the cognitive ability to manipulate words.

> Charles F. Hockett has suggested that . . . .

> In an elaboration of Hockett's theory, Julian Jaynes has explained that . . . .

> Commenting on Jaynes's theory, Mary Maxwell notes that . . . .

> Of course, none of these theories, no matter how persuasive they are, can be proved, for as Philip Lieberman observes:

These transitions and introductory phrases make the passage in Section 44a more readable. The version in Section 44b.1 is less coherent. It does not flow as smoothly without the transitions.

Identifying the sources for the reader by using introductory and connecting phrases makes the text of the paper easier to read. When every citation is relegated to parentheses following the information used, the effectiveness of the source material is diminished. In addition, introductory phrases make clear for the reader where a paraphrase or summary begins and help separate it from personal comments. Making clear where every bit of information comes from helps the reader understand the topic better.

44b.2 Using Effective Introductory Phrases and Transitions

Notice the effect of the boldfaced introductory transitional phrases in this rewritten passage.

> **Hockett writes** that the change from the limited system of primitive calls used by other animals to the "open and productive" system of the language used by humans "can be explained by the process of blending,"

which means recombining "discrete meaningful [sound] units into new combinations" (10). **Jaynes writes** that the blending may have occurred when early humans "modified the call system" by adding to established calls "intensified endings" that would have functioned as modifiers. Eventually, the endings could have been separated from the original and added to another call "to indicate the same kind of modification" (132). **Mary Maxwell writes** that Jaynes's theory is persuasive because it "is based on <u>emotional</u> distinction," because "<u>hearing</u> the difference in cries preceded the intentional changes of the cries made," and, finally, because "it argues for syntax, especially the manipulation of morphemes . . . right from the beginning of human language" (270–71).

> **Philip Lieberman writes:**
>
> Evolution proceeds in small steps, and the only reason that human language appears to be so disjoint from human communication systems is that the hominids who possessed "intermediate" languages are all dead. (5)

Although this version is better than the one in Section 44b.1, it is not as effective as the first version in Section 44a. The use of the same phrase to introduce each source is repetitive. Readers have an easier time reading the material if the introductory phrases are varied.

There are a great many different ways to vary introductory phrases. Look back at the passage in Section 44a and notice how introductory phrases are used. By paying attention to the transitions other writers use, you will discover effective ways of introducing information. The following are a few examples of ways you can vary introductory phrases.

Robertson and Cassidy in <u>The Development of Modern English</u> write: "But if the <u>how</u> of language can never be

known, there can be little doubt as to the <u>why</u>. Language
must have arisen out of a social necessity—the need for
communication between man and man" (9).

    As Robertson and Cassidy observe, even though we may
never know how language originated, we certainly can be
sure that it arose "out of a social necessity" (9).

    Robertson and Cassidy say that even though we may
never know how language originated, we certainly can be
sure that it arose "out of a social necessity" (9).

    **In an analysis of the origin of language, Robertson
and Cassidy suggest that** even though we may never know
the mechanisms that controlled how language developed, we
do know what caused it to develop. The cause, they
assert, is "social necessity" (9).

(For more information about transitional phrases, see Section 15d.)

44b.3 Citing Borrowed Sentences

A paper made up of a series of paragraphs, either quoted or paraphrased, with a citation at the end of each paragraph is not nearly as effective as a paper that fully integrates material from several sources together and offers interpretations of the material used. If every sentence contains a signal that clearly points to the source of the material used, the reader will have a better understanding of the relationship between the ideas presented.

Notice that in the following passage the source of the material is clearly evident.

    Although the mechanisms that produced language may
not be fully understood, there seems to be little question
that language developed because of social pressures. As
Robertson and Cassidy note in <u>The Development of Modern
English</u>, "But if the <u>how</u> of language can never be known,

```
there can be little doubt as to the why. Language must

have arisen out of a social necessity . . ." (9).

Certainly, there can be little question that language

arose "out of a social necessity," but just whether that

social necessity arose on the savannahs of central Africa

or later in northern Europe during the periods of

glaciation is not clear. Psychologist Julian Jaynes offers

the theory that because of the increased darkness during

the fourth glacial period, "vocal intentional signals gave

a pronounced selective advantage to those who possessed

them" (132).
```

In this passage the sources of the information are clearly marked. The first sentence is a personal observation of the writer. The second sentence is clearly attributed to a source. The third sentence is a personal observation. The fourth sentence is from a different source.

44b.4 When an Introduction for a Source Is Unnecessary

In most cases you will introduce paraphrases and summaries with a phrase identifying the source of the information. On occasion, however, you may not need to use an introductory phrase. Sometimes it is more important to integrate the information into the flow of your writing than to provide an introductory statement.

When the Source of the Information Is Not Important

Introducing a paraphrase is sometimes unnecessary if the information itself is more important than the person who wrote it and an introductory phrase would disrupt or complicate the flow of your writing. Of course, you would need to cite the source at the end of the paraphrase. The following example illustrates the technique.

```
Jaynes's theory of the origin of language is

persuasive to some scholars because he recognizes the

emotional nature of language, suggests that deliberate
```

```
changes occurred after differences in cries were

recognized, and establishes the importance of morphemes in

the development of syntax (Maxwell 270–73).
```

When Information Comes from Several Sources

When information comes from several sources, it would be awkward to cite them in an introductory phrase. Notice how the following example presents the information.

```
    A number of authorities agree that English spelling

is a major problem that could prevent English from

becoming a world language (Baugh and Cable 12; Robertson

and Cassidy 416).
```

CHAPTER

45

Documenting Sources

Depending on the academic area you are writing your paper in, you will use one of the four different styles of documentation: Modern Language Association or MLA (English and the humanities), American Psychological Association or APA (psychology and the other social sciences), Council of Biology Editors or CBE (the life sciences), and *The Chicago Manual of Style* or CMS (history and art history).

45a
CITING SOURCES WITHIN A PAPER

In much academic writing, parenthetical documentation has replaced the older style of footnoting or endnoting (placing a raised number in the text with a corresponding number and entry at the bottom of the page or at the end of the work). Parenthetical documentation makes reading easier because the reader doesn't have to keep flipping to the end of the essay to find out who's being quoted; it also simplifies typing and layout concerns since the writer doesn't have to design a page with space for footnotes at the bottom. Three styles of parenthetical documentation illustrate the patterns used in most disciplines. In Sections 45a.1 through 45a.3 you will find out how to use three forms of parenthetical documentation: the MLA style, the APA style, and the CBE style. In Section 45a.4 you will learn about the CMS style of documentation with footnotes.

45a.1 MLA Citations

For writing papers in English, languages, and some of the humanities, the style of documentation recommended by the Modern Language Association requires that you put the page number—where the information appeared in the original source—in parentheses after the quotation or paraphrase used in your work. If the source is not indicated by a phrase introducing the information, then the last name of the author is also included in the parentheses.

The following examples illustrate typical patterns of MLA citations for a number of different kinds of sources.

A WORK BY ONE AUTHOR

> Philip Lieberman emphasizes the importance of
> language when he observes, "Language affects and indeed
> structures virtually all aspects of human behavior" (1).

In this case, the page number is the only information enclosed in the parentheses; the author, Philip Lieberman, is identified in the introductory phrase. The following citation differs.

> Not only does language affect our actions, but it
> also structures practically every aspect of what we do as
> humans (Lieberman 1).

In this case, the author's name is included in the parentheses along with the page number because he is not identified in the text.

A WORK BY TWO OR THREE AUTHORS

When a work has two or three authors, they are all identified.

> Since language probably developed in humans as the
> brain and nervous system changed, the languages of
> primitive humans would have been simpler than our language
> today (Fromkin and Rodman 26).

A WORK BY FOUR OR MORE AUTHORS

For a source with four or more authors, you need put only the name of the first author followed by the Latin abbreviation *et al.* Notice that the abbreviation requires a period but is not italicized or underlined.

> Some historians have observed that during the 1980s
> in the fields of communications and electronics,
> "technological developments--miniaturization, satellite
> transmission, the videocassette recorder (VCR), and
> computers--affected almost every segment of American
> society, from the office, to homes, to schools" (Berkin
> et al. 893).

A GROUP AUTHOR

A source can be identified by the name of the group that serves as the author (a corporation, a government agency, an association, or a board, for example). It is usually better, especially if the name of the group is a long one, to incorporate it into an introductory phrase so that an extended parenthetical reference doesn't interrupt the reader.

> As early as 1972, the Conference Board, a New York-
> based business research group, issued a warning about the
> possible impact of the information technologies by saying
> that we could "create a new kind of rich-poor gap between
> those, regardless of economic status, who know how to
> command information and those who do not" (v).

In this example, since the group author (*Conference Board*) is identified in the passage, only the page number (*v*) is included in the parentheses at the end of the citation.

MORE THAN ONE VOLUME OF A WORK

In the following example, the number *1* in parentheses indicates the volume number. The number *2* is the page number. A colon separates the volume and page numbers.

> A nine-volume government report that analyzes the
> information economy defines information as "the data that
> has been organized and communicated" and information
> <u>activity</u> as "all the resources consumed in producing,
> processing and distributing information goods and
> services" (U.S. Department of Commerce 1: 2).

To cite a single volume of a multivolume work, put a comma after the author's name and include the abbreviation *vol.* (e.g., *U.S. Department of Commerce, vol. 1*). To indicate the volume number in the passage rather than in the parenthetical citation, spell out the word *volume* rather than abbreviating it.

WORKS BY AUTHORS WITH THE SAME LAST NAME

In the two passages below, the use of the author's first name in both the direct quotation and the paraphrase indicates that the paper contains another citation by an author with the same last name. To tell the reader which author named Thomas the citation refers to, the first name is included.

> Networking is not a new concept; indeed, biologist
> Lewis Thomas has noted that the "urge to form
> partnerships, to link up and form collaborative
> arrangements, is perhaps the oldest, strongest and most
> fundamental force in nature" (19).

> Networking is not a new concept; indeed, one
> biologist has suggested that collaborating and working
> together is perhaps one of the oldest and most powerful
> motivations in the world (Lewis Thomas 19).

MORE THAN ONE WORK BY THE SAME AUTHOR

If you have cited more than one work by the same author, you will need to distinguish between them by including information about the source either in the passage itself or in the parenthetical citation.

> One scholar has asserted that "every language mirrors
> and generates a possible world, an alternate reality"
> (Steiner, "The Coming Universal Language" 26).

> George Steiner contends that "every language mirrors
> and generates a possible world, an alternate reality"
> ("The Coming Universal Language" 26).

> George Steiner in "The Coming Universal Language"
> contends that "every language mirrors and generates a
> possible world, an alternate reality" (26).

A WORK FOR WHICH NO AUTHOR IS GIVEN

When no author is given, identify the source by the title of the article.

> The imbalance of information between the United
> States and much of the rest of the world is evidenced by
> the enormous amount of paper used to fuel the American
> information culture ("The Third World's Paper Gap" 1).

A NOVEL, A PLAY, OR A POEM

For a novel or a modern play, it is often helpful to include information such as the chapter or scene number in addition to the page number. Such works may have been printed in several editions.

> In Hemingway's <u>A Farewell to Arms</u>, Frederic's memory
> of Catherine is infused with metaphor: "She had
> wonderfully beautiful hair and I would lie sometimes and
> watch her twisting it up in the light that came in the

MLA

open door and it shone even in the night as water shines
sometimes just before it is really daylight" (118; ch.
17).

For classic plays—Shakespeare's, for example—cite act, scene, and
line numbers instead of page numbers.

At the end of act 1, we begin to be aware of
Hamlet's tragic situation when he says, "The time is out
of joint. Oh, cursed spite / That ever I was born to set
it right . . ." (1.5.189–90).

For a poem, cite line numbers. If a long poem is divided into parts,
books, or cantos, add that number before the line numbers.

In his Essay on Criticism, Pope reveals the
neoclassical emphasis on decorum when he writes, "Good
nature and good sense must ever join; / To err is human,
to forgive divine" (2.525–26).

AN INDIRECT SOURCE

When you cite a source quoted in another work, use the abbreviation *qtd. in.*

Bill Bates, a pioneer in electronic publishing, has
predicted that the difference in cost between traditional
publishing and electronic publishing will diminish and
that eventually "these two paths will cross and electronic
publishing is going to become very attractive" (qtd. in
Holt 32).

AN ENTIRE WORK

When you cite an entire work, it is preferable to put the author's name in
the text rather than in a parenthetical citation.

In 1962, economist Fritz Machlup, in a pioneering
study titled The Production and Distribution of Knowledge

<u>in the United States</u>, predicted that activities related to
information exchange would eventually become the dominant
part of the U.S. economy.

MORE THAN ONE WORK IN A SINGLE PARENTHETICAL CITATION

You can list several works in a single citation.

A number of authorities agree that English spelling
is a major problem that could prevent English from
becoming a world language (Baugh and Cable 12; Robertson
and Cassidy 416).

45a.2 APA Citations

In contrast to the MLA style of parenthetical documentation, the style recommended by the APA (American Psychological Association) emphasizes
the year of the publication rather than the page number of the source. It
is important that studies in the social sciences reflect the most recent schol-
arship. The year is usually put at the point of citation rather than at the
end of the passage. Some other differences exist, which you will discover
as you read the following examples. For example, a page number is
required for direct quotations. (A page number is not required for a paraphrase, but it is encouraged.)

A WORK BY ONE AUTHOR

Skinner (1969) identifies the essential ingredients
of stimulus-response theory when he notes that "adequate
formulation of the interaction between an [individual] and
[his or her] environment must always specify three things:
(1) the occasion upon which a response occurs, (2) the
response itself, and (3) the reinforcing consequences"
(p. 7).

A WORK BY TWO AUTHORS

Some researchers (Charniak & McDermott, 1985) believe
that "the ultimate goal of AI [Artificial Intelligence]

A
P
A

research is to build a person or, more humbly, an animal"
(p. 7).

A WORK BY THREE TO FIVE AUTHORS

Noncued avoidance conditioning has been demonstrated
in humans (Hefferline, Keenan, & Harford, 1959) as well as
in lower organisms.

A WORK BY SIX OR MORE AUTHORS

Research studies (Hayes et al., 1985) have shown that
public goals are more effective than private goals in
improving performance on tests.

A GROUP AUTHOR

The American Association on Mental Retardation
condemns "aversion procedures which cause physical pain or
illness" and "procedures which are dehumanizing--social
degradation, verbal abuse and excessive reactions" (AAMR,
1990).

A WORK FOR WHICH NO AUTHOR IS GIVEN

The Practice Directorate of the American
Psychological Association and the National Association
of School Psychologists have testified to Congress
to show their support for an amendment that would ban
the use of physical punishment for emotionally
disturbed children ("PD Supports Ban on Corporal
Punishment," 1990).

WORKS BY AUTHORS WITH THE SAME LAST NAME

The term behavior modification was first used by
R. I. Watson (1962).

An extreme form of environmentalism is reflected in this famous claim:

> Give me a dozen healthy infants, well-formed, and my own specified world to bring them up in and I'll guarantee to take any one at random and train him to become any type of specialist I might select-- doctor, lawyer, artist, merchant, chief, and, yes, even beggarman and thief, regardless of his talents, penchants, tendencies, abilities, vocations, and race of his ancestors. (J. B. Watson, 1930, p. 104)

MORE THAN ONE WORK IN THE SAME CITATION

The following citation identifies three works. Each is set up the same way as a citation for a single work. The entries are arranged alphabetically and are separated by semicolons.

> The advent of computers and electronic media has made self-paced and personalized instructional systems more efficient and easier for instructors to manage (Crosbie & Glenn, 1993; Crowell, Quintanar, & Grant, 1981; Hantula, Boyd, & Crowell, 1989; Rae, 1993).

The following citation refers to two different works by the same author in the same year.

> Behavioral strategies have been devised that help athletes cope with competition in sport (Orlick, 1986a, 1986b).

A CLASSICAL WORK

> William James (1892/1961) identified one aspect of self-consciousness when he wrote, "Whatever I may be thinking of, I am always at the same time more or less aware of myself, of my personal existence" (p. 43).

C B E

45a.3 CBE Citations

Like the MLA and APA systems of documentation, the CBE (Council of Biology Editors) system lists information about the sources in parentheses. With some variations, the CBE system is widely used in sciences other than biology. When using the CBE system, you will have to choose from two formats: the name-year system and the number system (in order of appearance).

The Name-Year System of Citations

The CBE name-year system is similar to the APA system in that it uses dates rather than page numbers at the point of citation. Note that a period is not used after the abbreviation *p* for *page* or *pages*.

A WORK BY ONE AUTHOR

> Pusey (1980) has observed that in the Gombe National Park in Tanzania, free-ranging female chimpanzees practiced both incest avoidance and exogamy.

A WORK BY TWO AUTHORS

> Researchers (Eisenburg and Kuehn 1966) have noted that in primate societies, removal of dominant individuals increases aggression among subordinates.

> Eisenburg and Kuehn (1966) noted that in primate societies, removal of dominant individuals increases aggression among subordinates.

A WORK BY THREE OR MORE AUTHORS

> Studies have shown that subjects who have effects from placebos also fail to distinguish between the effectiveness of different analgesics. Further, those who don't react to placebos are more likely to prefer one analgesic over another (Beecher and others 1953).

A Work by a Group Author

> Oil and gas emit smaller amounts of carbon dioxide than coal for the same efficiencies (National Research Council 1977, p 61).

A Work for Which No Author is Given

> One study (Anonymous 1976, p 174–8) estimated the potential capacity of a wave conversion device in the water.

The Number System of Citations

In the number system of citations, numbers are used to identify references that are listed at the end of the document.

> Preliminary evidence[1,2] suggests that weightlessness may allow some unique industrial processes to take place on a space station.

The references are listed at the end of the paper in numerical order, in the sequence in which they appear in the paper. If the source is used in the paper more than once, it is always cited by the number of its original entry. (See Section 45b.3 for the forms of different kinds of sources.)

45a.4 CMS Citations

The traditional way to indicate that you have cited another source is to use a note number (a number raised above the line at the end of the material being quoted, paraphrased, or summarized). This form of citation is based on *The Chicago Manual of Style* and is usually used in history, art, and some other areas of the humanities. The examples in this book are based on *A Manual for Writers of Term Papers, Theses, and Dissertations* by Kate L. Turabian, which incorporates most of the principles advocated by *The Chicago Manual of Style*.

> During the seventeenth century, the Quakers were enormously successful in spreading their religious doctrine throughout England, Ireland, and America.[1] The

```
Quaker settlements in colonial America attest to that

fact.
```

The references are put either at the bottom of the page as footnotes or at the end of the paper as endnotes (see Section 45b.4 for form).

45b
LISTING SOURCES AT THE END OF A PAPER

After you have finished writing your paper, list on a separate page at the end of the work any sources you have used. This list of sources serves as a convenience for the reader. By the very act of writing, you have joined a group of people who are interested in the topic you have addressed. You have, in essence, joined a community of collaborators who are separated by many miles and sometimes many years. These individual readers will find many statements and ideas in your written work intriguing and challenging. They may want to follow up on these ideas by reading the sources you cited.

The reference list, therefore, is essential because it gives the reader all necessary information about the sources you have used. Although the information contained in an entry is generally the same for each documentation style, the information is presented in different ways. Each method has some features in common. The MLA, APA, CBE name-year, and CMS bibliography formats all require that sources be listed at the end of the work in alphabetical order by the last name of the author. The CBE number and CMS note formats require that the sources be listed in numerical order.

45b.1 MLA Reference List

Books

An entry for a book in a reference list using the MLA style will have the following elements: *author* (last name first, followed by a comma, then first name and any initials); *title* (underlined); *city of publication*; *publisher* (generally shortened to one word); *date of publication* (most recent copyright date).

The following examples illustrate the general pattern of a book entry. Additional information is included when needed.

A BOOK WITH ONE AUTHOR

```
Lieberman, Philip. On the Origins of Language. New

     York: Macmillan, 1975.
```

A BOOK WITH TWO OR THREE AUTHORS

For a book by two or three authors, add a comma after the name of the first author (as listed on the book), then the names of the other authors, first name first.

```
Fromkin, Victoria, and Robert Rodman. An Introduction

     to Language. New York: Holt, 1974.
```

A BOOK BY MORE THAN THREE AUTHORS

When a book has more than three authors, you can list them either of two ways: first author followed by the Latin abbreviation *et al.* (not underlined and with no period after *et*), or all authors.

```
Berkin, Carol, et al. Making America: A History of the

     United States. Boston: Houghton, 1995.
```

```
Berkin, Carol, Christopher L. Miller, Robert W.

     Cherny, and James L. Gormly. Making America: A

     History of the United States. Boston: Houghton,

     1995.
```

A BOOK WITH NO AUTHOR NAMED

The first element in a listing for a book with no author is the title of the book.

```
Texas Travel Handbook. Austin: State Dept. of Highways

     and Public Transportation, 1986.
```

The entry is alphabetized in the list of references by the first word of the title (disregarding the words *a, an,* and *the*).

M
L
A

A Book with a Group Author

Conference Board. Information Technology: Some Critical

  Implications for Decision Makers, Rept. 537. New

  York: Conference Board, 1975.

A Government Publication

U.S. National Commission on Libraries and Information.

  National Information Policy. Rept. to the

  President submitted by the staff of the Domestic

  Council on the Right of Privacy. Washington: GPO,

  1975.

An Anthology or Edited Book

Finch, Robert, and John Elder, eds. The Norton Book of

  Nature Writing. New York: Norton, 1990.

A Book with a Title Within a Title

When a title of a work that is usually underlined (e.g., King Lear, a play by Shakespeare) appears in the title of a book, the title of that work is not underlined.

Adelman, Janet, ed. Twentieth Century Interpretations

  of King Lear: A Collection of Critical Essays.

  Englewood Cliffs: Prentice, 1978.

An Edition Other Than the First

Baugh, Albert C., and Thomas Cable. A History of the

  English Language. 3rd ed. Englewood Cliffs:

  Prentice, 1978.

A Translated Work

Aristotle. The Art of Rhetoric. Trans. H. C. Lawson-

  Tancred. London: Penguin, 1991.

A MULTIVOLUME WORK

Abrams, M. H., et al., eds. <u>The Norton Anthology of</u>

    <u>English Literature</u>. 5th ed. 2 vols. New York:

    Norton, 1986.

A SELECTION IN AN ANTHOLOGY

The three entries that follow illustrate different patterns of recording information about a selection from an anthology. The last two entries show how to list reprints.

Booth, Stephen. "On the Greatness of <u>King Lear</u>."

    <u>Twentieth Century Interpretations of</u> King Lear:

    <u>A Collection of Critical Essays</u>. Ed. Janet

    Adelman. Englewood Cliffs: Prentice, 1978.

    98—111.

Spilka, Mark. "Of George and Lennie and Curley's Wife:

    Sweet Violence in Steinbeck's Eden." <u>Modern</u>

    <u>Fiction Studies</u> 20.2 (1974): 169—79. Rpt. in

    <u>Contemporary Literary Criticism</u>. Vol. 21. Detroit:

    Gale, 1982. 381.

Mack, Maynard. "The World of <u>King Lear</u>." <u>Twentieth</u>

    <u>Century Interpretations of</u> King Lear: <u>A</u>

    <u>Collection of Critical Essays</u>. Ed. Janet Adelman.

    Englewood Cliffs: Prentice, 1978. 56—69. Rpt. of

    "Action and World." King Lear <u>in Our Time</u>.

    Maynard Mack. Berkeley: U of California P, 1965.

    98—117.

AN ARTICLE IN A REFERENCE BOOK

McGaw, Charles. "Acting." <u>The Encyclopedia Americana</u>.

    1993 ed.

AN INTRODUCTION, A PREFACE, A FOREWORD, OR AN AFTERWORD

Lee, Hermione. Introduction. <u>Three Guineas</u>. By Virginia
Woolf. London: Hogarth, 1986. vii–xvii.

A PAMPHLET OR BROCHURE

<u>San Francisco: Quick Guide</u>. San Francisco: Guest
Informant, 1995.

Periodicals

AN ARTICLE IN A NEWSPAPER

Cater, Douglass. "A Communications Revolution?" <u>Wall
Street Journal</u> 6 Aug. 1973: 18.

AN EDITORIAL

"So Long Calvin and Hobbes." Editorial. <u>Austin
American-Statesman</u> 31 Dec. 1995: D2.

A LETTER TO THE EDITOR

Powell, Colin L. Letter. <u>New Yorker</u> 30 Oct. 1995: 10.

A REVIEW

Morris, Anne. Rev. of <u>All Rivers Run to the Sea</u>, by
Elie Wiesel. <u>Austin American-Statesman</u> 17 Dec.
1995: E7.

AN ARTICLE IN A MAGAZINE

Elmer-Dewitt, Philip. "Battle for the Soul of the
Internet." <u>Time</u> 25 July 1994: 50–56.

AN ARTICLE IN A JOURNAL WITH CONTINUOUS PAGINATION

Dawkins, John. "Teaching Punctuation as a Rhetorical
Tool." <u>College Composition and Communication</u> 46
(1995): 533–48.

An Article in a Journal Paginated by Issue

Hunter, John O. "Technological Literacy: Defining a
New Concept for General Education." <u>Educational
Technology</u> 32.3 (1992): 26–29.

An Article with No Author Named

"The Third World's Paper Gap." <u>Washington Post</u> 1 Sept.
1977: 1.

Other Sources

A Radio or Television Program

"The Red Circle." <u>The Memoirs of Sherlock Holmes</u>. By
Sir Arthur Conan Doyle. Adapt. Jeremy Paul. Dir.
Sarah Hellings. Perf. Jeremy Brett and Edward
Hardwicke. Mystery. Introd. Diana Rigg. PBS.
KLRU, Austin. 11 Jan. 1996.

A Film or Videotape

<u>Henry V</u>. Dir. Kenneth Branagh. Perf. Kenneth Branagh,
Paul Scofield, Derek Jacobi, and Ian Holm. Samuel
Goldwyn, 1989.

A Sound Recording

Eagles. <u>Hell Freezes Over</u>. Geffen, 1994.

A Live Performance

<u>Jeffrey Bernard Is Unwell</u>. By Keith Waterhouse. Dir.
Ned Sherrin. Perf. Peter O'Toole. Apollo Theatre,
London. 18 Oct. 1989.

A LECTURE, SPEECH, OR ADDRESS OR PUBLISHED PROCEEDINGS

```
Selzer, Richard. Address. NCTE Convention. Hyatt

     Regency Hotel, San Antonio. 21 Nov. 1986.
```

AN INTERVIEW

```
Vonnegut, Kurt. Interview with Michael Schumacher.

     Writer's Digest. Nov. 1985: 22—27.
```

A LETTER, A MEMO, OR AN EMAIL COMMUNICATION

```
Gnerre, Alison. Email to the authors. 16 Sep.

     1998.
```

A PUBLICATION ON DISKETTE

```
Lanham, Richard D. The Electronic Word: Democracy,

     Technology, and the Arts. Diskette. Chicago: U of

     Chicago P, 1993.
```

A PUBLICATION ON CD-ROM

```
Pei, Mario. "English Language." Encarta. CD-ROM.

     Redmond: Microsoft, 1994.
```

Sources from the World Wide Web

An entry for a source from the World Wide Web should include all available information that is relevant to the entry: *author; title; publication information* for any print version of the source; *date of electronic publication* (update or posting date); *name of list or form* (if applicable); *number of pages, paragraphs, or sections,* if numbered; *date researcher accessed source; electronic address* in angle brackets.

PROFESSIONAL SITE

```
The H.D. International Society. 30 March 1998

     <http://www.well.com/user/heddy/hdsoc.html>.
```

M
L
A

PERSONAL SITE

Rosenberg, Jim. Home page. 30 March 1998

    <http://www.well.com/user/jer/index.html#menu>.

BOOK

Turner, Mark. <u>Death Is the Mother of Beauty: Mind,</u>

    <u>Metaphor, Criticism</u>. Chicago: U of Chicago Press,

    1987. <u>Mark Turner's Home Page</u>. 30 March 1998

    <http://www.wam.umd.edu/~mturn/WWW/DMB.WWW/

    dmbfront.html>.

POEM

DuPlessis, Rachel Blau. "Draft XXX: Fosse." <u>Drafts 15-</u>

    <u>XXX, The Fold</u>. Elmwood, CT: Potes & Poets, 1997.

    <u>The Electronic Poetry Center</u>. SUNY Buffalo. 30

    March 1998 <http://wings.buffalo.edu/epc/authors/

    duplessis/fosse.html>.

ARTICLE IN A REFERENCE DATABASE

"CHAD--A Country Study." <u>Library of Congress Country</u>

    <u>Studies</u>. Nov. 1997 Library of Congress. 30 March

    1998 <http://lcweb2.loc.gov/cgi-bin/query2/

    r?frd/cstdy:@field(DOCID+td0012)>.

ARTICLE IN A JOURNAL

Joyce, Michael. "Notes Toward an Unwritten Non-Linear

    Electronic Text, 'The Ends of Print Culture' (a

    work in progress)." <u>Postmodern Culture</u> 2.1 (1991):

    45 pars. 27 Oct. 1997 <http://www.press.jhu.edu/

    journals/postmodern_culture/v002/2.1joyce.html>.

ARTICLE IN A NEWSPAPER

Winik, Marion. "The Originator, Not the Imitator: My

    Luncheon with Anna Quindlen." <u>Austin Chronicle</u>.

    27 March 1998. 30 March 1998 <http://www.austin

    chronicle.com/current/books.quindlen.html>.

How to Create a Reference List Using the MLA Style

To create a works cited page, list the sources cited in the paper in alphabetical order on a separate page after the last page of text. Center the title "Works Cited" at the top of the page. Set up the entries using reverse indentation, also known as a *hanging indent*: start the first line of each entry at the left margin and indent succeeding lines five spaces. All lines are double spaced. If you list two or more works by the same author, replace the name of the author with three hyphens in the second and any succeeding entries. If the person named is an editor, translator, or compiler, the abbreviation *ed., trans.,* or *comp.* must be repeated for each entry. If the author is unknown, alphabetize by the first word of the title. (An initial *A, An,* or *The* is disregarded.) Notice how the principles discussed above have been incorporated into the sample works cited page below.

Works Cited

Hockett, Charles F. "The Origin of Speech." <u>Human

    Communication</u>. Ed. William S-Y. Wang. San

    Francisco: Freeman, 1982.

Jaynes, Julian. <u>The Origin of Consciousness in the

    Breakdown of the Bicameral Mind</u>. Boston:

    Houghton, 1990.

Lieberman, Philip. <u>On the Origins of Language</u>. New

    York: Macmillan, 1975.

Sapir, Edward. "Conceptual Categories in Primitive

    Languages." <u>Language in Culture and Society</u>. Ed.

    Dell Hymes. New York: Harper, 1964.

---. <u>Language: An Introduction to the Study of Speech</u>.

    New York: Harcourt, 1921.

Yule, George. <u>The Study of Language</u>. Cambridge:

  Cambridge UP, 1985.

45b.2 APA Reference List

Books

An entry for a book in a reference list using the APA style will have the following elements: *author* (last name first, followed by a comma, then initials); *date* (last copyright date listed, in parentheses); *title* (underlined, with only the first word of both the main title and subtitle as well as all proper nouns capitalized); *city of publication* (add the abbreviation for the state if the city is not well known for publishing*); publisher* (shortened to a few words).

A BOOK WITH ONE AUTHOR

Skinner, B. F. (1969). <u>Contingencies of reinforcement:</u>

  <u>A theoretical analysis.</u> New York: Appleton-

  Century-Crofts.

A BOOK WITH TWO AUTHORS

Cherniak, E., & McDermott, D. (1985). <u>Introduction to</u>

  <u>artificial intelligence.</u> Reading, MA: Addison-

  Wesley.

A BOOK WITH NO AUTHOR NAMED

<u>National Catholic almanac.</u> (1980). Huntington, IN: Our

  Sunday Visitor.

A BOOK WITH A GROUP AUTHOR

United Nations. (1974). <u>Demographic yearbook.</u> New York:

  United Nations Publications.

A GOVERNMENT PUBLICATION

U.S. National Center for Social Statistics. (1980).

  <u>Adoptions in 1970, adoptions in 1975</u> (Report E-

  10). Washington, DC: Government Printing Office.

AN ANTHOLOGY OR EDITED BOOK

Dews, P. (Ed.). (1970). <u>Festschrift for B. F. Skinner.</u>
    New York: Appleton-Century-Crofts.

AN EDITION OTHER THAN THE FIRST

Thorpe, W. H. (1963). <u>Learning and instinct in animals</u>
    (2nd ed.). London: Methuen.

A TRANSLATED WORK

Inhelder, B., & Piaget, J. (1958). <u>The growth of</u>
    <u>logical thinking from childhood to adolescence.</u>
    (A. Parsons & S. Milgram, Trans.). New York:
    Basic Books.

A MULTIVOLUME WORK

Thomas, W. I., & Znaniecki, F. (1918). <u>The Polish</u>
    <u>peasant in Europe and America.</u> (Vols. 1–2).
    Chicago: University of Chicago Press.

A SELECTION IN AN ANTHOLOGY

Murdock, G. P. (1945). The common denominator of
    culture. In R. Linton (Ed.), <u>The science of man</u>
    <u>in the world crisis</u> (pp. 124–142). New York:
    Columbia University Press.

AN ARTICLE IN A REFERENCE BOOK

Hay, W. M., & Hay, L. R. (1993). Behavior
    modification. In <u>Encyclopedia Americana</u> (Vol. 3,
    pp. 466–467). Danbury, CT: Grolier.

A PAMPHLET OR BROCHURE

The Centre for Alternative Technology. (1989).
    <u>Guidebook.</u> [Brochure]. Machynlleth, Powys, Wales:
    Author.

A
P
A

Periodicals

AN ARTICLE IN A NEWSPAPER

Walker, Kelli. (1995, December 31). Shelter is relic
of Cold War fears. Austin American-Statesman, pp.
B1, B3.

A LETTER TO THE EDITOR

Sawyer, T. C. (1990, August 12). The census: Why we
can't count [Letter to the editor]. New York
Times Magazine, p. 8.

A REVIEW

Coles, R. (1979, August 27). Unreflecting egoism.
[Review of the book The culture of narcissism].
The New Yorker, 98—105.

AN ARTICLE IN A MAGAZINE

Smith, A. (1975, October). Sport is a western yoga.
Psychology Today, 48—51, 74—76.

AN ARTICLE IN A JOURNAL WITH CONTINUOUS PAGINATION

Skinner, B. F. (1966). The phylogeny and ontogeny of
behavior. Science, 153, 1205—1213.

AN ARTICLE IN A JOURNAL PAGINATED BY ISSUE

Cooper, P. A. (1993). Paradigm shifts in designed
instruction: From behaviorism to cognitivism to
constructivism. Educational Technology, 33(5),
12—19.

AN ARTICLE WITH NO AUTHOR NAMED

On-line not political space. (1995, December 10).
Austin American-Statesman, p. C2.

Other Sources

A
P
A

A RADIO OR TELEVISION PROGRAM

Keenan, J. (1996). The matchmaker (D. Lee, Director).

    In C. Lloyd (Producer), Frasier. New York:

    National Broadcasting Corporation.

A FILM OR VIDEOTAPE

Sharman, B. (Producer), & Kenneth Branagh (Director).

    (1989). Henry V [Film]. (Available from Samuel

    Goldwyn)

A SOUND RECORDING

Beck, J. (1995). Goodbye pork pie hat. On Best of Beck

    [CD]. New York: Epic Records Group.

A LECTURE, SPEECH, ADDRESS, OR PUBLISHED PROCEEDINGS

Marty, M. (1980, February). Overcoming curricular

    poverty. Proceedings of the Community College

    Humanities Association, 34—41. Cranford, NJ.

A PUBLICATION ON CD-ROM

Bijou, S. W. (1994). Behavior modification.

    [CD-ROM]. Encarta. Redmond: Microsoft.

A JOURNAL ARTICLE ON THE WORLD WIDE WEB

Joyce, M. (1991). Notes toward an unwritten nonlinear

    electronic text, the ends of print culture (a

    work in progress). Postmodern Culture 2.1.

    Retrieved March 30, 1998 from the World Wide

    Web: http://www.press.jhu.edu/journals/postmodern_

    culture/v002/2.1joyce.html

A NEWSPAPER ARTICLE ON THE WORLD WIDE WEB

Winik, M. (1998, March 27). The originator, not the

    imitator: My lunch with Anna Quindlen. Austin

    Chronicle [Newspaper, selected stories on line].

    Retrieved March 30, 1998 from the World Wide Web:

    http://www.austinchronicle.com/current/

    books.quindlen.html

How to Create a Reference List Using APA Style

In unpublished manuscripts, the APA style allows reference lists to be indented in the same way as paragraphs (the first line of each entry indented with subsequent lines beginning at the margin). But for final copies (printed articles and student papers), reverse indentation (shown below) is ordinarily required. List the sources cited in your paper in alphabetical order on a separate page after the last page of text. Center the title "References" at the top of the page. Set up the entries using reverse indentation. Start the first line of each entry at the left margin and indent succeeding lines five spaces. All lines are double spaced. Notice how these principles are incorporated into the sample references page below.

References

Humphrey, N. (1992). A history of the mind. New York:

    Simon & Schuster.

Ornstein, R. E. (1977). The psychology of

    consciousness. San Francisco: W. H. Freeman.

Ornstein, R. E. (1991). The evolution of

    consciousness. New York: Simon & Schuster.

45b.3 CBE Reference List

You can list sources on a references page in one of two ways, using the name-year system or the number system.

Books

An entry for a book in a reference list using the CBE name-year style has the following elements: *author* (last name first, followed by a comma, then initials, with a period after the last initial only); *date* (last copyright date listed); *title* (not underlined, with only the first word and proper nouns capitalized); *city of publication* (add the state only if the city is not well known); *publisher*; *number of pages* (followed by *p.*). Note that the date follows the publisher in the CBE number system.

A Book with One Author

N-Y.

> Gould SJ. 1991. Bully for brontosaurus: reflections in natural history. New York: WW Norton. 540 p.

Num.

> 1. Gould SJ. Bully for brontosaurus: reflections in natural history. New York: WW Norton; 1991. 540 p.

A Book with Two Authors

N-Y.

> Motz L, Weaver JH. 1993. The story of mathematics. New York: Plenum. 356 p.

Num.

> 2. Motz L, Weaver JH. The story of mathematics. New York: Plenum; 1993. 356 p.

A Book with No Author Named

N-Y.

> [Anonymous]. 1969. The ocean. San Francisco: WH Freeman. 140 p.

Num.

> 3. [Anonymous]. The ocean. San Francisco: WH Freeman; 1969. 140 p.

A Book with a Group Author

N-Y.

> [NRC] National Research Council. 1977. Energy and climate. Washington: National Academy of Sciences. 356 p.

Num.

> 4. National Research Council [NRC]. Energy and climate. Washington: National Academy of Sciences; 1977. 356 p.

A GOVERNMENT PUBLICATION

N-Y.

> [NCHS] National Center for Health Statistics (US). 1980. Vital statistics of the United States. Washington: Government Printing Office. 485 p.

Num.

> 5. National Center for Health Statistics (US) [NCHS]. Vital statistics of the United States. Washington: Government Printing Office; 1980. 485 p.

AN ANTHOLOGY OR EDITED BOOK

N-Y.

> Barth F., editor. 1969. Ethnic groups and boundaries: the social organization of cultural differences. Boston: Little, Brown. 451 p.

Num.

> 6. Barth F., editor. Ethnic groups and boundaries: the social organization of cultural differences. Boston: Little, Brown; 1969. 451 p.

AN EDITION OTHER THAN THE FIRST

N-Y.

> Levin HL. 1988. The earth through time. 3rd ed. Philadelphia: Saunders College Publishing. 593 p.

Num.

> 7. Levin HL. The earth through time. 3rd ed. Philadelphia: Saunders College Publishing; 1988. 593 p.

C
B
E

A Translated Work

N-Y.

> Pavlov IP. 1927. Conditioned reflexes: an investigation
> of the physiological activity of the cerebral cortex.
> Anrep GV, translator. London: Oxford Univ Pr. 520 p.

Num.

> 8. Pavlov IP. Conditioned reflexes: an investigation
>   of the physiological activity of the cerebral
>   cortex. Anrep GV, translator. London: Oxford Univ
>   Pr; 1927. 520 p.

A Multivolume Work

N-Y.

> Oberholser H. 1974. The bird life of Texas. Volume 2.
> Austin: Univ of Texas Pr. 538 p.

Num.

> 9. Oberholser H. The bird life of Texas. Volume 2.
>   Austin: Univ of Texas Pr; 1974. 538 p.

A Selection in an Anthology

N-Y.

> Blumberg BS, Hesser JE. 1976. Anthropology and
> infectious disease. In: Physiological anthropology.
> Damon A, editor. Oxford: Oxford Univ Pr. p 260–94.

Num.

> 10. Blumberg BS, Hesser JE. Anthropology and
>   infectious disease. In: Physiological anthropology.
>   Damon A, editor. Oxford: Oxford Univ Pr; 1976.
>   p 260-94.

AN ARTICLE IN A REFERENCE BOOK

N-Y

> Coupland RT, Van Dyne G. 1982. Grassland ecosystem.
> In: McGraw-Hill Encyclopedia of Science &
> Technology. Volume 6. 5th ed. New York: McGraw-Hill.
> p 366—9.

Num.

> 11. Coupland RT, Van Dyne G. Grassland ecosystem. In:
>   McGraw-Hill Encyclopedia of Science & Technology.
>   Volume 6. 5th ed. New York: McGraw-Hill; 1982.
>   p 366—9.

AN INTRODUCTION, A PREFACE, A FOREWORD, OR AN AFTERWORD

N-Y.

> Sagan C. Introduction. 1988. In: Hawking SW. A brief
> history of time: from the big bang to black holes.
> Toronto: Bantam Books. p ix-x.

Num.

> 12. Sagan C. Introduction. In: Hawking SW. A
>   brief history of time: from the big bang to
>   black holes. Toronto: Bantam Books; 1988.
>   p ix—x.

A PAMPHLET OR BROCHURE

N-Y.

> [Anonymous]. 1989. HIV infection and AIDS [pamphlet].
> American Red Cross. 21 p.

Num.

> 13. [Anonymous]. HIV infection and AIDS [pamphlet].
>   American Red Cross; 1989. 21 p.

Periodicals

AN ARTICLE IN A NEWSPAPER

N-Y.

> Crider K. 1996 Jan 11. Uncle Sam's diet plan. Austin
> American-Statesman;Sect F:5(col 2).

Num.

> 14. Crider K. Uncle Sam's diet plan. Austin American-
>   Statesman 1996 Jan 11;Sect F:5(col 2).

AN EDITORIAL

N-Y.

> Hoffman P. 1995 May. A visionary rocket [editorial].
> Discover:8.

Num.

> 15. Hoffman P. A visionary rocket [editorial].
>   Discover 1995 May:8.

A LETTER TO THE EDITOR

N-Y.

> Bach DH. 1995 May. Beer physics [letter to the
> editor]. Discover:8.

Num.

> 16. Bach DH. Beer physics [letter to the editor].
>   Discover 1995 May:8.

A REVIEW

N-Y.

> Adams PL. 1991 Aug. Brief reviews: African
> silences by Peter Matthiesen [review].
> Atlantic:104.

Num.

> 17. Adams PL. Brief reviews: African silences by Peter Matthiesen [review]. Atlantic 1991 Aug:104.

AN ARTICLE IN A MAGAZINE

N-Y.

> Begley S. 1994 Apr 25. Beyond vitamins. Newsweek:44—9.

Num.

> 18. Begley S. Beyond vitamins. Newsweek 1994 Apr 25:44—9.

AN ARTICLE IN A JOURNAL WITH CONTINUOUS PAGINATION

N-Y.

> Pusey AE. 1980. Inbreeding avoidance in chimpanzees. Animal Behavior 28:543—52.

Num.

> 19. Pusey AE. Inbreeding avoidance in chimpanzees. Animal Behavior 1980;28:543—52.

AN ARTICLE IN A JOURNAL PAGINATED BY ISSUE

N-Y.

> Winn W, Bricken W. 1992. Designing virtual worlds for use in mathematics education: the example of experiential algebra. Educational Technology 32(12):12—9.

Num.

> 20. Winn W, Bricken W. Designing virtual worlds for use in mathematics education: the example of experiential algebra. Educational Technology 1992;32(12):12—9.

C
B
E

AN ARTICLE WITH NO AUTHOR NAMED

N-Y.

> [Anonymous]. 1995 May. Naked (and hungry) quasars.
> Discover:23.

Num.

> 21. [Anonymous]. Naked (and hungry) quasars. Discover
>   1995 May:23.

Other Sources

A RADIO OR TELEVISION PROGRAM

N-Y.

> Campbell-Jones S. 1966. Earthquakes [television
> program]. Campbell-Jones S, and Campbell-Jones
> S, producers. Boston: WGBH. (Nova). Available
> from: WGBH P.O. Box 2284, S. Burlington VT
> 05407

Num.

> 22. Earthquakes [television program].

A FILM OR VIDEOTAPE

N-Y.

> Broyles, Jr. W. 1995. Apollo 13 [motion picture].
> Grazer B, producer. Universal City (CA): Universal
> City Studios.

Num.

> 23. Apollo 13 [motion picture]. Broyles, Jr. W,
>   screenwriter. Grazer B, producer. Universal City
>   (CA): Universal City Studios; 1995.

A SOUND RECORDING

N-Y.

> Luce W. 1993. Lucifer's child [audiocassette].
> Olsen LD, producer/director. Auburn (CA): Audio
> Partners.

Num.

> 24. Lucifer's child [audiocassette]. Luce W. Olsen LD,
>   producer/director. Auburn (CA): Audio Partners;
>   1993.

A LECTURE, SPEECH, ADDRESS, OR PUBLISHED PROCEEDINGS

N-Y.

> Graybiel A. 1964. The labyrinth of space flight. In:
> Proceedings of the 3rd international symposium on
> bioastronautics and the exploration of space; 1964
> Nov 16-18; San Antonio TX.

Num.

> 26. Graybiel A. The labyrinth of space flight. In:
>   Proceedings of the 3rd international symposium on
>   bioastronautics and the exploration of space; 1964
>   Nov 16—18; San Antonio TX.

AN INTERVIEW

N-Y.

> Schumacher M. 1985 Nov. Vonnegut on writing
> [interview]. Writer's Digest:22—7.

Num.

> 27. Schumacher M. Vonnegut on writing [interview].
>   Writer's Digest 1985 Nov:22—7.

C
B
E

A Letter, A Memo, or an Email Communication

N-Y.

> Newton I. 1958. Newton's letter to Boyle, Feb. 28, 1678. In: Isaac Newton's papers & letters on natural philosophy. Cohen IB, editor. Cambridge: Harvard University Press. p 250—3.

Num.

> 28. Newton I. Newton's letter to Boyle, Feb. 28, 1678. In: Isaac Newton's papers & letters on natural philosophy. Cohen IB, editor. Cambridge: Harvard University Press; 1958. p 250—3.

A Publication on Diskette

N-Y.

> Microsoft. 1994. Microsoft Windows [computer program]. Version 3.1. Redmond (WA): Microsoft Corporation. 8 computer disks: 3 1/2 in. Accompanied by: 1 user's guide. System requirements: IBM PC family or fully compatible computer; DOS 3.1 or higher; 640K of conventional memory plus 256K of extended memory; 6 MB of free disk space (9 MB is recommended); at least 1 floppy drive; a display adapter that is supported by Windows.

Num.

> 29. Microsoft Windows [computer program]. Version 3.1. Redmond (WA): Microsoft Corporation; 1994. 8 computer disks: 3 1/2 in. Accompanied by: 1 user's guide. System requirements: IBM PC family or fully compatible computer; DOS 3.1 or higher; 640K of conventional memory plus 256K of extended memory;

```
6 MB of free disk space (9 MB is recommended); at
least 1 floppy drive; a display adapter that is
supported by Windows.
```

A PUBLICATION ON CD-ROM

N-Y.

```
Landis F. 1993. Jet propulsion. In: Encarta [CD-ROM].
Redmond (WA): Microsoft Corporation.
```

Num.

```
30. Landis F. Jet propulsion. In: Encarta [CD-ROM].
Redmond (WA): Microsoft Corporation; 1993.
```

How to Create a Reference List Using the CBE Name-Year Style

To create a reference list using the name-year method, list the sources cited in the paper in alphabetical order on a separate page after the last page of text. Center the title "Literature Cited" or "References" at the top of the page. All lines are double spaced.

```
                    Literature Cited
Graybiel A. 1964. The labyrinth of space flight. In:
Proceedings of the 3rd international symposium on
bioastronautics and the exploration of space; 1964 Nov
16–18; San Antonio TX.

Hoffman P. 1995 May. A visionary rocket [editorial].
Discover:8.

Landis F. 1993. Jet propulsion. In: Encarta [CD-ROM].
Redmond (WA): Microsoft Corporation.
```

How to Create a Reference List Using the CBE Number Style

To create a reference list using the number method, list the sources in numerical order (in the sequence they appeared in the paper) on a separate page after the last page of text. Center the title "References" or "Literature Cited" at the top of the page. All lines are double spaced.

C
B
E

Literature Cited

1. Graybiel A. The labyrinth of space flight. In:
   Proceedings of the 3rd international symposium on
   bioastronautics and the exploration of space; 1964
   Nov 16-18; San Antonio TX.

2. Landis F. Jet propulsion. In: Encarta
   [CD-ROM]. Redmond (WA): Microsoft Corporation;
   1993.

45b.4 CMS Reference List

C
M
S

According to *The Chicago Manual of Style*, sources can be listed in one of two ways: in the form of the footnotes themselves or in alphabetical order. The entries are single spaced. The examples that follow are based on Kate L. Turabian's book *A Manual for Writers of Term Papers, Theses, and Dissertations*. For the most part, Turabian's guidelines are consistent with those suggested by *The Chicago Manual of Style*. Where there are differences, Turabian's guidelines are recommended for student writers.

Books

An entry for a book in a reference list using the CMS style has the following elements: *author* (last name first, followed by a comma, then first name and any initials); *title* (underlined); *city of publication*; and *date of publication*. (The city, publisher, and date are enclosed in parentheses in the note method.) Entries are single spaced, with a double space between them.

A BOOK WITH ONE AUTHOR

Note

> 1. R. H. Tawney, <u>Religion and the Rise of
> Capitalism</u> (New York: Harcourt, Brace and World,
> 1962), 62.

Bib.

> Tawney, R. H. <u>Religion and the Rise of Capitalism</u>. New
> York: Harcourt, Brace and World, 1962.

A BOOK WITH TWO AUTHORS

Note

    2. Gabriel A. Almond and Sidney Verba, The Civic Culture (Boston: Little, Brown, 1963), 44.

Bib.

Almond, Gabriel A., and Sidney Verba. The Civic Culture. Boston: Little, Brown, 1963.

A BOOK WITH THREE AUTHORS

Note

    3. Jaroslav Pelican, J. Kitagawa, and S. Nasr, Comparative Work Ethics: Judeo-Christian, Islamic, and Eastern (Washington, D. C.: Library of Congress, 1985), 119.

Bib.

Pelican, Jaroslav, J. Kitagawa, and S. Nasr. Comparative Work Ethics: Judeo-Christian, Islamic, and Eastern. Washington, D.C.: Library of Congress, 1985.

A BOOK WITH MORE THAN THREE AUTHORS

Note

    4. Carol Berkin and others, Making America: A History of the United States (Boston: Houghton Mifflin, 1995), 893.

Bib.

Berkin, Carol, Christopher L. Miller, Robert W. Charny, and James L. Gormly. Making America: A History of the United States. Boston: Houghton Mifflin, 1995.

C
M
S

A BOOK WITH NO AUTHOR NAMED

Note

> 5. A Uniform System of Citation (Cambridge:
> Harvard Law Review Association, 1986),
> 44.

Bib.

> A Uniform System of Citation. Cambridge:
>   Harvard Law Review Association, 1986.

A BOOK WITH A GROUP AUTHOR

Note

> 6. Conference Board, Information Technology:
> Some Critical Implications for Decision Makers,
> Report no. 537 (New York: Conference Board,
> 1975), 45.

Bib.

> Conference Board. Information Technology:
>   Some Critical Implications for Decision Makers,
>   Report no. 537. New York: Conference Board,
>   1975.

AN ANTHOLOGY OR EDITED BOOK

Note

> 7. S. N. Eisenstadt, ed., The Protestant Ethic and
> Modernization: A Comparative View (New York: Basic
> Books, 1968), 67.

Bib.

> Eisenstadt, S. N., ed. The Protestant Ethic and
>   Modernization: A Comparative View. New York: Basic
>   Books, 1968.

A BOOK WITH A TITLE WITHIN A TITLE

Note

> 8. Jay Gellens, ed., <u>Twentieth Century
> Interpretations of "A Farewell to Arms,"</u>
> (Englewood Cliffs: Prentice-Hall, 1970),
> 3.

Bib.

> Gellens, Jay, ed. <u>Twentieth Century Interpretations
> of "A Farewell to Arms</u>." Englewood Cliffs:
> Prentice-Hall, 1970.

AN EDITION OTHER THAN THE FIRST

Note

> 9. Leo Strauss and Joseph Cropsey, eds.,
> <u>History of Political Philosophy</u>, 2d ed.
> (Chicago: Rand McNally, 1972), 10.

Bib.

> Strauss, Leo, and Joseph Cropsey, eds. <u>History of
> Political Philosophy</u>, 2d ed. Chicago: Rand McNally,
> 1972.

A TRANSLATED WORK

Note

> 10. Georg W. F. Hegel, <u>The Phenomenology of Mind</u>,
> trans. J. B. Baillie (New York: Harper & Row, 1967),
> 89–94.

Bib.

> Hegel, Georg W. F. <u>The Phenomenology of Mind</u>.
> Translated by J. B. Baillie. New York: Harper
> & Row, 1967.

C
M
S

A MULTIVOLUME WORK

Note

> 11. Robert A. Divine and others, <u>America:</u>
> <u>Past and Present</u>, vol. 1, <u>To 1877</u> (Glenview,
> Ill.: Scott, Foresman, 1984), 53.

Bib.

> Divine, Robert A., T. H. Breen, George M.
>   Frederickson, and R. Hal Williams. <u>America:</u>
>   <u>Past and Present</u>. Vol. 1, <u>To 1877</u>.
>   Glenview, Ill.: Scott, Foresman,
>   1984.

A SELECTION IN AN ANTHOLOGY

Note

> 12. J. H. Rowe, "Inca Culture at the Time of the
> Spanish Conquest," in <u>Handbook of South American</u>
> <u>Indians</u>, ed. J. Steward (Washington, D.C.: Bureau of
> American Ethnology, 1946), 92.

Bib.

> Rowe, J. H. "Inca Culture at the Time of
>   the Spanish Conquest." In <u>Handbook of South</u>
>   <u>American Indians</u>, ed. J. Steward, 183–330.
>   Washington, D.C.: Bureau of American Ethnology,
>   1946.

AN INTRODUCTION, A PREFACE, A FOREWORD, OR AN AFTERWORD

Note

> 13. Aristotle, <u>On Man and the Universe</u>, ed. with
> an introduction by Louise Ropes Loomis (New York:
> Walter J. Black, 1943), 61.

Bib.

> Aristotle. <u>On Man and the Universe</u>. Edited with an
>   introduction by Louise Ropes Loomis. New York:
>   Walter J. Black, 1943.

When you are primarily interested in the introduction, cite it first in the entry.

Note

> 14. Louise Ropes Loomis, ed., introduction to <u>On Man and the Universe</u>, by Aristotle (New York: Walter J. Black, 1943), xix.

Bib.

> Loomis, Louise Ropes, ed. Introduction to <u>On Man and the Universe</u>, by Aristotle. New York: Walter J. Black, 1943.

AN ARTICLE IN A REFERENCE BOOK

Note

> 15. George T. Dickie, "Aesthetics," in <u>Encyclopedia Americana</u>, 1993 ed.

Bib.

> Dickie, George T. "Aesthetics." <u>Encyclopedia Americana</u>. 1993 ed.

A GOVERNMENT PUBLICATION

Note

> 18. Congress, Senate, Committee on the Judiciary, <u>Communism in Labor Unions</u>, 83d Cong., 2d sess. (Washington, D.C.: Government Printing Office, 1954), 40.

Bib.

> U.S. Congress. Senate. Committee on the Judiciary. <u>Communism in Labor Unions</u>. 83d Cong., 2d Sess. Washington, D.C.: Government Printing Office, 1954.

C
M
S

A PAMPHLET OR BROCHURE

Note

> 19. <u>Country Walks around Bourton-on-the-Water</u> (Cheltenham, Eng.: Cotswolds Walkers, 1989), 15.

Bib.

> <u>Country Walks around Bourton-on-the-Water</u>. Cheltenham, Eng.: Cotswolds Walkers, 1989.

Periodicals

AN ARTICLE IN A NEWSPAPER

Note

> 20. Dick Stanley, "Campsite Tells Tale of Central Texas' Ancient Past," <u>Austin American-Statesman</u>, 17 December 1995, sec. B, pp. 1 and 3.

Bib.

> Stanley, Dick. "Campsite Tells Tale of Central Texas' Ancient Past." <u>Austin American-Statesman</u>. 17 December 1995, sec. B, pp. 1 and 3.

AN ARTICLE IN A MAGAZINE

Note

> 24. David Roberts, "The Decipherment of Ancient Maya," <u>Atlantic</u>, September 1991, 90.

Bib.

> Roberts, David. "The Decipherment of Ancient Maya," <u>Atlantic</u>, September 1991, 87–100.

AN ARTICLE IN A JOURNAL WITH CONTINUOUS PAGINATION

Note

> 25. Jacqueline Banerjee, "Mending the Butterfly: The New Historicism and Keats's 'Eve of St. Agnes,' " <u>College English</u> 57 (September 1995): 530.

C
M
S

Bib.

> Banerjee, Jacqueline. "Mending the Butterfly:
> The New Historicism and Keats's 'Eve of St.
> Agnes.' " <u>College English</u> 57 (September 1995):
> 529–45.

AN ARTICLE IN A JOURNAL PAGINATED BY ISSUE

Note

> 24. Preciously Norton, "When Technology Meets the
> Subject-Matter Disciplines in Education: Part One:
> Exploring the Computer as Metaphor," <u>Educational</u>
> <u>Technology</u> 32, no. 6 (1992): 40.

Bib.

> Norton, Preciously. "When Technology Meets
> the Subject-Matter Disciplines in Education:
> Part One: Exploring the Computer as
> Metaphor." <u>Educational Technology</u> 32, no. 6
> (1992): 38–46.

Other Sources

A LECTURE, SPEECH, ADDRESS, OR PUBLISHED PROCEEDINGS

Note

> 28. Arthur M. Cohen, "Help for the Humanities
> Is on the Way," in <u>Challenges before the Humanities</u>
> <u>in Community Colleges: Review and Proceedings</u>
> <u>of the Community College Humanities Association</u>,
> ed. Donald D. Schmeltekopf and Anne D. Rassweiler
> (Cranford, N.J.: Community College Humanities
> Association, 1980), 33.

Bib.

> Cohen, Arthur M. "Help for the Humanities Is on the
> Way." In <u>Challenges before the Humanities in</u>
> <u>Community Colleges: Review and Proceedings of the</u>
> <u>Community College Humanities Association</u>, edited by

```
Donald D. Schmeltekopf and Anne D. Rassweiler,
27—33. Cranford, N.J.: Community College Humanities
Association, 1980.
```

How to Create a Reference List for the CMS Endnotes Style

To create an endnotes page, list the footnotes on a separate page after the last page of text. Center the title "Notes" at the top of the page.

```
                      Notes

    1. Arthur M. Cohen, "Help for the Humanities
Is on the Way," in Challenges before the Humanities
in Community Colleges: Review and Proceedings of
the Community College Humanities Association,
ed. Donald D. Schmeltekopf and Anne D. Rassweiler
(Cranford, N.J.: Community College Humanities
Association, 1980), 33.
    2. Preciously Norton, "When Technology Meets the
Subject-Matter Disciplines in Education: Part One:
Exploring the Computer as Metaphor," Educational
Technology 32, no. 6 (1992): 40.
```

How to Create a Reference List for the CMS Bibliography Style

To create a bibliography page, list the sources cited in the paper in alphabetical order on a separate page after the last page of text. Center the title "Bibliography" or "Works Cited" at the top of the page. Use reverse indentation, also known as a hanging indent. That means that you will start the first line of each entry at the left margin and indent each succeeding line five spaces. Single-space all lines. If you list two or more works by the same author, replace the name of the author with an eight-space underline in the second and any succeeding entries.

C
M
S

Bibliography

Almond, Gabriel A., and Sidney Verba. <u>The Civic Culture</u>. Boston: Little, Brown, 1963.

Aristotle. <u>On Man and the Universe</u>. Edited with an Introduction by Louise Ropes Loomis. New York: Walter J. Black, 1943.

Hegel, Georg W. F. <u>The Phenomenology of Mind</u>. Translated by J. B. Baillie. New York: Harper & Row, 1967.

Jaeger, Werner. <u>Early Christianity and Greek Paideia</u>. London: Oxford University Press, 1961.

————. <u>Paideia: The Ideals of Greek Culture</u>. Vol. 1, <u>Archaic Greece, the Mind of Athens</u>. Translated by Gilbert Highet. New York: Oxford University Press, 1945.

Strauss, Leo, and Joseph Cropsey, eds. <u>History of Political Philosophy</u>, 2d ed. Chicago: Rand McNally, 1972.

Sample Paper Using MLA Format

Alcaraz 1

Alicia Alcaraz

Professor Davis

English 101

20 June 1996

Understanding Homelessness

Homeless people are all around us. The problem of homelessness has risen in the last twenty years to the point where it is now one of our society's major problems (Weir). The term <u>homelessness</u> has a negative connotation but at the same time has a profound and powerful impact in our world. According to Landau, our society continues to stereotype the image of homeless people (4). For example, a female homeless person is called a "bag lady" and the male homeless person a "wino" because our society portrays them that way. Landau also states that "homelessness is currently the term most often used to describe the relatively recent widespread appearance of destitute people in need of shelter" (5). Many people today still think the majority of homeless people choose to be homeless. On the contrary, Kendall states that under 6 percent of homeless people choose to live on the streets (160). Whatever the circumstances or situations that led them to be homeless, most of them want out of that life-style. Societal, governmental, and

continued on next page

personal factors contribute to the causes of homelessness (Foster, Landes, and Jacobes 16). It is true that many things cause or contribute to homelessness, but the most significant causes of homelessness are poverty, insufficient housing, and mental illness. Each of these can cause homelessness by itself, but often the three are interrelated.

Poverty is considered to be one of the important causes of homelessness. The National Coalition for the Homeless (NCH) states that "homelessness and poverty are inextricably linked. Being poor means being an accident, an illness, or a paycheck away from living in the streets." On the other hand, Foster, Landes, and Jacobes claim that although the country's homeless are poor, few of the poor are homeless (38). They also maintain that the two trends associated with homeless people in poverty are unemployment and insufficient minimum-wage employment (46). Therefore, the people who are susceptible to homelessness are either jobless or work for minimum wage (NCH). Thus, seeking money doesn't get a person out of poverty in households where income is low. Furthermore, Kendall indicates that many of the homeless have jobs but cannot afford to pay rent or provide the family with basic needs due to low-income jobs. In fact, 18 percent of the homeless fall into this category (163).

A lack of affordable housing is another major contributor to homelessness. Foster, Landes, and Jacobes

continued on next page

state that while the nation's housing shortage began in the late 1970s, the public was largely unaware of the problem until the 1980s when it was actually faced with the plight of homeless people wandering the nation's streets (23). Today, inadequate housing is linked to homelessness more than a need for family (Weir). Therefore, according to the NCH, "the leading cause of homelessness in the United States is the inability of poor people to afford housing." This not only forces some to be homeless but puts a large percentage at risk of becoming homeless. In our society, housing costs have gone up significantly in recent years, and it's scary. On this note, some people now have a difficult time purchasing a house for the first time, unlike their parents, who purchased homes at a time when housing costs had not yet soared. Robert Scheer, author of "America: Land of the Homeless," provides a specific example:

> I know of a single mother in Saint Paul, for one, who receives a welfare payment of $532 a month for herself and two children, but $440 was the lowest rent she could find and the utility bill took another $60. She also needed to spend some money on clothing and food for her family to supplement food stamps. The inevitable result was that she fell behind on the rent, was evicted, and now the family survives by going from shelter to shelter. (205)

continued on next page ⟶

Wright and Lam argue that "low-cost housing has been demolished at the same time as increasing numbers of Americans have slipped below the poverty line, making housing costs out of reach for many" (65). Therefore, it is clear that the decline in the availability of affordable housing and the increasing number of homeless persons are interrelated. According to Landau, the structure of a family will definitely break down if they are evicted (11). This is a tragic experience for anyone.

Besides poverty and the high cost of housing, mental illness is a stereotypical image of homelessness. Society needs to provide a stable home for the mentally ill because they are at high risk of being homeless (NCH). The fact is that approximately one-third of the single adult homeless population suffer from some form of severe and persistent mental illness (NCH). According to Lamb and Talbott, there are certain attributes that easily make the mentally ill homeless. For example, few can reliably pay rent on time, and are evicted (55). In addition, Foster, Landes, and Jacobes indicate that "over the last decade, the policy of deinstitutionalization (letting people who pose no threat to themselves or other people leave the institution, that is, a mental hospital) has resulted in large numbers of mentally ill persons living on the streets of many cities" (20). These researchers point out a problem with hospitals

continued on next page

releasing these mentally ill patients, and that is they will not have a place to stay to keep safe and warm (61). Furthermore, the NCH states that "people with mental illness must be able to live as independently as possible with the help of expanded comprehensive, community-based mental health services and other support."

There is no single solution to the complexity of homelessness facing our country and it will only continue to be a crisis. The NCH seems to agree, saying that "it is clear, however, that ending homelessness will require a concerted effort, by government, labor and the private sector, to ensure that all Americans who can work have an opportunity to obtain a job which pays a living wage." First, society as a whole can help the homeless people by providing better jobs that have better wages to cover rent, food, clothes, and bills. Second, government needs to provide more affordable housing for the working poor. Last, the government can fund the building of more hospitals for the mentally ill. Landau reminds us that "under adverse circumstances anyone can become homeless . . . unfortunately, no one is immune to misfortune" (95). On a final note, Snyder and Hombs emphasize that "our security, and, very possibly, our survival as a nation may depend on our ability--and our willingness--to come to grips with . . . homelessness in America" (17). The homeless cannot be ignored!

continued on next page ⟶

Works Cited

Foster, Carol D., Alison Landes, and Nancy R. Jacobes, eds. <u>Homeless in America--How Could It Happen Here?</u> Wylie: Information Plus, 1993.

Kendall, Diana. <u>Sociology: In Our Times</u>. Belmont: Wadsworth, 1996.

Lamb, Richard H., and John A. Talbott. "Mental Illness Causes Homelessness." <u>The Homeless: Opposing Viewpoints</u>. Ed. Lisa Orr. San Diego: Greenhaven, 1990. 55—59.

Landau, Elaine. <u>The Homeless</u>. New York: Messner, 1987.

National Coalition for the Homeless. <u>NCH Fact Sheet</u>. June 17, 1996 <http://www.nch.ari.net/facts.html>.

Scheer, Robert. "America: Land of the Homeless." <u>Cosmopolitan</u> 218 (1995): 204—207.

Snyder, Mitch, and Mary Ellen Hombs. "Homelessness Is Serious." <u>The Homeless: Opposing Viewpoints</u>. Ed. Lisa Orr. San Diego: Greenhaven, 1990. 17—20.

Weir, Daniel S. <u>Why Are Americans Homeless? A Review of Research Findings</u>. June 17, 1996 <gopher://csf.Colorado.EDU:70/00/psn/homeless/ Frequently-asked-questions/why-are-americans-homeless>.

Wright, James D., and Julie A. Lam. "Lack of Affordable Housing Causes Homelessness." <u>The Homeless: Opposing Viewpoints</u>. Ed. Lisa Orr. San Diego: Greenhaven, 1990. 65—70.

Sample Page from Paper Using APA Format

. . . Today, inadequate housing is linked to homelessness more than a need for family (Weir 1996). Therefore, according to the NCH (1996), "the leading cause of homelessness in the United States is the inability of poor people to afford housing." This not only forces some to be homeless but puts a large percentage at risk of becoming homeless. In our society, housing costs have gone up significantly in recent years, and it's scary. On this note, some people now have a difficult time purchasing a house for the first time, unlike their parents, who purchased homes at a time when housing costs had not yet soared. Robert Scheer (1995), author of "America: Land of the Homeless," provides a specific example:

> I know of a single mother in Saint Paul, for one, who receives a welfare payment of $532 a month for herself and two children, but $440 was the lowest rent she could find and the utility bill took another $60. She also needed to spend some money on clothing and food for her family to supplement food stamps. The inevitable result was that she fell behind on the rent, was evicted, and now the family survives by going from shelter to shelter. (p. 205)

Wright and Lam (1990) argue that "low-cost housing has been demolished at the same time as increasing

continued on next page

numbers of Americans have slipped below the poverty line, making housing costs out of reach for many" (p. 65). Therefore, it is clear that the decline in the availability of affordable housing and the increasing number of homeless persons are interrelated. . . .

Sample Page from Paper Using CBE Format

If the migratory instinct is heritable, how is it triggered? Most researchers believe that migratory birds possess an internal clock that controls its activities. The means of clock calibration, however, is not generally agreed upon. Baker (1984) cites several studies that found migratory restlessness occurred in caged birds with controls for constant day length and temperature, indicating a presence of other factors as the calibrating mechanisms. Able reached a similar conclusion, but he also found, by simulating the longitudinal magnetic fields that free-living individuals would experience along the migration route, that his caged birds showed intensified restlessness (1991). However, Sutherland claims that it is exactly day length that sets the annual clock, based on studies that showed blackcaps exposed to photoperiods simulating natural conditions were more likely to show migratory restlessness than individuals kept in constant light conditions (1992).

continued on next page

Perhaps the idea of backup systems provides the answer. Baker has proposed that the internal program cycles circannually, at least the first two or three years in the lab, but under natural conditions the program would be calibrated by photoperiod and temperature (1984). Gwinner agrees and adds that circannual calibrating mechanisms act in conjunction with natural conditions (1990). If this is true, then long-term alterations of the natural light cycle should result in biological rhythms being thrown out of phase and consequent changes in the cycling of bird behavior. There seems to be no definite answer yet, but researchers agree that more work needs to be done on free-living birds so that the effects of natural conditions on genetic controls can be better understood.

Sample Page from Paper Using CMS Format

. . . Today, inadequate housing is linked to homelessness more than a need for family.[12] Therefore, according to the NCH, "the leading cause of homelessness in the United States is the inability of poor people to afford housing."[13] This not only forces some to be homeless but puts a large percentage at risk of becoming homeless. In our society, housing costs have gone up

continued on next page

significantly in recent years, and it's scary. On this note, some people now have a difficult time purchasing a house for the first time, unlike their parents, who purchased homes at a time when housing costs had not yet soared. Robert Scheer, author of "America: Land of the Homeless," provides a specific example:

> I know of a single mother in Saint Paul, for one, who receives a welfare payment of $532 a month for herself and two children, but $440 was the lowest rent she could find and the utility bill took another $60. She also needed to spend some money on clothing and food for her family to supplement food stamps. The inevitable result was that she fell behind on the rent, was evicted, and now the family survives by going from shelter to shelter.[14]

Wright and Lam argue that "low-cost housing has been demolished at the same time as increasing numbers of Americans have slipped below the poverty line, making housing costs out of reach for many."[15] Therefore, it is clear that the decline in the availability of affordable housing and the increasing number of homeless persons are interrelated. . . .

10

Document Design

Manuscript Design

The Latin roots of the term *manuscript* indicate a work that is hand (*manus*) written (*scriptus*). In modern terms, it is possible to distinguish between two types of manuscripts. The first type includes prepublished pieces of work, such as school essays, creative works that may or may not be sent to a publisher for review, technical or business reports used in work sessions, and home pages on the World Wide Web. To a certain extent, we expect all these works to be changed or adapted by suggestions from their readers.

The second type, while still being literally unpublished in that it is not printed and offered to the general public, includes pieces of writing such as memos, résumés, or business letters that readers treat as final, unchangeable works.

These two types of manuscripts are sometimes treated in different ways. In all cases, though, writers need to treat manuscripts as works other people will read. As a result, manuscripts require appropriate design.

46a
MANUSCRIPT DESIGN AND WRITING PROCESSES

In most cases, a manuscript's design is imposed on you early in the writing process. All memos look more or less alike, as do most résumés or student papers; therefore, what you write should be appropriate for the general format. Experienced readers, after all, have grown accustomed to reading memos or résumés in certain ways. You may choose to deviate from readers' expectations and conventions, but you do so at a risk. So knowing your audience well is important. Hostile, overworked, or bored audiences want to focus on the issues and ideas, not on your innovative presentation.

Deviant or unusual design can serve two purposes, however. As a form of protest, it tells the audience that you will not comply with their expectations. As a form of entertainment, it tells the audience that you want to communicate something more than information.

Beyond general format, you seldom begin thinking about the design of the body of your document until you have completed much of your written work. Headings and subheadings, typeface, spacing, and leading are all design components that grow from the overall structure and message, as well as from general concepts about design.

Sometimes, however, you will actually know how you want your finished report to look. If so, that very look may suggest ideas about content. For instance, if you know that you have to put everything on one page, you might begin by thinking that you want to use bullets or dashes to list important ideas. You might know that you want to make only two or three points. This fact would limit how you think of the topic and what you say about it.

46b
MANUSCRIPT BASICS

We live in a world of overlapping technologies. Some people spend hours every week sending and receiving email messages. Others have not yet learned basic typewriting skills; everything they produce is handwritten. In a single day you may deal with various communications that are handwritten, typed, word processed, and emailed. Each tool you use—pencil, typewriter, computer—dictates a few basics in manuscript preparation.

Typewriting and word processing skills, however, have become essential for college-level students and for professionals. If you cannot type, you would be wise to take a typing class or to practice by using commercially available software programs.

46b.1 Paper

When computers and voice-mail systems first appeared, many people predicted the advent of the "paperless society." Such predictions have not come true.

You will probably circulate only typed or printed communications on the job, but a few instructors still allow students to submit handwritten essays. If you are handwriting an essay, use 8 1/2" x 11" lined white paper.

For typed and word-processed work, use 8 1/2" x 11" white paper without lines. Recycled paper is usually available. Paper should be medium-weight. Onionskin and erasable bond papers are usually too light, and cover stock is usually too heavy and too expensive.

46b.2 Ink and Printers

Have you ever had trouble understanding someone who has a soft voice and doesn't speak up? The same problems occur visually when someone writes in pencil or uses a typewriter or printer ribbon that is old and faded. Black or blue ink is preferable for handwritten work. Colored pencil or ink makes a paper less formal. Avoid using ink that easily smudges and never use pens with blunted tips.

For typed and word-processed works, simply make sure that your ribbons or ink cartridges produce dark, clear letters. Laser printers are preferable and are usually available in the workplace or in college libraries or word processing centers.

46b.3 Margins and Spacing

We've all read books in which as many words as possible were crammed onto the page; and we know how pleasant it is to read a page with adequate "white space"—that is, space on the page without words or pictures. In a manuscript, the greatest factors contributing toward adequate white space are the margins from the edges of the paper to the type and the spaces between lines of type.

When handwriting your work on lined paper, use the top lines and the vertical line on the left-hand side of the page for your guides; then leave about an inch for the right and bottom margins. This means you probably won't write on the last line or two. When writing an essay by hand, you will probably want to skip every other line. This is equivalent to double spacing in typing. And remember, out of consideration for the reader, to write on only one side of the paper.

Most word processing programs and printing software have "default" settings that usually produce margins of one inch on all sides of the paper. If you are typing your work, you will want to follow the same guidelines. Finally, you will want to print on only one side of the paper.

46b.4 Corrections and Insertions

Try as you might, time limitations sometimes prevent you from producing a perfectly clean manuscript. Most readers will accept a few, but only a few, handwritten changes.

Your guiding principle should be legibility. If you need to delete something in a handwritten paper, draw a single line through that material. This deleted material should be no more than a few words. If you have more than a full line to strike out, the best course is to recopy the page. If you need to insert a word or two, write above the line and indicate with a caret (^) where the material should be inserted. For example:

William Carlos Williams's "The Red Wheelbarrow" is startling ^in its

simplicity.

With the ease of using laser and ink-jet printers, there is no reason for any problems to remain in a manuscript. What will it take to correct any problem and reprint—two minutes? Insertions and changes are acceptable in academic writing only when a student catches something at the last minute. Use a caret as described above. In professional and business writing, handwritten corrections are usually unacceptable.

46c
STUDENT PAPERS

At their best, college classes that include writing begin to introduce students to the world of professional communication. College essays are not much different from formal reports or presentations in a business or government office. The instructor, like a supervisor on the job or an editor in a publishing firm, asks the student to write a thoughtful, considered opinion about a certain topic. Although relationships between students and instructors vary in formality, in most cases a student essay is less a discussion among friends than a professional communication.

46c.1 Student Essay With Cover Page

Some instructors ask that you include a cover page with your essay. Cover pages are aesthetically pleasing in that they look like the title pages of books, and they lend essays a formality and weight sacrificed by other manuscript formats. Figure 46.1 shows a typical cover page. Instructors who ask you to follow the Modern Language Association (MLA) guidelines do not require a cover page; instead, they will ask you to follow the guidelines in Section 46c.2. However, the formats suggested by the American Psychological Association (APA), the Council of Biology Editors (CBE), and *The Chicago Manual of Style* (CMS) include cover pages. If you are required to follow those formats, consult their most recent style manuals.

46c.2 Student Essay Without Cover Page

Some instructors ask you not to use a cover page. Essays written without a cover page tend to look more informal and force both the writer's and the reader's attention to the content of the essay by playing down the formality of presentation. In addition, in a world concerned with environmental issues, some people object to the use of extra paper simply for formality. Many instructors who follow MLA style guidelines for research papers encourage you to follow the format shown in Figure 46.2. Place your name, your instructor's name, the course name, and the date at the upper left-hand corner of the first page. Figure 46.3 illustrates the MLA format for subsequent pages of class essays and research papers.

Civilizing the Wild Man:

The Sacred Prostitute in <u>The Epic of Gilgamesh</u>

Center title
about 3″ from
top of page

by

James Franklin   Author of paper

Course   English 2713 World Literature I

Essay Number   Essay 3

Instructor   Professor Mary Jamison

Date   12 March 1998

Figure 46.1 Cover Page

J. Franklin 1

James Franklin

Professor Jamison

English 2713

12 March 1998

First initial, last name, and page number, flush with right margin, 1/2" from top of page

Title centered

Civilizing the Wild Man:

The Sacred Prostitute in The Epic of Gilgamesh

In The Epic of Gilgamesh, a Sumerian tale dating

back to 2000 B.C., the citizens of Uruk ask their

1" margin

gods to protect them from the tyranny of their

king, Gilgamesh. Gilgamesh, who is said to be two-

thirds god and one-third human, routinely performs

acts of cruelty upon his people. . . .

1" margin

Paper is double spaced

1" from bottom of page

Figure 46.2 MLA Format for First Page of Student Essay

Franklin 2

1" margin

while contemporary interpretations of the
prostitute's "taming" of Enkidu raise important
issues concerning masculine and feminine roles. . . .

Last name,
and page
number,
1/2" from top
of page

Figure 46.3 MLA Format for Subsequent Pages of Student Essay

46d
RÉSUMÉS

Few experiences are as grueling or as frustrating as applying for work. It seems that every employer you talk with has different personal criteria for judging applicants. All, however, want accurate information. For most jobs, then, you will find yourself writing a résumé and cover letter telling who you are and showing why you meet the stated criteria for the job.

46d.1 Features of a Résumé

All applicants for a position hope they are qualified. Otherwise they would not apply. So what can you do to stand out? Following the suggestions below will help.

Be honest.	Be thorough.
Be self-assured.	Be professional.
Be brief.	Be friendly.

Do these suggestions sound contradictory? They are. Yet writing a résumé is no more contradictory than most other writing assignments. Nowadays most people recommend that instead of trying to make one résumé fit all jobs, you tailor your résumé for each particular employer and position. This makes sense because it is much easier and usually more effective to communicate to a single, narrow audience than to general audience.

The format of the résumé has become fairly standardized. It should always be typed, almost always condensed to one or at most two pages. Key information is clearly indicated with headings and hanging indentations. No matter who the employer is or what the circumstances are, the following information is always called for.

Who you are and how you can be reached

Your professional goals

Your education

Your work experience

In addition, in some cases you may wish to include the following information.

Special features

Awards

Clubs/offices

Publications

Committee work

Hobbies and interests

Professional and personal references

Figure 46.4 shows a sample résumé with some of these features highlighted.

46d.2 Types of Résumés

All résumés do not have to look the same, especially since not all jobs are alike, not all employers are alike, and not all applicants are alike. Yet as noted in Section 46d.1, most résumés include certain basic information. How that information is presented, including the organization and focus, is your decision. Generally, there are three basic types of résumés: chronological, skills, and creative.

Chronological Résumé

The chronological résumé highlights the professional development of the applicant. Its organization features the applicant's most recent employment and works backwards in time. Figure 46.4 shows a chronological résumé.

Skills Résumé

The skills résumé places less emphasis on employment history and education and more on abilities. The skills résumé is organized according to topic, and examples are typically listed chronologically within each topic. If you have developed skills that are transferable from one job to another, whether they be management skills or creative skills, emphasize those first. Then detail previous accomplishments. Finally, include work history and education.

Creative Résumé

Creative résumés are those that in some way reflect the skills and habits of mind that a prospective job requires. Examples include a painting or collage by an applicant for a magazine art directorship, a greeting card by someone applying for a job designing cards, and a menu for someone wanting to be manage a trendy restaurant.

Harriet Monroe
2222 De La Garza Boulevard
Tulsa, Oklahoma 74103
(918) 555-5619

Objective: Restaurant Manager of Jackson's Riverside
Bistro.

Summary: Nine years in restaurant work in three
successful venues. Focus on quality food and
dedicated service. Active participant in two
award-winning management teams. Additional
training in accounting and management.

Experience:

1993-present   Manager. The Flying Fish. Tulsa, Oklahoma.
Supervising staff of 28. Increased monthly
earnings 98% from $35,652 to $69,784 in first
twelve months; continued growth of 63% per
year since.

1991-1993   Assistant Manager. Romeo's. Tulsa, Oklahoma.
Hired and supervised wait staff. Developed and
implemented wait staff orientation program.
Staff won the 1992 and 1993 "Most Efficient
Business Lunch" award in city poll sponsored
by local newspaper.

1988-1991   Wait Staff. Chicken Fried. Fayetteville,
Arkansas. Worked lunch and dinner shifts,
weekdays and weekends, while attending college.
Wait staff named in 1991 "Friendliest Eatery"
by student newspaper.

Education:

1996-1997   University of Oklahoma at Tulsa. 18 hours of
accounting classes.

1988-1991   B.S. Business Management and English.
University of Arkansas 1991. Graduated with
double major.

References: Upon request.

Figure 46.4 Sample Résumé

46d.3 Cover Letter

The formal nature of a résumé—its exclusive focus on information and its lack of reference to a specific audience or context—creates the need for a **cover letter**, a personal letter that accompanies the résumé and suggests to this specific reader ways to read the document. Figure 46.5 illustrates a sample cover letter.

46e
MEMOS

Memos (sometimes called memorandums or memoranda) are documents used within an organization to communicate a wide range of ideas and information. Essentially, they are letters from one employee to another or to a group of employees. The ideas and information are put into writing because the employee or the organization needs some record of the communication. Memos can range in tone from formal to very informal, depending on their purposes and intended readers. Most often they are brief, two pages at most. Very often memos serve as cover letters to longer, more complicated documents. Figure 46.6 illustrates the design of a typical memo.

46f
BUSINESS LETTERS

As memos are the most prominent form of written communication within a company or business, the **business letter** is the most prominent form of written communication from a business to the public, from a business to another business, and from an individual to a business.

A partial list of types of business letters includes letters of acceptance, acknowledgment, collection, complaint, credit, inquiry, order, reference, and sale. The following sections examine how to open and close business letters and how to indicate divisions and subdivisions in the text.

46f.1 Opening

After indicating the date of the letter and the name and address of the person you are writing to, you open the letter itself with a **salutation**, a greeting to the reader.

Most salutations will look like the following:

Dear Mr. Williams:

Dear Ms. Williams:

```
                        Harriet Monroe
                2222 De La Garza Boulevard
                     Tulsa, OK 74103


February 19, 1998


Ms. Elizabeth Jackson
Jackson Enterprises
909 South Taylor Ave.
St Louis, MO 63103


Dear Ms. Jackson:


I consider myself fortunate to have met you last week at the
Great Chefs Round-Up. St. Louis can certainly be proud of the
number of fine restaurants it supports. I was particularly
interested in your description of your new venture, Jackson's
Riverside Bistro. As I promised you, I am sending you my résumé
for you to consider.


I feel I have been very fortunate over the last nine years to
have worked where I have. All three establishments have been
strongly supported by a committed management team and dedicated
owners. If I have learned anything, it would be that successful
restaurants--no matter what size or kind--never rest on the
shoulders of one person. Success is the result of many people
working together. I know that the success of The Flying Fish in
Tulsa has truly been the result of a team effort.


I am confident that I could help you build this kind of team
at Jackson's. I look forward to talking with you again. I can
be reached at (918) 555-5619, and I am very willing to drive
to St. Louis to meet with you.


Sincerely,

Harriet Monroe

Harriet Monroe


enc.
```

Figure 46.5 Sample Cover Letter (Block Format)

Memorandum
Bill's Bungee Adventures

To: All Customer Service Reps
From: Bill Seeker
Date: 4 April 1997
Re: Customer Concern About Safety

I assume by now that you have all read or at least heard about the article in last Sunday's newspaper. It seems to be all everyone is talking about, especially our customers. So if a customer expresses concern about his or her safety, I ask you to treat the concern with politeness.

What you can tell the customers:

— Not one jumper has ever been injured at Bill's. Since opening in 1990, Bill's has averaged 50 jumps a day and not one person has been injured.

— Bungee jumping is highly regulated by the Sports Safety Board.

— Our course exceeds the standards in every case.

— We use the strongest cords available, capable of holding a 300-pound man from the height of our course.

— We use five strands of cord, not one, and one can support the jumper.

— Cords are checked every day and replaced every month, regardless of visible wear.

Finally, you may be interested to know—though you don't necessarily need to tell customers—that the article was written by a mother whose daughter was injured in a jump. The article originally appeared in a newspaper two months ago in New Jersey, where the daughter was injured. For some reason unknown to me, our paper here reprinted the article, mentioned our name in it, but never called us for information.

As you know from your own jumps when you were training, safety is our number one objective. Please let the customers know how much we care about them and their safety.

Figure 46.6 Sample Memo

Dear Dr. Williams:

Dear President Williams:

Dear Senator Williams:

Dear Professor Williams:

Dear Representative Williams:

Dear Reverend Williams:

Dear Sister Williams:

In all cases here, a colon follows the name. This is the typical practice in a formal business letter. Occasionally, when you are very familiar with the reader, you can follow the name with a comma. A new practice called "open punctuation" allows you to leave off any punctuation in the salutation.

46f.2 Closing

After you have stated the purpose of your letter and explained the subject thoroughly, you will need to close the letter. This is accomplished with a **complimentary closing** followed by a comma, your signature, and your typed name.

These examples of closings go from formal to informal.

Respectfully yours, Respectfully, Yours very truly,	For individuals in positions that command respect
Yours truly, Sincerely yours, Sincerely,	For most situations
Best regards, Cordially yours, Cordially,	For close business associates

46f.3 Paragraphing

In preparing your manuscript, you have the choice of three paragraphing formats: block, modified block, and indented. (Figures 46.5, 46.7, and 46.8, respectively, illustrate these three formats.) Which of these to use remains your decision, based on your intended purpose and tone. Generally speak-

2222 De La Garza Boulevard
Tulsa, OK 74103
February 19, 1998

Ms. Elizabeth Jackson
Jackson Enterprises
909 South Taylor Ave.
St Louis, MO 63103

Dear Ms. Jackson:

I consider myself fortunate to have met you last week at the Great Chefs Round-Up. St. Louis can certainly be proud of the number of fine restaurants it supports. I was particularly interested in your description of your new venture, Jackson's Riverside Bistro. As I promised you, I am sending you my résumé for you to consider.

I feel I have been very fortunate over the last nine years to have worked where I have. All three establishments have been strongly supported by a committed management team and dedicated owners. If I have learned anything, it would be that successful restaurants--no matter what size or kind--never rest on the shoulders of one person. Success is the result of many people working together. I know that the success of The Flying Fish in Tulsa has truly been the result of a team effort.

I am confident that I could help you build this kind of team at Jackson's. I look forward to talking with you again. I can be reached at (918) 555-5619, and I am very willing to drive to St. Louis to meet with you.

Sincerely,

Harriet Monroe

Harriet Monroe

enc.

Figure 46.7 Business Letter (Modified Block Format)

2222 De La Garza Boulevard
Tulsa, OK 74103
February 19, 1998

Ms. Elizabeth Jackson
Jackson Enterprises
909 South Taylor Ave.
St. Louis, MO 63103

Dear Ms. Jackson:

    I consider myself fortunate to have met you last week at
the Great Chefs Round-Up. St. Louis can certainly be proud of
the number of fine restaurants it supports. I was particularly
interested in your description of your new venture, Jackson's
Riverside Bistro. As I promised you, I am sending you my résumé
for you to consider.

    I feel I have been very fortunate over the last nine years
to have worked where I have. All three establishments have been
strongly supported by a committed management team and dedicated
owners. If I have learned anything, it would be that successful
restaurants--no matter what size or kind--never rest on the
shoulders of one person. Success is the result of many people
working together. I know that the success of The Flying Fish in
Tulsa has truly been the result of a team effort.

    I am confident that I could help you build this kind of
team at Jackson's. I look forward to talking with you again. I
can be reached at (918) 555-5619, and I am very willing to
drive to St. Louis to meet with you.

                              Sincerely,

                              Harriet Monroe

                              Harriet Monroe

enc.

Figure 46.8 Business Letter (Indent Format)

ing, the block format is the most modern and has an efficient feel to it since every portion of the letter begins at the left margin. Block-format paragraphs are not indented, and they are separated by a blank line. This format was created to save typists time and effort. The indented format is more traditional; and because the typist must make efforts to tab or indent paragraphs and other material, the indented format tends to have a more personal feel. The modified block format incorporates both elements and feels contemporary while not being quite as cold as the pure block format.

CommonSense Guide

The Parts of Formal Written Communications

Formal written communications usually include the following parts.

Announcement	Includes matters such as the writer's name, the intended audience, the subject, and the time and place of the writing.
Opening (if needed)	Clarifies the subject and the context of the discussion to follow.
Text	Presents the information and ideas the writer wants to communicate.
Subdivisions of text	Indicates through paragraphs, headings, and subheadings the organization of the text.
Closing (if needed)	Summarizes and suggests consequences of information in text.

CHAPTER

47

Illustrations

In your own writing at school or on the job, you may find yourself faced with a large number of facts that have clear but complex relationships with each other. But writing all the information seems to complicate the relationships instead of clarifying them. In these instances, presenting the information graphically often helps you communicate with the reader more efficiently and more effectively.

47a
CHOOSING VERBAL VERSUS GRAPHICAL INFORMATION

Do you remember a time you were invited to a party at someone's house or apartment, but it was a place you had never been before? What kind of directions were given to you? Were you given a paragraph describing the trip out to the place? Or were you given a list of streets and turns and addresses? Or were you given a map? Which would be most useful?

Most of us would agree that a map would be the most useful way to tell strangers how to get from one place to another. Presenting information graphically serves several purposes. Graphics help readers by

Organizing long lists of numerical data,

Simplifying complicated relationships among data,

Helping define,

Portraying visual information, and

Illustrating processes.

Presenting information graphically also indicates your concern for the audience in several ways. Readers who are experts in subjects often prefer information presented graphically. Because experts understand the relationships inherent in the information, they can read great quantities of graphical information quickly. Additionally, readers who are new to subjects almost always enjoy graphical information. Because they may be fearful of a new, complicated subject, novices appreciate being able to visualize data and the relationships revealed.

Finally, readers who are performing a task while reading instructions, such as those for building model airplanes, benefit from illustrations. Because they are already focused visually on the physical aspects of the work being performed, these readers more easily transfer illustrated information into action.

47b
PRESENTING ILLUSTRATIONS IN MANUSCRIPTS

Reading confusing prose is difficult and frustrating enough. However, encountering illustrations whose purpose and information are unclear is doubly frustrating, especially since we expect graphics to clarify and simplify. Readers have come to rely on certain practices concerning how illustrations are presented.

Place Illustrations Near the Discussion That Refers to Them

In your document, an illustration should be placed near your discussion of the material it refers to. Usually this means locating it directly below the discussion. If your illustration requires a full page, you will most often place it on the first available full page after the discussion.

Clearly Refer in the Discussion to the Illustration

In all cases, when you discuss an illustration, clearly tell your reader where you have placed the illustration in the manuscript. Often you can accomplish this by labeling the illustration—for example, *Figure 6* or *Table 12.4*. Then as you discuss the data, refer to the illustration with statements like these.

> As Figure 6 indicates, . . .

> The steps for this process are listed in Figure 6.

> Table 12.4 shows that Babe Ruth hit sixty home runs in 1927.

Focus the Reader on Your Interpretation of the Illustration

Illustrations are simply information. And the information is basically meaningless until you interpret it. Since you will include an illustration either to explain a topic or to make a point, simply make that point clear. There are two places to do so: in your text as you refer to the illustration and in the illustration itself, either as a title or as a caption.

Accurately Label the Illustration with a Heading

The reader can find an illustration only if you identify it with a label. Tables are illustrations that contain columns and rows. Figures include all charts, graphs, drawings, diagrams, maps, and photographs. Both tables and figures are numbered in sequence. The first figure you include is labeled *Figure 1* (for example, "Figure 1: Percentages of Men and Women Practicing Law"). The next figure is labeled *Figure 2*, and so on. If your document is long and divided into chapters, you might want to number them by chapter (for example, "Figure 3.1: Percentages of Men and Women Practicing Law").

Name and Define Everything in the Illustration

The purpose of most illustrations is to clarify a complicated topic, so be conscientious in providing complete details concerning measurements, dimensions, names of parts, angles of perception, and scale. In addition, in almost all cases, spell out words, and do not rely on abbreviations. If you must use abbreviations, choose only standard ones.

Identify the Source

Always identify the source of an illustration. If you have taken the illustration from another publication, include complete bibliographical information: author, title of article, title of book or magazine, publisher, date, and page number.

List Illustrations

Generally, when readers return to a document looking for an illustration, they can do so, provided there are not very many. But if your document contains more than five illustrations, provide a list of tables or a list of figures, usually following the table of contents. Like tables of contents, these lists are ordered by page number and heading.

47c
WORKING WITH DIFFERENT KINDS OF ILLUSTRATIONS

You can add a variety of illustrations to your writing. All of them—tables, graphs, charts, diagrams, drawings, maps, and photographs—add a different kind of information to your manuscript.

47c.1 Tables

Tables present information arranged in columns and rows. This arrangement allows readers to scan the material and quickly locate the data they are interested in. Another advantage of using tables is that they present a large amount of information quickly. Whereas most tables present numeric information, some tables contain words, and a few contain both numbers and words (see Table 47.1).

47c.2 Graphs

Graphs present information indicating the relationships between two sets of data. They can be designed in a number of ways—among them line graphs (see Figure 47.2), scatter graphs, bar graphs (see Figure 47.3), pictorial graphs, and pie graphs. Except for pie graphs, all are designed using

			Table of Honors English Classes at Violet Crown College Spring Semester 1997			
Section	Course Number	Course Name	Day & Time	Building	Room	Teacher
0001	1613	Comp. I	MWF 9:00 a.m.— 9:50 a.m.	English Building	2323	Lostracco
0002	1613	Comp. I	MWF 2:00 p.m.— 2:50 p.m.	English Building	2323	Huerta
0003	1613	Comp. I	TTH 12:00 p.m.— 1:15 p.m.	English Building	2323	Kinslow
0004	1623	Comp. II	MWF 10:00 a.m.— 10:50 a.m.	English Building	1323	Ward
0005	1623	Comp. II	MWF 1:00 p.m.— 1:50 p.m.	English Building	1323	Polnac
0006	1623	Comp. II	TTH 1:30 p.m.— 2:45 p.m.	English Building	1324	Grant
0007	1653	Creative Writing	TTH 9:00 a.m.— 10:15 a.m.	English Building	1223	Cameron
0008	2643	American Lit. I	MWF 11:00 a.m.— 11:50 a.m.	English Building	2223	Lundy
0009	2653	American Lit. II	TTH 10:30 a.m.— 11:45 a.m.	English Building	1223	Huerta
0010	2663	World Lit. I	MWF 12:00 p.m.— 12:50 p.m.	English Building	2213	Ward

Table 47.1 Table with Words and Numbers

the same principles. Information is presented using two axes, one vertical and one horizontal. Most often graphs present numerical information; therefore, the vertical axis indicates increased quantity going up, and the horizontal axis indicates increased quantity going to the right. Often the

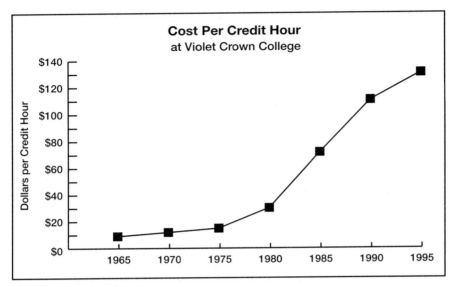

Figure 47.2 Line Graph

horizontal axis depicts the passage of time, usually with time moving forward to the right.

Pie graphs illustrate percentages. For instance, you could easily depict the percentages of grades in a given class. In designing a pie graph, the first thing to remember is that the circle or "pie" represents 100 percent of the topic being discussed and that 1 percent of the whole is 3.6 degrees of the circle.

47c.3 Charts

Charts are excellent for illustrating a process or a classification system. Flow charts can very clearly depict the steps in a process. In most cases, components of the processes are illustrated with boxes, circles, triangles, and the like, and the movement between steps is indicated by arrows. If you include different shapes, use them consistently.

Charts that illustrate classification systems include organizational charts, family trees, and biological trees. One important factor to remember in designing this type of chart is that most readers read from the top of the page to the bottom. Therefore, whatever you place at the top of the page should be most important.

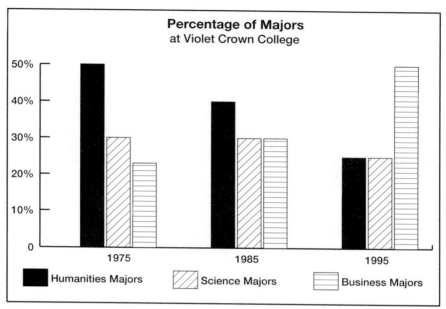

Figure 47.3 Bar Graph

47c.4 Drawings

Drawings present objects as they actually appear. They can range in detail, depending on how realistic a depiction is needed. Very often drawings lessen the need for extensive description, especially when you want to show the relationship of an object's parts to the object as a whole.

Drawings are always simple depictions of the object as it actually looks. At one time or another, you might also need to use the following:

Cutaway drawings   *allowing the viewer to see inside an object*

Exploded drawings   *allowing the viewer to see more clearly the relationship of all the parts, including those inside, with each other*

Perspective drawings   *allowing the viewer to see the object from different directions, such as from above, from below, and from the sides*

Action drawings   *allowing the viewer to see how the object works*

47c.5 Maps

Maps are most useful in depicting geographical information, but their uses are far more varied than you might think. For instance, maps can indicate relationships and comparisons between political entities. By using various graphical techniques with dots, shading, and lines, you can present various kinds of statistics.

47c.6 Photographs

Photographs are the most realistic representations of objects. When using photographs, remember that you can manipulate them in many ways by cropping, enlarging, and reducing them. You can highlight portions by enlarging only part of a photograph and laying it over the original. You can also direct your viewer's attention by using lines and arrows as you would with a drawing.

CHAPTER

48

Layout

The invention of the computer, laser printers, photocopy machines, and computerized publishing software has greatly changed the way we present our manuscripts to readers. In some cases, we are able to bypass the manuscript phase of publishing and produce final "published" products without ever going to a printer for typesetting. The ability to publish quickly is very exciting for those of us who lack access to large, expensive typesetting and printing devices.

In the future you may be asked to design a flier or brochure, an in-house newsletter, or a class poetry or literary journal. You might also produce your own invitations, fliers, party announcements, or club newsletters.

For professional-quality work, you should still rely on well-trained and experienced graphic artists. The following guidelines, however, introduce a few techniques and concerns about layout for general purposes.

48a
THE TASKS OF LAYOUT

To approach designing a booklet or another type of document, you need to learn about the tasks involved. Again, as with the writing tasks, you can imagine the tasks of layout in a step-by-step fashion, even though they often occur concurrently.

Examine Text and Illustrations

One task you will face is examining the pile of material you have to work with. How much is text? Is it all one piece, or is it a series of separate pieces? Are the pieces of equal value? Or are some pieces very important while others are of lesser importance—for example, annotations or captions? Is it all text, or are there photographs or illustrations? This information will give you an idea of how long the document will be and how complicated it will be to design.

Evaluate Purpose and Audience

Another task is to decide on the feel or tone you want your project to have. Do you want to create a calm, formal, uncluttered feel on the page, or do you want an arresting, informal, busy design? Or perhaps you want something that incorporates elements of both. How you face this task will depend greatly on whether you want to use the document primarily to express yourself, to entertain the audience, to persuade the audience, or to inform the audience. Also important is the audience itself. An annual report for IBM might look different from one for Ben and Jerry's because their investors have different values.

CommonSense Guide

Principles of Graphical Composition

The effectiveness of any graphic material is the product of the choices the designer makes. Those choices are often determined by which principles of graphics the designer highlights.

Balance	Do you want text and illustrations to give the page an even feel?
Proportion	Do you want to assign text and illustrations a size and density appropriate to their relative importance in providing meaning?
Rhythm	Do you want the viewer's eyes to move across the page quickly or slowly?
Movement	In what directions do you want your viewer's eyes to move across the page: up and down, right to left?
Unity	Do you want your text and illustrations to create a single tone, or do you want to create distractions and confusion for the viewer?

→

continued from previous page

Clarity	Do you want the text and illustrations to help the viewer understand your message quickly, or do you want to create ambiguity?
Simplicity	Do you want a few important elements with simple relationships, or do you want more elements with complicated relationships?

If you are a beginner, it is best to strive for a balanced, proportionate, slow-paced, unified, clear, simple presentation. Then with practice, you can add more complications to your design work.

Conceive Overall Design

It is always a good idea to look at the overall design of your project. If your work is longer than one page, not only will you design each page to reflect your vision, but also you will want to make sure the individual pages look good together. One technique that is helpful in attaining an overall balanced and unified design is using **thumbnail sketches**. A thumbnail sketch is a quick rendition of how you want the pages to look and in what order you want the materials to be presented. Some people like to make a group of small thumbnails, and others prefer to work from actual-sized thumbnails. As you make your thumbnail sketches, you will be forced to consider other matters in designing your document. These considerations—discussed in the remainder of the chapter—include paper size, page design, typefaces, graphical elements, and other special devices. The box on commonsense principles of graphical composition offers guidelines for designing your project.

48b
PAGE SIZE

Perhaps the first thing we notice about any piece of printed material is its size. Is it a poster hanging on the wall, a flier stapled to a telephone pole, a letter, a paperback book that will fit into a back pocket? Is it square, or is it taller than it is wide or wider than it is tall? So the first thing you will decide is the size and shape of your final product.

One of the limitations of current personal computer systems is that your page size will be determined by the size of paper that your printer and photocopy machine can handle. If you purchase more sophisticated software programs and equipment, you will be able to deliver your design to a printer on disk. Most of us work with legal-size paper (8 1/2" x 14") or standard-size paper (8 1/2" x 11"). Most computers and printers can work with either a vertical or horizontal layout on these standard paper sizes.

In addition, most programs allow you to design pages to your own specifications. If you print on legal-size paper, you can design a 2" x 14" flier (or any other size smaller than 8 1/2" x 14"). You will simply have to cut the paper to size after printing. Using the copy-and-paste feature of your publishing program, you may be able to place several copies on one sheet.

48c
PAGE DESIGN

After you have decided on the size of page you want to work with, the next step will be to choose a basic page design, including the number of columns, the size of margins, the kind of justification, and the positioning of images.

48c.1 Columns

The number of columns you use is influenced by the page size of your publication. One column of type works well with pages smaller than 8 1/2" x 11", such as most novels and other publications that people can hold in one hand. (A manuscript is another matter because it is usually double spaced.) Formats larger than 8 1/2" x 11" that also contain a large amount of text, such as magazines and newspapers, usually need to be divided into two or more columns. Another factor influencing the number of columns you chose is type size (see Section 48d.2).

48c.2 White Space and Margins

Wide margins and ample white space also create a leisurely and visually pleasing feel to the page. Most word processing and desktop publishing programs set adequate margins automatically. Notice that if you are working with a multiple-page layout, your pages have different margins set for the sides of the page. The reason for this difference is that if you plan to bind the pages, as you would for a book or magazine, part of the inside of the page will be curved and more difficult to read. So for any bound material, you will want to make the inside margin about half an inch larger than the outside margin.

48c.3 Justification

After you choose the number of columns you would like to work with, you can decide how you would like the lines of type to stand in the columns. **Justification** is the relationship of your margins to the beginning and ending letters of your line of type. You have four choices.

1. Center each line.
2. Justify the lines at the left margin, but leave the right margin unjustified. (This approach is sometimes called *ragged right*.)
3. Justify the lines at the right margin, but leave the left margin unjustified. (This method is sometimes called *ragged left*.)
4. Justify the lines at both the left and right margins. (This method is often called *full justification*.)

Most often you will choose left justification or full justification. Left justification is most prevalent; it gives your document an informal feel but is very readable because the line breaks differ in location and help the reader's eyes scan down the page. Full justification has a more formal feel because it gives the text clean vertical lines; but with long lines of type, it is slightly more difficult to read than left justification. Centering is usually saved for titles, captions, and some poems. In long passages of prose, centering serves little purpose and makes for difficult reading. Right justification is seldom employed except for purely artistic purposes.

48d
TYPEFACES

Perhaps the most important factor in a pleasing layout is the typeface. Two important features of typefaces are type style and type size.

48d.1 Type Style

Your choice of the kinds and numbers of **type styles** to use in your document depends largely on your purpose. If you mean to entertain, especially to entertain through design more than through language, you are as free as your imagination allows. But if your purpose is to persuade or to explain, your choices are more limited. A good rule of thumb is that in any typical design project, you will want to use no more than three or four type styles, each one being used for a specific purpose. You will want one style for the main text and perhaps a second style for a second kind of text. Headings and subheadings will most often be a bold or underlined version of the text type style. You may want a separate style for the titles as well.

One important distinction between type styles is that some letters are designed with "serifs" or "feet" at the bottom of the letters. Sans serif type styles are designed without feet. The effect of these feet is to establish a connection from one letter to the next, a kind of line on which the letters stand, making reading easier and less tiring.

Sans serif type is generally considered more contemporary. A page of sans serif letters seems lighter, with more white space than a page of serif type, but the eye does not move as easily from each letter or word to the next. Sans serif type styles are used more often for shorter texts and very often for titles.

Typefaces often suggested include

Serif	Baskerville, Bookman, Caledonia, Century Schoolbook, Cheltenham, Garamond, Goudy, Times Roman
Sans serif	Futura Light, Helvetica, Universal

48d.2 Type Size

If you are designing a newsletter or brochure, your major concern will probably be the readability of the type. But this is not the only consideration; you also need to think about how long your line of print is. How wide do you want your columns to be? Typically, readers find that an average of seven to ten words per line is a comfortable length to read for long stretches. On word processing and desktop publishing software, this means that you will generally use 9- or 12-point type.

48d.3 Leading

When laying out your text, one of the factors to consider is **leading**. In preparing manuscripts, you deal with leading when you choose to single-space or double-space a page. In designing a brochure or newsletter, you also consider the spacing between lines of type. The space between lines of type is called leading because in early printing presses, strips of lead were placed between lines of type. Lines spaced together too closely can cause the page to look too dark or too busy or crowded and cause the reader to read lines over and over. Lines of type laid out too far apart make the words seem to float on the page, and the readers can again lose track of which line they are reading, sometimes even skipping lines.

Most word processing or desktop publishing programs have set automatic defaults for leading for each type size. You may want to change that setting on the rare occasions when you want to crowd or loosen your type. For example, you may find that a word or line of type from the end of a paragraph appears by itself at the top of a page or column. Sometimes a slight adjustment of the leading of the paragraph, so slight that most readers will not notice the change, will save enough space to bring the line back to the bottom of the previous page or column.

48e
GRAPHICAL ELEMENTS

The printed page simultaneously communicates verbally and graphically. For instance, as a writer you strive to show the relationship of your ideas through patterns of organization (Chapter 14), transitions (Section 16c), and similar techniques. As graphic designer, you attempt to show relationships by the way you lay out your pages. Among the many graphical techniques that help define the relationships between blocks of type are lines, rules, boxes, titles and headings, and headers and footers.

48e.1 Lines, Rules, and Boxes

Lines, rules, and boxes define the relationships between the many parts of your writing. The challenge is to help the parts retain their independence while still contributing to the overall effect of your writing.

There are several reasons for employing lines, rules, and boxes.

To decorate and enliven the text

To separate different kinds of text

To emphasize something in the text

To lead the reader's eyes across the page

48e.2 Titles and Headings

Titles and headings are important means for both informing readers about content and pleasing them with boldness or grace.

Titles—that is, the names of articles, essays, or poems contained in your publication—are as important for their eye-catching design as for any other reason. Therefore, the typeface of a title is almost always larger than the typeface of the text. How much larger will depend on how dramatic you want your design to be.

You are also free to choose a typeface for your titles that is different from the text typeface. Sans serif typefaces and decorative, flowing typefaces can be particularly pleasing. In choosing a typeface for titles, you may want to select one that reflects the tone of the title.

Where you place titles will depend on your overall design. For instance, if your page contains the text of only one work, then the title will very often be centered across the top. However, if the page contains more than one essay or article, you will want to place titles only over the appropriate columns. Although you will most often place titles at the top of the page, you need not always follow that practice.

Headings, such as names of sections of an article or essay, can be almost as important as titles for attracting the eyes of a reader. Readers very often scan an article looking for topics of special interest. For this reason, headings are usually treated with more restraint than titles. They are in a smaller typeface than the title, sometimes just slightly larger than the text typeface. In addition, headings are placed where they naturally occur in the text, either "heading" the relevant text or occasionally, if margins allow, beside the text.

48e.3 Headers and Footers

Headers and **footers** are names for the material that appears at the top and bottom of a page, respectively. These are the places where you put page numbers. And sometimes you may include the name of the publication or some subdivision of the publication, such as a chapter title. For a periodical, you may use the date of the publication. But whatever you put in a header or a footer will be consistent from page to page. In most cases, page numbers are placed on the outer edge of the page or in the center. Readers will quickly learn how to read your publication for page numbers and other information and will expect it to be in the same place every time.

11

The Internet

Internet Resources

The Internet has been called a network of networks. Linking millions of people on millions of computers all over the world, this enormous system is continuously expanding and developing. And even now, its potential as a resource for communication and research has not been fully realized.

On the Internet you will be able to communicate directly with individuals and organizations through email, through interactive chat groups, through virtual reality environments, and through a kind of global bulletin board called Usenet. In addition, you will have access to a mind-boggling amount of research information on almost any topic, information that includes online versions of print materials as well as materials available only through the Internet.

The Internet can be overwhelming, especially when you are just beginning to explore. Fortunately, many resources are available to you. Be patient, and don't be afraid to leap into cyberspace.

49a WORLD WIDE WEB

The **World Wide Web** is currently the most extensively used of all Internet resources. It has replaced the earlier methods of accessing the information on the Internet. Even if you want to get information from any of the other tools on the Internet (Gopher, FTP, Usenet, and Telnet), you can do it through the Web. Its popularity is understandable because the Web allows easier access to information than did any of the earlier Internet methods.

Information on the Web is found on **Web pages** that can have graphics and sound as well as text. These pages are collected at **Web sites**, which can be accessed by **Web browser** software such as *Netscape Navigator* or *Microsoft Internet Explorer*. To access a particular Web site, you enter the electronic address, called a **URL** (uniform resource locator), in the browser's dialog box. For example, the address http://www.si.edu is the location of the Web site for the Smithsonian Institution. The browser will connect you to the Web page located at that address. When you select a highlighted word or icon at that site, you will move to other related Web sites. By using this method, you can "browse" the Web, jumping from site to site as your interest and curiosity lead you.

To locate Web sites relevant to topics you may be researching, you will need to use a **search engine**. Browsers have built-in links to some search engines. Which ones you choose will depend in part on your personal preferences, in part on your experience with Internet resources, and in part on what kind of research you are doing.

Search engines locate information about a topic either by keyword or by category. Some, like AltaVista and HotBot, are keyword-only search engines. Others combine directory searches of categories with keyword searches. Each method has its advantages and disadvantages. The keyword searches access much more information, but when you use keyword searches on some kinds of topics, you run the risk of getting more "hits" (finding Web pages with that keyword) than you can possibly investigate. Directory searches allow you to narrow the search by first identifying categories of information before you do a keyword search. As a result, starting with a directory search before using the keyword search will usually be faster. However, search engines that use directories usually have more limited databases than those that search with keywords only, so you may miss some good sources unless you check keywords too.

There is no single best strategy for all occasions, so you should try to use several search engines rather than limiting yourself to one. The following descriptions will help you make choices. Before trying to use a search engine, read the help screens on its home page to learn how to take full advantage of its capabilities.

AltaVista   http://www.altavista.digital.com

Because it is fast and complete, AltaVista is a very popular search tool. It is the purest of the search engines. You simply enter a query and it responds. It searches more than thirty million pages.

Excite   http://www.excite.com

In addition to searches, Excite provides access to news and reviews of Web sites.

HotBot   http://www.hotbot.com

Like AltaVista, HotBot is a pure keyword search engine. It searches more than fifty million Web pages. It is consistently rated as one of the best search engines.

Infoseek   http://www.infoseek.com

Infoseek combines an enormous directory for searching categories with a powerful keyword search engine.

Lycos   http://www.lycos.com

In addition to basic search features, Lycos offers other attractive information resources such as reviews of Web sites, road maps, corporate profiles, and classified ads.

WebCrawler   http://www.webcrawler.com

WebCrawler is fast and easy to use. If you want to find basic information on a topic quickly, WebCrawler is a good resource.

Yahoo!   http://www.yahoo.com

Yahoo is one of the most popular search engines; Netscape Navigator *and* Microsoft Internet Explorer *contain built-in links to it. Because it is easy to use, it is highly recommended for beginners. It combines directory searches by category and keyword searches. (Yahoo uses AltaVista for broader keyword searches.)*

CommonSense Guide

Search Techniques

Don't expect your first search to find everything you need. If a directory search doesn't turn up much information, you may want to use a keyword search engine, such as Alta Vista, that has a greater reach. Identify a number of possible keywords. The listing activities in Chapter 7 may help you identify possibilities. For example, if your topic is "the environmental movement," you might use the keywords "environmental," "ecology," "conservation," and "nature."

Some search engines let you look for related terms by shortening the keyword to its basic root and adding a special character such as a question mark or asterisk. For example, searching for "environment*" will find "environmental," "environmentalism," and "environmentalists."

To refine your search, some browsers let you use two words connected with AND or NOT or enclosed in quotation marks. AND will return results that include all the terms listed. (For example, "environmentalism AND ecology" would get results for both words.) NOT allows you to exclude words that don't relate to your topic. (For example, "pollution NOT air" would return results about pollution, but not those dealing with air pollution.) Enclosing two words in quotation marks will return hits that include those two words appearing together in that order. (For example, "environmental ethics" would return those results in which the term *environmental ethics* appears.)

 **49b**
GOPHER

On your journeys through cyberspace, you may run across a **Gopher**. There are about 7500 Gopher servers all over the world that have information on just about every subject, although Gopher is rapidly becoming obsolete. In some ways, searching on Gopher is simpler than searching on the Web. You deal with simple lists, and in many cases Gopher searches are much faster than Web searches.

Gopher, developed at the University of Minnesota (whose mascot is the gopher), is a system of Internet protocols that allow you to connect to other computers, access their directories, and download files. You can search Gopher sites for directory names, titles of files, and file texts. What you will receive on your computer screen will be pure text. For the most part, Gopher files do not include graphics.

The search tool **Veronica** was developed to access Gopher sites on computers connected through the Gopher system. You type one or more keywords that define the topic you are interested in researching. Veronica searches for any files that match your keywords.

49c
FTP

Whereas Gopher servers contain mostly text-based files, an **FTP** (File Transfer Protocol) can retrieve software as well. One of the important uses of FTP is transferring software files. FTP allows you to transfer large data files between computers. Some sites require a password, but most allow "anonymous" users. Once connected, you are able to move hierarchically through the site's files. If you find any files that you would like to copy to your own computer, you can do so. Also, in many cases, you can use the site's search tools to locate information at other sites throughout the world.

Archie was the first tool that could locate data in a number of computers at once. The Archie system maintains a database of files available without a password. Archie allows you to type in keywords that you want to search, then lists the file names it locates throughout the world that include those keywords. Additionally, you can tell Archie whether you want to search for an exact match or a partial match of your keywords.

49d
TELNET

Telnet is a "terminal emulation protocol" that allows you to log on to remote computer systems (that is, computers located at distant sites). Unlike FTP, which essentially lets you search through a distant computer's files, Telnet makes it possible to actually work on the distant computer. For this reason, many computers require passwords for users who connect through Telnet. Once logged on, you can work on the distant computer as if you were sitting in front of it.

Telnet can be a valuable tool because it allows you to search catalogs of libraries around the world, access multiuser games and online stores, and access your email from remote computers. A Web site called Hytelnet at http://library.usask.ca/hytelnet gives information about accessing Telnet.

49e
USENET

The **Usenet** system is simply part of the information that moves over the Internet. It is composed of **newsgroups** in which computer users carry on discussions about almost any topic you can imagine. A newsgroup is like a bulletin board where members can post and respond to messages.

You must evaluate carefully the information you get from a newsgroup. There are no guarantees about the reliability of the information. But a newsgroup can give you ideas and information that you can follow up with further research. A valuable tool that will allow you to monitor and select information from newsgroups is a search engine called DejaNews at http://www.dejanews.com.

49f
LISTSERVS

Listservs are basically mailing lists using email. Like newsgroups, they provide a great body of information on many topics. Finding an appropriate mailing list can be a daunting task; more than 7500 lists are available. There is a way to make some sense of all the possibilities. A comprehensive list of all listservs, PAML (Publicly Accessible Mailing Lists), can be searched at http://www.NeoSoft.com/internet/paml. It is also available at ftp://rtfm.mit.edu, an FTP site.

49g
EMAIL

The first thing most people will probably learn when they go online is how to use email. Internet service providers have all the information users need for sending and receiving email. But you should be aware of some strategies you can use to make using email more productive.

- **Be polite.** That sounds obvious, but email does create opportunities for offending people, or at least for making it inconvenient for recipients to read your mail. For example, nesting a great many forwarded messages can irritate your reader. Have a reason for forwarding a message.

- **Take some time composing your message.** Because email is fast, many people have a tendency to be sloppy. Compose offline so you can consider more carefully what you want to say.

- **Never send anything on email that you want to keep private.** Any email message may well be read by someone other than the person it was intended for.

CommonSense Strategy

Internet Addresses in Other Protocols

Sometimes links on the Web take you to Gopher or FTP sites. If you have a specific address of a document not in the HTML format, you can access that address through the Web by entering the file type followed by the address.

gopher://address

ftp://address

telnet://address

news://address

CHAPTER

50

Choosing and Evaluating Internet Sites

Internet sites provide you with the opportunity to access a great body of information. But you must remember that almost anyone can put almost anything on the Internet and the World Wide Web. Evaluating Internet sources is even more important than evaluating traditional sources of information. The sites listed in the sections that follow are credible sources that you may be able to use as a starting point for some of your research.

50a
MAGAZINES AND NEWSPAPERS ONLINE

Traditional print sources are becoming readily available online. Since you may already have had some experience with them in your library research, they will help you begin to understand how to make use of online sources.

The Christian Science Monitor   http://www.csmonitor.com

Provides an online version of The Christian Science Monitor. *The* Monitor *is known for its objectivity in reporting.*

Electronic Journals   gopher://gopher.cic.net

Lists electronic journals on the Internet.

The Electronic Poetry Center at the University of Buffalo at http://wings.buffalo.edu/internet/library/e-journals/ub/rift/ provides an electronic poetry journal and access to other resources.

Newspapers Online   http://www.newspapers.com

Lists Web sites for hundreds of newspapers; also includes some other publications such as trade journals.

The New York Times   http://www.nytimes.com

Provides an online version of the New York Times.

Pathfinder   http://www.pathfinder.com

Provides access to a collection of Web sites affiliated with Time-Warner: Time, Life, Fortune, Sports Illustrated, People, The Weather Channel, *and CNN.*

Reuters News Service   http://www.reuters.com

Provides wire service information used by many other news sources.

USA Today Online   http://www.usatoday.com

The online version of USA Today *has a good financial section and provides an index for browsing past feature articles.*

50b
LIBRARIES

Libraries are making their presence known on the Internet. Through them you can find indexes, links to databases, and some full-text documents.

Internet Public Library   http://ipl.sils.umich.edu

Provides access to reference librarians for answers to questions.

Library Catalogs Worldwide   gopher://libgopher.yale.edu

Provides connections to libraries around the world.

Library of Congress   http://www.loc.gov

Provides links to various collections, online texts, and services.

LIBCAT   http://www.metronet.lib.mn.us/lc/lc1.html

Provides links to more than a thousand libraries with Web and Gopher access.

Libweb   http://sunsite.berkeley.edu/Libweb

Offers links to libraries around the world.

The WWW Virtual Library   http://www.tissot.org/vl/Overview.html

Provides links to a wide range of academic subjects.

50c
FULL-TEXT DOCUMENTS

Some sites, particularly at universities, have been trying to make full-text documents available, especially documents that are in the public domain.

Alex   http://www.lib.ncsu.edu/stacks/alex-index.html

Gives access to thousands of electronic texts in the public domain.

Electronic Books   gopher://vatech.lib.vt.edu

Provides access to many full-text electronic books.

Project Gutenberg   http://promo.net/pg/lists/list.html

Provides access to a large number of works in public domain, including light literature, classics, and reference works.

University of Virginia Electronic Text Center   http://etext.lib.virginia.edu

Contains thousands of electronic texts.

50d
REFERENCE WORKS

Basic reference sources such as dictionaries and atlases are readily available online. Government sites are especially helpful when you are looking for collections of data.

Bureau of the Census   http://www.census.gov

Provides census information having to do with population, the economy, and geography.

City.Net   http://www.city.net

Provides travel information for more than two thousand cities worldwide.

Online Dictionaries   http://www.bucknell.edu/~rbeard/diction.html

Lists online dictionaries.

Research It!   http://www.iTools.com/research-it/research-it.html

Searches for dictionary, thesaurus, King James Bible, and other reference materials useful in research.

THOMAS   http://thomas.loc.gov

Provides access to congressional legislation and to documents with links to other government sites.

The World Fact Book   http://www.odci.gov/cia/publications/nsolo/wfb-all.html

Provides information on geography, politics, demographics, and so on for nearly every country in the world. Compiled by the CIA.

50e
SELECTED ACADEMIC SITES

Academic institutions have long been repositories of information in many disciplines. Most academic sites are usually credible sources of information for researchers.

BIOSCI   http://www.bio.net

Provides links to newsgroups and journals in the biological sciences.

The English Server   http://english-server.hss.cmu.edu

Provides resources in fiction, drama, and other areas in the humanities.

Historical Documents and Speeches   gopher://dewey.lib.ncsu.edu:70/11/library/stacks/historical-documents-US

Contains historical documents and texts of speeches.

Humanities Hub   http://www.gu.edu.au/gwis/hub/hub.home.html

Provides links to Web sites for anthropology, architecture, cultural sciences, film, gender studies, government, history, computing, sociology, women's studies, and philosophy.

Purdue University Online Writing Lab (OWL)   http://owl.english.purdue.edu

Covers the basics of grammar, writing, research, and business writing.

World Guide to Biology   http://www.theworld.com/SCIENCE/BIOLOGY/SUBJECT.HTM

Provides links to biology resources around the world (including, but not limited to, university sites).

WWW Virtual Library Chemistry   http://www.chem.ucla.edu/chempointers.html

Provides links to chemistry resources worldwide, including sites of universities, commercial organizations, and nonprofit organizations.

Glossary of Usage

When you make choices about which words to use, you will need to consider the appropriateness of that choice. The following explanations will help you make informed decisions about some of the finer points of usage.

a, an   Use *a* before words that begin with a consonant sound, even when the sound is spelled with a vowel (*a* cat, *a* dog, *a* European, *a* union). You will always want to use *an* before words that begin with a vowel sound, including words that begin with a silent *h* (*an* arbor, *an* ear, *an* ogre, *an* hour).

accept, except   When *accept* is used as a verb, it means "to receive." *Except* means "to exclude" or "excluding."

actually   This term is frequently overused as a modifier (*Actually*, I didn't mean to do it). It is most accurately used to refer to matters having to do with fact or reality (She *actually* saw the accident).

advice, advise   *Advice* means "recommendation." *Advise* means "to recommend."

affect, effect   In the majority of cases, *affect* is used as a verb meaning "to influence," and *effect* is used as a noun meaning "a result." *Affect* has a limited use (usually in psychology) as a noun to mean "a feeling." *Effect* can be used as a verb to mean "to produce as a result" or "to bring about." See Section 36a.

aggravate   *Aggravate* is most accurately used to mean "to make worse" (You will *aggravate* your condition if you don't rest). To use it to mean "to annoy or irritate" is considered informal.

ain't   *Ain't* is a colloquial form of *am not*, but it has been extended to *is not, are not, has not,* and *have not*. It is never seen in writing except as dialogue reflecting a dialect or for effect—to create a comical, facetious, or folksy tone.

a lot   *A lot* is always two words. It can be overused; there is usually a better expression than *a lot*. *Lots* is even more informal than *a lot*.

all ready, already   *All ready* means "prepared." *Already* means "by this time."

all together, altogether   *All together* refers to "everyone being assembled in a group." *Altogether* means either "entirely," "wholly," or "completely."

allusion, illusion   An *allusion* is a passing reference to something, often a literary work or an event in history. An *illusion* is an unreal, misleading, or deceiving appearance.

bare, bear   When used as an noun or adjective, *bare* means "naked." When used as a verb, it means "to expose." When used as a noun, *bear* is the name of an animal. When used as a verb, it means "to carry" or "to endure."

being as, being that   These phrases are generally avoided in formal writing. Either *because* or *since* would be a better choice.

brake, break   When used as a noun, *brake* means "a device for stopping." When used as a verb, it means "to slow down or stop." When used as a noun, *break* means "an interruption." When used as a verb, it means "to smash" or "to interrupt."

breadth, breath, breathe   *Breadth* means "width." *Breath*, a noun, means "air taken into and let out of the lungs." *Breathe* is a verb meaning "to inhale and exhale."

capital, capitol, Capitol   The word *capital* means "primary in importance," "punishable by death," "wealth," "center of government," or "uppercase letter." The word *capitol* means "a building in which a state legislature meets." The word *Capitol* refers to the building in which the U.S. Congress meets.

cite, sight, site   The word *cite* means "to quote" or "to refer to." *Sight* means "a view," "vision," or "something seen." *Site* means "a place" or "a locale."

coarse, course   The adjective *coarse* means "rough." The noun *course* means either "a direction" or "an academic offering."

conscience, conscious   The noun *conscience* means "a moral sense of right and wrong." The adjective *conscious* means "having awareness."

consensus of opinion   This phrase is redundant. There is no reason to use the word *opinion* with the word *consensus* since *consensus* means "collective opinion." It is better to use the word *consensus* alone.

continual, continuous   *Continual* can refer to uninterrupted sequence, but now is usually restricted to an activity occurring at repeated intervals. *Continuous* means "without interruption," either in space or time.

council, counsel   The noun *council* means "a committee." When used as a noun, *counsel* means "advice" or "an attorney." When used as a verb, it means "to advise."

desert, dessert   When used as a noun, *desert* means "a barren area." When used as a verb, it means "to abandon." The noun *dessert* means "the last course in a meal."

dyeing, dying   The verb or adjective *dyeing* means "coloring." The verb or adjective *dying* means "expiring" or "drawing to an end."

emigrate, immigrate   The verb *emigrate* means "to leave one place in order to settle in another." It is usually followed by the word *from*. The verb *immigrate* means "to enter and settle in a country where a person is not a native." It is usually followed by the word *to*.

fewer, less   The word *fewer* is used to refer to anything that can be counted. The word *less* is used to refer to things thought of collectively.

formally, formerly   The adverb *formally* means "with regard to ceremony." The adverb *formerly* means "at an earlier time."

hear, here   The verb *hear* means "to perceive sound" or "to listen." The adverb *here* means "at," "in," or "at this place."

hole, whole   The noun *hole* means "an opening." The adjective *whole* means "entire" or "complete."

its, it's   *Its* is the possessive form of *it*. *It's* is a contraction of *it is*. See Section 36a.

later, latter   The adjective *later* means "at an advanced time" or "after some time." When used as a noun or adjective, *latter* means "the second of two things mentioned." It is also used as an adjective to mean "near the end."

lead, led   When used as a verb, *lead* means "to guide." When used as a noun, it means "a dense metallic element." The verb *led* means "guided."

loose, lose   The adjective *loose* means "not fastened or restrained." The verb *lose* means "to misplace or accidentally leave behind" or "to fail to win."

moral, morale   When used as a noun, *moral* means "an object lesson." When used as an adjective, it means "ethical." The noun *morale* means "confidence" and "cheerfulness."

OK, O.K., okay   All three forms of this expression are acceptable; however, they are generally avoided altogether in formal writing.

passed, past   The verb *passed* means "went by." When used as an adjective, *past* means "gone by" or "previous." When used as an adverb, it means "beyond."

patience, patients   The noun *patience* means "calm endurance." The plural noun *patients* means "those under medical care."

peace, piece   The noun *peace* means "the absence of war" or "serenity." The noun *piece* means "a part of something."

precede, proceed   The verb *precede* means "to go or come before." The verb *proceed* means "to go forward."

presence, presents   The noun *presence* means "immediate proximity." The plural noun *presents* means "gifts." The verb *presents* means "introduces" or "gives."

pretty   In academic writing, the words *very* and *rather* are preferable.

principal, principle   When used as an adjective, *principal* means "most important." When used as a noun, it means "the chief person or head." The noun *principle* means " a basic assumption" or "a rule or standard."

quiet, quite   The adjective *quiet* means "silent." The adverb *quite* means "entirely."

sense, since   The noun *sense* means "any of the functions of perception." As an adverb, *since* means "from then until now." As a conjunction, it means "because."

than, then   The conjunction *than* is used in comparative statements. The adverb *then* means "at that time" or "accordingly."

their, there, they're   The pronoun *their* means "belonging to them." When used as a noun, *there* means "that place." As an expletive, it is used to begin a sentence but has no grammatical function or meaning. *They're* is a contraction of *they are*. See Section 36a.

to, too, two   The preposition *to* means "toward." The adverb *too* means "also" or "excessively." The adjective *two* means "the number two." See Section 36a.

wait on, wait for   The expression *wait on* is sometimes used to refer to the act of waiting, but it is more accurately used to refer to the act of waiting on tables. It is more exact to say *wait for* when you want to refer to the act of waiting.

weather, whether   The noun *weather* means "the state of the atmosphere at a given time." The subordinating conjunction *whether* means "if."

where   It is inaccurate to use *where* to mean "that" (I saw on the news *that* [not *where*] there was a huge storm in the Northeast).

which, witch   The pronoun *which* means "the particular one or ones." The noun *witch* means "a woman who practices sorcery."

who's, whose   *Who's* is a contraction of *who is* or *who has*. *Whose* is the possessive form of *who* or *which*.

yore, your, you're   The noun *yore* means "the far past." *Your* is the possessive form of *you*. *You're* is a contraction of *you are*. See Section 36a.

Glossary of Terms

Many of the terms that follow are technical terms that may have been explained in other ways in the text.

absolute phrase   See **phrase**.

abstract noun   See **noun**.

accusative   Another term for the objective case. See **case**.

acronym   A word (that is pronounced as a word) formed from the first letters of a series of words.

Examples:

> *SADD* (pronounced like the word *sad*) is formed by the initial letters of the organization *S*tudents *A*gainst *D*runk *D*riving.

> *Radar* is formed from the initial letters of the phrase *ra*dio *d*etecting *a*nd *r*anging.

See Sections 38c.5 and 38d.2.

active voice   See **voice**.

adjectival   A term used for a word or word group that functions as an adjective. See **adjective**.

adjective   A word that modifies a noun, a pronoun, or a group of words functioning as a noun. Usually an adjective tells *which one, what kind*, or *how many*.

Examples:

> the *green* tree [Which tree?]

> a *curious* look [What kind of look?]

> *three* birds [How many birds?]

See also **phrase** and **clause**.

adjective clause   See **clause**.

adjective phrase   See **phrase**.

adverb   A word that modifies a verb, an adjective, or another adverb.

Examples:

> He thought *quickly*. [*Quickly* modifies the verb *thought*.]

> The *incredibly* quick fox disappeared. [*Incredibly* modifies the adjective *quick*.]

> The fox disappeared *incredibly* quickly. [*Incredibly* modifies the adverb *quickly*.]

adverb clause   See **dependent clause**.

adverbial conjunction   See **conjunctive adverb**.

adverb phrase See **phrase**.

agreement The correspondence between subject and verb or between pronoun and antecedent in number and in person. See Chapters 30 and 31.

antecedent The word to which a pronoun refers.

Example:

John discovered that he had left his wallet at home. [The noun *John* is the *antecedent* of the pronouns *he* and *his*.]

See Chapter 31.

appositive A word or group of words that identifies or renames a noun or pronoun immediately preceding it.

Example:

Harvey, my brother, is untrustworthy. [*My brother* is the appositive.]

auxiliary verbs Verbs that combine with other verbs to express **voice**, **mood**, or **tense**. Auxiliary verbs are forms of *be* (*is* blown), forms of *have* (*has* made), forms of *do* (*did* live), and modal auxiliaries.

auxiliary See **auxiliary verbs**.

article *An, an* (indefinite articles), and *the* (definite article).

case The change in the form of a noun or a pronoun to indicate that it functions as a **subject**, as an **object**, or as a possessive. Some grammarians use the term *accusative* to refer to the case of a **direct object**, *dative* to refer to the case of an **indirect object**, and *possessive* to refer to the case of a noun or pronoun that shows possession.

clause A group of words that has a **subject** and a **predicate**. Clauses may be either independent or dependent. **Dependent clauses** are also called subordinate clauses. An **independent clause**, because it is grammatically complete, can stand alone as a sentence. (In a **complex sentence** with one independent clause, that clause is called the *main clause*.)

Example:

He made up his mind.

A dependent clause, because it depends on the independent clause to complete its meaning, cannot stand alone as a sentence.

Example:

When he makes up his mind.

See also **fragment**.

A dependent clause will be of one of three types.

1. An *adjective clause* (introduced by a relative pronoun, a relative adjective, or a relative adverb) functions as an adjective and modifies a noun or a noun substitute.

   Examples:

   > John, *who could never make up his mind*, missed his chance. [The adjective clause *who could never make up his mind* modifies the proper noun *John. Who* is a relative pronoun.]

   > The man, *whose tie was on fire*, ran from the restaurant. [*Whose* is a relative adjective.]

   > We went to a place *where we could be alone*. [*Where* is a relative adverb.]

2. An *adverb clause* (introduced by a subordinating conjunction, a relative adverb, or correlative adverbs) functions as an adverb and modifies a verb, an adjective, or another adverb.

   Example:

   > *After he made up his mind*, he acted decisively. [The adverb clause *After he made up his mind* modifies the verb *acted.*]

3. A *noun clause* (introduced by a subordinating conjunction, a relative pronoun, or a relative adjective) functions as a noun.

   Example:

   > *That he could act on his own decisions* never occurred to him. [The noun clause *That he could act on his own decisions* acts as the subject of the sentence.]

collective noun   A noun that, though it is singular in form, names a group of people or things.

comma fault   See **comma splice**.

comma splice   A faulty sentence in which two independent clauses are connected by a comma.

Example:

The sun is shining, it will not rain today.

comparative degree   See **degree**.

complement   A word that completes the meaning of the verb. Complements are predicate nominatives, predicate adjectives, **direct objects**, and **indirect objects**.

complete predicate   See **predicate**.

complete subject   See **subject**.

complex sentence   A sentence that has one independent clause and one dependent clause. See also **clause**.

compound sentence   A sentence that has at least two independent clauses. See also **clause**.

compound-complex sentence   A sentence that has two or more independent clauses and one or more dependent clauses.

conjunction   A word that connects sentences or sentence parts. There are three kinds of conjunctions.

1. A *coordinating conjunction* is a word that joins equal sentence elements without making one of them a modifier. The seven coordinating conjunctions are *and, but, or, nor, for, so,* and *yet*.

2. A *correlative conjunction* is a pair of words that connect equal sentence elements. Correlative conjunctions include *not only . . . but also, either . . . or, neither . . . nor,* and *both . . . and*.

3. A *subordinating conjunction* is a word that joins two clauses, making the one it introduces a modifier. Some common subordinating conjunctions are *because, since, when, if,* and *although*.

conjunctive adverb   An adverb that connects two independent clauses.

Example:

He knew the score; *therefore,* he made his exit. [Notice that the two independent clauses are separated by a semicolon.]

Typical conjunctive adverbs are *therefore, however, nevertheless, then,* and *besides*.

contraction   A shortened form of a word or words created by omitting some of the letters. The omitted letters are indicated by an apostrophe.

Examples:

can't for *cannot, isn't* for *is not*.

coordinating conjunction   See **conjunction**.

correlative conjunction   See **conjunction**.

cumulative sentence   A sentence in which the subject appears before the verb and its complements and modifiers.

Example:

[subject] [verb]   [complement]   [modifier]

He   hit   the ball   hard.

This kind of sentence is the most commonly used sentence pattern in English. It also called a *loose sentence*.

dangling modifier   A modifier that does not modify anything in the sentence clearly.

Example:

Looking through the door, the light was clearly visible. [There is no word in the sentence for the participial phrase *Looking through the door* to modify, so it is said to be dangling.]

dative case   Another term for the objective case when it is used for an indirect object. See **case**.

declarative sentence   A sentence that makes a statement rather than asking a question or making an exclamation.

Example:

The shelf is filled with books.

degree   The form of an adjective or an adverb that shows its relative intensity. There are three forms.

1. The *positive degree* is the uncompared form, such as *quiet* or *quietly*.
2. The *comparative degree* indicates that the term modified is greater than one other thing in its class, such as *quieter* or *more quietly*.
3. The *superlative degree* indicates that the term modified is greater than any other thing in its class, such as *quietest* and *most quietly*.

demonstrative adjective   A demonstrative pronoun functioning as an adjective.

demonstrative pronoun   See **pronoun**.

dependent clause   A **clause** that cannot stand alone as a sentence and must depend on another clause to complete its meaning. Dependent clauses are usually introduced by relative pronouns, relative adjectives, or subordinating conjunctions.

direct object   A noun or a noun substitute that receives the action of the verb.

Example:

John hit the ball. [The noun *ball* is the direct object of the verb *hit*.]

double negative   Having two negatives in the same sentence.

Example:

It *don't* make *no* difference.

expletive   The words *there* and *it* when they are used to postpone the appearance of the subject.

Example:

There are two birds on the wire. [*There* is an expletive. *Birds* is the subject that follows the verb *is*.]

fragment   A group of words punctuated as a sentence, but lacking elements necessary for those words to be considered a sentence.

fused sentence   A sentence constructed incorrectly by combining two independent clauses with neither a conjunction nor a mark of punctuation.

Example:

It is raining I will not go to town.

future tense   A verb form that indicates an action will take place in the future.

Example:

He *will go* to town.

gender   The classification of personal pronouns as masculine (*he*), feminine (*she*), and neuter (*it*).

genitive case   Another term for the possessive case. See **case**.

gerund   See **verbal**.

helping verb   See **auxiliary verbs**.

imperative mood   See **mood**.

indefinite pronoun   See **pronoun**.

independent clause   A group of words that contains a **subject** and a **predicate** and can stand alone as a sentence.

indicative mood   See **mood**.

indirect object   A noun or noun substitute that receives the action of the verb indirectly.

Example:

He hit John the ball. [The noun *John* is the indirect object.]

infinitive   The basic form of a verb preceded by the preposition *to*.

infinitive phrase   See **phrase**.

intensive pronoun   See **pronoun**.

interjection   A word or words used to express a strong emotion. It has no grammatical relationship to the rest of the sentence. Typical interjections are *oh, ah, yeah,* and *wow*.

interrogative adjective   An interrogative pronoun that, when combined with a noun, asks a question.

Example:

Whose paper is this? [*Whose* is the interrogative pronoun.]

interrogative pronoun   See **pronoun**.

interrogative sentence   A sentence that asks a question as opposed to making a statement or making an exclamation.

intransitive verb   A verb that expresses action or condition but does not take a complement.

Example:

He laughed.

See also **transitive verb** and **linking verb**.

irregular verb   A verb that does not create the past tense form and the past participle form by adding *-d* or *-ed* to the verb.

linking verb   A verb that connects its subject with a **subject complement**. Typical linking verbs are *be, seem, appear, become, feel, sense, grow, taste, look,* and *sound*.

loose sentence   See **cumulative sentence**.

main clause   See **clause**.

mixed construction   A sentence that has two or more parts that are grammatically incompatible.

Example:

By washing the car will keep it looking new.

See Section 34g.

modifier   A word or group of words that limits or qualifies the meaning of another word or group of words. See **adjective** and **adverb**.

mood   The form of a verb that indicates the manner or attitude of the speaker.

1. The *imperative mood* is the form of a verb indicating that a command is being expressed.

Example:

Make up your mind.

2. The *indicative mood* is the form of a verb indicating that the act expressed by the verb is a fact.

Example:

He finally *made* up his mind.

3. The *subjunctive mood* is the form of a verb that expresses wishes, speculations, recommendations, or indirect requests.

Example:

I wish I *were* on vacation.

nominative case   Another term for the subjective case. See **case**.

noun   A word that names a person, place, thing, or idea.

Example:

boy [person]

garden [place]

table [thing]

geometry [idea]

A noun may be either common [dog] or proper [Rover].

noun clause   See **clause**.

number   The property of a noun, pronoun, or verb that indicates whether it is referring to one (*singular*) or more than one (*plural*).

object of preposition   See **object**.

object   A noun or noun substitute that receives the action of a verb or verbal (direct object, object of a gerund, object of a participle or object of an infinitive), is indirectly affected by the action of a verb (indirect object), or follows a preposition (object of a preposition).

Examples:

She bought a new car. [*Car* is a direct object of the verb *bought*.]

Running a marathon is difficult. [*Marathon* is the object of the gerund *running*.]

Running a marathon, he damaged his knee. [*Marathon* is the object of the participle *running*.]

To run a marathon requires a great deal of preparation. [*Marathon* is the object of the infinitive *to run*.]

She gave Harvey a kiss. [*Harvey* is the indirect object of the verb *gave*.]

The hood of the car was scratched. [*Car* is the object of the preposition *of*.]

objective case   The form of a pronoun indicating that it should be used as the object of a verb, the object of a preposition, or the object of an infinitive.

parallelism   The structure that results when matching parts of a sentence are equivalent in form.

participle phrase   See **phrase**.

participle   See **verbal**.

passive construction, passive voice   See **voice**.

person   The forms of pronouns and verbs used to indicate whether someone is speaking (first person), being spoken to (second person), or being spoken about (third person).

personal pronoun   See **pronoun**.

phrase   A group of closely related words that do not have both a subject and a predicate. A phrase may be one of the following types.

1. A *noun phrase* is a noun and its modifiers.

Example:

> The *meadow soaked by rain and snow* became a treacherous bog that made the hike a challenging adventure. [The noun is *meadow*. Its modifiers are *The* and *soaked by rain and snow*.]

2. A *verb phrase* is a verb and its complements and modifiers.

Example:

> The meadow soaked by rain and snow *became a treacherous bog that made the hike a challenging adventure*. [The verb is *became*. Its complements and modifiers are *a treacherous bog that made the hike a challenging adventure*.]

3. A *prepositional phrase* is a preposition followed by a noun or noun substitute.

Example:

> The man *in the black fedora* looked mysterious. [The prepositional phrase *in the black fedora* modifies the noun *man*.]

4. A *gerund phrase* consists of a gerund, its object, and/or its modifiers.

Example:

> *Playing a rough game* is the way to win.

5. A *participial phrase* consists of a participle, its object, and/or its modifiers.

Example:

> *Playing a rough game*, the team finally won.

6. An *infinitive phrase* consists of an infinitive, its object, and/or its modifiers.

Example:

> *To play a rough game* is the only way to win.

7. An *absolute phrase* is a noun or pronoun phrase (usually followed by a participle and perhaps some modifiers) that is grammatically independent of the rest of the sentence.

Example:

The decision having been made, they all left.

plural   See **number**.

positive degree   See **degree**.

predicate   The **verb** and its **complements**.

prefix   A syllable or syllables added to the beginning of a word to modify its meaning.

preposition   A word that connects a noun or noun substitute (its object) to another part of the sentence, creating a phrase that functions as a **modifier**.

prepositional phrase   See **phrase**.

pronoun   A word used in place of a **noun**.

1. A *demonstrative pronoun* (*this, that, these, those*) points out the word it refers to.

Example:

This is the right trail.

2. An *indefinite pronoun* (*everybody, all, whoever,* etc.) refers to an unspecified person or thing.

Example:

Everything is going well.

3. An *intensive pronoun* (*himself, herself, themselves,* etc.) emphasizes the noun or pronoun preceding it.

Example:

I *myself* have done the same thing.

4. An *interrogative pronoun* (*who, which, what,* etc.) introduces a question.

Example:

Who did that?

5. A *personal pronoun* (*I, me, he, his, him, they,* etc.) refers to one or more persons or things.

Example:

We told *them* to mind *their* own business.

6. A *reciprocal pronoun* (*each other, each other's, one another, one another's*) refers to separate parts of a plural noun or pronoun.

Example:

We gave *each other* presents.

7. A *reflexive pronoun* (*myself, himself, themselves,* etc.) renames or reflects back upon a preceding noun or pronoun. It differs from an intensive pronoun in that it can serve as an object.

Example:

He gave *himself* a present. [*Himself* functions as the indirect object of the verb *gave.*]

8. A *relative pronoun* (*who, whom, which, that*) introduces an adjective clause (also called a *relative clause*) and refers to the noun or pronoun that precedes it.

Example:

The dog *that* had the bone growled.

reflexive pronoun   See **pronoun**.

relative adjective   A word such as *whose* or *which* that introduces an subordinate clause. See **clause**.

relative adverb   A word such as *when, where, why,* or *how* that introduces a subordinate clause. See **clause**.

relative clause   An adjective clause. See **clause**.

relative pronoun   See **pronoun**.

run-on sentence   See **fused sentence**.

run-together sentence   See **fused sentence**.

sentence fragment   See **fragment**.

singular   See **number**.

space order   In descriptions, the arrangement of details according to their physical relationship to each other.

spatial order   See **space order**.

split infinitive   An infinitive with an element between *to* and the verb.

Example:

He wanted *to* correctly *make* the decision.

standard edited American English   Patterns of usage that conform to traditional rules and conventions.

subject   The word or group of words in a sentence or a clause about which the **verb** makes a statement. A subject may be either simple, complete, or compound.

subject complement   A noun or an adjective after a linking verb that describes or renames the **subject** of the sentence.

subject-verb agreement The requirement that a verb and its subject have forms that agree in both **number** and **person**. See Chapter 30.

subjective case The form of a **pronoun** used as a **subject**.

subordinate clause See **dependent clause**.

subordinating conjunction See **conjunction**.

subjunctive mood See **mood**.

substantive A word, phrase, or clause that functions as a noun.

suffix A syllable or syllables added to the end of a word to modify its meaning.

summary A shortened version of a work.

superlative degree See **degree**.

syllogism In deduction, a series of three statements that form a logical sequence and lead to a valid conclusion.

synonym A word that means the same or almost the same as another.

syntax The principle governing the grammatical relationships between words in a sentence.

synthesis An element of reasoning that involves putting ideas together to form a new idea.

tag question A question appended to a sentence.

tense The time indicated by a verb—past, present, or future.

tense sequence A principle governing the choice of verbs to show the logical relation between them when a sentence has more than one verb.

thesis The main idea of informative writing and of arguments that explain a topic.

thesis statement A statement of the **thesis**.

tone The writer's attitude toward the materials and the reader as revealed by word choice.

topic The subject of a piece of writing.

topic sentence The sentence in a paragraph that contains the main idea.

transition A word, phrase, sentence, or paragraph that makes a connection between ideas in a piece of writing.

transitional expression A word or phrase that shows a connection between ideas and helps to create coherence.

transitive verb A verb that takes a **direct object**.

understatement A statement that makes the situation alluded to seem less important than it really is. Understatement is used to create irony in satirical and literary works.

unity The close connection existing between the main idea of a paragraph or a whole work and the elaborative details that develop the idea.

verb A word that expresses an action or a condition.
Examples:

> The birds *flew*. [action]
>
> The flowers *are* beautiful. [condition]

verb phrase A verb and its modifiers. A verb phrase is one of the two essential parts of a complete sentence.

verbal A form of a verb—gerund, participle, or infinitive—that functions as another part of speech.

1. A *gerund* is a verb ending in -*ing* that functions as a noun.
Example:

> *Running* is good exercise.

2. A *participle* is a verb ending in -*ed* or -*ing* that functions as an adjective.
Example:

> *Running* in the woods, he saw many animals.

3. An *infinitive* is a verb that is preceded by the preposition *to* and that may function as a noun, an adjective, or an adverb.
Example:

> *To see* him was a pleasure. [The infinitive *to see* functions as a noun.]

verbal phrase A **verbal**—gerund, participle, or infinitive—and its modifiers.

verb tense See **tense**.

voice One of two forms of verbs that shows that a subject acts (*active voice*) or is acted upon (*passive voice*).
Example of active voice:

> Harvey ate fig preserves each morning.

Example of passive voice:

> Fig preserves were eaten by Harvey each morning.

word order   The arrangement of words in a sentence. The normal word order of an English sentence is subject, verb, complement. In English, grammatical relationship and meanings are usually determined by word order.

word processing   Writing by using a computer program that allows the writer to manipulate (edit, delete, rearrange) texts on the computer screen before printing.

writing process   The activities that writers engage in to produce written texts. These activities include editing, drafting, and proofreading.

Index

Symbols for Editing and Revising
Numbers refer to sections of this book

abbr	abbreviation problem	38a-38d
agr	agreement	
	verbs	30a-30h
	pronouns	31g
	sentence elements	34e
awk	awkward	
cap	capital letter needed	38a-38d, 39a-39c
case	problem with noun or pronoun case	32a-32i
coh	problem with coherence	16a-16d
comp	inaccurate comparison	35b-35c
coord	problem with coordination or coordination needed	20d
cs	comma splice	24c
dev	development needed	13b
dm	dangling modifier	33d
frag	fragment	23b
fs	fused sentence	23c
hyph	problem with hyphenation	36c, 36h
ital	problem with the use of italics	38a-38d, 39a-39c, 41a-41c
jar	problem with jargon	17a
lc	lowercase letter needed	
mixed	mixed construction	34g
mm	misplaced modifier	33c
p	punctuation needed	22a-28c
pass	problem with passive voice	19a
ref	problem with pronoun reference	31a-31f
shift	inappropriate shift	34a-34d
sp	spelling error	36a-36h
sub	problem with subordination or subordination needed	20e
sxl	sexist language	21a-21e
trans	problem with transition or transition needed	16c
v	problem with the form or tense of a verb	29a-29f
var	need sentence variety	20a-20b
w	wordy	18b-18e
wc	word choice	17a, 19d
ww	wrong word	
//	problem with parallelism	20c
,	problem with the use of commas	22c
;	problem with the use of semicolons	22b
:	problem with the use of colons	22b
	problem with the use of apostrophes	32g, 36g
""	problem with the use of quotation marks	39a-40d

Contents